Contemporary Quantity Recipe File

JOHN C. BIRCHFIELD
MARILYN McCAMMON DAVENPORT
NORMAN D. HILL
RICHARD M. WINGARD
JOHN C. BIRCHFIELD, EDITOR

CAHNERS BOOKS
A Division of Cahners Publishing Company, Inc.
89 Franklin St., Boston, Massachusetts 02110
Publishers of Institutions/VF Magazine

Library of Congress Cataloging in Publication Data
Main entry under title:

Contemporary quantity recipe file.

   Includes indexes.
   1. Cookery for institutions, etc. I. Birchfield,
John C.
TX820.067   641.5'7   75-12917
ISBN 0-8436-2065-X

ISBN 0-8436-2065-X

Printed in the United States of America

CONTENTS

1. ACKNOWLEDGEMENT   1

2. INTRODUCTION TO THE USE OF
    THE RECIPES   3
    Purpose   3
    Use of the Recipes   4
    Standard Recipes—Key to Control   5
    Developing a Standard Recipe   7
    Recipe Constraints   10
    Flexibility   11

3. MODERN FOOD PRODUCTION
    TECHNIQUES   12
    Utilizing Food Purchased in a Form
        that Requires Minimum Effort to
        Bring to Serving Temperature   12
    Preparing Foods Just Prior to and
        During Serving Time   13
    Utilizing Production Equipment
        and Service Techniques
        that Will Reduce Labor   14
    Developing an On-Going Training Program   15
    Implementing an Effective Cost Control System   17
    Batch Cookery   18

4. FOOD FACILITIES LAYOUT AND
    EQUIPMENT DESIGN   19
    The Convenience Kitchen   20
    Storage   21
    Pre-Preparation   21
    Final Preparation   25
    "Small Spaces" Concept   26
    Self-Service   28
    Dining Room Floor Space   29

5. DATA PROCESSING AND COST CONTROL   31
    Elements of a Food Service System   31
    The Computer   33
    Cost Control   40
    Doing Pre-Cost and Post-Cost by Hand   41

6. PURCHASING AND STANDARDS   47
    Centralized Purchasing   47
    Food Buying   47
        Find Out What Is Offered   47
        Determine Needs   48
        Establish Written Specifications
            Concerning Your Needs   48
        Develop a Buying Procedure and
            Take a Course of Action   50
        Spot-Check and Inspect All Deliveries   53

7. RECIPES   55-320
    Sauces and Gravies   55
    Entrees   71
    Vegetables   165
    Hot Fruits   225
    Salads   232
    Breakfast Items   294
    Fruits and Melons   301
    Miscellaneous   315

8. APPENDIX   321
    Charts and Conversion Tables   321
    Purchasing Documents   334

9. GLOSSARY   342

INDEX TO RECIPES   344

1/ ACKNOWLEDGEMENT

The University of Tennessee Food Services Department launched this research project to develop an up-dated standard recipe file that would reflect modern food production techniques. As the project progressed, the department decided to computerize these recipes so that the advantages of food cost control and of being able to make frequent changes in the recipe file would be available.

The development of the project covered a period of three years, utilizing the efforts of many devoted people in this fine department. The administrative support offered by the University of Tennessee and the time and effort of its computer resources were of invaluable assistance in this effort. The members of the management staff committed themselves professionally to a standard recipe project that would: (1) incorporate the finest modern food production techniques, and (2) develop recipes that had been carefully tested in both small and large quantities.

This effort was planned to answer a need in the food services industry for a set of quantity recipes that provide:

Large variations in quantity
Easily understood preparation method
  printed on each recipe
The flexibility of frequent up-dates
The capability of conversion
  to a computerized recipe|system
Carefully tested recipes in both small and large quantities

The operational results that occurred through writing, testing and computerizing the set of recipes were recipes that could be easily converted to the metric system. The recipes were so outstanding that soon it became clear that the end-product should be shared with other members of the food service industry. This significant recipe research project undertaken by the University of Tennessee Food Services Department is gratefully acknowledged.

The National Association of College and University Food Services appointed a Recipe and Menu Development Committee which gave additional impetus to the development of this set of standard recipes. Recipes were contributed from other regions and areas of the United States by the membership. Thus the food products presented represent an excellent cross section of cookery from many areas of the United States. The support and encouragement of N.A.C.U.F.S. and the continued availability of members of this association to provide an up-dating of the recipes themselves are reason enough to designate this standard recipe project as a professional effort under the association's on-going activities.

Cahners Books has also offered support and encouragement in the compilation of this research project, as has Mrs. Jule Wilkinson, editor. The authors gratefully acknowledge this help and support.

John C. Birchfield
Vice President of Business Affairs
Westminster Choir College
Princeton, New Jersey

Marilyn McCammon Davenport, R.D.
Staff Dietitian, Food Services
University of Tennessee
Knoxville, Tennessee

Norman D. Hill
Director of Food Services
University of Tennessee
Knoxville, Tennessee

Richard M. Wingard
Director of Food Services
Auburn University
Auburn, Alabama

Contemporary touches for safe food handling on the line are the fresh plastic gloves and colorful bandana head covers worn by the servers.

2/ INTRODUCTION TO THE USE OF THE RECIPES

THE STANDARD RECIPES[1] presented in this book offer a contemporary solution to the food service problems faced by modern operators of large quantity food services. However, these recipes are also designed to translate the research results of a large quantity, future-oriented food service operation into a form that will prove profitable for smaller operators.

These recipes are written to take full advantage of the latest developments in equipment, food components, and ingredients. The computer has contributed to their development and testing, and the approaches used in that phase of the development of these recipes are explained for possible adaptation by other operators. Finally, these recipes have been fully operation-tested to a degree only dedication and access to the computer could make possible.

In the past, the food service industry has had access to many standard recipes developed by the commercial sector, by professional food management companies, and by individual food service operators. Branches of the armed forces, home economics departments, and leading university institutional management departments have also made important contributions to the standardized recipe files that are presently available to the industry.

Such recipes were usually directed to a specific audience. For instance, most of the standard recipes produced by leading food companies were written for small quantities and directed specifically to small and medium-sized food service establishments. For institutions producing 100, 200, or as many as 1000 portions of a single food item, these recipes often are not easily adaptable.

Many schools of institutional management have developed standardized recipe files for the purpose of training young men and women in basic food production techniques. These recipes reflect the "cooking from scratch" approach. As an example, the student is expected to roll out a pie crust, peel and core the apples, add the seasonings, place an attractive crust over the apples, and bake the apple pie. Such recipes are excellent training tools but are not satisfactory for use in large quantity food production.

Other basic standardized recipe files published over the years have been directed to the "medium quantity" market,

---

[1]Throughout this book, the term standard recipes is used to describe what are sometimes described as standardized recipes.

i.e., operations such as school lunch programs, medium-sized extended health care facilities, hospitals, and other institutions that prepare foods for groups of people ranging in size from 50 to 200.

The Need

After studying the various standard recipes that are available, it became apparent that the food service industry did not seem to have a set of standard recipes that both (1) reflected the increasing number of labor-free foods currently offered by food manufacturers, and (2) met the needs of the operation producing quantity foods in large volume.

Commercial food processors have referred to their labor-free products as "convenience foods," "ready foods," and sometimes by other designations indicating that the component is purchased in a form that requires little hand labor in order to be incorporated into an end product that is ready for service.

The Solution

This set of standard recipes was developed to take advantage of the excellent work that the food manufacturers are doing in providing labor-saving food products, and to use these in a recipe file that can span both the small and large quantity recipe needs of the industry.

To accomplish this, the recipes are written with a range of approximately 25 to 1,000 portions. This range meets the recipe requirements of food facilities such as the larger restaurants, hospitals, colleges and universities, and other institutions serving food in large quantity. However, this material is also highly appropriate for the small operation where 25 to 100 portions might be needed. Here the food service industry will find, for the first time, a set of carefully tested small and large quantity recipes in which convenience food products have been combined using operationally-proven methods.

For the future, Cahners Books and the food services staff of the University of Tennessee have the on-going capability of keeping this quantity standardized recipe file up-dated through the technology of the computer and the resources of an excellent publisher.

USE OF THE RECIPES

Although the recipe format selected is one that lends itself to being computerized, it should be strongly emphasized that these standard recipes are designed to be used without further aid from the computer. These recipes represent an unprecedented combination of variation in quantity, easy-to-understand preparation methods, and operation-tested end products. An example of the recipe format used in final development of the standard recipes in this book appears on the facing page.

Included in each recipe are these five basic factors:

Basic Factors of Recipe Format

1. the name
2. menu category and recipe number
3. serving standards, i.e., the serving pan, portions per pan, portion size, serving utensil, and serving temperature
4. ingredients in a range of quantities
5. procedure

This same recipe format had been used successfully before the recipes were computerized. The only changes made when converting the recipes to the computer were to add a stock number to identify the ingredient and to add line numbers for both the ingredient and the procedure sections.

The description used for the ingredients as printed on the recipe comes directly from the description used in purchasing.

The procedure section is written so that a production person with a minimum amount of experience can follow it. In addition, experience in several operations has demonstrated that only a small amount of training is necessary to familiarize the cook with the abbreviations and the use of decimals in the recipes. (See Appendix for conversion tables.)

In the ingredient and quantity sections of the recipes, no abbreviations occupy more than three spaces. This was done to get as much information as possible into a limited amount of space in the computer and on the recipe cards.

When early preparation is necessary for a food item, this fact is indicated by an E* and is explained in the procedure section of the recipe.

MEAL -- LUNCH MEAL DATE -- NOV. 20, 1974 ESTIMATED 2075 CUSTOMERS SERVING UNIT PRESIDENTIAL CAFETERIA

RECIPE 4570 FROZEN FRUIT SALAD   PORTION SIZE 4.5 OZ WT   TEMPERATURE 32 F   UTENSIL
                                                   PORTIONS/PAN   PAN

SERVINGS   400

NO.	STOCK ITEM	AMOUNT	UNIT
74801	GELATIN,PLAIN,12/1LB.CS.	1.	LB
17950	WATER, COLD	2.	QT
74120	PINEAP. CRU, HVY SRP,HAW,XSTD,6/10	4.	CAN
74550	ORANGE,MAND,SECT,HVY.SRP,FCY,6/10	4.	CAN
73905	PEACHES,YC,SLI.FNCY, 6/10 /CS.	4.	CAN
17955	WATER, HOT 180 DEG.	1.	GAL
		3.	QT
39525	WHIP TOPPING,12/32FOZ.CAN	4.	CAN
75440	SALAD DRESSING,4/1GAL./CS.	2.	QT
61050	BANANAS,20LB.BOX,FRESH	24.	LB
74690	PECANS,MED.FNCY.30LB./CS	6.	LB
73820	RED MARASCHINO,HLVS.FNCY 6/.5GAL.	2.	QT
72001	MARSHMALLOW,MINIATURE,12/1LB.	4.	LB

PREPARATION INSTRUCTIONS

1. SPRINKLE GELATIN OVER COLD WATER AND SOAK 10 MIN.
2. DRAIN CRUSHED PINEAPPLE, MANDARIN ORANGES, AND SLICED PEACHES AND SUBSTITUTE JUICES FOR BOILING WATER IN RECIPE.
3. HEAT FRUIT JUICE AND POUR OVER GELATIN AND DISSOLVE.
4. COOL MIXTURE AND LET THICKEN SLIGHTLY.
5. WHIP THE WHIP TOPPING AND FOLD INTO THE GELATIN MIXTURE.
6. FOLD IN THE SALAD DRESSING.
7. DICE BANANAS, WEIGHT OF BANANAS IS A.P. (3 LB OF BANANAS A.P.EQUALS 2 LB E.P.)
8. FOLD IN REMAINING INGREDIENTS AND POUR INTO INDIVIDUAL 4 OZ MOLDS. FREEZE.
9. UNMOLD ON LETTUCE LEAF.

STANDARD RECIPES KEY TO CONTROL

What Is a Standard Recipe?

A standard recipe is a recipe that lists the food ingredients to be used in the production of a pre-determined food item. The listing includes the quantity of each ingredient, the method of combining the ingredients, and the standard expected in the final product. It might be assumed that standard recipes have been widely accepted in the kitchens of today's food service operations. However, in spite of the fact that standardization has been widely accepted, food operators have not been consistent in insisting that food production personnel prepare menu items from a recipe.

There are, of course, many problems in the use of a standard recipe. The single, most important decision that must be made, if food costs are to be controlled and the high quality of the product is to be assured, is the decision to acquire standard recipes and to use them. If every employee, supervisor, and manager is convinced that the standard recipe is the only method that assures cost and quality control, then it follows that every time a food product is prepared in the kitchen, a standard recipe must be in full view of the production personnel and must be followed by them. Management's insistence that a recipe be used each and every time that a food item is prepared is a most difficult, yet most important, first step in cost and quality control.

An interesting segment of the food industry—in that it needs no standard recipes—is the fast food business. Many fast food companies have engineered their food products so that all standards of quality and quantity are established by the food manufacturer. The employees in these operations make very few decisions concerning either preparation or portion size. Sophisticated kitchen equipment that is automatically timed, combined with portioned food products, allows the fast food chain to use unskilled and semi-skilled employees and supervisors in the kitchen.

There is an important lesson to be learned in viewing this limited-menu segment of the food industry. Where a standard recipe cannot be developed and implemented, the only alternative is to standardize the food product itself before it arrives at the back door of the kitchen. In other words, if we fail to accomplish cost control with standard recipes, then the only alternative for a profitable food service operation is to use high quality convenience foods, such as pre-prepared entrees, that require no preparation in the kitchen. For most food service operations, the total use of convenience products is not feasible because of limited product availability and cost.

Summary

In summary: (1) standard recipes are necessary to control the quality and quantity of each food item produced, and (2) if the standard recipe system is adopted, a standard recipe must be used each time a food product is prepared in the kitchen.

ADVANTAGES OF STANDARDIZATION

1. Quality Control

For many years, the truly successful food or lodging operator in the hospitality industry demonstrated to the public that a standard of excellence prevailed in his establishment. Succesful hotel and motel chains guaranteed the public a clean room, good service, and an acceptable price. Leading restaurant chains guaranteed cleanliness and an excellent food product from a familiar menu. The businessman or the family traveling on the road patronized most often that food or lodging establishment with a reputation for good quality.

If a cafeteria or a restaurant serves the customer a tender steak during the first visit and a tough piece of meat—presented in a sloppy and unattractive manner the next time—repeat business is unlikely. The standard recipe is the only tool available to production personnel that guarantees a consistent, high quality product. The assurances of consistency as a result of the use of standard recipes cover:

—seasoning
—method of combining
  ingredient
—temperature

—appearance and garnish
—yield
—method of service
—degree of doneness

2. Employee Training

The professional chef is indeed in short supply in the United States, and this scarcity has been in effect for many years. Food service managers have been forced to turn to semi-skilled and unskilled employees who possess only basic food preparation knowledge. Training, in consequence, has become not just desirable, but rather an essential part of management's responsibility. The semi-skilled worker must be constantly exposed to proper food handling techniques, acceptable methods of preparation, and good service. The single most reliable source for food handling techniques can be found in the well-written standard recipe. In other words, the standard recipe is a most valuable training resource both for day-to-day improvement of the skills and for the long-range professional development of the food production worker.

3. Quantity Control (Yield)

The words "over production" are often used to describe one of the causes of food waste and loss of profit. Ideally, the amount of food prepared should equal the amount of food to be consumed by the customers—but, actually, this equation is seldom achieved.

Normally, standard recipes provide for variations in quantity of the item produced, by listing separate ingredient quantities for perhaps 25, 50, or 200 portions. Additionally, the portion size is indicated and the recommended serving utensil is described, so that a consistent yield can be obtained.

Without this valuable information, the advantage offered by the standard recipe is lost. To control the quantity of food used in the recipe but not to control the yield through proper portioning, is self-defeating.

Quantity control is a four-step process when the standard recipe is used as a guide. These steps are:

  A. establish the number of portions needed
  B. purchase the exact quantity called for in the standard recipe
  C. use correctly-sized serving utensils
  D. make effective use of leftovers, if unavoidable overproduction occurs

4. Cost Control

It is usual for manufactured products to be sold on the basis of the processing cost, plus a markup for overhead and profit. This technique is not often used in the food service industry. A typical method of establishing the selling price of a food product in a restaurant is to base the price on the amount charged by the restaurant next door. Another technique often used is known as "charge what the traffic will bear." This technique sets the price for the item to be sold on the basis of the amount of money that can be extracted without complaint from the customer.

The standard recipe allows management to cost the food product very easily; all that is required is simply to add the costs of each of the ingredients. A recipe seldom has cost information permanently printed on it because of the wide variations in the cost of food ingredients from season to season, or from year to year. It is imperative that each item on the menu be examined frequently for the relationship between its cost and its selling price. A formula frequently used for establishing a selling price is to multiply the food cost by 2.5 or 3. For instance, if the ingredient costs per serving of beef stew are \$.47, the selling price might be in the range of \$1.20 to \$1.40 per serving.

Another method for expressing this relationship between cost and selling price is the "percentage food cost." In the example above, the beef stew that sold for \$1.20 would yield a 39.2 percent food cost, ($\frac{.47}{1.20}$ = 39.2%), while the \$1.40 selling price would yield a 33.5 percent food cost ($\frac{.47}{1.40}$ = 33.5%).

DEVELOPING A STANDARD RECIPE

Food service operators often want to develop their own recipes or to rewrite recipes collected from outside sources. To begin with, it is essential to understand the component parts of the process. The following is a detailed guide to the step-by-step process used to develop a standard recipe.

Step I: MAKING A FORM—A standard blank form should be used that provides for all of the data in the recipe that is suggested below. (An example of a recipe form, with each step indicated can be seen in the illustration on page 9.)

Step II: TITLE—The title of the recipe should be easily understood and should also be worded to simplify filing and indexing. For instance, recipes are normally filed under major food groups such as meats, vegetables, salads, fruits, etc. Under meats, they are divided further into beef, poultry, lamb, and other major meat designations. The title, then, should make filing the recipes under these categories as easy as possible.

Step III: RECIPE NUMBER—For indexing and cross-referencing, a recipe number is invaluable. For instance, a tomato sauce recipe may appear under "spaghetti," or as a sauce for meat loaf. Referring to the tomato sauce recipe by number makes it easy for the cook to find the recipe whenever he needs it, and makes it unnecessary to place the same recipe under several categories in the file.

Step IV: SERVING STANDARDS—This part of the standard recipe indicates the size of the pan from which the food will be served and the number of portions that may be expected. In addition, the portion size and the serving utensil are indicated. Finally, the appropriate temperature for serving is given, often in designations such as cold, hot, or room temperature, rather than in degrees.

Step V: YIELD—In selecting a standard recipe, the yield expected is the key to cost control. It should be noted that in the recipes in this book the yield varies from one recipe to the next. This is desirable because it makes possible the use, as packaged, of the major recipe ingredient; i.e., a full can or other complete unit of purchase is specified. This eliminates partially used containers which are too often wasted. Yield should be developed in a range of portions to fit the quantity of food to be sold in each food establishment. Yields often are stated in a range between 25 and 500 portions.

Step VI: INGREDIENTS—The ingredients should be listed in an easy-to-understand manner, using the most important word first in the description. As an example, ground paprika should be listed "Paprika, ground," or light tuna should be listed as "Tuna, light." Ingredients should also be listed in a manner consistent with that used in functions carried out in other departments of the food operation, such as in food purchasing specifications and inventory listings. The description

Recipe No.	Recipe Name					Category
Serving Standards:	Pan	Portions/Pan	Portion Size	Utensil	Temperature	

Ingredients	Portions				Procedure

	STEP III		STEP II			
4535	CONGEALED FRUIT					SALADS-GELATINS
Recipe No.	Recipe Name					Category

Serving Standards: STEP IV _____ _____ 4 OZ. _____ COLD

| Pan | Portions/Pan | STEP V Portion Size | Utensil | Temperature |

STEP VI Ingredients	Portions				Procedure STEP VIII
	50	STEP VII 100	300	500	
GELATIN, CHERRY 12/24 OZ/CS	1 BOX	2 BOXES	6 BOXES	10 BOXES	1) DISSOLVE GELATIN IN HOT WATER.
WATER, HOT	1/2 GAL.	1 GAL.	3 GAL.	5 GAL.	2) ADD COLD WATER AND STIR.
WATER, COLD	1 QT.	2 QT.	1 GAL. 2 QT.	2 GAL. 2 QT.	3) ADD ICE AND STIR UNTIL DISSOLVED.
ICE, CRUSHED	2 LB.	4 LB.	12 LB.	20 LB.	4) CHILL AND ALLOW TO THICKEN SLIGHTLY.
FRUIT COCKTAIL, FNCY, 6/10	1 CAN	2 CANS	6 CANS	10 CANS	5) DRAIN FRUIT COCKTAIL.
					6) WHEN GELATIN HAS CONGEALED SLIGHTLY, ADD FRUIT COCKTAIL. MIX WELL.
					7) POUR 1/2 CUP GELATIN MIXTURE INTO MOLDS.
					8) REFRIGERATE.
					9) UNMOLD ON LETTUCE.
					EARLY PREP.: PREPARE GELATIN ONE DAY AHEAD OF SERVING DAY.

of the desired ingredient should be sufficiently detailed to assure that the same quality is duplicated in future purchases.

Potatoes, canned, are purchased in a case of six No. 10 cans; white pepper, in a pound box, or mayonnaise, in four one-gallon jars. To this description of ingredient and pack should be added a brief description of the desired quality, as an example, "Potatoes, canned, tiny whole, 100-120 count." In most instances, these standards of purchase should be listed in lower case letters following the ingredients. Examples of these listings can be seen in the standard recipes that appear in this book.

Step VII: AMOUNT AND UNIT OF THE INGREDIENT—The quantity is usually printed in decimal equivalents and the unit letters in an abbreviated form; they appear in this order immediately following the ingredient. Periods after the abbreviation are unnecessary (i.e., gal not gal. for gallon or gallons, or lb not lbs. for pound or pounds).

Step VIII: PROCEDURE OR METHOD—With the exception of the accuracy of the quantity, the procedure or method is the most important part of the recipe. The method must be carefully written, based on observation of the best techniques that have been developed for preparing the recipe. Discussion with kitchen personnel and research as to the most satisfactory and expedient method are both necessary. Words that can be easily misinterpreted should be avoided, and simple, short sentences should be used.

After writing the procedure or method, it is imperative that two steps be taken to test the accuracy of the description:

First—test the recipe method by preparing it exactly as it is written.

Second—give the recipe to a semi-skilled food worker and silently watch the worker as he assembles the recipe.

Do not make any remarks or offer any assistance. If the recipe can be successfully prepared by a semi-skilled food worker, it is well written!

Summary

It has been demonstrated that a well-written standard recipe reflects the skills of an excellent cook and further the formula allows for variations that will satisfy regional and personal taste differences to make such recipes adaptable in a wide range of foodservice operations.

Other variations should be developed within a standard recipe file to accommodate:

—seasonal changes
—raw product availability
—changes in ingredient costs
—availability of hard-to-obtain food ingredients
—customer preference in method of preparation or in seasoning
—new and interesting garnishes

A good cook will sometimes reject the standard recipe concept because he/she feels threatened since a less skilled person just by following the recipe might also be able to prepare an excellent product. Some cooks do not like the idea of writing down their "secrets" for others to see and understand. Cooks and other highly skilled food production personnel must be made to understand that the standard recipe is being introduced as a basic tool needed to ensure cost control and consistency.

Most of the outstanding chefs of the world are pleased to have their recipes published because of the recognition that it brings to them as well as to their profession. This makes it possible to sell the idea of recipe standardization to all employees in a way that emphasizes both pride in the skills of cooking and the importance of excellence in every recipe formula since these formulas are to be passed on, serving as a training device for others in the industry.

RECIPE CONSTRAINTS

In developing this set of large quantity recipes a few constraints were adopted. As the first constraint, the recipes are not designed to be extended to all possible numbers of portions. One reason for this is that some extensions would result in quantities of ingredients that the cooks would have difficulty in measuring.

To solve the measurement problem, the recipes were written so that if a basic recipe is for 100 portions, it specifies four No. 10 cans of a particular ingredient. However, if that recipe were to be extended to 105 portions, the four cans would have to be increased to 4.2 cans of the ingredient. This .2 of a can would be difficult to measure. Also, what would the cook do with the other .8 of a can? For that reason, these recipes were planned for specific extensions only.

The second constraint was that the most expensive ingredient in the recipe is usually used in whole units, For example, in tuna fish salad a whole can of tuna is used in the basic recipe and the yield is for 40 portions. Of course, it is not possible to have every ingredient in a recipe come out to whole cans; in cases where only a small amount of some ingredient may be needed, partial cans or packages will have to be used. However, the major ingredient is always specified in its entirety as packaged.

The third constraint is based on a long-standing concern in quantity cookery, the effect on salt, pepper, and other spices when a small recipe, say for 25 or 50 portions, is extended to 1,000 portions. In such recipes, when converting from one quantity to another, all ingredients are extended by the same mathematical factor. However, the recipes in this file were all tested in the largest quantities. These varied anywhere from 200 to 1,500 portions, depending upon the production requirements of the testing operation. The largest recipes were developed first and then divided to supply the recipes for smaller quantities.

All of the standard recipes in this *Contemporary Quantity Recipe File* have been tested over a four-year period, in all quantities listed. Seasonings, such as salt and pepper, in the recipes were kept on the light side, since it is easier to add these at the table to satisfy individual preferences.

FLEXIBILITY

Another constraint in the development of these recipes was that the smallest quantity would have to be an amount that could be extended only by an exact multiple. For example, if the smallest quantity of the original recipe was for 100 portions, the quantity for 150 portions would not be developed since it would not make possible the use of whole cans and/or quantities of ingredients that assure easy measurements for the preparer.

For these reasons, in many recipes the smallest quantity is for 20 to 25 portions, the amount from one No. 10 can. These smaller recipes can be especially helpful at certain times of the year when the number of customers served is smaller than usual because of holidays, weekends, or other slow periods. These recipes also reflect the fact that, in the case of less popular foods, preparation of only a minimum number of portions may be all that is required.

With the many new food products that are appearing on the market daily, it is not an easy task to maintain standard recipes, but with an excellent recipe file as a basis, recipes can be easily altered by deleting certain products and adding others. The recipe can be prepared with the new product, and if it is acceptable, the new item can sometimes be inserted into the computerized recipe or on the recipe card by changing only one line. Another design feature of the recipe card file (available as an accompaniment to this book) is that one column has been left blank so that special quantities or changes can be inserted by the food service operation that is using the file.

3/ MODERN FOOD PRODUCTION TECHNIQUES

IN TODAY'S ECONOMY with its rapidly fluctuating costs, the success of any food operation is due largely to the use of standard recipes combined with up-to-date production techniques. An operation cannot afford to use methods from the past, offering as an explanation these well-worn words, "We have always done it that way." Unless convinced that there is no better way, it is the responsibility of progressive food service managers to seek out new and more efficient methods for the production of quality food products.

KEYS TO SUCCESSFUL OPERATION

The basic operational philosophy of this standardized recipe research project must be understood if the best use is to be made of the results that are published here. The key concepts which the authors feel are essential to a successful food service program, are that the operation must be set up to:

1. purchase all food in a form requiring a minimum of effort to bring it to proper serving temperature
2. prepare foods just prior to and during serving time
3. utilize production equipment and service techniques that will reduce labor

4. develop an on-going training program for all levels of staff
5. implement an effective cost control system that provides necessary information speedily to those who have budget responsibility
6. use small quantity or batch cooking where possible

These are the essential concepts that management must adopt to gain maximum benefit from this system. These concepts are so important in light of the current emphasis on efficiency and quality that each should be examined in greater depth.

1. FOOD PURCHASED IN A FORM THAT REQUIRES MINIMUM EFFORT TO BRING IT TO SERVING TEMPERATURE—This approach is designed to keep labor costs to a minimum. With constantly increasing wages, it becomes essential to avoid unnecessary expenditure of time and dollars in performing tasks that others can do more efficiently and at less cost.

The many companies that make up the national food processing industry have made great strides in the past several years in developing quality products for use in the institutional market. This is not a reference to pre-prepared entrees as much as it is to items such as dehydrated potatoes, soups and vegetables or frozen items such as pre-cooked bacon, coffee, or turkey breasts—to name only a few.

Why spend valuable time laboriously peeling potatoes and other vegetables, or filling many sheet pans with slices of bacon, when this work has already been done by the food processing industry. Bacon panning time could much better be spent in ensuring that the bacon that is put out on the serving line meets the standards that have been set.

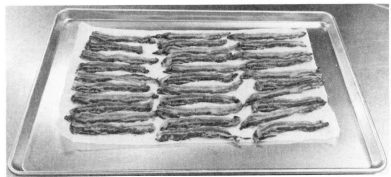

A convenient food product—"Pre-cooked Bacon."

The many types of labor-saving food items available today are limited only by the willingness of food service management to seek them out. Imagination, resourcefulness, and a genuine desire to take advantage of these new products are the essential ingredients for success in this area.

2. PREPARE FOODS JUST PRIOR TO AND DURING SERVING TIME—This concept is aimed at improving the quality of the food offered to the customer. Too frequently food products are produced hours before serving time and then are transferred for the intervening period to some sort of warming device. It takes little imagination to visualize the deterioration in quality that has occurred by the time a product handled in this way is served to the customer.

The consumer has become increasingly conscious of high quality, freshly prepared food, and if this quality is in any way lacking, a loss in future sales will result. Proof of the importance of this concept is shown by the success of many fast food operations. These food facilities, serving a high quality product prepared at the last minute, are demonstrating ever-increasing dollar volume sales.

The recent trend toward all-day service in many cafeteria food service programs makes the application of the concept of last-minute food preparation essential. This highly popular approach to meal service dictates the production of items in small quantities over a long period of time. The result is better products and more satisfied customers.

With or without all-day service, it is possible to develop last-minute food preparation techniques in all food service operations. This concept requires that personnel concerned with production must be convinced that freshly prepared food is

Food can be prepared just prior to and during serving time when pass-through window provides easy, direct access to cafeteria line.

important. To further reinforce this concept, the reduction of available holding equipment should be part of the process.

3. UTILIZE PRODUCTION EQUIPMENT AND SERVICE TECHNIQUES THAT WILL REDUCE LABOR—Any food service manager who is able to give input to the layout and design of an operation for which he/she is responsible is, indeed, fortunate. Unhappily this is seldom the case, as more often than not a food service manager is asked to operate a facility without having had the benefit of assisting in the design.

Although exclusion from planning can, at times, make it difficult to introduce new concepts in kitchen design, it should not be used as an excuse to forego a continuing search for

Self-service reduces labor and is enjoyed by the customer (right).

Quick recovery fryers (below) with conveniently located work surfaces are an illustration of production equipment that will reduce labor.

Self-service dessert counter makes an appealing display that leads to increased volume; such self-service cuts labor costs (right below).

Training done at the management and supervisory level must be a day-to-day process. Food production personnel meet to discuss the meal preparation for the coming week.

more efficient methods of operation through careful equipment selection and improved service techniques.

The proper selection and utilization of food production equipment is so important an element in the use of these standard recipes that it is treated in a separate section.

4. DEVELOP AN ON-GOING TRAINING PROGRAM— The food service industry has been struggling with the dilemma of its unskilled labor force for many years. Large amounts of time and money have been spent in the search for ways to perfect a training process for the many workers involved in the numerous phases of food service.

Training is a prime goal in almost every operation, but it is seldom accomplished with measurable results or continuity. Management seminars and professional food service meetings almost always have a panel or discussion revolving around the central theme of training. Training booklets and manuals offering training techniques that are effective, if properly utilized, are developed and produced in great numbers. It is generally accepted that a quality food service operation cannot be maintained unless continuing on-the-job training is part of the standard operating procedure.

The Busy Manager

Unfortunately for most food service facilities, training is frequently done on a sporadic and inconsistent basis. Somehow, ordering the food, overseeing its preparation, checking on the quality of its service, and supervising the clean-up seems to consume more time than the average food service manager is able to find in his work day. As a consequence, time to be spent in planning a training session is not available and that important activity is continually being postponed for another day which somehow never comes.

The standard recipe can be used both as a training aid and as a guide to quality and cost control in food production.

The truth is, of course, that many of the steps necessary in the process of serving food to our customers would require less supervision if the manager made one of his prime goals the setting up of an on-going and continuous training program.

Training Goals

Before an effective training program can be launched, it is important to establish a few goals for the project. The following objectives illustrate what good training should be designed to accomplish. It should be planned to:

a. give each employee a thorough knowledge of his/her working situation and conditions of employment

b. train each individual in the responsibilities and techniques of his/her job in a way that will make excellent performance and, thus, job satisfaction possible

c. keep each employee familiar with and updated in every phase of his/her job

d. give every employee the opportunity, as well as the tools and know-how, to expand job knowledge and increase his opportunity for advancement

e. develop "esprit de corps" through a consistent and progressive system of individual and group development

f. keep training a dynamic process, that is, construct a program that is flexible so it can be changed as needed to meet the changing demands of the job or of society.

A Training Aid

One possible solution to the training dilemma is to have a set of standard recipes that can be easily understood by anyone who has basic reading skills. If the method of preparation listed with the recipe is carefully written, then presumably a semi-skilled food service worker can take that recipe and produce a quality standardized food product.

The failure of most recipe writers is explained by the fact that their own skills in the food preparation area make it difficult for them to write a recipe at a level easily understood by a semi-skilled worker. Because the recipe writer understands how to thicken a sauce or make a gravy, he/she is apt to insert into the method only the words, "After adding the cooked cubes of meat, thicken the product with flour." Obviously, such a recipe fails to direct the cooks clearly and completely as to the correct method of combining the ingredients.

The cook called upon to follow a recipe written in this way must either have the necessary skills or work out the technique on his/her own. Thus, at a critical stage in the production process, important decisions are made without management control; these frequently result in a less than satisfactory product for the customer.

A common frustration for the semi-skilled cook is the traditional system of abbreviation so frequently used in quantity recipes. As an example, the designation "A. P." may not be understood, and the cook may not know how to interpret "as purchased" for the particular food product, even if it is defined. The translation of such information by the cook into an exact amount of food to be added to a particular recipe can be confusing because of yield variations in basic food commodities. The result can be a costly mistake and the loss of quality control.

Convenience Foods as an Aid to Training

The food processors have made a major contribution to the industry by solving a part of the training dilemma in advance. Food products often come to the kitchen in a form that can be readily combined, as delivered, with other ingredients in a recipe, or even may need only to be heated before being placed directly on the serving counter. This convenience food development has received much attention and has been discussed in great detail in recent years and, therefore, needs no further elaboration here. However, it is extremely important to note that the harmonious combination of these labor-saving

foods into a well-developed standard recipe can now solve a sizable part of the training problem for the food service industry.

A well-written, easily understood standard recipe can play a significant role in assisting management to overcome the difficulties formerly encountered by its food preparation labor. With those difficulties no longer a factor, training becomes a function of teaching kitchen personnel the basic food handling techniques that assure a sanitary product assembled with a minimum amount of labor. Food management personnel must train the food handler to read and understand a standard recipe that follows a logical pattern in assembling ingredients.

In summary, training cannot be totally eliminated from the kitchens but it can be greatly simplified when food preparation personnel have confidence that if carefully followed, the standard recipe will yield a high quality product. If a recipe cannot be easily understood and fails to yield an excellent menu item for the customer, then the employee's confidence in the system, which is so important, will have been partially destroyed and additional effort will be required to restore it.

5. IMPLEMENT AN EFFECTIVE COST CONTROL SYSTEM—An effective method of cost control is described in detail in another chapter; however, the significance of the cost control system as a modern production technique merits its discussion at this point as one of the important elements of these essential operational concepts.

With today's rapidly changing market situation, the food service manager who is not completely informed of the current financial status of his/her operation is in trouble Available information should, at a minimum, include food and labor costs and should be received as soon as possible following the accounting period concerned.

The pre-cost system (i.e., predicting food cost in advance) is particularly effective in keeping costs in line. Knowing the cost of a certain combination of items on a menu in the quantity required, prior to the actual service of that menu, allows the manager to react *in advance* if costs are out of line. This ability to predict food costs accurately, at least four to six weeks in advance, is vital in maintaining a favorable budget position. The pre-cost method, as a planning tool that allows

Batch Cookery—cooking while the meal is in progress—eliminates over-production and waste. This high speed vegetable steamer can cook frozen broccoli in 2-1/2 minutes. Note use of steam table pan for cooking and serving in the same utensil.

a look at food costs a few weeks before the menu is prepared and served, is far superior to the commonly found practice of looking back at a financial statement that reflects accounting operational data thirty or forty days old.

Whatever system is employed, the important point is that the information be rapidly received by those who need to know. Information has little effect and is of limited value if allowed to sit on the desk in an accounting office when it should be in the hands of those responsible for food service operations.

6. *BATCH COOKERY*—The concept of cooking in small quantities has long been recognized as a means of (a) preserv-ing the quality and appearance of foods and (b) eliminating over-production in the kitchen. However, even though this cooking method has been around a long time, all too often food production personnel "cook a little extra," or "cook ahead to get ready for the big rush."

Batch cookery, as a production concept, is written into these standardized recipes. Equipment that is convenient for this cooking technique should be designed into the modern kitchen. The manager must recognize that even though the kitchen and the recipe are directed toward small quantity, high speed cooking, constant supervision of the food service staff is required if the advantages of batch cookery are to be realized.

4/ FOOD FACILITIES LAYOUT AND EQUIPMENT DESIGN

MODERN STANDARD RECIPES and a kitchen designed and equipped to handle the basic cookery of twenty years ago are, of course, incompatible.

It is pretty well established today that for most institutional kitchens a vegetable preparation room or a root cellar would not be compatible with the use of labor-saving frozen or canned foods as specified in a modern set of recipes.

Standard recipes must not only be written to take advantage of the latest types of food products available from the commercial processor, but must also be written with modern

THE FUNCTION ➡	MUST HAVE ➡	BUT ALSO
The Menu	Variety, without creating production problems	Must fit the equipment on hand plus available food from the supplier
The Recipe	Easy production methods that give cost and quality control	Must fit the variety of equipment found in different types of food establishments
The Kitchen Design and Equipment	The versatility to handle a variety of food products	Must work well with the recipe preparation method and handle the demands of today's menu

high speed cooking equipment in mind. However, every production kitchen may not have or need all kinds of equipment, so the modern recipe must be written so that it is adaptable to more than one kind of foodservice equipment.

The Convenience Kitchen

The goal is to design the menu, the recipe, and the kitchen to fit the specific needs of the food establishment. These variations have been summarized on page 19.

As a foundation for making optimal use of a set of standard recipes, the idea must be accepted that the supply of skilled chefs is very limited and, therefore, greater reliance must be placed on the use of labor-saving products. If this idea is accepted, the next step is to have the kitchen and its equipment

A convection oven is a high speed oven that uses very little floor space.

laid out in a logical manner that will expedite the use of modern food products in the most effective manner.

Kitchen Layout

The food service operator who inherits a large, older kitchen should not be discouraged. Convenience food products can be effectively used in an older kitchen. However, to take full advantage of these products, the purchase of certain more efficient pieces of equipment should be considered. Discarding outdated equipment and replacing it with modern usually requires that a determined effort over some period of time be made by the manager. Examples of some pieces of equipment that might profitably be replaced are:

Conventional Equipment	Possible Replacement
Hot Top Range	High Speed Vegetable Steamer
Deck Oven	Convection Oven
Stock Pot	Medium Size Steam Jacketed Kettle
Frying Pans	Tilting Kettle

Moving a stainless steel work table that is no longer useful out of a large meat or vegetable preparation area, and disposing of it for far less than cost, is not an easy decision for management. Closing down a butcher shop in favor of the use of portioned meats and consequent reliance on a local or regional meat processing plant is also a difficult but necessary decision being faced by most institutions today.

The following concepts are the basis of one approach to kitchen layout and equipment selection to take advantage of the labor-saving techniques reflected in these standard recipes. There are, of course, many justifiable approaches to good layout and design; the piece of equipment that is efficient and useful in one situation, such as a fast food operation, may be totally out of place in a large institutional kitchen.

The approach that is emphasized here is that management must be convinced and then must convince the employees of the value of a plan that, although it reduces man-hours, will increase productivity in the kitchen and service areas.

The kitchen equipment ideas reviewed here are not presented as rigid rules or guidelines but instead are offered to provide:

a.   better understanding of the labor-saving concept of these recipes

b.   stimulation for a new approach to food production, kitchen layout, and equipment selection

Each of the following areas or functions in a typical food facility is described briefly to give further emphasis and understanding of the concepts and ideas behind modern food production techniques:

- Storage
- Pre-Preparation Area
- Final Preparation
- "Small Space" Concept
- Self-Service
- Dining Room Floor Space

STORAGE

There has been a recent movement in the food service industry toward greater and greater dependence on frozen and freeze-dried foods. Other methods of preservation are under development, and the degree of dependence, common in the past, on canned foods or fresh foods is lessening. The design of the receiving facilities and the storage area must reflect this trend to the use of food products resulting from many new and different preservation methods being adopted now or that will be developed in the future.

Walk-in freezers in the past were quite small; sometimes so small and crowded that it was not possible to walk in. Today, providing a walk-in freezer that will store two or three days' supply of perishable food (or in some cases a two-week supply) is considered to be a necessity.

Health codes and good sanitary practices demand that these walk-ins have clear open shelving providing easy access by food preparation personnel. Maintaining walk-in freezers at a temperature of -10°F., with increases in temperature during the day up to 10°F. to meet load variance, is considered normal in food service operations.

These requirements for refrigeration have been recognized for many years, yet all too often new kitchen facilities are not designed to provide either equipment that maintains adequate temperatures or enough space for refrigerated storage.

In summary, the standardized recipe file reflects a great dependence on both frozen and freeze-dried food products that reduce labor costs; storage areas must be provided that will maintain the high quality of these foods.

PRE-PREPARATION

Pre-preparation, in the context of this book, should be thought of as both an area of the kitchen and as the function of work done to the food ahead of actual preparation of the meal. In past years, an example of pre-preparation would have been the butchering of meat or the peeling of potatoes. Pre-preparation in today's food service operation is the combining

This storage area is designed to be compact and easy to clean. With greater use of frozen foods, dry storage areas can be smaller.

In this well-designed pre-preparation area steam jacketed kettles, work table, mixer, and serving utensils are placed in a close working arrangement. Note sink designed into work table.

Morrill Cafeteria, University of Tennessee, pre-preparation area offers conveniently located work space for the combination of labor-saving foods with other ingredients to produce finished dishes in minimum time.

of labor-saving foods with other ingredients so that the food product can be readied for final service to the customer with as little labor as possible. Examples of pre-preparation activities are:

- mixing water with instant gelatin
- hydrating dehydrated onions
- putting together the ingredients in a meat loaf
- assembling the parts of an attractive salad
- roasting meat
- cleaning lettuce
- thawing ground beef patties

Haphazard approaches to work spaces in kitchens which do not provide pre-preparation areas lead to disorganization and waste of labor. To test the efficiency of this point in a particular kitchen, first determine if the pre-preparation area is located logically near dry and refrigerated storage areas.

Pre-preparation involves the removal of a food product from refrigeration and, according to schedule, the transfor-

mation of this basic ingredient to a finished product. It follows then that pre-preparation areas should be located between storage and final preparation. (See arrow on the following chart.)

LOGICAL SEQUENCE OF KITCHEN FUNCTIONS

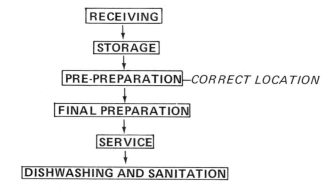

RECEIVING
↓
STORAGE
↓
PRE-PREPARATION—*CORRECT LOCATION*
↓
FINAL PREPARATION
↓
SERVICE
↓
DISHWASHING AND SANITATION

Many kitchens are set up with a cooking station that has fryers, ovens, and worktables arranged around the cook's work area in what seems to be a convenient manner. This is a basic mistake since it provides for the functions of pre-preparation and final preparation in the same area. Under this arrangement, the cook must often walk some distance to the storage section of the kitchen and then bring a food product back to the work area for pre-preparation. This same work area is then later used for the final preparation of, for instance, a meat loaf that is to be formed.

A worktable surface that is used for basic preparation, with a mixer and food chopper nearby, does not provide a satisfactory place for dishing up foods into cafeteria pans, or for the final preparation of french fries and hamburgers. In other words, the two functions of pre-preparation and of final service preparation are not compatible in the use either of equipment or work space. The following schematic drawing illustrates this point:

SCHEMATIC DRAWING OF CORRECT ARRANGEMENT IN A FOOD PREPARATION AREA

KETTLES	WORK TABLES	FOOD CHOPPER

PRE-PREPARATION

OVEN

WORKTABLE

FRYERS	SPREADER	GRILL	HIGH SPEED STEAMER

FINAL PREPARATION

POINT OF SERVICE

↓

SCHEMATIC DRAWING OF INCORRECT ARRANGEMENT IN A FOOD PREPARATION AREA

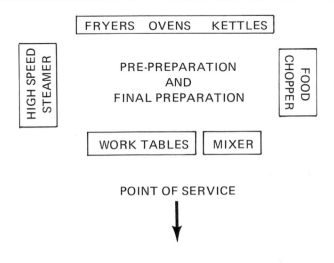

FRYERS   OVENS   KETTLES

HIGH SPEED STEAMER

PRE-PREPARATION
AND
FINAL PREPARATION

FOOD CHOPPER

WORK TABLES   MIXER

POINT OF SERVICE

↓

If proper grouping of areas for the functions of mixing, cleaning, chopping, and stewing of the basic food ingredients has been achieved, then many steps will be saved and greater efficiency will result. The kitchen layout must follow a logical arrangement in the groupings of mixers, ovens, steam jacketed kettles, work tables, and a variety of chopping and cutting equipment if the pre-preparation area is to be fully functional.

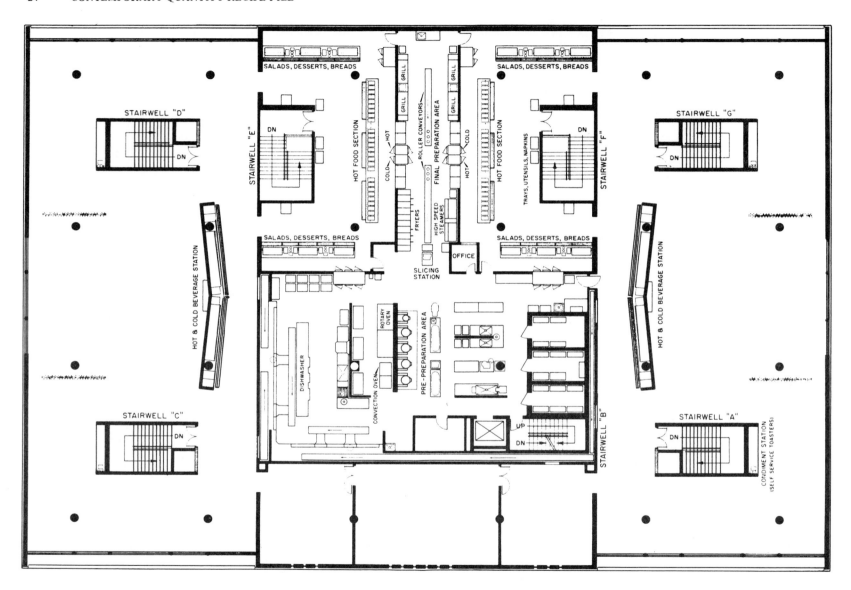

PRESIDENTIAL DINING HALL
(Second Floor)

THE UNIVERSITY OF TENNESSEE

At Morrill Cafeteria equipment for final preparation is arranged in area that can handle a full menu for 2000 meals per day.

FINAL PREPARATION

The final preparation area is the place in the kitchen where (a) high-speed cooking equipment is grouped, and (b) foods that require longer cooking periods are made ready for final service to the customer. The type of equipment located in the final preparation area should ensure that foods are prepared as close as possible to the time when the customer walks into the establishment. When this practice is followed, the freshly prepared food product can be served at the proper temperature, and there is an additional bonus in the elimination of overproduction.

For example, a fryer or grill is a piece of equipment used in final production. The fryer is normally used to prepare french fries or deep-fried seafood products. If either the french fries or the deep-fried seafood items are cooked well before the meal period, the result will be an unacceptable food item for the customer. The obvious solution to peak service for such foods is to be sure that the cooks prepare them at the last minute in only the amount needed, and that they are then served to the customer hot and crisp. This very obvious solution, however, is often not possible because of kitchen design and equipment layout. Fryers and grills are often located at great distances from the serving counters; or, an even greater obstacle, holding equipment is located adjacent to the grill or fryer which, of course, encourages the cooks to prepare these "last minute" food items too far in advance.

"Last Minute" Cookery

The epitome of last minute food preparation can be observed in the fast food industry. Well-known hamburger chains with very high volume food production requirements have managed to engineer their facilities so that food is never cooked too far in advance, yet the customer is seldom kept waiting.

If the customer orders food in a unit of a typical fast food chain, a conveyor broiler cooks the hamburger within moments of the time it is ordered. The food product is assembled within seconds, and is then placed in the small space designed for holding. Thus, the customer is assured of a high quality, recently prepared product, and the cook is constrained by the kitchen design from "getting a little bit ahead." However, last minute preparation of food in large quantities is also possible and should be planned for in the design of the kitchen floor space and equipment.

Some food products offered in an institution do not lend themselves to high-speed, last-minute cookery. Roast meats used for the evening meal or the less expensive casserole items and, of course, such items as meat loaf, chicken salad, spaghetti, or barbeque-on-a-bun are examples of food products that cannot normally be prepared in a few seconds. Again, the solution for serving these products at the last moment, at the peak of quality, is to (a) see that they are placed in an acceptable holding unit as close as possible to the point of service, and (b) not to complete the product in its final form until the last few moments before service.

The final preparation area must have, as a part of its design, a good slicing station or other assembly work area that allows the food preparation staff to dish up or complete only the amount of items necessary for the particular meal.

Holding Equipment

Good holding equipment should be available only in the sizes actually needed, so that the cooks are not encouraged to overproduce food. Hot or cold holding units should be selected that incorporate humidity control and convenient movement to the point of service.

Too much capacity in holding units can waste many food dollars. As an example, there is a great difference between a piece of roast beef, pre-prepared in the kitchen and held unsliced, and the same amount of roast beef after it has been sliced, placed in a steam table pan, and held in a heated pass-through unit. In one instance, the unsliced roast beef will have excellent retention of quality and can be used for another meal. However, once sliced, the same roast beef deteriorates rapidly in the holding equipment or on the steam table line.

"Small Space" Concept

Construction costs have reached such high levels that now, more than ever, every square foot of space in new or renovated facilities must be justified. Storage rooms, kitchens, dishwashing areas, service and dining room floor space must be sized in an exact manner; operators can no longer afford a haphazard approach to the sizing of food facilities spaces, if, indeed, they ever could. The luxury, if it was a luxury, of the large kitchen is a thing of the past.

Holding equipment provides a convenient method for keeping food hot, but its use should not result in cooking food too far ahead of meal time.

This receiving dock is small enough for two trucks, trash disposal and steps for employees. Three or four bays are unnecessary if there is only one receiving clerk.

The "small space" concept is successful only if the designer, in conjunction with management, agrees that each area of the food facility should be:

a. adequate
b. no larger than necessary

Some typical questions that might be asked in the examination of space requirements are:

RECEIVING

Question: How many trucks can your receiving clerk unload at once?

Comment: If he can handle only one truck, or two at the most, why must the receiving area be designed to accommodate four trucks?

Question: How much space does the receiving clerk need for unloading?

Comment: A receiving dock the width of two trucks and approximately 10 feet in depth is quite adequate.

Question: After the food is received, how much space is needed in the corridor leading to storage?

Comment: A corridor with limited "break-out" space is quite sufficient. This space is the holding area used briefly before placing the food into storage; it should be kept small, with only enough space for weighing foods prior to storage.

Question: How big should the dry storage area be?

Comment: The space requirement for dry storage is different for each food facility in every section of the country. The proper sizing is tied, of course, to frequency of delivery. Watch out for the trap in purchasing of "If you'll take a full truck load, I can save you a lot of money." This trap will lead to greatly oversized storage spaces and may result in slow inventory turnover.

PRE-PREPARATION

Question: Do you really need a vegetable preparation room?

Comment: Canned vegetables and the frozen food industry have almost eliminated the justification for in-house pre-preparation of fresh vegetables. Many areas of the country today provide produce, such as lettuce, that is cleaned and made ready for salad preparation before it is delivered to the food service operator.

Question: Can a space-consuming deck oven be justified in this area?

Comment: Modern convection ovens or smaller rotary ovens have high capacity in relationship to the floor area consumed.

Question: Are high speed, vertical cutters, which require large floor space for adjacent work surfaces and clean-up, justifiable in terms of the volume of food produced?

Comment: These excellent pieces of equipment must be carefully analyzed to be sure they are truly labor-saving. Many smaller pieces of chopping and cutting equipment do an adequate job and are easier to clean. Even more important, they consume less floor space. Be sure that the size of the equipment fits the needs and size of the kitchen.

Question: In batch cookery using high speed, high pressure vegetable steamers are large numbers of steam jacketed kettles needed?

Comment: For bringing soups up to proper serving temperature or for preparation of hot casseroles, a steam jacketed kettle is usually a necessity. However, cooks who use kettles for large quantity vegetable cookery are often using a steam jacketed kettle inappropriately. The vegetables are being cooked too far in advance and in too great a quantity. High speed vegetable steamers provide high capacity while occupying a small amount of kitchen floor space.

FINAL PREPARATION AREA

Question: Are there small spreader plates located beside fryers and grills for placement of the raw, uncooked product?

Comment: Many fry stations or grills are left with no work space nearby and the cook must place the raw ingredients in a box on the floor or on a nearby cart with much waste of labor, time and space. Convenient small work surfaces are economical and are very much appreciated by the cooks.

Question: Are hot-top ranges with small ovens underneath still being used in the kitchen?

Comment: The hot-top range in most quantity kitchens seems to be the collection place for melting butter, keeping gravy hot, or, even less desirable, for vegetable cookery. Occasionally, a large pot of soup will be kept hot on this piece of equipment. These ranges are space consuming and often inefficient in the medium or large volume food facility. The small or medium size tilting kettle and a vegetable steamer will effectively take the place of the hot-top range in most kitchens.

SELF-SERVICE

The customer walks into many food operations, locates the menu board, picks up the eating utensils and napkin, selects the hot food items he/she wants, makes his own salad and applies the dressing, selects from among many different kinds of beverages, and after eating, takes the dirty dishes or disposables to a trash can or a dish-return area.

The public has become accustomed to this pattern, yet full advantage of the acceptance of this process has not been taken by the food service industry. It is, of course, a development that should be exploited because of the degree of labor reduction that results from self-service.

Even a very fine restaurant often incorporates self-service into its lavish meal service. The oyster bar and the preparation of a salad by the customer are very obvious examples. The psychology at play in self-service is often overlooked. Most people enjoy the activity of making a choice from foods that they can actually see.

The cafeteria and the fast food restaurant with colorful foods cooked in plain view have captured a significant segment of the eating-out business by taking advantage of food visibility and eye appeal. Incorporating self-service, then, into any type of food operation not only saves labor but appeals to the basic human desire to be able to see and select the food product about to be consumed. Economy in food facility design can certainly be enhanced by taking advantage of the self-service concept.

Pictured on the facing page are some of the types of self-service set-ups that can be adapted for many kinds of foodservice operation. The self-service salad bar is a popular attraction in many service restaurants today.

Making "help yourself" an attractive procedure pays off in self-service beverage station which reduces labor and speeds service (above); the enticing, self-service salad bars (above right and below).

DINING ROOM FLOOR SPACE

Dining table size has not been explored sufficiently by the food service industry to assure the maximum efficiency and potential savings in use of floor space. Kitchen designers tend to see the dining room table as a plastic-laminated surface designed to accommodate diners around its four sides.

The size of a table top and its configuration can have a dramatic impact on the size of the dining room. For instance, if four people sit on the four sides of a square table, much space is wasted because (a) the four corners of the table are not utilized, (b) the center of the table is much too large for the condiments, and (c) no natural aisle space is created when the customers' chairs project on each of the four sides of the table.

The solution to this specific dining room table problem is to seat the same four people on two sides of a table having a rectangular shape. This allows four people to converse easily and naturally·but, even more importantly, the entire table surface can be comfortably utilized. Aisle space is created because no chairs interfere with traffic on two sides of the table.

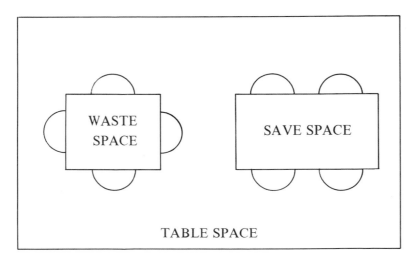

WASTE
SPACE

SAVE SPACE

TABLE SPACE

The use of this type of table can reduce a dining room requirement of 13 to 14 sq. ft. per chair to 10 to 11 sq. ft. per chair. This resulting space saving in a 200 seat restaurant or a 1,000 seat cafeteria can reduce construction costs by thousands of dollars. This approach to dining room layout also results in dining spaces that are more pleasant and comfortable for the customer to walk through.

SUMMARY

Excellent publications are available on the broad subject of kitchen layout and design. If maximum benefit is to be realized from the quality, labor-saving standard recipes presented here, management is urged to think in terms of achieving high productivity through the use of high quality equipment chosen to meet the specific production needs of the operation.

This production line at the University of Tennessee's Presidential Court Cafeteria is equipped to handle featured menu items in amounts necessary to meet requirements.

5/ DATA PROCESSING AND COST CONTROL

THE PHRASE "being snowed under by paper work" is one heard frequently, as many people do not understand the end result of the hours of labor they have to spend on reports and forms. They often feel this labor would be more productive if spent on other projects.

However, when the information collected from such reports is made available to improve food production and to keep costs under control, the importance of collecting and processing data becomes clear.

The use of data processing in the management of business operations is not new, since data processing has long been done effectively by hand. Automated accounting systems and various types of reports have been used for some time to develop data. In some operations, computer time is available. However, whether produced by a manual or a computerized system, in the food service industry, the data has generally been available only *after* the purchase of food components and their combination into a meal, too late to be of assistance in those important areas.

In both commercial and noncommercial food services, where the number of transactions is relatively constant, a daily food cost and/or a monthly financial statement have been sufficient in the past to give adequate control. In fact, a number of computer systems have been developed and are in use for the data processing of daily food service cost control. Other systems have been developed for use in large institutions as a basis for control of what customers eat and for the compiling of statistics on various aspects of food service.

ELEMENTS OF A FOOD SERVICE SYSTEM

What a Pre-Cost System Offers

The first steps in developing cost control techniques for food service are a system of forecasting expenses and a way of comparing the expected with the actual cost of a menu. Such a system is called a pre-cost.

A pre-cost system requires a detailed cost breakdown of the menu, covering all the major ingredients that go into each item. This is where the standard recipe makes its first contribution. To get this breakdown, prior to the purchase of food for the production of the meal, the unit manager indicates the number of customers expected and the quantities of each item needed. This menu breakdown is priced, and the costs are compared to pre-determined budget guidelines. It is

FIGURE 1. FLOW CHART OF PLANNING, ORDERING, AND FOOD PRODUCTION

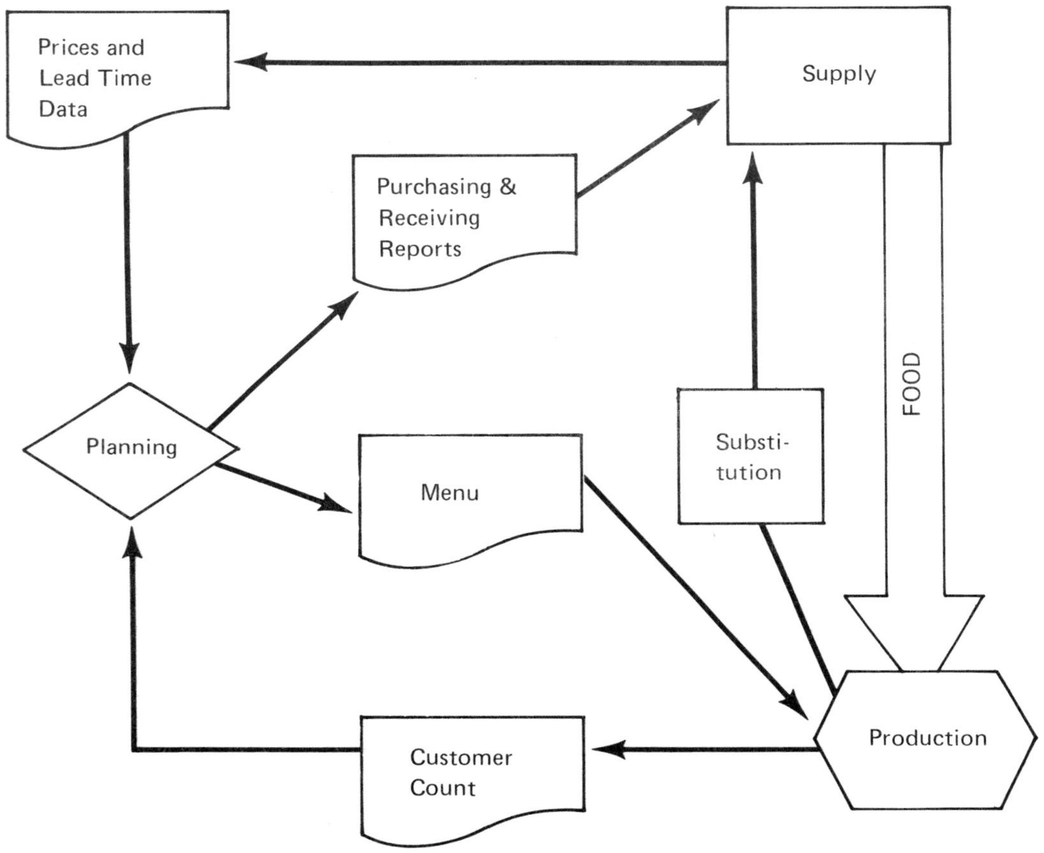

then possible (1) to determine the feasibility of introducing new menu items, (2) to decide the frequency with which expensive items should be served and (3) to make any necessary changes prior to obligating funds.

The functions of planning, ordering and production are more effectively accomplished through the use of the feedback from the pre-cost system which can also be used to determine future requirements as seen in Figure 1.

In the planning stage, data from previous production, customer counts from past records, availability of a food item, and the cost of an item in relation to pre-determined budget constraints are all required if sound decisions are to be made.

The process of obtaining this information through the use of a computer is outlined first. The steps required in a manual system set up to provide the same information are presented later in this section.

THE COMPUTER

No attempt will be made in this book to present a primer on the computer and all of its possible technical uses in the food service industry. However, to have the reader understand how this modern management tool is used in the development of a standard recipe, some understanding of a basic computer system is essential. The way the computer is used in developing standard recipes is outlined below.

Computer Components

As an initial step the two components of the system, the "standard recipe file" and the "stock file," are stored in the computer.

The recipe file contains recipes for all the items on the menu. The stock file describes all the ingredients required for the recipes, with cost and source information for each ingredient.

Figure 2 illustrates the way a basic computer system works —what the inputs of information to the computer are and the outputs to be derived. What may not be apparent in Figure 2 is that in actual operation, many of the steps or functions go on simultaneously. The basic computer system is designed to allow flexibility in its use. It should also be dynamic, providing continued avenues for improvement of the data it supplies for an operation.

To indicate some of the more elaborate functions that a computer system that utilizes standardized recipe data can offer in the way of useable management information, further possible developments of the system are described below.

The Flow Chart

A natural way to begin a more detailed study of such a computer system is with a flow chart. The flow chart is perhaps the easiest and most logical way to understand the scheme of operations required by a computer. In Figure 3 the flow chart illustrates the ways data can feed into the computer. To obtain useful data from the computer, data stored in its memory bank must hold true for some period of time. The data relating to the standard recipe file that has been stored includes a listing of all recipes for products used, and a stock file enumerating all the ingredients; this serves as a base for calculations by the computer when the operation is geared to a cycle menu.

Cycle Menu

A cycle menu is a menu for a given period of time that lists all the food items to be served during that period. A cycle menu can be repeated as indicated—at daily, weekly, or monthly intervals. With a cycle menu, management can refine and improve a well-worked-out menu, rather than being forced to rewrite it periodically.

The cycle menu, often written for three- or four-week periods, offers a continuing opportunity to introduce new products, seasonal variations, and customer preferences. In food operations using a cycle menu system, the management, by going over the menu planning form (Figure 4), is able to review the menu weekly. The menu planning form lists the estimated number of portions and the customer count anticipated for the week; this input into the computer is also used to obtain an estimated cost for a particular meal. The pre-cost information obtained from the computer is also reviewed by management. If adjustments are needed, the pre-costed menu can be sent to the computer for re-costing. All of this is done before purchase and production of menu items begins.

Output

In the system that has been described, the computer assembles and sorts, from its stored data, information which is then used to produce seven important documents. These seven basic output documents (print-outs) are: (1) production recipes, (2) issue plans, (3) preliminary order work form, (4) final receiving reports, (5) food cost summary report, (6) standard recipe summary report, and (7) stock file vendor listing report.

Some of these documents are used simultaneously in various phases of the operation. Others are produced only after a preliminary form has been used and further data has been developed. With the speed with which a computer can handle the data fed into it, the new form can be quickly put in the hands of the persons who need it in the receiving area and the kitchen itself. The seven documents and their uses are:

1. *Production Recipes.* Production recipes are, in reality, the standard recipes. They list all the ingredients for the number of servings specified in the menu planning stage. All information regarding the production of an item is printed out by the computer for the production supervisor and/or cooks, so that information about pre-determined portions, serving utensils, and preparation procedures is available for use during preparation.

2. *Issue Plan.* The issue plan lists all items that are to be sent to production on a given day. The scheduling of food products to be delivered for "early prep" is arranged after the print-out is received.

The issue plan serves a second basic function, i.e., it provides receiving personnel with a document telling how to make up the food issues to the kitchen for a given meal. The print-out of the issue plan also assists the receiving personnel in accounting for all goods leaving the storeroom. Any differences between the issue plan and actual issue are entered on the form that the computer provides.

3. *Preliminary Order Work Form.* This document is also used by receiving personnel, since it provides lists of all items to be used in the recipes by the day and by the week. Before placing an order for stock that will be required during the coming week, the receiving supervisor reviews the preliminary order work form. He checks the following:

    a. those items that can be used from par stock

    b. over- and under-usage of items scheduled for previous menus which left either an unanticipated depletion or excess in stock

    c. stock required by current week's production

    d. items not automatically ordered which have a relatively low usage rate, such as spices

4. *Final Receiving Report.* The final receiving report is used by the purchasing staff to place orders with the appropriate purveyors who deliver the food to the various units on the designated delivery dates. As the goods arrive at the unit food facility, the receiving supervisor uses the copy of the final receiving report that has come to him from the computer to verify the products that are being received. All invoices are attached to the final receiving report and together with the actual issue plan are sent to the Bookkeeping Department to be used as an input into the computer, becoming part of the food cost summary.

5. *Food Cost Summary Report.* The food cost summary report, or "post-cost report," lists by unit, day and meal the number of meals served and their cost, both average and total.

A statistical analysis of commodities is also provided by this print-out which may be used for input when a computer run is made for the next cycle menu.

6. *Standardized Recipe Summary Report.* The recipe summary report is a listing of all recipes with a breakdown of the unit cost and the standard number of portions per mix. It is periodically updated to reflect changes in the cost of ingredients (stock file). This print-out is also used in the menu planning phase so that management is always in a position to adjust the selling prices of food products on the menu.

7. *Stock File Vendor Listing Report.* The vendor listing is a report that lists all vendors, the products on which they have quoted prices, the brand names, and the priority of selection. This report is used by management to review suppliers, their products and price.

Summary—this, in brief, is a summary of the data that can be used in a food service system. One must remember that much of the computer operation is performed simultaneously with a good deal of overlap between functions. The system must not be viewed as a step-by-step process where the whole scheme of operation must be completed before the cycle can be started again. The system is designed to be a continuous process, making data available when they need it to those who need it—the clerk, the cook, and management—in order to make the food service operation more efficient and beneficial to the customer.

Chart illustrating the flow of data into a basic computer system and the output from the computer appears on facing page.

FIGURE 2. BASIC COMPUTER SYSTEM

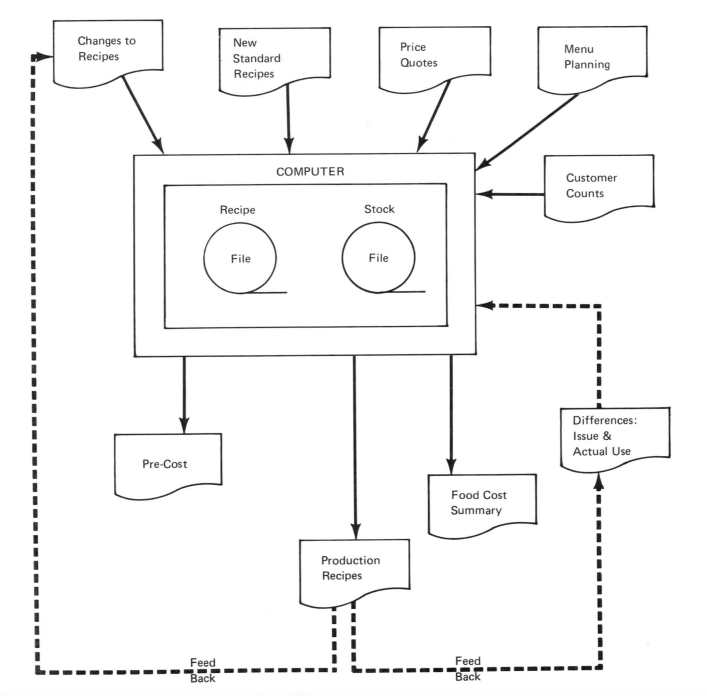

FIGURE 3. COMPUTER SYSTEM FLOW CHART

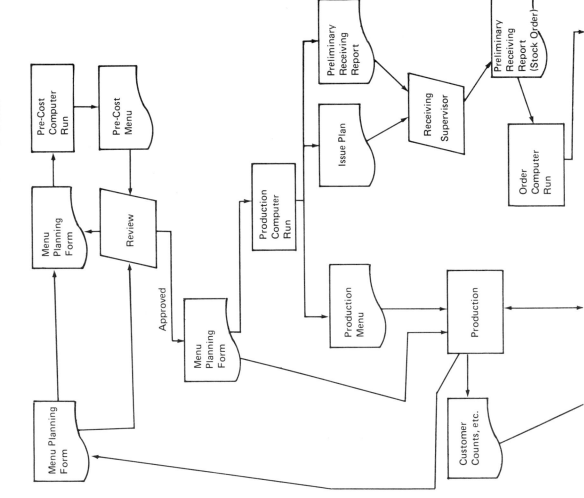

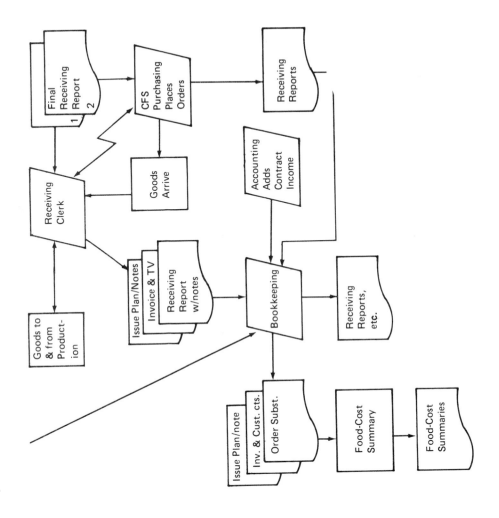

FIGURE 4—MENU PLANNING FORM

Central Food Services Dept.

MENU PLANNING FORM
NO. 46-008

UNIT_____ WEEK____20____

DAY___Monday___

UNIT NO.	MEAL DATE
1-2	3-8
30	2-26-73

BREAKFAST — Header Card

Recipe Name	M 9	10	Portion Estimate 11-14	Recipe No. 15-18	Portions Served
Orange Juice					
Grapefruit Juice					
Sliced Peaches			50	7630	
Dry Cereal			100	6112	
EGGS TO ORDER			144	6010	
SCRAMBLED EGGS			400	6016	
Cream of Wheat			22	6154	
Sausage Patties			164	1650	
Waffles to Order					
			50	6062	
Cake Donuts			144	5202	
Yeast Donuts			84	5213	
Biscuits			96	5076	
Toast/Marg/Jelly			60	6072	
Whole Wheat Toast			42	6076	
Beverages			330	5538	

Breakfast Customer Estimate: H 330

LUNCH — Header Card

Recipe Name	M 9	10	Portion Estimate 11-14	Recipe No. 15-18	Portions Served
Punch/Apple Juice					
Chicken Gumbo Soup			150	0040	
Gr. Cheese Sandwich			450	2660	
Beef Stroganoff/w/					
Noodles			300	1340	
Brussels Sprouts			120	3192	
Cinnamon Pears			288	3432	
Potato Chips			252	3042	
Tossed Salad			350	4055	
Blackberry Isle			90	4515	
Fruit Mallow Salad			368	4350	
Butterwash Rolls			300	5126	
White Bread			90	5032	
Whole Wheat Bread			56	5034	
Golden Del. Apples			200	7510	
Carrot Cake			378	7015	
Cherry Gel Parfait			153	4596	
Assorted Ice Cream			144	7235	
Beverages			770	5558	
Cottage Cheese			130	4210	
Eggs			204	4225	
Garnish Head Lettuce			50	4052	

Lunch Customer Estimate: H 770

DINNER — Header Card

Recipe Name	M 9	10	Portion Estimate 11-14	Recipe No. 15-18	Portions Served
Punch/Grapefruit Ju.					
Tomato Soup			150	0340	
Fr. Haddock/Tar.Sau.			320	1950	
Italian Spaghetti			792	1220	
Broccoli Spears			360	3186	
Spiced Applesauce			540	3422	
Tossed Salad			350	4055	
Frosted Fruit Salad			180	4560	
Mand. Orange/Coconut Toss			480	4359	
Garnish Head Lettuce			50	4052	
Italian Bread			540	5024	
Purple Plums			40	7670	
Cherry Cobbler			300	7434	
Assorted Ice Cream			144	7235	
Beverages			950	5551	
Cottage Cheese			520	4210	

Dinner Customer Estimate: H 950

Notes:

Notes:

Notes:

FIGURE 5—BUDGET REQUEST

BUDGET REQUEST

Dining Hall

unt Number   282828

(Cents Omitted)

	Actual			FY 74 (Step 1)			
	Amount	Per Unit	% of Rev.	Amount	Per Unit	% of Rev.	Inc. (Dec.)
REVENUE							
Contracts	1,107,697		89.5	999,919		79.9	(24,048)
Grill	78,636		6.4	99,900		8.0	15,880
Guests	50,843		4.1	151,256		12.1	16,564
Other							
TOTAL REVENUE	1,237,176		100.0	1,251,075		100.0	8,405
COST OF SALES	532,644		43.1	530,232		42.4	(9,086)
EXPENDITURES							
SALARIES							
Prof. Salaries	42,526		3.4	53,700		4.3	5,569
Clk. & Supp.	11,979		1.0	8,500		.7	-0-
Total Salaries	54,505		4.4	62,200		5.0	5,569
TEMP. HELP	241,295		19.5	247,924		19.8	(1,440)
Total Sal. & Temp. H.	295,800		23.9	310,124		24.8	4,128
PERATING & MISC.							
dm. Charge	65,364		5.3	80,513		6.4	8,64
es & Prtg.	56,172		4.5	42,000		3.4	
	-0-		-0-	150		-0-	
	1,964		.2	3,700			

FOOD COST

LABOR COST

FIGURE 6–STATEMENT OF OPERATION

OF OPERATION
ON DINING HALL
MARCH, 1974

	YEAR TO DATE			
	BUDGET 1974	%	ACTUAL 1974	
et Sales	$750,645		$795,150	
Cost of Sales	318,273	42.4	334,758	42.1 ← FOOD COST
Gross Profit	$432,371	57.6	$460,392	57.9
Operating Expenses				
Salaries	76,650	6.3	34,987	4.4 ← LABOR COST
Temporary Wages	144,014	19.1	182,615	22.9 ←
Employee Meals	6,416	.9	6,953	.9
Staff Benefits	15,089	2.0	14,713	1.9
Supplies & Printing	24,498	3.3	25,666	3.2
Laundry	7,674	1.0	7,144	.9
Maint. & Repairs	15,833	2.1	14,098	1.8
Utilities	22,077	2.9	22,077	2.
Equipment	2,500	.3	154	
elephone	1,069	.1	1,069	
rance	2,775	.4		
	200			
	75			

COST CONTROL

Budgets

A budget is the essential first step in a cost control system. A budget is a pre-determined plan of anticipated future financial performance and is also a basic document in food control. In developing a budget, consideration is given to income and expenses, and historical data about the operation is listed and compared. Budgets are normally prepared well in advance of the date that they become effective.

After all the essential information has been compiled, the budget can be developed with a high degree of accuracy. The primary budget concerns are food and labor costs. The standard recipe is a particularly effective technique for controlling these costs. In the budget request in Figure 5, page 39, the focus is put on food and labor costs, the two most important cost control figures.

Operational Statement

This is a financial statement of operations which compares actual performance with the budget. A portion of an operational statement is illustrated in the example shown in Figure 6 which lists both budgeted and actual expenditures.

It is beyond the scope of this book to describe in detail the way that budgets and operational statements are developed. However, food and labor costs in these documents are shown to focus attention on these tools as a part of cost control. In the examples, food costs are 42.4 percent. Living within this budget as projected on the financial statement is the responsibility of food service personnel with supervisory responsibility whatever their level in the organization. Thus the 42.4 percent illustration might be a target for a food cost percentage in an operation.

DOING A PRE-COST AND POST-COST BY HAND

Since most food service operations do not have a computer or have access to one, the pre-cost, post-cost system described here is probably the most significant concept in this section. The manual system can provide a sound basis for cost control, as many operations without computer back-up have demonstrated by performing quite effectively.

Basically a manual pre-cost system contains the same elements that are used in a data processing system. A stock file must be maintained and standard recipes must be followed. After the planning of a cycle menu, a document listing all menu items and their major ingredients is developed. There is an example of a handwritten pre-cost on page 42. As an aid

to understanding the handwritten pre-cost system, the example is presented in steps labeled first, second, third, etc.

Summary

Since the manual pre-cost and post-cost system is basic to cost control, most operations first work out the system that meets their needs effectively when it is done by hand. As the operation becomes larger and/or more complex, parts of the system are automated.

Whether the data needed for cost control is provided manually or by computer, the critical ingredient in the implementation of those controls is the people who operate within the system.

The use of a computer print-out provides both a method of inventory control and a food order form.

FIGURE 7—THE MANUAL PRE-COST

FIRST—THE CYCLE MENU

FOOD SERVICES DEPARTMENT

WEEK 26

BREAKFAST	LUNCH	DINNER
Orange Juice	Punch and Apple Juice	Punch and Grapefruit Juice
Grapefruit Juice	Chicken Gumbo Soup	Cream of Tomato Soup
Pineapple Tidbits	GRILLED CHEESE SANDWICH	FRIED FLOUNDER WITH TARTAR SAUCE
Dry Cereal	BEEF STROGANOFF WITH NOODLES	ITALIAN SPAGHETTI
EGGS TO ORDER	HAM COLD PLATE	Fordhook Limas
SCRAMBLED EGGS	Green Peas	Broccoli Spears
BLUEBERRY PANCAKES	Broiled Peaches	Spiced Applesauce
Cream of Wheat	Potato Chips	Tossed Salad
Sausage Patties	Cole Slaw	Frosted Fruit Salad
Waffles to Order	Blackberry Isle Congealed	Orange-Coconut Toss
Glazed Donuts and Biscuits	Fruitmallow Salad	Italian Bread
Toast/Margarine/Jelly	White Bread and Whole Wheat	Purple Plums
Beverages	Fresh Apples	Cherry Cobbler
	Carrot Cake	Assorted Ice Cream
	Cherry Gelatin Parfait	Beverages
	Assorted Ice Cream	
	Beverages	

SECOND—THE PRE-COST FORM

FOOD SERVICES DEPARTMENT

DATE _____   UNIT _____   WEEK _____

Breakfast - Est. _____   Actual _____   Cost/Meal _____   TOTAL _____

THIRD—MAJOR INGREDIENTS OF RECIPES ARE LISTED WITH UNITS OF ISSUE

FOOD SERVICES DEPARTMENT

DATE _____   UNIT _____   WEEK 26 _____

Breakfast - Est. _____   Actual _____   Cost/Meal _____   TOTAL _____

Orange Juice	___ ___	cns	___ ___ ___		
Grapefruit Juice	___ ___	cns	___ ___ ___		
Pineapple Tidbits	___ ___	cns	___ ___ ___		
Dry Cereal	___ ___	cs	___ ___ ___		
Eggs-Fresh	___ ___	dz	___ ___ ___		
-Frozen	___ ___	lb	___ ___ ___		
Pancake Mix	___ ___	bx	___ ___ ___		
Blueberries	___ ___	cn	___ ___ ___		
Cream of Wheat	___ ___	bx	___ ___ ___		
Sausage Patties (3 oz.)	___ ___	lb	___ ___ ___		
Biscuits	___ ___	dz	___ ___ ___		

Donuts, Glazed	___ ___	dz	___ ___ ___		
White Bread	___ ___	lv	___ ___ ___		
W. Wheat Bread	___ ___	lv	___ ___ ___		
Jelly, Assorted	___ ___	cs	___ ___ ___		
Syrup, Indiv.	___ ___	cs	___ ___ ___		
Margarine	___ ___	lb	___ ___ ___		
Reddies	___ ___	lb	___ ___ ___		
Coffee	___ ___	cn	___ ___ ___		
Milk-Whole	___ ___	cn	___ ___ ___		
-Skim	___ ___	cn	___ ___ ___		
-Choc	___ ___	cn	___ ___ ___		

FOURTH—ESTIMATED NUMBER OF CUSTOMERS TO BE SERVED IS DETERMINED

FOOD SERVICES DEPARTMENT

DATE _____   UNIT _____   WEEK 26 _____

Breakfast-Est.   900   Actual _____   Cost/Meal _____   TOTAL _____

Orange Juice	___ ___	cns	___ ___ ___		
Grapefruit Juice	___ ___	cns	___ ___ ___		
Pineapple Tidbits	___ ___	cns	___ ___ ___		
Dry Cereal	___ ___	cs	___ ___ ___		
Eggs-Fresh	___ ___	dz	___ ___ ___		
-Frozen	___ ___	lb	___ ___ ___		
Pancake Mix	___ ___	bx	___ ___ ___		
Blueberries	___ ___	cn	___ ___ ___		
Cream of Wheat	___ ___	bx	___ ___ ___		
Sausage Patties (3 oz.)	___ ___		___ ___ ___		
Biscuits	___ ___	dz	___ ___ ___		

Donuts, Glazed	___ ___	dz	___ ___ ___		
White Bread	___ ___	lv	___ ___ ___		
W. Wheat Bread	___ ___	lv	___ ___ ___		
Jelly, Assorted	___ ___	cs	___ ___ ___		
Syrup, Indiv.	___ ___	cs	___ ___ ___		
Margarine	___ ___	lb	___ ___ ___		
Reddies	___ ___	lb	___ ___ ___		
Coffee	___ ___	cn	___ ___ ___		
Milk-Whole	___ ___	cn	___ ___ ___		
-Skim	___ ___	cn	___ ___ ___		
-Choc	___ ___	cn	___ ___ ___		

FIFTH—ESTIMATED QUANTITIES (BASED ON PAST RECORDS OF STANDARD RECIPES) ARE ENTERED BY PERSON RESPONSIBLE FOR PRODUCTION

FOOD SERVICES DEPARTMENT

DATE ___ April 3 _____   UNIT ___ Presidential Court ___   WEEK 26 _____

Breakfast-Est. ___ 900 _____   Actual _____ Cost/Meal _____   TOTAL _____

Orange Juice	36	cns	.84		Donuts, Glazed	60	dz	.45
Grapefruit Juice	8	cns	.46		White Bread	6	lv	.31
Pineapple Tidbits	4	cns	1.33		W. Wheat Bread	4	lv	.22
Dry Cereal	2	cs	1.46		Jelly, Assorted	2	cs	2.25
Eggs-Fresh	14	dz	.35		Syrup, Indiv.	2	cs	2.60
-Frozen	160	lb	.36		Margarine	6	lb	.19
Pancake Mix	4	bx	1.02		Reddies	6	lb	.33
Blueberries	1	cn	1.76		Coffee	1/2	cn	3.67
Cream of Wheat	4	bx	.48		Milk-Whole	6	cn	6.00
Sausage Patties (3 oz.)	110	lb	.58		-Skim	2	cn	3.75
Biscuits	30	dz	.36		-Choc	1	cn	6.00

SIXTH—LATEST PRICES BY PURCHASES ARE ADDED

SEVENTH—THE QUANTITY AND PRICE ARE EXTENDED TO GIVE COST FOR EACH MENU ITEM

EIGHTH--THE COST OF ALL FOOD FOR THIS MEAL IS TOTALED

FOOD SERVICES DEPARTMENT

DATE ___ April 3 _____   UNIT ___ Presidential Court ___   WEEK ___ 26 _____

Breakfast-Est. ___ 900 _____   Actual _____ Cost/Meal .3127   TOTAL 281.48 _____

Orange Juice	36	cns	.84	30.24	Donuts, Glazed	60	dz	.45	27.00
Grapefruit Juice	8	cns	.46	3.68	White Bread	6	lv	.31	1.86
Pineapple Tidbits	4	cns	1.33	5.32	W. Wheat Bread	4	lv	.22	.88
Dry Cereal	2	cs	1.46	2.92	Jelly, Assorted	2	cs	2.25	4.50
Eggs-Fresh	14	dz	.35	4.90	Syrup, Indiv.	2	cs	2.60	5.20
-Frozen	160	lb	.36	57.60	Margarine	6	lb	.19	1.14
Pancake Mix	4	bx	1.02	4.08	Reddies	6	lb	.33	1.98
Blueberries	1	cn	1.76	1.76	Coffee	1/2	cn	3.67	1.84
Cream of Wheat	4	bx	.48	1.92	Milk-Whole	6	cn	6.00	36.00
Sausage Patties (3 oz.)	110	lb	.58	58.00	-Skim	2	cn	3.75	7.50
Biscuits	30	dz	.36	10.80	-Choc	1	cn	6.00	6.00

NINTH—THE TOTAL COST PER MEAL *TO BE SERVED* **IS COMPUTED**

TENTH—THE TOTAL ESTIMATED CUSTOMER COUNTS AND COSTS OF MEALS FOR THE WEEK ARE TABULATED

FOOD SERVICES DEPARTMENT

DATE _____ April 3, Monday _____ UNIT _____ Presidential Court _____ WEEK 26

Breakfast-Est. 900   Actual _____ Cost/Meal .3127 TOTAL 281.48

Orange Juice	36	cns	.84	30.24	
Grapefruit Juice	8	cns	.46	3.68	
Pineapple Tidbits	4	cns	1.33	5.32	
Dry Cereal	2	cs	1.46	2.92	
Eggs-Fresh	14	dz	.35	4.90	
-Frozen	160	lb	.36	57.60	
Pancake Mix	4	bx	1.02	4.08	
Blueberries	1	cn	1.76	1.76	
Cream of Wheat	4	bx	.48	1.92	
Waffle Mix	4	bx	1.60	6.40	
Sausage Patties (3 oz.)	100	lb	.58	58.00	
Biscuits	30	dz	.36	10.80	

Donuts, Glazed	60	dz	.45	27.00
White Bread	6	lv	.31	1.86
W. Wheat Bread	4	lv	.22	.88
Jelly, Assorted	2	cs	2.25	4.50
Syrup, Indiv.	2	cs	2.60	5.20
Margarine	6	lb	.19	1.14
Reddies	6	lb	.33	1.98
Coffee	1/2	cn	3.67	1.84
Milk-Whole	6	cn	6.00	36.00
-Skim	2	cn	3.75	7.50
-Choc	1	cn	6.00	6.00

AND

are summarized for the week:

FOOD SERVICES DEPARTMENT
DINING HALLS
COST SUMMARY

WEEK ENDING APRIL 9   WEEK 26

	PRE-COST			POST-COST		
	Estimated to be served	Cost	Cost/Meal served	Actual	Cost	Cost/Meal
Breakfast	4875	1555.83	.3191			
Lunch	9633	5100.00	.5294			
Dinner	10,975	6467.20	.5892			
TOTAL	25,483	13,123.03	.5149			

FOOD COST _____

FIGURE 8–THE MANUAL POST-COST

The documents used in the pre-cost of a menu are used to develop this vital performance information

FIRST—THE ACTUAL NUMBER OF MEALS SERVED IS ENTERED

FOOD SERVICES DEPARTMENT

DATE __April 3, Monday__   UNIT __Presidential Court__   WEEK __26__

Breakfast-Est. __900__   Actual __891__   Cost/Meal __.3187 / .3127__   TOTAL __284.00 / 281.48__

Orange Juice	35	36	cns	.84	30.24	29.40	Donuts, Glazed	60	dz	.45	27.00
Grapefruit Juice		8	cns	.46	3.68		White Bread	6	lv	.31	1.86
Pineapple Tidbits		4	cns	1.33	5.32		W. Wheat Bread	4	lv	.22	.88
Dry Cereal	2.25	2	cs	1.46	2.92	3.28	Jelly, Assorted	2	cs	2.25	4.50
Eggs-Fresh		14	dz	.35	4.90		Syrup, Indiv.	2	cs	2.60	5.20
-Frozen		160	lb	.36	57.60		Margarine	6	lb	.19	1.14
Pancake Mix		4	bx	1.02	4.08		Reddies	6	lb	.33	1.98
Blueberries		1	cn	1.76	1.76		Coffee	1/2	cn	3.67	1.84
Cream of Wheat		4	bx	.48	1.92		Milk-Whole	6.5 6	cn	6.00	36.00 39
Sausage Patties (3 oz.)		110	lb	.58	58.00		-Skim	2	cn	3.75	7.50
Biscuits		30	dz	.36	10.80		-Choc	1	cn	6.00	6.00

SECOND –ONLY THE DIFFERENCES IN AMOUNTS OF FOOD SERVED ARE RECORDED

THIRD—NEW TOTAL AND AVERAGE COST PER MEAL SERVED ARE COMPUTED

FOURTH—THE COST SUMMARY IS COMPLETED TO GIVE MANAGEMENT A COMPARISON OF *PLANNED* PRODUCTION WITH THE ACTUAL MEAL COST

FOOD SERVICES DEPARTMENT
DINING HALLS
COST SUMMARY

WEEK ENDING __April 9__   WEEK __26__

	ESTIMATE	COST	COST/MEAL		ACTUAL	COST	COST/MEAL
Breakfast	4875	1555.83	.3191		4,738	1,585.50	**.3346**
Lunch	9633	5100.00	.5294		10,431	5,610.40	.5378
Dinner	10,975	6467.20	.5892		10,835	6,817.85	.6292
TOTAL	25,483	13,123.03	.5149		26,004	14,013.75	.5389

FOOD COST __.5389__
Per Meal Served

6/ PURCHASING AND STANDARDS

IN A RELATIVELY short span of time, the food service industry has become one of the largest industries in the business world. Some of the industry's major growth strides are being made through institutional food service systems and chains. Their high volume of food sales is the basis of a continuing demand for a readily available supply of food of high quality, in ample quantities.

CENTRALIZED PURCHASING

An excellent way for an operation to be assured of the necessary quantity of food is to centralize the food purchasing function, utilizing a person who has this expertise. However, the determination of quality should be assigned to those trained in food production and presentation.

Many institutional food services have their food purchased by an organization that is separate from the Food Service Department.

If handled internally through a separate department, however, such a purchasing function may be thought of as a profit center. This is based on the assumption that the savings realized by professional purchasing techniques have a major beneficial influence on the food cost or cost of sales in the operating units. The results of such an approach should be a consideration.

FOOD BUYING

There have been several approaches and generalizations recorded concerning successful food buying. The best and most simple approaches to successful food buying, as outlined by Frooman in *Five Steps to Effective Institutional Food Buying,* are: (1) find out what is offered; (2) determine what best fits your needs; (3) establish written specifications concerning your needs; (4) develop a buying procedure and take a course of action, and (5) spot-check and inspect all deliveries.[1]

1. *FIND OUT WHAT IS OFFERED*—The food buyer must keep alert to the ever changing market situation. Foods in plentiful supply, foods on the market in new forms, and fluctuations in market prices are but a few of the factors that demand attention. This necessary information is accumulated from such sources as local and federal market reports, news-

---

1. A. A. Frooman, *Five Steps to Effective Institutional Food Buying,* 2nd ed., (Chicago: Institutions Publications, Inc., 1953) pp. 6, 388-89. Out of print.

papers, technical and trade associations, meetings and magazines, research reports, talks with sales representatives, and visits to produce and wholesale firms.

2. *DETERMINING NEEDS*—Quantities of food needed are based on the number of persons to be served, the size of the portion to be given, and the amount of waste and shrinkage loss involved in the preparation of foods.

Records of meal census (Figure 9 on the facing page) may be used to good advantage to determine future numbers to be served. Standard recipes give portion sizes and quantities required for prepared foods. A knowledge of wholesale weights and sizes for various commodities helps the buyer translate quantity needs into appropriate units of purchase.

Food Purchasing as a Part of a Centralized Concept

If the centralized food purchasing concept is adopted. the size of the purchasing staff may vary from a single clerk to a full staff, including a purchasing manager, a buyer, a purchasing clerk, and a food technologist; or the staff may be even larger.

The purchasing staff keeps abreast of new developments offered by the food industry. They are aided in their search for information by displays and demonstrations of new products given personally by representatives from various food companies. Other valuable information is gained about new foods, marketing trends, and consumer demand by studying various publications, such as *Washington Report, National Restaurant Association News, Service World Reports, Institutions/VF Magazine,* USDA publications on meat and poultry, and others. The food buyer is also visited, in many cases daily, by area salesmen who contribute information and samples of food industry offerings.

Before food is actually purchased by the staff, the food needs of operating units must be determined. These needs can be determined in several ways. For instance, by referring to a cycle menu that is to be used over a given time period, the purchasing manager can determine what ingredients will need to be purchased. Such menus are often formulated by a staff dietitian in cooperation with the food service managers.

To determine the quantity of food to be bought, the dietitian and the food service managers must first decide on the portion sizes, basing these on the standard recipes. With information on the portion size and the number of customers to be served, a general food quantity can be obtained. The purchasing manager and the food buyer can then convert the quantity value into units of purchase. In the absence of a cycle menu, the buyer makes forecasts (based on past experiences) as to what future needs might be.

After the quantitative needs are determined, management decides on and informs the purchasing staff of the quality level of food needed for items or entrees served. The quality level needed for a specific ingredient can be partially determined by the way it is to be used in a particular meal plan or menu. For example, a vegetable used in a stew would not need to be superior in quality, whereas, the meat that is used as the primary ingredient of an entree would have to be of superior quality.

3. *ESTABLISH WRITTEN SPECIFICATIONS CONCERNING YOUR NEEDS*—A rigid set of quality specifications should be written for each quality of food to be purchased. Specifications for quality should include:

1. a description detailed enough to make competitive bidding possible
2. statement of exact amount of each item needed
3. a description of the expected condition of the food to be received

Such requirements for purchasing specifications provide an additional means of cost control at an early point in the food purchasing process. An operation's own set of specifications should be supplemented by those available from the USDA.

The use to be made of the product in the food service operation should also be reflected in the specifications written for it. For example, a fancy or extrastandard grade green bean may be acceptable for one menu situation, but if it is to be used on a serving line, a type of green bean should be selected that will resist steam table wilt or deterioration.

Specifications for a product can be established by using as a reference "USDA Quality Grade Standards" and "Food and Drug Standards of Identity, Quality and Fill." This informa-

FIGURE 9–FOOD SERVICES DEPARTMENT
DAILY MANAGER ON DUTY REPORT

UNIT _____

DAY_____ DATE_____

MEAL CENSUS

PROBLEMS AND EXCEPTIONS

BREAKFAST

ESTIMATE_____ ACTUAL_____

PAID _____ | cash | chg | total

FOOD QUALITY Sup ☐ Std ☐ Una ☐

ACCEPTANCE Sup ☐ Std ☐ Una ☐

MOD

CONTI-NENTAL

ESTIMATE_____ ACTUAL_____

PAID _____ | cash | chg | total

MOD

LUNCHEON

ESTIMATE_____ ACTUAL_____

PAID _____ | cash | chg | total

FOOD QUALITY Sup ☐ Std ☐ Una ☐

ACCEPTANCE Sup ☐ Std ☐ Una ☐

MOD

DINNER

ESTIMATE_____ ACTUAL_____

PAID _____ | cash | chg | total

FOOD QUALITY Sup ☐ Std ☐ Una ☐

ACCEPTANCE Sup ☐ Std ☐ Una ☐

MOD

ITEMS DISCARDED   DAILY WASTE REASONS   INITIALS

Copy to Director of Food Service

tion is reproduced annually in "The Almanac of the Canning, Freezing, Preserving Industries."[1]

An example of the use of "The Almanac" as a reference in establishing specifications illustrates how this publication can be used as a purchasing guide. In one large institution, all of the sizes of chunk carrots that could be purchased were listed, with all specified to be at the same level of quality. After conferences with the cafeteria managers and the food service staff dietitian, agreement on a desired size for a chunk carrot was reached. This size was then correlated with the sizes in "The Almanac," and product specifications were easily determined.

Well-written, concise food specifications are an essential tool for the buyer, the receiving clerk, and management.

4. *DEVELOP A BUYING PROCEDURE AND TAKE A COURSE OF ACTION*—One reason for having a central purchasing department is to relieve the food operations managers of the responsibilities and details encountered in purchasing. It is, therefore, strongly recommended for most food establishments that all purchasing of food be administered by a central purchasing office. The unit managers place their orders by sending data on their needs to the central office and the purchasing personnel then buy for all units collectively. In addition to making the cafeteria manager's job easier by allowing him/her to concentrate on operations management, savings can be realized by buying in larger quantities.

When the total food needs for all units have been determined and when written specifications have been formulated, then the food buyer is ready to purchase the food. In order to purchase most efficiently, the purchasing office must develop buying procedures. These procedures can be divided into two general classes, bid buying and non-bid, or open market, buying.

Bid Buying

Bid buying is done by the central purchasing office when it is advantageous to do so from a cost standpoint. For example, when canned food products are bought in large quantity, bid buying is used. By inviting bids for these products, more food suppliers will have a chance to market their product, greater competition will exist, and lower purchase prices should result. Also, since there will be a wider selection to choose from, management can be more selective and better quality can be obtained through this bid buying technique.

Bid buying will usually minimize any favoritism problem that exists in a food purchasing situation. Bid prices are announced privately or publicly, and the lowest price quoted for a particular item is ordinarily chosen. However, awarding the bid on the basis of price alone may not always be wise. Sometimes the lowest-priced product may not meet specifications or may cost more on a cost-per-serving basis.

Value Analysis

It is always essential to consider the end use and form of the product to be purchased.

Purchasing people have been known to say, "It is my job to buy at the right price. To do this, I must analyze cost." They do not necessarily mean that they intend to buy the product with the lowest price. What they mean is that they plan to use common sense in systematically analyzing the total cost of a product or service by considering its end use, form, and function. As an example, they will consider all aspects before making a decision on convenience foods rather than buying, just because their purchase price is lower, "straight-from-the-garden" potatoes that have to be washed, peeled, and processed.

Bid Procedure

When the items and the quantities to be bought have been determined, requests for bids are sent to approved food suppliers. The food suppliers quote their prices on bid sheets, seal and return them to the purchasing department where they are opened on a specified date. In addition, as stated in the bid conditions, the food suppliers send two samples of every product for which they have quoted a price. (Examples of general and special bid conditions may be seen in Appendix B.)

Bidding and Samples

The bid conditions should be constantly revised as changes

1. Edward E. Judge & Sons, *The Almanac of the Canning, Freezing, Preserving Industries,* Seventy-Nine Bond Street, Westminster, Maryland 21157.

and/or additions are made in any phase of the food selection procedures. For example, section SBC-5 of the special bid conditions (see Appendix) states that the samples required by the buyer should be of the same quality grade as the merchandise on which the bid was made. However, in addition to being the same quality, the samples should be from the same lot of product that would be shipped if the supplier's brand were selected for purchase. In other words, the samples submitted and the goods shipped should have almost identical manufacturer's code numbers, and these should be included on the government grader's certificate (Figure 10).

After the bid prices and samples are obtained, the purchasing staff and other members of the management staff evaluate the samples and select the brand to be purchased for each food item. The evaluation and selection can be separated into four separate procedures:

1. coding and obtaining preliminary technical information from the main samples.
2. evaluating and rating of samples by staff members
3. establishing price comparisons
4. making the selection

Coding

First, the staff must remove the labels from all the samples and give each sample a test code. The coding is done in order to eliminate any prejudices that might affect the evaluation process. After the cans are coded, preliminary technical information is obtained, such as product, style, brand, manufacturer's can code, supplier, label weight, grade, pack price, and other information that applies. This information is recorded on the product information sheet (Figure 11). A separate sheet is used for each sample.

Evaluation and Rating

Next, the evaluation and rating of the samples is done. Testing information is obtained and the samples are poured onto grading trays and are evaluated and rated as to their quality by staff members. To record the ratings, a modified government scoring sheet is used (Figure 12). This eliminates the high degree of variation that is inherent in a subjective evalua-

tion when terms such as "poor," "average" and "excellent" are used.

By using a modified government scoring sheet, a high degree of variation is almost certain to be eliminated. For each product evaluated, the government score sheet lists the factors of quality that determine its score. These factors are explained in detail in the USDA standards for that particular product. Then, a number score can be assigned to each quality factor. After all factors are evaluated, the sum of the points scored can be calculated for each sample, and these sums can be readily compared and the samples ranked in order.

Price Comparisons

The third procedure in evaluating and selecting food items is the establishment of price comparisons. After the samples are rated, the prices of the top three deemed acceptable for use are compared (see Appendix). Price comparisons are calculated for price per ounce and/or cost per serving.

Making the Selection

After the quality has been determined and price comparison calculated, the fourth step of the evaluation and selection process can be made. The food buyer selects the product that meets the quality standards and still keeps purchasing cost at a minimum.

After the final selection is made, the information sheets, the evaluation sheets and the price comparisons for each product that has been tested are placed in a folder and stored in a file at the central purchasing office.

Open Market Buying

Open market buying is used extensively by commercial and institutional food buyers. This type of buying is the simple and informal quoting of prices by the food supplier and a placement of an order by the food buyer. Two advantages of this type of buying are (1) negotiations between buyer and supplier sometimes result in lower purchase prices and (2) the convenience of buying at any time desired. Using this method, it would be possible for a buyer to take advantage of low seasonal prices on food items during their harvest season.

FIGURE 10—GOVERNMENT GRADING CERTIFICATE

FORM FV-146
(7-1-61)
COPY

U.S. DEPARTMENT OF AGRICULTURE
CONSUMER AND MARKETING SERVICE
CERTIFICATE OF QUALITY AND CONDITION
(PROCESSED FOODS)

This certificate is receivable in all courts of the United States as prima facie evidence of the truth of the statements therein contained. It does not excuse failure to comply with any applicable Federal or State laws. *WARNING: Any person who knowingly shall falsely make, issue, alter, forge, or counterfeit this certificate, or participate in any such actions, is subject to a fine of not more than $1,000 or imprisonment for not more than one year, or both. (7 U.S.C. 1622 (h)).*

DATE   November 6,

APPLICANT   *XYZ* Canning Company

ADDRESS

RECEIVER OR BUYER   - - - - - - - - - - -

ADDRESS   - - - - - - - - - - -

SOURCE OF SAMPLES
Officially Drawn

PRODUCT INSPECTED
CANNED WHITE POTATOES

CODE MARKS ON CONTAINERS

POTAT 3XP80,	POTAT 3XP71,	POTAT 3XN86,	POTAT 3XN94,	POTAT 3XP81,	POTAT 3XN59,	POTAT 3XP64

PRINCIPAL LABEL MARKS
Unlabeled

Net Weight:	Meets Net Weight of 106 ounces
Vacuum Readings:	6 to 9 inches
Drained Weight:	Sample Average 75.4 ounces
Style:	Whole
Count:	106 to 114
Size:	Small

GRADE: U.S. GRADE A or U.S. FANCY
Average Score 93 points

REMARKS: This certificate covers 800 cases 6/No. 10 cans (Packer's count). Containers drawn for quality are in good condition. Samples drawn from lot located *XYZ* Canning Company, and identified by code.

ADDRESS OF INSPECTION OFFICE

SIGNATURE OF INSPECTOR

Pursuant to the regulations issued by the Secretary of Agriculture under the Agricultural Marketing Act of 1946, as amended (7 U.S.C. 1621-1627), governing the inspection and certification of the product designated herein, I certify that the quality and condition of the product as shown by samples inspected on the above date were as shown, subject to any restrictions specified above.

PLEASE REFER TO THIS CERTIFICATE BY NUMBER AND INSPECTION OFFICE
U.S. GOVERNMENT PRINTING OFFICE: 1970 - 404-988

FIGURE 11–PRODUCT INFORMATION

A. Preliminary and Supplied Information

Product:
Style:
Brand:
Manufacturer's Can Code:
Supplier:
Label Weight:
Label Dr. Wt.:
Supplier's Count:
USDA Grade:
Size of Container:
Case Price:
Cost Per Pack:
Cost per oz:

B. Testing Information

Test Code:
Wt. of Container:
Net Weight:
Drain Weight:
Percent Fill:
Headspace:
Vacuum:
Defects of Container:
Defects of Product:
Sieve Size of Count:
Syrup Brix:
Clearness of Liquor:
Flavor/Odor:
Number of Servings:
Comments:

DATE_____ TECHNOLOGIST_____

5. *SPOT-CHECK AND INSPECT ALL DELIVERIES*—After a food item is bought, a buyer should spot-check the shipment of the purchased item on arrival or delivery to prevent the receipt and acceptance of an incorrect shipment.

If discrepancies are noted by the receiving clerk or the food service manager, these should be reported immediately to the purchasing manager and/or buyer so that a decision on the acceptance or rejection of the delivery can be made.

The end product of purchasing to standards is satisfied customers.

FIGURE 12–SCORING SHEET

FACTORS	SCORE POINTS	SAMPLE CODE NUMBERS												
COLOR	(A 21-25) 1-25													
CONSISTENCY	(A 22-25) 1-25													
ABSENCE OF DEFECT	(A 21-25) 1-25													
FLAVOR	(A 21-25) 1-25													
TOTAL SCORE	(A-B 85-100)													
	100													
FLAVOR/ODOR														

COMMENTS:

Signed _____

7/ RECIPES

(See Chapter 2—Introduction to the Use of Recipes for explanation of forms; for abbreviations, see Appendix.)

Sauces and Gravies

0520	BROWN GRAVY				SAUCES AND GRAVIES
Recipe No.	Recipe Name				Category

Serving Standards: _____ _____ __2 oz__ _____ __Hot__

Pan   Portions/Pan   Portion Size   Utensil   Temperature

Ingredients	Portions 16	320	640	1280	Procedure
Yield	.25 gal	5.00 gal	10.00 gal	20.00 gal	
MARGARINE, SOLID, 1 lb	2.00 oz	2.50 lb	5.00 lb	10.00 lb.	1. Melt margarine in steam kettle.
FLOUR, 25 lb bag	2.00 oz	2.50 lb	5.00 lb	10.00 lb	2. Stir flour into margarine to make a roux.
WATER, cold	3.62 cup	4.00 gal	9.00 gal	18.00 gal	3. Combine beef base with roux and blend well. Add
		2.00 qt.	1.00 cup	2.00 cup	other seasonings.
		.50 cup			4. Add water and stir rapidly.
BEEF SOUP BASE, 12/1 lb/cs	.75 oz	.75 lb	1.75 lb	3.75 lb	5. Simmer until thin, smooth sauce is formed, about
		3.00 oz	2.00 oz		10 min.
SALT, 100 lb bag	.31 tsp	2.00 tbs	.25 cup	.50 cup	6. Serve according to instructions.
		.25 tsp	.50 tsp	1.00 tsp	Cooking time: 10 min.
PEPPER, BLACK, GROUND,	.18 tsp	1.00 tbs	2.00 tbs	.25 cup	Cooking temp: simmer
6 lb.		.75 tsp	1.50 tsp	1.00 tbs	Equipment: steam kettle
GRAVY MIX, 4/1 gal/cs	1.25 tsp	.50 cup	1.00 cup	2.00 cup	*Variation:* For pork or veal make a light brown gravy
		1.00 tsp	2.00 tsp	1.00 tbs	by reducing gravy mix by 1/2.
				1.00 tsp	
MONOSODIUM GLUTAMATE,	.62 tsp	.25 cup	.50 cup	1.00 cup	
2 lb can		.50 tsp	1.00 tsp	2.00 tsp	

0530	CHICKEN (or TURKEY) GRAVY	SAUCES AND GRAVIES
Recipe No.	Recipe Name	Category

Serving Standards:

Pan	Portions/Pan	2 oz Portion Size	2 oz Ladle Utensil	Hot Temperature

Ingredients	Portions				Procedure
	16	320	640	1280	
Yield	.25 gal	5.00 gal	10.00 gal	20.00 gal	
MARGARINE, SOLID, 1 lb	.25 lb	5.00 lb	10.00 lb	20.00 lb	1. Melt margarine in steam kettle.
FLOUR, 25 lb bag	2.00 oz	2.50 lb	5.00 lb	10.00 lb	2. Stir flour into margarine to make a roux.
CHICKEN SOUP BASE,	1.00 oz	1.25 lb	2.50 lb	5.00 lb	3. Add chicken base and blend well.
12/1 lb/cs					4. Add water and stir rapidly.
WATER, cold	3.33 cup	4.00 gal	8.00 gal	16.00 gal	5. Add salt and monosodium glutamate. Mix well.
		2.66 cup	1.00 qt	2.00 qt	6. Simmer until a thin, smooth sauce is formed, about
			1.32 cup	2.64 cup	10 min.
SALT, 100 lb bag	.33 tsp	2.00 tbs	.25 cup	.50 cup	Cooking time: 12 to 15 min.
		.66 tsp	1.32 tsp	2.64 tsp	Cooking temp: simmer
MONOSODIUM GLUTAMATE,	.50 tsp	3.00 tbs	.25 cup	.75 cup	Equipment: steam kettle
2 lb can		1.00 tsp	2.00 tbs	1.00 tbs	
			2.00 tsp	1.00 tsp	

0610	BARBECUE SAUCE				SAUCES AND GRAVIES
Recipe No.	Recipe Name				Category

Serving Standards:

		3 oz	3 oz Ladle	
Pan	Portions/Pan	Portion Size	Utensil	Temperature

Ingredients	Portions				Procedure
	48	96	192	480	
Yield	1.00 gal	2.00 gal	4.00 gal	10.00 gal	
					1. Rehydrate onions in specified amount of water.
ONIONS, DEHYD CHOP	1.00 oz	2.00 oz	.25 lb	10.00 oz	2. Combine all ingredients except the last item, water,
2.5 lb XSTD 6/10					in a steam kettle and blend thoroughly.
WATER, cold	.50 cup	1.00 cup	2.00 cup	1.00 qt	3. Simmer for 30 min.
				1.00 cup	4. Add hot water and stir well.
TOMATO CATSUP, 6/10 cs	1.00 can	2.00 can	4.00 can	10.00 can	5. Serve according to desired use.
VINEGAR, COLORED,	1.50 cup	3.00 cup	1.00 qt	3.00 qt	Cooking time: 30 min
DIST 4/1 gal/cs			2.00 cup	3.00 cup	Cooking temp: simmer
MUSTARD, GROUND, 1 lb	.75 oz	1.50 oz	3.00 oz	7.50 oz	Equipment: steam kettle
WORCESTERSHIRE SAUCE,	.75 cup	1.50 cup	3.00 cup	1.00 qt	
4/1 gal/cs				3.50 cup	
SALT, 100 lb bag	1.00 oz	2.00 oz	.25 lb	10.00 oz	
LEMON JUICE,	.25 cup	.75 cup	1.50 cup	1.00 qt	
RECONSTITUTED, 12/qt jars	2.00 tbs	1.00 tbs	2.00 tbs	1.00 tbs	
	1.50 tsp				
HOT SAUCE, 4/gal/cs	2.00 tbs	.25 cup	.50 cup	1.25 cup	
SUGAR, GRAN, 100 lb	2.00 oz	.25 lb	.50 lb	1.25 lb	
WATER, hot, 180°F.	1.50 cup	3.00 cup	1.00 qt	3.00 qt	
			2.00 cup	3.00 cup	

0620	CHEESE SAUCE				SAUCES AND GRAVIES
Recipe No.	Recipe Name				Category

Serving Standards:

		1 oz		Hot
Pan	Portions/Pan	Portion Size	Utensil	Temperature

Ingredients	Portions				Procedure
	64	128	640	1280	
Yield	2.00 qt	1.00 gal	5.00 gal	10.00 gal	1. Grate cheese.
CHEDDAR CHEESE, WHEEL	.75 lb	1.50 lb	8.00 lb	16.25 lb	2. Melt margarine in steam kettle.
	1.00 oz	2.00 oz	2.00 oz		3. Add flour to make a roux and cook for 5 min., stir-
MARGARINE, SOLID, 1 lb	.25 lb	.75 lb	4.00 lb	8.00 lb	ring until smooth.
	2.50 oz	1.00 oz	1.00 oz	2.00 oz	4. Turn steam off.
FLOUR, 25 lb bag	3.25 oz	.25 lb	2.00 lb	4.00 lb	5. Add water to roux. Mix until smooth.
		2.50 oz	.50 oz	1.00 oz	6. Add dry milk to mixture, stirring constantly; turn
WATER, hot, 180°F.	1.50 qt	3.00 qt	3.00 gal	7.00 gal	on steam and cook for 6 to 12 min. until thickened.
			3.00 qt	2.00 qt	7. Add cheese, salt, white pepper and Worcestershire
MILK, INST NONFAT DRY,	.25 lb	.75 lb	3.75 lb	7.50 lb	sauce and stir until cheese is melted.
6/5 lb	2.00 oz				8. Serve according to desired use.
SALT, 100 lb bag	1.75 tsp	1.00 tbs	.25 cup	.50 cup	*Note:* 1 gal cheese sauce wt is 8.5 lb.
		.50 tsp	1.00 tbs	3.00 tbs	Cooking time: 15 min. total
			2.50 tsp	2.00 tsp	Equipment: steam kettle
PEPPER, WHITE, GROUND,	.02 tsp	.05 tsp	.25 tsp	.50 tsp	
1 lb					
WORCESTERSHIRE SAUCE,	2.25 tsp	1.00 tbs	.25 cup	.75 cup	
4/1 gal/cs		1.50 tsp	3.00 tbs	3.00 tbs	
			1.50 tsp		

0622	CUSTARD SAUCE				SAUCES AND GRAVIES
Recipe No.	Recipe Name				Category

Serving Standards:

Pan	Portions/Pan	1 oz Portion Size	1 oz Ladle Utensil	Temperature

Ingredients	Portions				Procedure
	50	100	200	500	
Yield	.40 gal	.80 gal	1.60 gal	4.00 gal	
WATER, cold	1.25 qt	2.50 qt	1.00 gal 1.00 qt	3.00 gal .50 qt	1. Place cold water in mixing bowl; add dry milk and dissolve.
MILK, INST NONFAT DRY, 6/5 lb	5.00 oz	10.00 oz	1.25 lb	3.00 lb 2.00 oz	2. Add pudding mix and stir with wire whip until well mixed.
PUDDING, INSTANT VANILLA, 12/2 lb	.25 box	.50 box	1.00 box	2.50 box	3. Portion with 1 oz ladle.

0640	WHITE SAUCE (MEDIUM)				SAUCES AND GRAVIES
Recipe No.	**Recipe Name**				**Category**

Serving Standards: _____ _____ __1 oz__ _____ _____

| | Pan | Portions/Pan | Portion Size | Utensil | Temperature |

Ingredients	Portions				Procedure
	32	**128**	**640**	**1280**	
Yield	.25 gal	1.00 gal	5.00 gal	10.00 gal	1. Melt margarine in steam kettle.
MARGARINE, SOLID, 1 lb	3.50 oz	14.00 oz	4.00 lb	8.75 lb	2. Add flour and stir with a wire whip and cook for 5
			6.00 oz		min.
FLOUR, 25 lb bag	1.75 oz	7.00 oz	2.00 lb	4.00 lb	3. Turn off steam and add hot water and mix until
			3.00 oz	6.00 oz	smooth.
WATER, hot, 180°F.	3.25 cup	3.00 qt	4.00 gal	8.00 gal	4. Add dry milk and stir until dissolved.
		1.00 cup	1.00 cup	2.00 cup	5. Turn on steam and simmer until thickened, 6 to 12
MILK, INST NONFAT DRY, 6/5 lb	3.25 oz	13.00 oz	4.00 lb	8.00 lb	min.
			1.00 oz	2.00 oz	6. Add salt.
SALT, 100 lb bag	.75 tsp	1.00 tbs	.25 cup	.50 cup	7. Serve according to desired use.
			1.00 tbs	2.00 tbs	Equipment: steam kettle

0660	COCKTAIL SAUCE				SAUCES AND GRAVIES
Recipe No.	Recipe Name				Category

Serving Standards: _____   _____   __1 oz__   __1 oz Ladle__   __Cool__

Pan   Portions/Pan   Portion Size   Utensil   Temperature

Ingredients	Portions				Procedure
	50	**100**	**200**	**400**	
Yield	1.62 qt	3.33 qt	6.66 qt	13.33 qt	
CHILI SAUCE, 6/10	.50 can	1.00 can	2.00 can	4.00 can	1. Combine all ingredients in mixing bowl. Stir well.
HORSERADISH, 12/qt/cs	.50 cup	1.00 cup	2.00 cup	1.00 qt	2. Chill immediately.
WORCESTERSHIRE SAUCE,	2.00 tbs	.25 cup	.50 cup	1.00 cup	3. Serve according to desired use.
4/1 gal/cs					
HOT SAUCE, 4/gal/cs	.25 tsp	.50 tsp	1.00 tsp	2.00 tsp	
CELERY SEED, 1 lb	1.50 tsp	1.00 tbs	2.00 tbs	.25 cup	

0670	CREOLE SAUCE				SAUCES AND GRAVIES
Recipe No.	Recipe Name				Category

Serving Standards: _____   _____   __2 oz__   _____   __Hot__
                          Pan   Portions/Pan   Portion Size   Utensil   Temperature

Ingredients	Portions				Procedure
	40	160	320	640	
Yield	2.50 qt	2.50 gal	5.00 gal	10.00 gal	
ONIONS, DEHYD CHOP, 2.5 lb XSTD 6/10	.25 oz	1.00 oz	2.00 oz	.25 lb	1. Rehydrate green peppers and onions in specified amt of water for 45 min.
PEPPERS, DEHYD DICED, GRN, 1.25 lb XSTD 6/10	.25 oz	1.00 oz	2.00 oz	.25 lb	2. Melt margarine in steam kettle. Add onions and green peppers and saute 10 min. Do not brown.
WATER, cold	.50 cup	2.00 cup	1.00 qt	2.00 qt	3. Add flour, stirring constantly with a wire whip. Cook slowly 5 min., stirring occasionally.
MARGARINE, SOLID, 1 lb	5.00 oz	1.25 lb	2.50 lb	5.00 lb	
FLOUR, 25 lb bag	3.00 oz	.75 lb	1.50 lb	3.00 lb	4. Add tomatoes and stir with a wire whip to break them up.
TOMATOES, BROKEN, dr wt 64 oz XSTD 6/10	.75 can	3.00 can	6.00 can	12.00 can	5. Add water and simmer about 15 min.
WATER, cold	.50 cup	2.00 cup	1.00 qt	2.00 qt	6. Add salt and sugar and stir.
SALT, 100 lb bag	.50 oz	2.00 oz	.25 lb	.50 lb	7. Turn off steam and serve according to desired use.
SUGAR, GRAN, 100 lb	.75 oz	3.00 oz	6.00 oz	.75 lb	Cooking time: 30 min.
					Cooking temp: simmer
					Equipment: steam jacketed kettle

0690	GREEN PEA SAUCE				SAUCES AND GRAVIES
Recipe No.	Recipe Name				Category

Serving Standards:

		2 oz	2 oz Ladle	Hot
Pan	Portions/Pan	Portion Size	Utensil	Temperature

Ingredients	Portions				Procedure
	32	64	320	640	
Yield	.50 gal	1.00 gal	5.00 gal	10.00 gal	
MARGARINE, SOLID, 1 lb	6.00 oz	.75 lb	3.75 lb	7.50 lb	1. Melt margarine in steam kettle.
FLOUR, 25 lb bag	3.00 oz	6.00 oz	1.00 lb 14.00 oz	3.75 lb	2. Add flour while stirring with a wire whip and cook for 5 min.
WATER, hot, 180°F.	1.50 qt	3.00 qt	3.00 gal 3.00 qt	7.00 gal 2.00 qt	3. Turn steam off. 4. Add hot water and mix until smooth.
MILK, INST NONFAT DRY, 6/5 lb	6.00 oz	.75 lb	3.75 lb	7.50 lb	5. Add dry milk, stirring constantly. 6. Turn on steam and cook for 6 to 12 min. until thickened.
SALT, 100 lb bag	1.12 tsp	2.25 tsp	3.00 tbs 2.25 tsp	.25 cup 3.00 tbs 1.50 tsp	7. Add salt. 8. Cook green peas in high speed steam cooker for 1 min.
PEAS, SM FNCY, 20 lb box	6.00 oz	.75 lb	3.75 lb	7.50 lb	9. Drain peas and fold into sauce. 10. Place sauce in serving pans and serve according to desired use. Equipment: steam kettle, high speed steam cooker

0708	SAUERBRATEN SAUCE				SAUCES AND GRAVIES
Recipe No.	Recipe Name				Category

Serving Standards: _____   _____   2 oz   _____   Hot

Pan   Portions/Pan   Portion Size   Utensil   Temperature

Ingredients	Portions				Procedure
	32	320	640	1280	
Yield	.50 gal	5.00 gal	10.00 gal	20.00 gal	
ONIONS, YELLOW, MED, 50 lb FNCY	.50 lb	5.00 lb	10.00 lb	20.00 lb	1. Wash and peel onions. Weight is AP.
CARROTS, FNCY BULK, 50 lb, no tops	.25 lb	2.50 lb	5.00 lb	10.00 lb	2. Wash and trim carrots. Weight is AP. 3. Slice onions and carrots one-eighth inch thick using slicer.
WATER, hot, 180°F.	1.00 qt .25 cup	2.00 gal 2.00 qt 2.50 cup	5.00 gal 1.00 qt 1.00 cup	10.00 gal 2.00 qt 2.00 cup	4. Steam carrots and onions in high speed steam cooker until tender, about 1.5 min. Drain liquid and save.
VINEGAR, RED WINE, DIST, 4/1 gal/cs	.66 cup	1.00 qt 2.66 cup	3.00 qt 1.32 cup	1.00 gal 2.00 qt 2.64 cup	5. Place hot water, red wine vinegar, sherry, spices and raisins in steam kettle and bring to boil. 6. Add liquid from carrots and onions from Step 4.
COOKING SHERRY, gallons	1.00 cup	2.00 qt 2.00 cup	1.00 gal 1.00 qt	2.00 gal 2.00 qt	7. Skim the fat from the top of the beef drippings. Measure remaining drippings and add water if neces-
CLOVES, WHOLE, 1 lb	.37 tsp	1.00 tbs .75 tsp	2.00 tbs 1.50 tsp	.25 cup 1.00 tbs	sary to get the amount of drippings specified. Add to steam kettle.
PEPPER, BLACK, GROUND, 6 lb	.37 tsp	1.00 tbs .75 tsp	2.00 tbs 1.50 tsp	.25 cup 1.00 tbs	8. Crush the ginger snaps and add while stirring with a wire whip. Continue to simmer until thickened, 8
MUSTARD SEEDS, 20 oz	.50 tsp	1.00 tbs 2.00 tsp	3.00 tbs 1.00 tsp	.25 cup 2.00 tbs 2.00 tsp	to 10 min. 9. Fold into mixture the cooked carrots and onions.
RAISINS, SEEDLESS, FNCY, 30 lb box	6.00 oz	3.75 lb	7.50 lb	15.00 lb	10. Pour over sliced roast beef in counter pans. Keep warm in holding cabinet.
BEEF DRIPPINGS from cooked meat	.75 cup	1.00 qt 3.50 cup	3.00 qt 3.00 cup	1.00 gal 3.00 qt 2.00 cup	Cooking time: 10 min. Cooking temp: simmer Equipment: steam kettle, high speed steam cooker
GINGER SNAPS, 6/14 oz/cs	.25 lb	2.50 lb	5.00 lb	10.00 lb	

0730	TOMATO SAUCE	SAUCES AND GRAVIES
Recipe No.	Recipe Name	Category

Serving Standards:

		2 oz	2 oz Ladle	Hot
Pan	Portions/Pan	Portion Size	Utensil	Temperature

Ingredients	Portions				Procedure
	80	160	320	640	
Yield	1.25 gal	2.50 gal	5.00 gal	10.00 gal	
					1. Rehydrate onion in specified amt of water for 45
ONIONS, DEHYD CHOP,	.50 oz	1.00 oz	2.00 oz	.25 lb	min.
2.5 lb XSTD 6/10					2. Melt margarine in steam kettle. Add onion and
WATER, cold	.25 cup	.50 cup	1.00 cup	2.00 cup	saute 10 min. Do not brown.
MARGARINE, SOLID, 1 lb	10.00 oz	1.25 lb	2.50 lb	5.00 lb	3. Add flour, stirring constantly with a wire whip;
FLOUR, 25 lb bag	6.00 oz	.75 lb	1.50 lb	3.00 lb	cook slowly 5 min. stirring occasionally.
TOMATOES, BROKEN,	1.50 can	3.00 can	6.00 can	12.00 can	4. Add tomatoes and stir with a wire whip to break
dr wt 64 oz XSTD 6/10					them up.
WATER, cold	1.50 cup	3.00 cup	1.00 qt	3.00 qt	5. Add water and simmer about 15 min.
			2.00 cup		6. Add salt and sugar and stir.
SALT, 100 lb bag	1.00 oz	2.00 oz	.25 lb	.50 lb	7. Turn off steam and serve according to desired use.
SUGAR, GRAN, 100 lb	1.50 oz	3.00 oz	6.00 oz	.75 lb	Cooking time: 30 min.
					Cooking temp: simmer
					Equipment: steam jacketed kettle

0731   **ITALIAN TOMATO SAUCE**   **SAUCES AND GRAVIES**

Recipe No.   Recipe Name   Category

Serving Standards: _____ _____ 2 oz _____ Hot

       Pan   Portions/Pan   Portion Size   Utensil   Temperature

Ingredients	44	264	528	1056	Procedure
Yield	2.75 qt	16.50 qt	8.25 gal	16.50 gal	1. Rehydrate onions in specified amt of water.
ONIONS, DEHYD CHOP, 2.5 lb XSTD 6/10	1.00 oz	.25 lb 2.00 oz	.75 lb	1.50 lb	2. Melt margarine in steam kettle; add rehydrated onions and saute for 5 min.
WATER, cold	.50 cup	3.00 cup	1.00 qt 2.00 cup	3.00 qt	3. Add flour and mix well. Cook about 5 min.
MARGARINE, SOLID, 1 lb	.25 lb	1.50 lb	3.00 lb	6.00 lb	4. Add second amt of water, diced tomatoes in puree and spice mix and mix well.
FLOUR, 25 lb bag	2.00 oz	.75 lb	1.50 lb	3.00 lb	5. Simmer about 20 min.
WATER, cold	1.00 qt	1.00 gal 2.00 qt	3.00 gal	6.00 gal	6. Serve according to desired use.
TOMATOES, DICED, HVY PUREE, FNCY, 6/10	1.00 can	6.00 can	12.00 can	24.00 can	Cooking time: total 30 min. Cooking temp: simmer
ITALIAN SPICE MIX, 14 oz bag	.25 oz	1.50 oz	3.00 oz	.25 lb 2.00 oz	Equipment: steam kettle

0805	CARAMEL SAUCE (FOR BANANAS, FOR ICE CREAM)				SAUCES AND GRAVIES
Recipe No.	Recipe Name				Category

Serving Standards: _____ _____ **1 tsp** _____ **Cold**

         Pan   Portions/Pan   Portion Size   Utensil   Temperature

Ingredients	Portions				Procedure
	360	720	1080	2160	
Yield	1.87 qt	3.75 qt	5.62 qt	11.25 qt	
SUGAR, LIGHT BROWN, 24/1 lb/cs	2.00 lb	4.00 lb	6.00 lb	12.00 lb	1. Place brown sugar, white corn syrup and water in steam kettle.
SYRUP, LIGHT CORN, 6/64 oz	2.00 cup	1.00 qt	1.00 qt 2.00 cup	3.00 qt	2. Cook until the soft ball stage, 230°F. Test thermometer and adjust the end point temperature accordingly. For example, if water boils at 208°F.
WATER, cold	1.00 cup	2.00 cup	3.00 cup	1.00 qt 2.00 cup	on your thermometer instead of 212°F., subtract 4° from the 230°F. and cook to 226°F. instead.
MARGARINE, SOLID, 1 lb	.50 lb	1.00 lb	1.50 lb	3.00 lb	3. Remove from kettle and add the margarine and
MARSHMALLOWS, REGULAR, 12/1 lb	1.87 oz	3.75 oz	.25 lb 1.62 oz	.50 lb 3.25 oz	marshmallows and stir until melted, using a wire whip. (8 marshmallows equal 1.875 oz.)
MILK, EVAPORATED, 48/14.5 oz	2.00 cup	1.00 qt	1.00 qt 2.00 cup	3.00 qt	4. Add evaporated milk gradually, stirring constantly. Cool.

Cooking temp: end point 230°F.

Equipment: steam kettle

0810	FRUIT SAUCE				SAUCES AND GRAVIES
Recipe No.	Recipe Name				Category

Serving Standards:

	Pan		Portions/Pan	1 oz Portion Size	1 oz Ladle Utensil	Hot Temperature

Ingredients	Portions				Procedure
	40	120	240	480	
Yield	1.25 qt	3.75 qt	7.50 qt	3.75 gal	
PINEAPPLE JUICE, 12/46 foz can	3.00 cup	2.00 qt 1.00 cup	1.00 gal 2.00 cup	2.00 gal 1.00 qt	1. When pineapple appears on the menu, the juice should be saved and substituted for canned pineapple juice here.
SUGAR, GRAN, 100 lb	2.50 oz	7.50 oz	15.00 oz	1.00 lb 14.00 oz	2. Place pineapple juice in steam kettle but do not turn on steam.
CORNSTARCH, 24/1 lb/cs	1.00 oz	3.00 oz	6.00 oz	.75 lb	3. Combine sugar and cornstarch and gradually add to cold pineapple juice, stirring constantly.
FRUIT COCKTAIL, FNCY, 6/10 can	2.00 cup	1.00 qt 2.00 cup	3.00 qt	1.00 gal 2.00 qt	4. Bring to boil and simmer 10 min.
RAISINS, SEEDLESS, FNCY, 30 lb box	2.00 oz	6.00 oz	.75 lb	1.50 lb	5. Place raisins in pressure steamer for 2 min. to puff them up.
CLOVES, GROUND, 1 lb	.06 tsp	.18 tsp	.37 tsp	.75 tsp	6. Add undrained fruit cocktail, raisins and ground cloves to sauce and stir just enough to combine. Simmer about 2 min.
					7. Fruit sauce may be poured over ham in counter pans or it may be placed in counter pans and 1 oz served over ham on plate if desired.

Cooking time: 15 min.

Equipment: steam kettle

0820	LEMON SAUCE				SAUCES AND GRAVIES
Recipe No.	Recipe Name				Category

Serving Standards:

	Pan	Portions/Pan	2 oz Portion Size	2 oz Ladle Utensil	Cool Temperature

Ingredients	Portions				Procedure
	36	216	432	864	
Yield	2.25 qt	13.50 qt	6.75 gal	13.50 gal	
SUGAR, GRAN, 100 lb	1.00 lb 10.00 oz	9.75 lb	19.50 lb	39.00 lb	1. Combine sugar, cornstarch and salt in steam kettle.
CORNSTARCH, 24/1 lb/cs	2.50 oz	15.00 oz	1.00 lb 14.00 oz	3.75 lb	2. Add cold water gradually while stirring to dissolve other ingredients.
SALT, 100 lb bag	.37 tsp	2.25 tsp	1.00 tbs 1.50 tsp	3.00 tbs	3. Turn on steam and cook approximately 10 min. until thick and clear, stirring frequently.
WATER, cold	1.50 qt	2.00 gal 1.00 qt	4.00 gal 2.00 qt	9.00 gal	4. Add lemon juice, margarine and yellow food color.
LEMON JUICE, RECONSTITUTED, 12/qt jars	.50 cup 1.00 tsp	3.00 cup 2.00 tbs	1.00 qt 2.00 tbs 2.00 tsp	3.00 qt .50 cup	5. Mixture then needs to be cooled to be thick enough. *Note:* To serve hot add 1 lb cornstarch per 20 lb sugar. Cooking time: 10 min.
MARGARINE, SOLID, 1 lb	.87 oz	5.25 oz	10.50 oz	1.00 lb 5.00 oz	Cooking temp: simmer Equipment: steam kettle
YELLOW CONC, qt	.08 tsp	.50 tsp	1.00 tsp	2.00 tsp	

0830	VANILLA SAUCE	SAUCES AND GRAVIES
Recipe No.	Recipe Name	Category

Serving Standards:

		2 oz	2 oz Ladle	Cool
Pan	Portions/Pan	Portion Size	Utensil	Temperature

Ingredients	Portions				Procedure
	54	216	432	648	
Yield	13.50 cup	13.50 qt	6.75 gal	10.00 gal	
					1. Combine sugar, cornstarch and salt in steam kettle.
SUGAR, GRAN, 100 lb	2.50 lb	10.00 lb	20.00 lb	30.00 lb	2. Add cold water gradually while stirring to dissolve
CORNSTARCH, 24/1 lb/cs	.25 lb	1.00 lb	2.00 lb	3.00 lb	other ingredients.
SALT, 100 lb bag	.62 tsp	2.50 tsp	1.00 tbs	2.00 tbs	3. Turn on steam and cook approximately 10 min.
			2.00 tsp	1.50 tsp	until thick and clear, stirring occasionally.
WATER, cold	2.50 qt	2.00 gal	5.00 gal	7.00 gal	4. Add margarine, yellow food color and vanilla. Mix
		2.00 qt		2.00 qt	well.
MARGARINE, SOLID, 1 lb	1.25 oz	5.00 oz	10.00 oz	15.00 oz	5. Sauce then needs to be cooled to be thick enough.
YELLOW CONC, pt	.12 tsp	.50 tsp	1.00 tsp	1.50 tsp	*Note:* To serve hot add 1 lb extra cornstarch per 20
VANILLA, 12 qt case	2.00 tbs	.50 cup	1.00 cup	1.50 cup	lb sugar.
					Cooking time: 10 min.
					Cooking temp: simmer
					Equipment: steam kettle

Entrees

1030	CHARCOAL BROILED STRIP STEAK				ENTREES—Beef
Recipe No.	**Recipe Name**				**Category**

Serving Standards: 20- by 12- by 2.5-in.   6 to 7 oz   Solid Spatula   Hot
Pan   Portions/Pan   Portion Size   Utensil   Temperature

Ingredients	Portions				Procedure
	50	**200**	**500**	**1000**	
LOIN, STRIP, CHO, whl, bnls, 13 lb	21.87 lb	87.50 lb	218.75 lb	437.50 lb	1. Trim excess fat from loin strip.
SALT, 100 lb bag	1.50 oz	6.00 oz	15.00 oz	1.00 lb 14.00 oz	2. Cut loin strips into 6 to 7 oz steaks using the slicer. Weigh steaks occasionally and change slicer setting as needed to get 6 to 7 oz portions.
PEPPER, BLACK, GROUND, 6 lb	.75 tsp	1.00 tbs	2.00 tbs 1.50 tsp	.25 cup 1.00 tbs	3. Cook steaks on charcoal grill for 7 min. on one side. Turn and cook for 5 min.
GARLIC POWDER, 1 lb	.25 tsp	1.00 tsp	2.50 tsp	1.00 tbs 2.00 tsp	4. Mix salt, pepper and garlic powder. Sprinkle over steaks. Seasoning is optional.
					5. Place in 20- by 12- by 2.5-in. counter pans to serve. Cooking time: 12 min. Equipment: charcoal grill

1050	COUNTRY FRIED STEAK				ENTREES—Beef
Recipe No.	Recipe Name				Category

Serving Standards: 20- by 12- by 2.5-in. ____ 4 oz ____ Solid Spatula ____ Hot ____

| | Pan | Portions/Pan | Portion Size | Utensil | Temperature |

Ingredients	Portions				Procedure
	40	120	480	960	
Yield	10.00 lb	30.00 lb	120.00 lb	240.00 lb	
STEAK, CH-CUB, 4 oz, 6 percent T.V.P.	10.00 lb	30.00 lb	120.00 lb	240.00 lb	1. Mix flour and seasonings and dredge frozen steaks in mixture.
FLOUR, 25 lb bag	.75 lb	2.25 lb	9.00 lb	18.00 lb	2. Oil grill and brown steaks on both sides at 350°F., or place 20 steaks on sheet pan and cook for 15 min. at 325°F. in conv oven.
SALT, 100 lb bag	1.25 oz	3.75 oz	15.00 oz	1.00 lb 14.00 oz	
PEPPER, BLACK, GROUND, 6 lb	.50 tsp	1.50 tsp	2.00 tbs	.25 cup	3. Rehydrate sliced onions in specified amt of water.
SHORTENING, LIQUID, for deep fat, 5 gal	1.25 cup	3.75 cup	3.00 qt 3.00 cup	1.00 gal 3.00 qt 2.00 cup	4. Make a brown gravy: melt margarine in steam kettle. Add flour and make a roux.
ONIONS, DEHYD, sliced 6/10	.25 lb	.75 lb	3.00 lb	6.00 lb	5. Add beef base and blend well, then add water and stir rapidly. 6. Simmer until a thin smooth sauce is formed.
WATER, cold	2.00 cup	1.00 qt 2.00 cup	1.00 gal 2.00 qt	3.00 gal	7. Add seasonings and gravy mix and stir well; turn off steam.
MARGARINE, SOLID, 1 lb	6.00 oz	1.00 lb 2.00 oz	4.50 lb	9.00 lb	8. Using 40 browned steaks and 3 qt of brown gravy make 2 layers of slightly overlapping steaks with re-
FLOUR, 25 lb bag	6.00 oz	1.00 lb 2.00 oz	4.50 lb	9.00 lb	hydrated onions and brown gravy over each layer. 9. Place in 300°F. conv oven for about 45 min.
BEEF SOUP BASE, 12/1 lb/cs	2.50 oz	7.50 oz	1.00 lb 14.00 oz	3.75 lb	*Note:* For each 10 lb of steak, .75 gal of gravy is re- quired.
WATER, cold	2.75 qt	2.00 gal .25 qt	8.00 gal 1.00 qt	16.00 gal 2.00 qt	Cooking time: total about 1 hr Cooking temp: see above
SALT, 100 lb bag	1.00 tsp	1.00 tbs	.25 cup	.50 cup	Equipment: grill, conv oven
PEPPER, BLACK, GROUND, 6 lb	.50 tsp	1.50 tsp	2.00 tbs	.25 cup	
GRAVY MIX, 4/1 gal/cs	1.00 tbs 1.00 tsp	.25 cup	1.00 cup	2.00 cup	
MONOSODIUM GLUTAMATE, 2 lb can	.75 tsp	1.00 tbs 2.25 tsp	.25 cup 3.00 tbs	.75 cup 2.00 tbs	

1052	WESTERN STEAK				ENTREES—Beef
Recipe No.	Recipe Name				Category

Serving Standards: <u>20- by 12- by 2.5-in.</u> <u>4 oz</u> <u>Solid Spatula</u> <u>Hot</u>
Pan   Portions/Pan   Portion Size   Utensil   Temperature

Ingredients	Portions				Procedure
	40	120	480	960	
ONIONS, DEHYD, CHOP, 2.5 lb XSTD 6/10	2.00 oz	.25 lb 2.00 oz	1.50 lb	3.00 lb	1. Rehydrate onions with specified water.
WATER, cold	1.00 cup	3.00 cup	3.00 qt	1.00 gal 2.00 qt	2. Combine flour, chili powder, monosodium glutamate, salt, black pepper, garlic powder and paprika.
FLOUR, 25 lb bag	.50 lb	1.50 lb	6.00 lb	12.00 lb	3. Reconstitute milk with water and stir in eggs with wire whip.
CHILI POWDER, 1 lb	.50 oz	1.50 oz	6.00 oz	.75 lb	4. Dredge frozen steaks in flour mixture, dip in egg-milk batter and roll in bread crumbs to which the onions have been added.
MONOSODIUM GLUTAMATE, 2 lb can	.50 oz	1.50 oz	6.00 oz	.75 lb	
SALT, 100 lb bag	1.00 oz	3.00 oz	.75 lb	1.50 lb	5. Place on sheet pans and bake in conv oven at 350°F. for 15 to 17 min.
PEPPER, BLACK, GROUND, 6 lb	.25 oz	.75 oz	3.00 oz	6.00 oz	6. Arrange in counter pans.
GARLIC POWDER, 1 lb	.50 oz	1.50 oz	6.00 oz	.75 lb	*Note:* Steaks may be breaded 1 day in advance and placed in refrigerator.
PAPRIKA, GROUND, 6 lb	.50 oz	1.50 oz	6.00 oz	.75 lb	Cooking time: 15 to 17 min.
MILK, INST NONFAT DRY, 6/5 lb	1.50 oz	4.50 oz	1.00 lb 2.00 oz	2.25 lb	Cooking temp: 350°F.
WATER, cold	1.50 cup	1.00 qt .50 cup	1.00 gal 2.00 cup	2.00 gal 1.00 qt	Equipment: conv oven
EGGS, 6/5 lb/cs	6.00 oz	1.00 lb 2.00 oz	4.50 lb	9.00 lb	
BREAD CRUMBS	1.50 lb	4.50 lb	18.00 lb	36.00 lb	
STEAK, CH-CUB, 4 oz, 6 percent T.V.P.	10.00 lb	30.00 lb	120.00 lb	240.00 lb	

1060	FLANK STEAK				ENTREES—Beef
Recipe No.	Recipe Name				Category

Serving Standards:

20- by 12- by 2.5-in.		2.5 oz	Tongs	Hot
Pan	Portions/Pan	Portion Size	Utensil	Temperature

Ingredients	Portions				Procedure
	50	100	200	500	
STK, FLANK GOOD GRADE, 16 oz	12.00 lb	24.00 lb	48.00 lb	120.00 lb	1. Place about 10 flank steaks on a sheet pan.
SALT, 100 lb bag	1.25 oz	2.50 oz	5.00 oz	12.50 oz	2. Sprinkle seasonings over meat.
PEPPER, BLACK, GROUND, 6 lb	.25 tsp	.50 tsp	1.00 tsp	2.50 tsp	3. Pour 0.25 cup of oil over ea pan of steaks.
					4. Cook in conv oven at 400°F. until the internal temp is 150°F., about 10 to 15 min.
GARLIC POWDER, 1 lb	.25 tsp	.50 tsp	1.00 tsp	2.50 tsp	5. Slice on No. 15 so that 6 to 8 slices weigh 2.5 oz for one serving.
MONOSODIUM GLUTAMATE, 2 lb can	2.25 tsp	1.00 tbs	3.00 tbs	.25 cup	
		1.50 tsp		3.00 tbs	6. Place in 20- by 12- by 2.5-in. counter pans.
				1.50 tsp	7. Serve with au jus or other desired sauce.
PAPRIKA, GROUND, 6 lb	.75 tsp	1.50 tsp	1.00 tbs	2.00 tbs	Cooking time: 10 to 15 min.
				1.50 tsp	Cooking temp: 400°F.
SHORTENING, LIQUID, for deep fat 5 gal	.33 cup	.66 cup	1.32 cup	3.30 cup	Equipment: conv oven

1079	GRILLED STEAK WITH DILL PICKLE	ENTREES—Beef
Recipe No.	Recipe Name	Category

Serving Standards: 20- by 12- by 2.5-in. / **Pan**   40 / **Portions/Pan**   4 oz / **Portion Size**   Solid Spatula / **Utensil**   Hot / **Temperature**

Ingredients	Portions				Procedure
	40	**200**	**520**	**1000**	
STEAK, CH-CUB, 4 oz, item 24, 10 lb/box	10.00 lb	50.00 lb	130.00 lb	250.00 lb	1. Start grill at 300°F. and coat with 1 cup oil. None is needed after that.
SALT, 100 lb bag	1.00 oz	5.00 oz	13.00 oz	1.00 lb 9.00 oz	2. Combine seasonings and use to season steaks as they are being grilled.
PEPPER, BLACK, GROUND, 6 lb	.50 tsp	2.50 tsp	2.00 tbs .50 tsp	.25 cup .50 tsp	3. Place frozen steaks on grill and cook until brown, about 4 min.
MONOSODIUM GLUTAMATE, 2 lb can	.20 tsp	1.00 tsp	2.60 tsp	1.00 tbs 2.00 tsp	4. Turn steaks over and cook other side until brown, about 3 min. Do not press. Turn only once.
PICKLES, THICK DILL CHIPS, 4/1 gal/cs	.12 gal	.61 gal	1.59 gal	3.07 gal	5. Place steaks in counter pans and garnish each with a dill pickle chip.
*BROWN GRAVY, Recipe 0520	.50 gal	2.50 gal	6.25 gal	12.50 gal	Cooking time: 7 min.
					Cooking temp: 300°F.
					Equipment: grill
					*Variation: Add brown gravy.

1090	SMOTHERED STEAK ON BUN (HALF)	ENTREES—Beef
Recipe No.	Recipe Name	Category

Serving Standards: 20- by 12- by 2.5-in. / **Pan**   / **Portions/Pan**   4 oz / **Portion Size**   / **Utensil**   Hot / **Temperature**

Ingredients	Portions				Procedure
	40	**120**	**480**	**960**	
COUNTRY FRIED STEAK, Recipe 1050	10.00 lb	30.00 lb	120.00 lb	240.00 lb	1. Prepare country fried steak.
ROLLS, HAMBURGER, pkg/12 4-inch, rd	1.66 doz	5.00 doz	20.00 doz	40.00 doz	2. Serve on warm bun half.

1095	CANTONESE STEAK (CHAR-BROILED)				ENTREES—Beef
Recipe No.	Recipe Name				Category

Serving Standards: 20- by 12- by 2.5-in. _____ 1 ea _____ Solid Spoon _____ Hot
                 Pan   Portions/Pan   Portion Size   Utensil   Temperature

Ingredients	Portions				Procedure
	30	120	240	960	
CANT BEEF STK, C.B. CHOP 2.6 oz sq	5.00 lb	20.00 lb	40.00 lb	160.00 lb	1. Place frozen fully-cooked char-broiled steak in steam table pans 20- by 12- by 2.5-in. so that air can circulate between them.
BROWN GRAVY, Recipe 0520	.50 gal	2.00 gal	4.00 gal	16.00 gal	2. Place in conv oven at 350°F. until thoroughly heated, about 8 min.
VEGETABLES, CHOW MEIN, 4/4 lb/cs	.50 lb	2.00 lb	4.00 lb	16.00 lb	3. Prepare brown gravy and hold.
					4. Cook chow mein vegetables in steamer until tender and add to gravy.
					5. Gravy may be poured over steak in counter pans or placed in separate pan to be served on request with 2 oz ladle.
					Cooking time: see above
					Cooking temp: 350°F.
					Equipment: conv oven, steam kettle and steamer

1101	SWISS STEAK	ENTREES—Beef
Recipe No.	Recipe Name	Category

Serving Standards: <u>20- by 12- by 2.5-in.</u>   <u>40</u>   <u>4 oz</u>   Solid Spoon   <u>Hot</u>
           Pan   Portions/Pan   Portion Size   Utensil   Temperature

Ingredients	Portions				Procedure
	40	120	480	960	
Yield	.75 gal	2.25 gal	9.00 gal	18.00 gal	
PEPPERS, DEHYD DICED, GRN, 1.25 lb XSTD 6/10	1.50 oz	4.50 oz	1.00 lb 2.00 oz	2.25 lb	1. Rehydrate green peppers and chopped onions in specified amt of water.
ONIONS, DEHYD CHOP, 2.5 lb XSTD 6/10	1.50 oz	4.50 oz	1.00 lb 2.00 oz	2.25 lb	2. Rehydrate sliced onions in second amt of water and set aside.
WATER, cold	1.50 cup	1.00 qt .50 cup	1.00 gal 2.00 cup	2.00 gal 1.00 qt	3. Prepare tomato gravy; melt margarine in steam kettle. Add flour and make a roux.
ONIONS, DEHYD, SLICED, 6/10	3.00 oz	9.00 oz	2.25 lb	4.50 lb	4. Add tomatoes and third amt of water and stir with a wire whip to break up the tomatoes. Stir until
WATER, cold	1.50 cup	1.00 qt .50 cup	1.00 gal 2.00 cup	2.00 gal 1.00 qt	thickened and simmer about 10 min.
MARGARINE, SOLID, 1 lb	1.50 oz	4.50 oz	1.00 lb 2.00 oz	2.25 lb	5. Add salt, sugar, rehydrated chopped onions and green peppers and stir. Turn off steam and hold.
FLOUR, 25 lb bag	1.50 oz	4.50 oz	1.00 lb 2.00 oz	2.25 lb	6. Mix second amts of flour and salt with black pepper and dredge frozen steaks in mixture.
TOMATOES, BROKEN, dr wt 64 oz XSTD 6/10	.50 can	1.50 can	6.00 can	12.00 can	7. Oil grill and brown steaks on both sides at 350°F. or place 20 steaks on sheet pan and cook for 15
WATER, cold	1.25 qt	3.75 qt	3.00 gal 3.00 qt	7.00 gal 2.00 qt	min. at 325°F. in conv oven.
SALT, 100 lb bag	1.00 tbs	3.00 tbs	.75 cup	1.50 cup	8. Using 40 browned steaks and 3 qt of tomato gravy from Step 5, make 2 layers of slightly overlapping
SUGAR, GRAN, 100 lb	1.00 tsp	1.00 tbs	.25 cup	.50 cup	steaks with rehydrated sliced onions and tomato
FLOUR, 25 lb bag	.75 lb	2.25 lb	9.00 lb	18.00 lb	gravy over each layer in 20- by 12- by 2.5-in. pans.
SALT, 100 lb bag	2.50 oz	7.50 oz	1.00 lb 14.00 oz	3.75 lb	9. Place in conv oven at 300°F. for about 45 min.
PEPPER, BLACK, GROUND, 6 lb	.75 tsp	2.25 tsp	3.00 tbs	.25 cup 2.00 tbs	*Note:* Yield is for tomato gravy. Cooking time: total about 1 hr Cooking temp: see above
STEAK, CH-CUB, 4 oz, 6 percent T.V.P.	10.00 lb	30.00 lb	120.00 lb	240.00 lb	Equipment: steam kettle, conv oven, grill

1103	ITALIAN STEAK PARMIGIANA				ENTREES—Beef
Recipe No.	Recipe Name				Category

Serving Standards: __20- by 12- by 2.5-in.__   __24__   __4 oz__   __Solid Spatula__   __Hot__
Pan   Portions/Pan   Portion Size   Utensil   Temperature

Ingredients	Portions				Procedure
	72	288	576	1152	
ITALIAN TOMATO SAUCE	2.75 qt	2.00 gal	5.00 gal	11.00 gal	1. Prepare Italian tomato sauce and hold.
Recipe 0731		3.00 qt	2.00 qt		2. Fill deep fat fryer with oil and heat to 350°F.
BRD ITALIAN BEEF STK	18.00 lb	72.00 lb	144.00 lb	288.00 lb	3. Place frozen Italian steaks in fryer basket and fry
6/6 lb/cs					in deep fat 4 to 5 min. or until golden brown.
					4. Place 24 steaks in counter pans 20- by 12- by 2.5-in.
					and pour 3.66 cups of Italian tomato sauce from
					Step 1 over each pan.
					Note: Amount of sauce is approx 1.25 oz/steak.
					Cooking time: 4 to 5 min.
					Cooking temp: 350°F.
					Equipment: deep fat fryer

1122	HOT ROAST BEEF SANDWICH				ENTREES—Beef
Recipe No.	Recipe Name				Category

Serving Standards: <u>20- by 12- by 2.5-in.</u>   <u>12</u>   <u>2 oz</u>   <u>Spatula</u>   <u>Hot</u>

             Pan   Portions/Pan   Portion Size   Utensil   Temperature

Ingredients	Portions				E*	Procedure
	30	120	480	960		
ROUND, GOOSENECK, US CHO No. 170, 20 lb	6.00 lb	24.00 lb	96.00 lb	192.00 lb		1. Season gooseneck round with salt and pepper on all sides.
SALT, 100 lb bag	.50 tsp	2.00 tsp	2.00 tbs 2.00 tsp	.25 cup 1.00 tbs 1.00 tsp		2. Roast in rotary oven at 300°F. until the internal temp is 140°F. approx 4 to 5 hr. Save drippings.
						3. Cool in refrigerator overnight. Roasts may be cut into smaller pieces for rapid cooling.
PEPPER, BLACK, GROUND, 6 lb	.25 tsp	1.00 tsp	1.00 tbs 1.00 tsp	2.00 tbs 2.00 tsp		4. Prepare brown gravy and hold. Beef drippings may be substituted for part of the margarine and water.
BROWN GRAVY, Recipe 0520	2.00 qt	2.00 gal	8.00 gal	16.00 gal		
BREAD, SANDWICH, WHITE, 32 oz	1.00 lf	4.00 lf	16.00 lf	32.00 lf		5. Slice roast into thin slices and place 2 oz on each slice of bread for an open-face sandwich.

6. Before placing on serving counter add 2 oz very hot gravy and place in holding cabinet.

Cooking time: 4 to 5 hr

Cooking temp: 300°F.

Equipment: rotary oven

*Early Prep: Cook roasts 1 day ahead of serving day to aid in thin slicing.

1132	SAUERBRATEN				ENTREES—Beef
Recipe No.	Recipe Name				Category

Serving Standards: __20- by 12- by 2.5-in.__ _____ __2.5 oz__ __Solid Spatula__ __Hot__
Pan   Portions/Pan   Portion Size   Utensil   Temperature

Ingredients	Portions				Procedure
	100	500	1000	1500	
ROUND, GOOSENECK, US CHO No. 170, 20 lb	25.00 lb	125.00 lb	250.00 lb	375.00 lb	1. Season gooseneck rounds with salt and pepper on all sides.
SALT, 100 lb bag	2.00 tsp	3.00 tbs 1.00 tsp	.25 cup 2.00 tbs 2.00 tsp	.50 cup 2.00 tbs	2. Roast in rotary oven at 300°F. until the internal temp is 140°F., approx 4 to 5 hr.
PEPPER, BLACK, GROUND, 6 lb	1.00 tsp	1.00 tbs 2.00 tsp	3.00 tbs 1.00 tsp	.25 cup 1.00 tbs	3. Remove from oven and place in holding cabinet until time to slice. 4. Prepare sauerbraten sauce.
SAUERBRATEN SAUCE Recipe 0708	1.50 gal	7.50 gal	15.00 gal	22.50 gal	5. Slice roast into 2.5 oz slices (slicer No. 11 or 12). 6. Place sliced meat in 20- by 12- by 2.5-in. counter pans and pour sauerbraten sauce over it. Cooking time: 4 to 5 hr Cooking temp: 300°F. Equipment: rotary oven

| 1140 | ROAST BEEF AU JUS | | | | ENTREES—Beef |
| Recipe No. | Recipe Name | | | | Category |

Serving Standards: 20- by 12- by 2.5-in.   45   2.5 oz   Tongs   Hot
                        Pan   Portions/Pan   Portion Size   Utensil   Temperature

| Ingredients | Portions | | | | Procedure |
	25	100	400	800	
Yield	3.75 lb	15.00 lb	60.00 lb	120.00 lb	
ROUND, GOOSENECK, US CHO No. 170, 20 lb	6.25 lb	25.00 lb	100.00 lb	200.00 lb	1. Season gooseneck round with salt and pepper on all sides.
SALT, 100 lb bag	.50 tsp	2.00 tsp	2.00 tbs 2.00 tsp	.25 cup 1.00 tbs 1.00 tsp	2. Roast in rotary oven at 300°F. until the internal temp is 140°F., approx 4 to 5 hr.
PEPPER, BLACK, GROUND, 6 lb	.25 tsp	1.00 tsp	1.00 tbs 1.00 tsp	2.00 tbs 2.00 tsp	3. Remove from oven and place in holding cabinet until time to slice.

3. Remove from oven and place in holding cabinet until time to slice.
4. Slice roast into 2.5 oz slices (slicer No. 11 or 12).
5. Place slices in 20- by 12- by 2.5-in. counter pan.
6. Use drippings from roast to make au jus. Pour enough over roast slices to prevent drying while in holding cabinet and on serving line.

Note: Yield is weight of usable meat after slicing losses are subtracted.

Cooking time: 4 to 5 hr
Cooking temp: 300°F.
Equipment: rotary oven

1145	COOKED ROAST BEEF					ENTREES—Beef
Recipe No.	Recipe Name					Category

Serving Standards:

	Pan		Portions/Pan		1.33 oz Portion Size	Utensil	Temperature

Ingredients	Portions				E*	Procedure
	30	180	720	1440		
Yield	2.50 lb	15.00 lb	60.00 lb	120.00 lb		
ROUND, GOOSENECK, US CHO No. 170, 20 lb	4.00 lb 2.00 oz	24.75 lb	99.00 lb	198.00 lb		1. Season gooseneck round with salt and pepper on all sides.
SALT, 100 lb bag	.33 tsp	2.00 tsp	2.00 tbs 2.00 tsp	.25 cup 1.00 tbs 1.00 tsp		2. Roast in rotary oven at 300°F. until the internal temp is 140°F., approx 4 to 5 hr.
PEPPER, BLACK, GROUND, 6 lb	.16 tsp	1.00 tsp	1.00 tbs 1.00 tsp	2.00 tbs 2.00 tsp		3. Remove from oven and cut roast into smaller pieces for rapid cooling. 4. Place in refrigerator until ready to use in specified item.

Note: Yield is weight of usable meat after slicing losses are subtracted.
Cooking time: 4 to 5 hr
Cooking temp: 300°F.
Equipment: rotary oven
*Early Prep: Cook roast beef 1 day ahead of serving day for item.

1180	BEEF TURNOVERS WITH GRAVY				ENTREES—Beef
Recipe No.	Recipe Name				Category

Serving Standards:

20- by 12- by 2.5-in.	16	3.75 oz	Spatula	Hot
Pan	Portions/Pan	Portion Size	Utensil	Temperature

Ingredients	Portions				E* Procedure
	50	**100**	**500**	**700**	
ONIONS, DEHYD CHOP, 2.5 lb XSTD 6/10	2.00 oz	.25 lb	1.25 lb	1.75 lb	1. Rehydrate onions in first amt of water for 20 min.
WATER, cold	1.00 cup	2.00 cup	2.00 qt 2.00 cup	3.00 qt 2.00 cup	2. Brown beef in steam kettle, stirring to break up lumps.
GRD BEEF BULK REG, 20 pcnt A fat, No. 136	6.25 lb	12.50 lb	62.50 lb	87.50 lb	3. Add onions, salt and pepper and cook 20 min. longer.
SALT, 100 lb bag	.50 oz	1.00 oz	5.00 oz	7.00 oz	4. Drain off excess fat and save to use later.
PEPPER, BLACK, GROUND, 6 lb	.75 tsp	1.50 tsp	2.00 tbs 1.50 tsp	3.00 tbs 1.50 tsp	5. Weigh out needed amt of beef fat saved in Step No. 4 and pour into mixing bowl.
BEEF DRIPPINGS from cooked meat	.25 lb	.50 lb	2.50 lb	3.50 lb	6. Stir flour into fat to make a roux. 7. Add beef base to roux and blend well.
FLOUR, 25 lb bag	3.00 oz	6.00 oz	1.00 lb 14.00 oz	2.00 lb 10.00 oz	8. Add hot water to beef mixture and stir. 9. Add roux to beef mixture; stir and cook 10 min.
BEEF SOUP BASE, 12/1 lb/cs	.25 lb	.50 lb	2.50 lb	3.50 lb	10. Cool thoroughly in shallow pans in refrigerator.
WATER, hot, 180°F.	1.00 qt	2.00 qt	2.00 gal 2.00 qt	3.00 gal 2.00 qt	11. Place a level No. 20 scoop of cooled beef mixture on pastry round. Seal.
PASTRY, ROUND, 6-in. diameter	4.00 doz 2.00 ea	8.00 doz 4.00 ea	41.00 doz 8.00 ea	58.00 doz 4.00 ea	12. Place turnovers on sheet pans and brush each with melted margarine.
MARGARINE, SOLID, 1 lb	.25 lb	.50 lb	2.50 lb	3.50 lb	13. Bake 30 min. in conv oven at 300°F.
BROWN GRAVY Recipe 0520	.50 gal	1.00 gal	5.00 gal	7.00 gal	14. Pour 2.5 cup brown gravy over 16 turnovers or place gravy on serving line in separate pans to be served on request.

Note: Remaining beef fat can be substituted for margarine in brown gravy served over turnovers. Portion size is total weight of raw turnover.

Cooking time: 40 min. in steam kettle
30 min. in conv oven

Cooking temp: 300°F

Equipment: steam kettle, conv oven

*Early Prep: Prepare meat mixture a day ahead and cool overnight under refrigeration.

1190	CHILIBURGERS				ENTREES—Beef
Recipe No.	Recipe Name				Category

Serving Standards: 10- by 12- by 6-in. / Pan   4 oz / Portion Size   No. 10 Scoop / Utensil   Hot / Temperature

Ingredients	Portions				Procedure
	75	225	525	1050	
Yield	2.18 gal	6.54 gal	15.26 gal	30.52 gal	
ONIONS, DEHYD CHOP, 2.5 lb XSTD 6/10	.25 lb	.75 lb	1.75 lb	3.50 lb	1. Rehydrate onion and green pepper in first amt of water.
PEPPERS, DEHYD DICED, GRN, 1.25 lb XSTD 6/10	2.00 oz	6.00 oz	14.00 oz	1.75 lb	2. Saute ground beef, onions and green pepper in steam kettle, stirring occasionally to prevent lumping.
WATER, cold	3.00 cup	2.00 qt 1.00 cup	1.00 gal 1.00 qt 1.00 cup	2.00 gal 2.00 qt 2.00 cup	3. When meat is browned, skim off excess fat (about 1.5 cup fat for each 12.5 lb beef).
GRD BEEF BULK REG, 20 pcnt A fat, No. 136	12.50 lb	37.50 lb	87.50 lb	175.00 lb	4. Add diced tomatoes in puree, salt and chili powder and simmer about 30 min.
TOMATOES, DICED, HVY PUREE, FNCY 6/10	1.00 can	3.00 can	7.00 can	14.00 can	5. Combine cornstarch and part of the second amt of water. Add remaining water to steam kettle and stir in the water-cornstarch mixture.
SALT, 100 lb bag	1.75 oz	5.25 oz	12.25 oz	1.00 lb 8.50 oz	6. Cook until thickened, about 10 min.
CHILI POWDER, 1 lb	2.00 oz	6.00 oz	14.00 oz	1.75 lb	7. Place in counter pans.
CORNSTARCH, 24/1 lb/cs	.25 lb	.75 lb	1.75 lb	3.50 lb	8. Serve a No. 10 scoop of mixture on warm hamburger bun.
WATER, cold	1.75 qt	1.00 gal 1.25 qt	3.00 gal .25 qt	6.00 gal .50 qt	*Note:* 35 (4 oz) portions per gal; wt is 8.75 lb per gal.
ROLLS, HAMBURGER, pkg/12, 4-in., rd	6.25 doz	18.75 doz	43.75 doz	87.50 doz	Cooking time: see above Cooking temp: simmer Equipment: steam kettle

1200	CHILI CON CARNE (WITH FRESH GROUND BEEF)				ENTREES—Beef
Recipe No.	Recipe Name				Category

Serving Standards: 20- by 12- by 6-in.   96   5.5 oz   4 oz Ladle   Hot

                Pan   Portions/Pan   Portion Size   Utensil   Temperature

Ingredients	Portions				Procedure
	60	360	540	1080	
Yield	2.50 gal	15.00 gal	22.50 gal	45.00 gal	
GRD BEEF BULK REG, 20 pcnt A fat, No. 136	6.50 lb	39.00 lb	58.50 lb	117.00 lb	1. Brown meat thoroughly in steam kettle. Stir occasionally to avoid lumping.
ONIONS, DEHYD CHOP, 2.5 lb XSTD 6/10	2.00 oz	.75 lb	1.00 lb 2.00 oz	2.25 lb	2. Add remaining ingredients and simmer for 1 hr. Do not drain kidney beans.
GARLIC POWDER, 1 lb	.62 oz	3.75 oz	5.62 oz	11.25 oz	*Note:* 1080 servings is the largest amount that can be
CHILI POWDER, 1 lb	1.75 oz	10.50 oz	1.00 lb	2.00 lb	made in a 60 gal steam kettle.
OREGANO, GROUND, 1 lb	.12 oz	.75 oz	1.12 oz	2.25 oz	Cooking time: 1-1/2 hr
SALT, 100 lb bag	1.87 oz	11.25 oz	1.00 lb .87 oz	2.00 lb 1.75 oz	Equipment: steam kettle
PEPPER, RED CAYENNE, GROUND, 1 lb	1.00 tsp	2.00 tbs	3.00 tbs	.25 cup 2.00 tbs	
WATER, cold	2.50 qt	3.00 gal 3.00 qt	5.00 gal 2.50 qt	11.00 gal 1.00 qt	
TOMATOES, DICED, HVY PUREE, FNCY 6/10	1.00 can	6.00 can	9.00 can	18.00 can	
BEANS, KID, DK, RED, FNCY, dr wt 70 oz 6/10	1.66 can	10.00 can	15.00 can	30.00 can	

1201   **CHILI CON CARNE (WITH FROZEN COOKED BEEF CRUMBLES)**   **ENTREES—Beef**

Recipe No.   Recipe Name   Category

Serving Standards: 20- by 12- by 6-in.   96   5.5 oz   4 oz Ladle   Hot

         Pan   Portions/Pan   Portion Size   Utensil   Temperature

Ingredients	Portions				Procedure
	60	360	540	1080	
Yield	2.50 gal	15.00 gal	22.50 gal	45.00 gal	
BEEF CRUMBLES, PRECOOKED, 2/5 lb/cs	5.00 lb	30.00 lb	45.00 lb	90.00 lb	1. Place frozen precooked beef crumbles in steam kettle.
WATER, cold	2.50 qt	3.00 gal 3.00 qt	5.00 gal 2.50 qt	11.00 gal 1.00 qt	2. Add water and turn on steam to thaw meat, stirring occasionally with a wire whip, 5 to 10 min.
ONIONS, DEHYD CHOP, 2.5 lb XSTD 6/10	2.00 oz	.75 lb	1.00 lb 2.00 oz	2.25 lb	3. Add seasonings, beans and diced tomatoes to beef and simmer for 45 min. Do not drain beans.
GARLIC POWDER, 1 lb	.62 oz	3.75 oz	5.62 oz	11.25 oz	4. Place 4 gal in 20- by 12- by 6-in. counter pans to serve.
CHILI POWDER, 1 lb	1.75 oz	10.50 oz	1.00 lb	2.00 lb	*Note:* 1080 servings is the largest amount that can be
OREGANO, GROUND, 1 lb	.12 oz	.75 oz	1.12 oz	2.25 oz	made in a 60 gal steam kettle. Yield is 24 servings
SALT, 100 lb bag	1.87 oz	11.25 oz	1.00 lb .87 oz	2.00 lb 1.75 oz	per gallon.
PEPPER, RED CAYENNE, GROUND, 1 lb	1.00 tsp	2.00 tbs	3.00 tbs	.25 cup 2.00 tbs	Cooking time: about 1 hr total Cooking temp: simmer
TOMATOES, DICED, HVY PUREE, FNCY 6/10	1.00 can	6.00 can	9.00 can	18.00 can	Equipment: steam kettle
BEANS, KID, DK, RD, FNCY, dr wt 70 oz 6/10	1.66 can	10.00 can	15.00 can	30.00 can	

1210	BURGER ON BUN				ENTREES—Beef
Recipe No.	**Recipe Name**				**Category**

Serving Standards: <u>20- by 12- by 2.5-in.</u>   <u>   </u>   <u>3 oz</u>   <u>Tongs</u>   <u>Hot</u>

                     Pan   **Portions/Pan**   **Portion Size**   **Utensil**   **Temperature**

Ingredients	Portions				Procedure
	27	**216**	**540**	**1080**	

GRD BEEF PATTIE, 3 oz
  20 pcnt A fat, No. 1136
ROLLS, HAMBURGER,
  pkg/12 4-in. rd
	5.00 lb
	
	2.25 doz
		40.00 lb
		
		18.00 doz
			100.00 lb
			
			45.00 doz
				200.00 lb
				
				90.00 doz
					1. Grill on one side at 300°F. for 4 min. until brown.
					2. Turn and brown on other side for 3 min. Be careful not to press or puncture the meat so the hamburger will cook in its own juices.
					3. Place hamburger in counter pans.
					4. Serve on warm bun. Cheese is optional.
					Note 1: Lettuce and tomato will be served on salad counter.
					Note 2: Portion size is raw weight.
					Cooking time: 7 min.
					Cooking temp: 300°F.
					Equipment: grill

1212	CHEESEBURGER				ENTREES—Beef
Recipe No.	Recipe Name				Category

Serving Standards: 20- by 12- by 2.5-in. _____   4 oz _____   _____   Hot _____
                        Pan   Portions/Pan   Portion Size   Utensil   Temperature

Ingredients	Portions				Procedure
	48	192	480	960	
GRD BEEF PATTIE, 4 oz 20 pcnt A fat, No. 1136	12.00 lb	48.00 lb	120.00 lb	240.00 lb	1. Grill on one side at 300°F. for 4 min. until brown.
ROLLS, HAMBURGER, pkg/12 4-in., rd	4.00 doz	16.00 doz	40.00 doz	80.00 doz	2. Turn and brown on other side for 3 min. Be careful not to press or puncture the meat so the burger will cook in its own juices.
SLICED TOMATOES W/LETTUCE, Recipe 4165	4.00 doz	16.00 doz	40.00 doz	80.00 doz	3. Place burger in counter pans.
AMERICAN CHEESE, pre-cut 6/5 lb	2.50 lb	10.00 lb	25.00 lb	50.00 lb	4. Serve on warm bun with cheese, lettuce and tomato. *Note:* Portion size is raw weight. Cooking time: 7 min. Cooking temp: 300°F. Equipment: grill

1213	GERMAN BURGER ON BUN				ENTREES—Beef
Recipe No.	Recipe Name				Category

Serving Standards: <u>20- by 12- by 2.5-in.</u>   <u>12</u>   <u>3 oz</u>   <u>Solid Spatula</u>   <u>Hot</u>
Pan   Portions/Pan   Portion Size   Utensil   Temperature

Ingredients	Portions				Procedure
	54	216	540	1080	
GRD BEEF PATTIE, 3 oz 20 pcnt A fat, No. 1136	10.00 lb	40.00 lb	100.00 lb	200.00 lb	1. Grill pattie on one side at 300°F. for 4 min. until brown.
ROLLS, HAMBURGER, pkg/12 4-in., rd	2.25 doz	9.00 doz	22.50 doz	45.00 doz	2. Turn and brown on other side for 3 min. Be careful not to press or puncture the pattie.
KRAUT, SHREDDED, FNCY 6/10	.62 can	2.50 can	6.25 can	12.50 can	3. Place bun halves on sheet pans with cut surfaces up.
SWISS CHEESE, pre-cut, 6/5 lb	2.00 lb 13.00 oz	11.25 lb	28.00 lb 2.00 oz	56.25 lb	4. Top with cooked pattie, 1 oz drained kraut and 1 sl Swiss cheese. 5. Place in conv oven at 350°F. until cheese begins to melt, 2 to 3 min.
PICKLES, THICK DILL CHIPS, 5 gal/can	2.00 cup	2.00 qt	1.00 gal 1.00 qt	2.00 gal 2.00 qt	6. Place 12 open-faced sandwiches in pan 20- by 12- by 2.5-in. 7. Garnish each sandwich with a dill pickle chip. Cooking time: about 10 min. total Cooking temp: 300°F. grill. 350°F. oven Equipment: grill, conv oven

1220	ITALIAN SPAGHETTI				ENTREES—Beef
Recipe No.	Recipe Name				Category

Serving Standards:

20- by 12- by 2.5-in.	32	6.75 oz	4 oz Ladle	Hot
Pan	Portions/Pan	Portion Size	Utensil	Temperature

Ingredients	Portions				Procedure
	72	288	576	864	
Yield	2.25 gal	9.00 gal	18.00 gal	27.00 gal	
ONIONS, DEHYD CHOP, 2.5 lb XSTD 6/10	2.00 oz	.50 lb	1.00 lb	1.50 lb	1. Rehydrate onions in first amt of water.
WATER, cold	1.00 cup	1.00 qt	2.00 qt	3.00 qt	2. Saute rehydrated onions and ground beef in steam kettle. Cook until meat is well browned, stirring occasionally to prevent lumping. Skim off excess fat.
GRD BEEF BULK REG, 20 pcnt A fat, No. 136	7.50 lb	30.00 lb	60.00 lb	90.00 lb	
ITALIAN SPICE MIX, 14 oz bag	.25 bag	1.00 bag	2.00 bag	3.00 bag	3. Add spice mix, tomato paste, diced tomatoes in puree and water to browned meat and simmer for 2 hr stirring occasionally to prevent sticking.
TOMATO PASTE, HVY, 33 pcnt sld 6/10	2.00 cup	2.00 qt	1.00 gal	1.00 gal 2.00 qt	
TOMATOES, DICED, HVY, PUREE, FNCY 6/10	2.00 can	8.00 can	16.00 can	24.00 can	4. Break spaghetti two times and cook in boiling salted water until tender, approx 20 min. Rinse and drain.
WATER, cold	1.00 qt	1.00 gal	2.00 gal	3.00 gal	5. Combine cooked spaghetti with meat sauce and place 1.75 gal of mixture in counter pans 20- by 12- by 2.5-in.
SPAGHETTI, LONG THIN, 20 lb	3.00 lb 6.00 oz	13.50 lb	27.00 lb	40.50 lb	6. Bake at 350°F. for 30 min. in conv oven.
PARMESAN CHEESE, grated, 12/1 lb	9.00 oz	2.25 lb	4.50 lb	6.75 lb	7. Garnish each pan with 4 oz Parmesan cheese.

7. Garnish each pan with 4 oz Parmesan cheese.
Note: Yield is for gallons of meat sauce.
Cooking time: 2 hr in steam kettle
                     30 min. in conv oven
Cooking temp: 350°F. conv oven
Equipment: steam kettle, conv oven

1221	SPAGHETTI WITH ITALIAN MEAT BALLS	ENTREES—Beef
Recipe No.	Recipe Name	Category

Serving Standards: 20- by 12- by 2.5-in.	20	5 ea	Solid Spoon	Hot
Pan	Portions/Pan	Portion Size	Utensil	Temperature

Ingredients	Portions				Procedure
	38	114	456	912	
Yield	1.12 gal	3.37 gal	13.50 gal	27.00 gal	1. Place diced tomatoes, tomato paste and water in steam kettle and stir.
TOMATOES, DICED, HVY, PUREE, FNCY 6/10	1.50 can	4.50 can	18.00 can	36.00 can	2. Add onions (not rehydrated), garlic powder, salt, beef base, ground oregano, basil leaves, ground thyme, black pepper and sugar and stir to mix well.
TOMATO PASTE, HVY, 33 pcnt sld 6/10	1.50 cup	1.00 qt .50 cup	1.00 gal 2.00 cup	2.00 gal 1.00 qt	
WATER, cold	3.75 cup	2.00 qt 3.25 cup	2.00 gal 3.00 qt 1.00 cup	5.00 gal 2.00 qt 2.00 cup	3. Simmer sauce for 1 hr stirring occasionally, but avoid breaking up the tomatoes.
ONIONS, DEHYD CHOP, 2.5 lb XSTD 6/10	1.50 oz	.25 lb .50 oz	1.00 lb 2.00 oz	2.25 lb	4. Heat the flame broiled meatballs in the conv oven at 350°F. until thoroughly heated, about 8 min.
GARLIC POWDER, 1 lb	.75 tsp	2.25 tsp	3.00 tbs	.25 cup 2.00 tbs	5. Place about 100 meatballs in counter pans 20- by 12- by 2.5-in. (approx half of a 6 lb box) and pour 2.5 qt of sauce from Step 3 over them.
SALT, 100 lb bag	2.25 tsp	2.00 tbs .75 tsp	.50 cup 1.00 tbs	1.00 cup 2.00 tbs	6. Break spaghetti twice and cook in boiling salted water until tender, approx 20 min. Rinse and drain and place in counter pans.
BEEF SOUP BASE, 12/1 lb/cs	2.25 oz	6.75 oz	1.00 lb 11.00 oz	3.00 lb 6.00 oz	
OREGANO, GROUND, 1 lb	1.12 tsp	1.00 tbs .37 tsp	.25 cup 1.50 tsp	.50 cup 1.00 tbs	7. Serve 5 meatballs with sauce (4 oz wt sauce) over 5.5 oz of spaghetti. Serve spaghetti with tongs.
BASIL, 1 lb can	1.50 tsp	1.00 tbs 1.50 tsp	.25 cup 2.00 tbs	.75 cup	*Note 1:* This sauce can be served without the meatballs over veal Parmigiana or other veal steaks.
THYME, GROUND, 1 lb can	.75 tsp	2.25 tsp	3.00 tbs	.25 cup 2.00 tbs	*Note 2:* Yield is for gal of tomato sauce; 3 oz ladle of sauce is 4 oz wt.
PEPPER, BLACK, GROUND, 6 lb	.75 tsp	2.25 tsp	3.00 tbs	.25 cup 2.00 tbs	Cooking time: see above Cooking temp: 350°F.
SUGAR, GRAN, 100 lb	2.25 tsp	2.00 tbs .75 tsp	.50 cup 1.00 tbs	1.00 cup 2.00 tbs	Equipment: steam kettle, conv oven
FLAME MEATBALLS, 6/6 lb/cs	6.00 lb	18.00 lb	72.00 lb	144.00 lb	
SPAGHETTI, LONG THIN, 20 lb	3.75 lb	11.25 lb	45.00 lb	90.00 lb	

1225	**SPAGHETTI WITH MEAT SAUCE**					**ENTREES—Beef**
Recipe No.	Recipe Name					Category

Serving Standards:

20- by 12- by 6-in.	88	4.5 oz	3 oz Ladle	Hot
Pan	Portions/Pan	Portion Size	Utensil	Temperature

Ingredients	Portions				Procedure
	65	130	520	780	
Yield	2.25 gal	4.50 gal	18.00 gal	27.00 gal	
ONIONS, DEHYD CHOP, 2.5 lb XSTD 6/10	2.00 oz	.25 lb	1.00 lb	1.50 lb	1. Rehydrate onions in first amt of water.
WATER, cold	1.00 cup	2.00 cup	2.00 qt	3.00 qt	2. Saute rehydrated onions and ground beef in steam kettle. Cook until meat is well-browned, stirring occasionally to prevent lumping. Skim off excess fat.
GRD BEEF BULK REG, 20 pcnt A fat, No. 136	7.50 lb	15.00 lb	60.00 lb	90.00 lb	
ITALIAN SPICE MIX, 14 oz bag	.25 bag	.50 bag	2.00 bag	3.00 bag	3. Add spice mix, tomato paste, diced tomatoes in puree and water to browned meat and simmer for 2 hr stirring occasionally to prevent sticking.
TOMATO PASTE, HVY, 33 pcnt sld 6/10	2.00 cup	1.00 qt	1.00 gal	1.00 gal 2.00 qt	
TOMATOES, DICED, HVY PUREE, FNCY 6/10	2.00 can	4.00 can	16.00 can	24.00 can	4. Place 3 gal meat sauce in counter pans 20- by 12- by 6-in.
WATER, cold	1.00 qt	2.00 qt	2.00 gal	3.00 gal	5. Break spaghetti twice and cook in boiling salted water until tender, approx 20 min. Rinse and drain. Place in counter pans.
SPAGHETTI, LONG THIN, 20 lb	6.50 lb	13.00 lb	52.00 lb	78.00 lb	6. Serve 3 oz ladle of meat sauce weight 4.5 oz over 5.5 oz of spaghetti. Serve spaghetti with tongs.

Note: Yield is for gallons of meat sauce.

Cooking time: see above

Cooking temp: see above

Equipment: steam kettles

1230	LASAGNE				ENTREES—Beef
Recipe No.	Recipe Name				Category

Serving Standards: 12- by 20- by 2.5-in. Pan | 24 Portions/Pan | 8 oz Portion Size | Solid Spoon Utensil | Hot Temperature

Ingredients	Portions				Procedure
	108	432	648	1296	
Yield	4.50 gal	18.00 gal	27.00 gal	54.00 gal	
NOODLES, LASAGNE, 10 lb	4.50 lb	18.00 lb	27.00 lb	54.00 lb	1. Add lasagne noodles to salted boiling water. Cook
GRD BEEF BULK REG,	15.00 lb	60.00 lb	90.00 lb	180.00 lb	20 min.
20 pcnt A fat, No. 136					2. Drain noodles and rinse with cold water. Drain
ONIONS, DEHYD CHOP,	.25 lb	1.00 lb	1.50 lb	3.00 lb	again.
2.5 lb XSTD 6/10					3. Rehydrate onions. Saute onions with ground beef.
WATER, cold	2.00 cup	2.00 qt	3.00 qt	1.00 gal	Cook until meat is well-browned. Stir occasionally
				2.00 qt	to prevent lumping. Skim off excess fat.
ITALIAN SPICE MIX, 14 oz bag	.50 bag	2.00 bag	3.00 bag	6.00 bag	4. Add spice mix, tomatoes and water to ground beef
TOMATO PASTE, HVY,	.33 can	1.33 can	2.00 can	4.00 can	and simmer 2 hr. Stir sauce with wire whip to pre-
33 pcnt sld 6/10					vent sticking.
TOMATOES, DICED, HVY,	4.00 can	16.00 can	24.00 can	48.00 can	5. Grease full steam table pans. Alternate layers of
PUREE, FNCY 6/10					noodles with mozzarella cheese, drained cottage
WATER, cold	2.00 qt	2.00 gal	3.00 gal	6.00 gal	cheese, parmesan cheese and meat sauce. Use 1 gal
COTTAGE CHEESE,	3.50 lb	14.00 lb	21.00 lb	42.00 lb	sauce to make 4 layers in each pan. End with moz-
25 lb bag in box					zarella cheese on top.
MOZZARELLA CHEESE,	4.00 lb	16.00 lb	24.00 lb	48.00 lb	6. Bake 1 to 1.25 hr at 250°F.
6/5 lb					*Note:* Sauce may be made the day before. Yield is
PARMESAN CHEESE,	1.50 lb	6.00 lb	9.00 lb	18.00 lb	for gal of meat sauce.
grated 12/1 lb					Cooking time: total 3.25 hr
					Cooking temp: simmer—250°F.
					Equipment: steam kettle and conv oven

1250	MEAT LOAF WITH TOMATO SAUCE				ENTREES—Beef
Recipe No.	Recipe Name				Category

Serving Standards:

12- by 20- by 2.5-in.	52	4 oz	Solid Spatula	Hot
Pan	Portions/Pan	Portion Size	Utensil	Temperature

Ingredients	Portions				Procedure
	106	318	636	954	
ONIONS, DEHYD CHOP,	2.00 oz	6.00 oz	.75 lb	1.00 lb	1. Rehydrate onion and green pepper in specified
2.5 lb XSTD 6/10				2.00 oz	amt of water for 45 min. Do not drain.
PEPPERS, DEHYD DICED,	.25 lb	.75 lb	1.50 lb	2.25 lb	2. In a large mixing bowl, combine all ingredients ex-
GRN, 1.25 lb XSTD 6/10					cept ground beef and tomato sauce. Mix thor-
WATER, cold	.75 qt	2.25 qt	1.00 gal	1.00 gal	oughly.
			.50 qt	2.75 qt	3. Add ground beef. Mix thoroughly to combine.
BREAD CRUMBS	2.00 lb	6.00 lb	12.00 lb	18.00 lb	*Note: Mixing can be done with an electric mixer,*
WATER, cold	1.00 qt	3.00 qt	1.00 gal	2.00 gal	*using the dough hook.* After ground beef is added
			2.00 qt	1.00 qt	to other ingredients, mix 2 min. on speed 1 and 30
EGGS, 6/5 lb cs	1.00 lb	3.00 lb	7.00 lb	10.00 lb	sec on speed 2.
	3.00 oz	9.00 oz	2.00 oz	11.00 oz	4. Shape into 4.5 lb loaves and bake uncovered at
TOMATO CATSUP, 6/10/cs	.33 can	1.00 can	2.00 can	3.00 can	350°F. until the internal temp is 160°F., about 1.5
MONOSODIUM GLUTAMATE,	1.33 oz	.25 lb	.50 lb	.75 lb	to 2 hr.
2 lb can					5. Cut each loaf into 13 to 14 slices. Pour 2.5 cups
SALT, 100 lb bag	2.00 tbs	.50 cup	1.00 cup	1.50 cup	of tomato sauce over each loaf.
	2.00 tsp				*Note:* Meat loaves can be mixed and shaped a day
PEPPER, BLACK, GROUND,	2.00 tsp	2.00 tbs	.25 cup	.25 cup	ahead.
6 lb				2.00 tbs	Cooking time: 1.5 hr
GRD BEEF BULK REG,	30.00 lb	90.00 lb	180.00 lb	270.00 lb	Cooking temp: 350°F.
20 pcnt A fat No. 136					Equipment: rotary oven, mixing bowl, electric mixer
TOMATO SAUCE, Recipe 0730	1.25 gal	3.75 gal	7.50 gal	11.25 gal	

1251	CHEESE MEAT LOAF WITH TOMATO SAUCE				ENTREES—Beef
Recipe No.	**Recipe Name**				**Category**

Serving Standards:

20- by 12- by 2.5-in.	52	4 oz	Solid Spatula	Hot
Pan	**Portions/Pan**	**Portion Size**	**Utensil**	**Temperature**

Ingredients	Portions				Procedure
	115	**345**	**690**	**1035**	
PEPPERS, DEHYD DICED, GRN, 1.25 lb XSTD 6/10	.25 lb	.75 lb	1.50 lb	2.25 lb	1. Rehydrate green pepper in specified amt of water for 45 min. Do not drain.
WATER, cold	2.00 cup	1.00 qt 2.00 cup	3.00 qt	1.00 gal 2.00 cup	2. In a large mixing bowl, combine all ingredients except beef, cheese and tomato sauce. Mix thoroughly.
BREAD CRUMBS	2.00 lb	6.00 lb	12.00 lb	18.00 lb	
WATER, cold	1.00 qt	3.00 qt	1.00 gal 2.00 qt	2.00 gal 1.00 qt	3. Cube cheese into 1/4 in. cubes.
EGGS, 6/5 lb/cs	1.00 lb 3.00 oz	3.00 lb 9.00 oz	7.00 lb 2.00 oz	10.00 lb 11.00 oz	4. Add ground beef and cubed cheese to mixture. Mix thoroughly. *Note: Mixing can be done with an electric mixer, using the dough hook.* After ground beef and cheese are added to other ingredients, mix 2 min. on speed 1 and 30 sec on speed 2.
TOMATO CATSUP, 6/10/cs	.33 can	1.00 can	2.00 can	3.00 can	
MONOSODIUM GLUTAMATE, 2 lb can	1.33 oz	.75 lb	.50 lb	.25 lb	
SALT, 100 lb bag	2.00 tbs 2.00 tsp	.50 cup	1.00 cup	1.50 cup	5. Shape into 4.5 lb loaves and bake uncovered at 350°F. until the internal temp is 160°F. or about 1.5 hr.
PEPPER, BLACK, GROUND, 6 lb	2.00 tsp	2.00 tbs	.25 cup	.25 cup 2.00 tbs	6. Cut each loaf into 13 to 14 slices.
CHEDDAR CHEESE, WHEEL	2.00 lb	6.00 lb	12.00 lb	18.00 lb	7. Pour 2.5 cups tomato sauce over each loaf.
GRD BEEF BULK REG, 20 pcnt A fat No. 136	30.00 lb	90.00 lb	180.00 lb	270.00 lb	*Note:* Meat loaf can be mixed and shaped a day ahead.
TOMATO SAUCE, Recipe 0730	1.25 gal	3.75 gal	7.50 gal	11.25 gal	Cooking time: 1.5 hr Cooking temp: 350°F. Equipment: rotary oven

1280	STUFFED PEPPER WITH TOMATO SAUCE				ENTREES—Beef
Recipe No.	Recipe Name				Category

Serving Standards: **20- by 12- by 2.5-in.**   **20**   **1 ea**   **Solid Spoon**   **Hot**
_____
Pan   Portions/Pan   Portion Size   Utensil   Temperature

Ingredients	Portions				Procedure
	56	112	224	448	
RICE, CONVERTED, 6/10 lb	1.00 lb 10.00 oz	3.25 lb	6.50 lb	13.00 lb	1. Cook rice in boiling water until tender, about 25 min. Drain. Cool.
ONIONS, DEHYD CHOP, 2.5 lb XSTD 6/10	.50 oz	1.00 oz	2.00 oz	.25 lb	2. Rehydrate onions in specified amt of water.
WATER, cold	.25 cup	.50 cup	1.00 cup	2.00 cup	3. Wash green peppers thoroughly in cold water, drain.
PEPPERS, HLVS, GRN, 25 CT FNCY 6/10	2.25 can	4.50 can	9.00 can	18.00 can	4. Combine cooked rice, rehydrated onions and raw ground beef. Add seasonings and tomato puree and mix well.
GRD BEEF BULK REG, 20 pcnt A fat No. 136	7.50 lb	15.00 lb	30.00 lb	60.00 lb	_Note: Mixing can be done with the electric mixer and dough hook._ Mix 1 min. on speed 1 and 1
SALT, 100 lb bag	1.50 oz	3.00 oz	6.00 oz	.75 lb	min. on speed 2.
PEPPER, BLACK, GROUND, 6 lb	.50 tsp	1.00 tsp	2.00 tsp	1.00 tbs 1.00 tsp	5. Fill peppers using a No. 10 scoop slightly heaped (4.75 oz of mixture).
TOMATO PUREE, 1.06 FNCY, 6/10/cs	.50 can	1.00 can	2.00 can	4.00 can	6. Bake at 350°F. for approx 1 hr.
TOMATO SAUCE, Recipe 0730	1.25 gal	2.50 gal	5.00 gal	10.00 gal	7. Place in counter pans and pour 1 qt tomato sauce over 11 pepper halves.

7. Place in counter pans and pour 1 qt tomato sauce over 11 pepper halves.

Note: Pre-prep rice may be cooked 1 day in advance and cooled in refrigerator.

Cooking time: 1 hr

Cooking temp: 350°F

Equipment: steam kettle, sheet pans, mixing bowl or electric mixer with dough hook and rotary oven.

1291	SALISBURY STEAK WITH GRAVY				ENTREES—Beef
Recipe No.	Recipe Name				Category

Serving Standards:	20- by 12- by 2.5-in.		4.25 oz	Solid Spatula	Hot
	Pan	Portions/Pan	Portion Size	Utensil	Temperature

Ingredients	Portions				E*	Procedure
	25	200	500	1000		
ONIONS, DEHYD CHOP, 2.5 lb XSTD 6/10	.50 oz	.25 lb	10.00 oz	1.25 lb		1. Rehydrate onions in first amt of water.
WATER, cold	.25 cup	2.00 cup	1.00 qt 1.00 cup	2.00 qt 2.00 cup		2. Dissolve milk in second amt of water. 3. In a large mixing bowl combine all ingredients and mix lightly.
MILK, INST NONFAT DRY, 6/5 lb	2.00 oz	1.00 lb	2.50 lb	5.00 lb		4. Portion with a No. 10 scoop to get a 4.5 oz raw portion.
WATER, cold	2.00 cup	1.00 gal	2.00 gal 2.00 qt	5.00 gal		5. Shape into oblong patties and place on sheet pans. 6. Cook in conv oven at 350°F. for 12 to 15 min. being careful not to overcook.
BREAD CRUMBS	.50 lb	4.00 lb	10.00 lb	20.00 lb		7. Prepare brown gravy.
SALT, 100 lb bag	1.00 tsp	2.00 tbs 2.00 tsp	.25 cup 2.00 tbs 2.00 tsp	.75 cup 1.00 tbs 1.00 tsp		8. Place steaks in counter pans and pour gravy over them or serve gravy separately.
GRD BEEF BULK REG, 20 pcnt A fat No. 136	5.00 lb	40.00 lb	100.00 lb	200.00 lb		*Note:* Gravy is 1.25 oz per portion or 1 qt per 25 portions.
PEPPER, BLACK, GROUND, 6 lb	.25 tsp	2.00 tsp	1.00 tbs 2.00 tsp	3.00 tbs 1.00 tsp		Cooking time: 12 to 15 min.
MONOSODIUM GLUTAMATE, 2 lb can	1.00 tsp	2.00 tbs 2.00 tsp	.25 cup 2.00 tbs 2.00 tsp	.75 cup 1.00 tbs 1.00 tsp		Cooking temp: 350°F. Equipment: conv oven *Early Prep: Steaks can be mixed and shaped 1 day ahead.
BROWN GRAVY, Recipe 0520	.25 gal	2.00 gal	5.00 gal	10.00 gal		

1330	BEEF STEW				ENTREES—Beef
Recipe No.	Recipe Name				Category

Serving Standards:

20- by 12- by 6-in.	82	6 oz	4 oz Ladle	Hot
Pan	Portions/Pan	Portion Size	Utensil	Temperature

Ingredients	Portions				Procedure
	62	248	496	992	
Yield	3.00 gal	12.00 gal	24.00 gal	48.00 gal	1. Drain carrots and potatoes and add enough water to this liquid to equal amt in recipe and place in steam kettle. Adjust water as needed.
CARROTS, CHK, FNCY, 69 dw, 6/10	1.00 can	4.00 can	8.00 can	16.00 can	
POTATOES, WHL, wtrpk ct 100 6/10	1.00 can	4.00 can	8.00 can	16.00 can	2. Add stew beef, dehyd onions, salt and pepper and simmer for 1 hr.
WATER, cold	2.75 gal	11.00 gal	22.00 gal	44.00 gal	3. Skim off fat if necessary and use in place of margarine to make a roux for thickening.
BEEF, STEW, 1 in., 90 pcnt lean No. 1195	12.50 lb	50.00 lb	100.00 lb	200.00 lb	
ONIONS, DEHYD CHOP, 2.5 lb XSTD 6/10	3.00 oz	.75 lb	1.50 lb	3.00 lb	4. Wash celery and slice into .25 inch slices; add to steam kettle and simmer 30 min. longer or until beef and celery are tender but firm. Weight of celery is EP.
SALT, 100 lb bag	1.00 oz	.25 lb	.50 lb	1.00 lb	
PEPPER, BLACK, GROUND, 6 lb	.25 oz	1.00 oz	2.00 oz	.25 lb	5. Make a roux with flour and margarine or substitute fat from Step 3 for margarine.
CELERY, FRESH, GRN, FNCY, pascal, bun	1.25 lb	5.00 lb	10.00 lb	20.00 lb	6. Add roux to stew slowly while stirring. Continue to stir and cook until thickened.
FLOUR, 25 lb bag	.25 lb	1.00 lb	2.00 lb	4.00 lb	7. Drain whole onions and add to stew.
MARGARINE, SOLID, 1 lb	.50 lb	2.00 lb	4.00 lb	8.00 lb	8. Add potatoes, carrots, green peas (not thawed) and gravy mix to stew.
ONIONS, WHOLE, SM, FNCY, 100 ct 6/10	.50 can	2.00 can	4.00 can	8.00 can	
PEAS, SM, FNCY, 20 lb box	1.25 lb	5.00 lb	10.00 lb	20.00 lb	9. Mix thoroughly but lightly and simmer for 20 min.
GRAVY MIX, 4/1 gal/cs	1.00 tbs	.25 cup	.50 cup	1.00 cup	10. Turn steam off.
					11. Place 4 gal of stew in counter pans 20- by 12- by 6-in.

Cooking time: total about 2 hr
Cooking temp: simmer
Equipment: steam kettle

1340	BEEF STROGANOFF WITH NOODLES				ENTREES—Beef
Recipe No.	Recipe Name				Category

Serving Standards: __20- by 12- by 6-in.__   __50__   __5 oz__   __3 oz Ladle__   __Hot__
                              Pan   Portions/Pan   Portion Size   Utensil   Temperature

Ingredients	Portions				Procedure
	50	**100**	**200**	**500**	
BEEF, STEW, 1 in., 90 pcnt lean No. 1195	12.50 lb	25.00 lb	50.00 lb	125.00 lb	1. Place oil in steam kettle.
SHORTENING, LIQUID, for deep fat 5 gal	.75 cup	1.50 cup	3.00 cup	1.00 qt 3.50 cup	2. Add beef. Brown 15 to 25 min. Stir. 3. Rehydrate onions in first amt of water for 20 min. 4. Add onions, mushrooms, flour and beef base to
ONIONS, DEHYD CHOP, 2.5 lb XSTD 6/10	1.00 oz	2.00 oz	.25 lb	10.00 oz	the beef, stirring frequently. Cook for 30 min. 5. Add to the mixture second amt water and tomato
WATER, cold	.50 cup	1.00 cup	2.00 cup	1.00 qt 1.00 cup	juice. Simmer until tender 1.5 to 1.75 hr. 6. Dissolve cornstarch in third amt of water. Add and
MUSHROOMS, STEMS/PCS, XSTD 24/16 oz dw	1.00 can	2.00 can	4.00 can	10.00 can	cook until thickened, 10 to 15 min. 7. Add sour topping and sherry. Simmer 15 min.
FLOUR, 25 lb bag	6.00 oz	.75 lb	1.50 lb	3.75 lb	8. Pour approx 2 gal of mixture into 20- by 12- by 6-
BEEF SOUP BASE, 12/1 lb/cs	6.00 oz	.75 lb	1.50 lb	3.75 lb	in. counter pans. 9. Serve over noodles.
WATER, cold	2.50 qt	1.00 gal 1.00 qt	2.00 gal 2.00 qt	6.00 gal 1.00 qt	Cooking time: 3 hr Cooking temp: simmer
CORNSTARCH, 24/1 lb/cs	2.00 oz	.25 lb	.50 lb	1.25 lb	Equipment: steam kettle
WATER, cold	.50 cup	1.00 cup	2.00 cup	1.00 qt 1.00 cup	
TOMATO JUICE, 12/46 foz can	.50 can	1.00 can	2.00 can	5.00 can	
NON-DAIRY SOUR CREAM, 1/2 gal 4/cs	.50 ctn	1.00 ctn	2.00 ctn	5.00 ctn	
COOKING SHERRY, gallons	.50 cup	1.00 cup	2.00 cup	1.00 qt 1.00 cup	
BUTTERED NOODLES, Recipe 3336	2.00 gal	4.00 gal	8.00 gal	20.00 gal	

| 1350 | BRAISED BEEF | | | ENTREES—Beef |
| Recipe No. | Recipe Name | | | Category |

Serving Standards:

| 20- by 12- by 6-in. | | 5 oz | 3 oz Ladle | Hot |
| Pan | Portions/Pan | Portion Size | Utensil | Temperature |

| Ingredients | Portions | | | | Procedure |
	50	200	300	500	
Yield	1.87 gal	7.50 gal	11.25 gal	18.75 gal	
BEEF, STEW, 1 in.,	12.50 lb	50.00 lb	75.00 lb	125.00 lb	1. Brown meat in steam kettle stirring occasionally
90 pcnt lean No. 1195					to prevent sticking, about 30 min.
ONIONS, DEHYD CHOP,	1.25 oz	5.00 oz	7.50 oz	.75 lb	2. Add water, onions, salt and pepper. Cover with a
2.5 lb XSTD 6/10				.50 oz	lid and simmer until tender, approx 1.5 hr.
WATER, cold	1.25 gal	5.00 gal	7.50 gal	12.50 gal	3. Skim off excess fat.
SALT, 100 lb bag	1.50 oz	6.00 oz	9.00 oz	15.00 oz	4. Add second amt of water.
PEPPER, BLACK, GROUND,	.12 oz	.50 oz	.75 oz	1.25 oz	5. Make a whitewash with flour, cornstarch, and last
6 lb					amt of water.
WATER, cold	1.25 qt	1.00 gal	1.00 gal	3.00 gal	6. Add whitewash to meat mixture stirring constant-
		1.00 qt	3.50 qt	.50 qt	ly. Cook until thickened, about 10 min.
FLOUR, 25 lb bag	.25 lb	1.00 lb	1.50 lb	2.50 lb	7. Add gravy mix and stir to mix.
CORNSTARCH, 24/1 lb/cs	.25 lb	1.00 lb	1.50 lb	2.50 lb	8. Pour into 20- by 12- by 6-in. counter pans.
WATER, cold	1.00 cup	1.00 qt	1.00 qt	2.00 qt	9. Using a 3 oz ladle serve over rice or noodles.
			2.00 cup	2.00 cup	Cooking time: 2.25 hr
GRAVY MIX, 4/1 gal/cs	2.00 tsp	2.00 tbs	.25 cup	.25 cup	Cooking temp: simmer
		2.00 tsp		2.00 tbs	Equipment: steam kettle
				2.00 tsp	
VARIATIONS					
BUTTERED RICE, Recipe 3350	1.25 gal	5.00 gal	7.50 gal	12.50 gal	
OR					
BUTTERED NOODLES,	2.00 gal	8.00 gal	12.00 gal	20.00 gal	
Recipe 3336					

1361	GRILLED LIVER WITH ONIONS				ENTREES—Beef
Recipe No.	Recipe Name				Category

Serving Standards: __20- by 12- by 2.5-in.__ __20__ __4 oz__ __Solid Spatula__ __Hot__
 Pan Portions/Pan Portion Size Utensil Temperature

Ingredients	Portions				Procedure
	48	96	288	576	
BEEF LIVER, SLICED, 4 oz	12.00 lb	24.00 lb	72.00 lb	144.00 lb	1. Dredge frozen liver in flour, salt, pepper mixture.
FLOUR, 25 lb bag	.75 lb	1.50 lb	4.50 lb	9.00 lb	2. Place on 300°F. oiled grill and cook until browned
SALT, 100 lb bag	2.00 tsp	1.00 tbs	.25 cup	.50 cup	on one side, about 5 min. Turn and cook on other
		1.00 tsp			side about 5 min. or until done.
PEPPER, BLACK, GROUND,	.25 tsp	.50 tsp	1.50 tsp	1.00 tbs	3. Place 20 servings of liver in 20- by 12- by 2.5-in.
6 lb					counter pan.
ONIONS, YELLOW, MED,	4.00 lb	8.00 lb	24.00 lb	48.00 lb	4. Saute sliced onions in oil on grill about 10 min.
FNCY 50 lb					Sprinkle over liver. Weight of onions is AP.
SHORTENING, LIQUID,	1.50 cup	3.00 cup	2.00 qt	1.00 gal	*Note:* If liver is frozen together, it will need to be
for deep fat 5 gal			1.00 cup	2.00 cup	thawed to be separated. Individually frozen liver
					should not be thawed prior to cooking.
					Cooking time: 10 to 12 min.
					Cooking temp: 300°F.
					Equipment: grill

1362	SMOTHERED LIVER WITH ONIONS				ENTREES—Beef
Recipe No.	Recipe Name				Category

Serving Standards:	20- by 12- by 2.5-in.	40	4 oz	Solid Spatula	Hot
	Pan	Portions/Pan	Portion Size	Utensil	Temperature

Ingredients	Portions				Procedure
	40	120	240	480	
BROWN GRAVY, Recipe 0520	3.00 qt	2.00 gal 1.00 qt	4.00 gal 2.00 qt	9.00 gal	1. Prepare brown gravy. 2. Peel and slice fresh onions. Weight is AP.
ONIONS, YELLOW, MED, FNCY, 50 lb	2.00 lb	6.00 lb	12.00 lb	24.00 lb	3. Dredge liver in flour, salt and pepper mixture. 4. Place on oiled 400°F. grill and cook until browned
BEEF LIVER, SLICED, 4 oz	10.00 lb	30.00 lb	60.00 lb	120.00 lb	on one side, about 2 min. Turn and cook on other
FLOUR, 25 lb bag	10.00 oz	1.00 lb 14.00 oz	3.75 lb	7.50 lb	side about 2 min. or until browned. 5. Place 20 servings of liver in 20- by 12- by 2.5-in.
SALT, 100 lb bag	2.00 tsp	2.00 tbs	.25 cup	.50 cup	counter pan and sprinkle with sliced fresh onion.
PEPPER, BLACK, GROUND, 6 lb	.25 tsp	.75 tsp	1.50 tsp	1.00 tbs	Add 1.5 qt of brown gravy and then add another 20 servings of liver, followed by onions and 1.5 qt
SHORTENING, LIQUID, for deep fat 5 gal	1.25 cup	3.75 cup	1.00 qt 3.50 cup	3.00 qt 3.00 cup	of gravy. 6. Place in conv oven at 300°F. for about 45 min.

Note: If liver is frozen together, it will need to be thawed to be separated. Individually frozen liver should not be thawed prior to cooking.
Cooking time: 4 min. plus 45 min.
Cooking temp: 400°F. grill; 300°F. oven
Equipment: grill, conv oven

1380	CORNED BEEF AND CABBAGE	ENTREES—Beef
Recipe No.	Recipe Name	Category

Serving Standards: 20- by 12- by 2.5-in. _____   2 oz _____   Slotted Spatula _____   Hot _____
Pan   Portions/Pan   Portion Size   Utensil   Temperature

Ingredients	Portions				E*	Procedure
	40	240	480	960		
CABBAGE, GREEN, FNCY, 50 lb	8.33 lb	50.00 lb	100.00 lb	200.00 lb		1. Wash cabbage. Weight is AP. 2. Remove unusable leaves saving all usable outer leaves.
SALT, 100 lb bag	1.00 tsp	2.00 tbs	.25 cup	.50 cup		3. Cut cabbage into quarters and remove core.
MARGARINE, SOLID, 1 lb	.25 lb	1.50 lb	3.00 lb	6.00 lb		4. Chop with French knife into long pieces about 1.5 inches wide.
CORNED BEEF, PRECOOKED, 10 lb	5.00 lb	30.00 lb	60.00 lb	120.00 lb		5. Slice corned beef into 2 oz portions and place in counter pan and pour a small amt of hot water over it and place in food warmer to heat it.

6. Cook cabbage in boiling salted water with margarine until tender, about 10 to 15 min., or sprinkle with salt and cook in high speed steam cooker until tender, about 2 min.

7. Drain cabbage and if cooked in high speed steam cooker, add melted margarine.

8. Serve 2 oz of cabbage with slotted spoon and 2 oz of corned beef.

Cooking time: see above

Equipment: high speed steam cooker or steam kettle

*Early Prep: Thaw corned beef one day in advance.

1390	HOT REUBEN SANDWICH				ENTREES—Beef
Recipe No.	Recipe Name				Category

Serving Standards: 12- by 20- by 2.5-in. _____   1 ea _____   Spatula _____   Hot _____
Pan — Portions/Pan — Portion Size — Utensil — Temperature

Ingredients	Portions				E*	Procedure
	24	192	480	1440		
CORNED BEEF, PRECOOKED, 10 lb	1.50 lb	12.00 lb	30.00 lb	90.00 lb		1. Slice corned beef on slicer into .5 oz slices. Use 2 slices per sandwich (total 1 oz).
TURKEY, ROLL, WHT, grade A, 9 lb	1.50 lb	12.00 lb	30.00 lb	90.00 lb		2. Slice turkey into 1 oz slices on slicer set on approx 8.
KRAUT, SHREDDED, FNCY 6/10	.25 can	2.00 can	5.00 can	15.00 can		3. Place 1 oz turkey on bun; top with 1 oz corned beef, 1 oz drained kraut and 1 slice cheese. Top with bun half.
SWISS CHEESE, pre-cut, 6/5 lb	1.25 lb	10.00 lb	25.00 lb	75.00 lb		4. Heat in conv oven at 350°F. for 2 to 3 min. until cheese melts.
KAISER ROLLS, PUMPER-NICKEL, doz	2.00 doz	16.00 doz	40.00 doz	120.00 doz		

Cooking time: 2 to 3 min.
Cooking temp: 350°F.
Equipment: conv oven
*Early Prep: Thaw turkey and corned beef in refrigerator 1 day ahead.

1510	BAKED HAM WITH FRUIT SAUCE				ENTREES—Pork
Recipe No.	Recipe Name				Category

Serving Standards: <u>12- by 20- by 2.5-in.</u>   <u>40</u>   <u>3 oz</u>   <u>Solid Spatula</u>   <u>Hot</u>
                        Pan   Portions/Pan   Portion Size   Utensil   Temperature

Ingredients	Portions				Procedure
	40	120	240	480	
HAM, BNLS, COOKED, CHO, 9 lb	9.00 lb	27.00 lb	54.00 lb	108.00 lb	1. Remove wrapper and place hams in roasting pans, fat side up.
SUGAR, LIGHT BROWN, 24/1 lb/cs	6.00 oz	1.00 lb 2.00 oz	2.25 lb	4.50 lb	2. Score about 1/8-in. deep in a diagonal pattern.
MUSTARD, GROUND, 1 lb	3.00 tbs	.50 cup 1.00 tbs	1.00 cup 2.00 tbs	2.25 cup	3. Place brown sugar in mixing bowl and crush all lumps of sugar.
CLOVES, GROUND, 1 lb	1.00 tsp	1.00 tbs	2.00 tbs	.25 cup	4. Add prepared mustard and cloves and mix well.
FRUIT SAUCE, Recipe 0810	1.25 qt	3.75 qt	1.00 gal 3.50 qt	3.00 gal 3.00 qt	5. Spread mixture on top of hams, approx 7 oz/ham.

6. Bake at 300°F. in rotary oven until internal temp is 130°F., approx 2.5 hr. The internal temp will continue to rise to approx 140°F. after removal from oven.

7. Slice ham on slicer into 3 oz portions.

8. Place 40 serv in ea 20- by 12- by 2.5-in. counter pan.

9. Prepare and pour fruit sauce over ham.

Cooking time: 2.5 hr

Cooking temp: 300°F.

Equipment: rotary oven

1520	ESCALLOPED HAM AND POTATOES				ENTREES—Pork
Recipe No.	Recipe Name				Category

Serving Standards:

20- by 12- by 2.5-in.	32	5.75 oz	Solid Spoon	Hot
Pan	Portions/Pan	Portion Size	Utensil	Temperature

Ingredients	Portions				Procedure
	64	256	384	512	
Yield	3.00 gal	12.00 gal	18.00 gal	24.00 gal	
ONIONS, DEHYD CHOP, 2.5 lb XSTD 6/10	.37 oz	1.50 oz	2.25 oz	3.00 oz	1. Rehydrate onions in specified amt of water.
WATER, cold	.25 cup	1.00 cup	1.50 cup	2.00 cup	2. Melt margarine in steam kettle.
MARGARINE, SOLID, 1 lb	1.00 lb 2.00 oz	4.50 lb	6.75 lb	9.00 lb	3. Add flour and blend together to make roux. Turn off steam.
FLOUR, 25 lb bag	.50 lb	2.00 lb	3.00 lb	4.00 lb	4. Add hot water and stir with a wire whip.
WATER, hot, 180°F.	1.00 gal	4.00 gal	6.00 gal	8.00 gal	5. Add dry milk and stir to dissolve.
MILK, INST NONFAT DRY, 6/5 lb	.75 lb	3.00 lb	4.50 lb	6.00 lb	6. Turn on steam and cook until a thin smooth sauce is formed, about 10 min.
SALT, 100 lb bag	1.00 tbs	.25 cup	.25 cup 2.00 tbs	.50 cup	7. Add salt. Turn off steam and hold. 8. In a separate steam kettle bring an ample amt of salted water to boil.
POTATOES, SLICED, DEHYD, 4/5 lb bag	2.50 lb	10.00 lb	15.00 lb	20.00 lb	9. Add dehydrated potatoes and simmer until tender, about 15 min. Do not overcook. Drain well.
HAM, PULLMAN, size 4x4, 6/11 lb	7.00 lb	28.00 lb	42.00 lb	56.00 lb	10. Slice ham twice on slicer set on No. 30, then cut with knife into half-inch cubes.
CHEDDAR CHEESE, WHEEL	1.00 lb	4.00 lb	6.00 lb	8.00 lb	11. Combine sauce, potatoes and ham and place 1.5 gal mixture in counter pans 20- by 12- by 2.5-in.

Procedure (continued):

12. Bake in conv oven at 350°F. 25 to 30 min.
13. Sprinkle 8 oz of grated cheese over each pan and return to oven until melted.

Cooking time: total about 1 hr
Cooking temp: 350°F.
Equipment: steam kettle, conv oven

| 1530 | GRILLED HAM STEAK | | | | ENTREES—Pork |
| Recipe No. | Recipe Name | | | | Category |

Serving Standards: __20- by 12- by 2.5-in.__   __3 oz__   __Solid Spatula__   __Hot__
                    Pan   Portions/Pan   Portion Size   Utensil   Temperature

Ingredients	Portions				Procedure
	48	96	480	960	
HAM, CELLO PK,	9.00 lb	18.00 lb	90.00 lb	180.00 lb	1. Remove covering from ham.
sbr US choice, 9 lb					2. Slice ham 3 oz on slicer.
SHORTENING, LIQUID,	.50 cup	1.00 cup	1.00 qt	2.00 qt	3. Place ham on preheated oiled 300°F. grill. Cook
for deep fat 5 gal			1.00 cup	2.00 cup	until lightly browned, about 3 min. Turn. Brown
					2 min. on other side.
					Cooking time: 5 min.
					Cooking temp: 300°F.
					Equipment: oiled grill
					If grill is not available, use conv or rotary oven.
					Note: Temp for rotary oven: 375°F.
					Temp for conv oven: 325°F.

1550	HAM AND CHEESE ON BUN				ENTREES—Pork
Recipe No.	Recipe Name				Category

Serving Standards:

12- by 20- by 2.5-in.	12	1 ea	.	Solid Spatula	Warm
Pan	Portions/Pan	Portion Size		Utensil	Temperature

Ingredients	Portions				Procedure
	96	192	480	960	
HAM, PULLMAN, size 4x4, 6/11 lb	7.50 lb	15.00 lb	37.50 lb	75.00 lb	1. Set automatic slicer on No. 9 and slice ham. Slices should weigh approx 1 oz.
SWISS CHEESE, pre-cut, 6/5 lb	5.00 lb	10.00 lb	25.00 lb	50.00 lb	2. Place 1 slice of ham and 1 slice of cheese on bottom half of bun. Top with top half of bun.
ROLLS, HAMBURGER, pkg/12-4 in., rd	8.00 doz	16.00 doz	40.00 doz	80.00 doz	3. Brush top of bun with melted margarine.
MARGARINE, SOLID, 1 lb	.50 lb	1.00 lb	2.50 lb	5.00 lb	4. Place in conv oven at 350°F. for 4 to 5 min.
					Cooking time: 4 to 5 min.
					Cooking temp: 350°F.
					Equipment: conv oven

1552	GRILLED HAM AND CHEESE SANDWICH				ENTREES—Pork
Recipe No.	Recipe Name				Category

Serving Standards: 20- by 12- by 2.5-in.   1 ea   Solid Spatula   Hot
_____
                    Pan   Portions/Pan   Portion Size   Utensil   Temperature

Ingredients	Portions				Procedure
	45	180	495	990	
HAM, PULLMAN, size 4x4, 6/11 lb	3.50 lb	14.00 lb	38.50 lb	77.00 lb	1. Set automatic slicer on No. 9 and slice ham. Slices should weigh approx 1 oz.
AMERICAN CHEESE, pre-cut 6/5 lb	2.00 lb 6.00 oz	9.50 lb	26.00 lb 2.00 oz	52.25 lb	2. Assemble 1 slice of ham and 1 slice of cheese between 2 slices of bread.
BREAD, SANDWICH, WHITE, 32 oz	3.00 lf	12.00 lf	33.00 lf	66.00 lf	3. Brush tops with melted margarine.
MARGARINE, SOLID, 1 lb	.75 lb	3.00 lb	8.25 lb	16.50 lb	4. Place on 300°F. grill for 7 min., margarine side down.
					5. Brush top with melted margarine.
					6. Turn and brown other side.
					7. Place in 20- by 12- by 2.5-in. counter pans.
					Cooking temp: 300°F.
					Equipment: grill

1560	HAM, MACARONI AND CHEESE				ENTREES—Pork
Recipe No.	Recipe Name				Category

Serving Standards:

20- by 12- by 2.5-in.	30	6 oz	4 oz Ladle	Hot
Pan	Portions/Pan	Portion Size	Utensil	Temperature

Ingredients	Portions				Procedure
	115	230	345	460	
Yield	6.00 gal	12.00 gal	18.00 gal	24.00 gal	
MACARONI, ELBOW, 20 lb box	5.00 lb	10.00 lb	15.00 lb	20.00 lb	1. Bring an ample amt of salted water to boil. Add macaroni. Cook 15 min. or until tender. Do not overcook. Drain and rinse with cold water to remove surface starch. Drain well.
MARGARINE, SOLID, 1 lb	1.25 lb	2.50 lb	3.75 lb	5.00 lb	
FLOUR, 25 lb bag	1.25 lb	2.50 lb	3.75 lb	5.00 lb	
WATER, hot, 180°F.	2.50 gal	5.00 gal	7.50 gal	10.00 gal	
MILK, INST NONFAT DRY, 6/5 lb	2.50 lb	5.00 lb	7.50 lb	10.00 lb	2. Melt margarine and blend in flour to make a roux. Turn off steam.
CHEDDAR CHEESE, WHEEL	3.00 lb	6.00 lb	9.00 lb	12.00 lb	3. Add hot water and stir with wire whip.
SALT, 100 lb bag	1.00 tbs	2.00 tbs	3.00 tbs	.25 cup	4. Add dry milk and stir to dissolve.
HAM, PULLMAN, size 4x4, 6/11 lb	10.00 lb	20.00 lb	30.00 lb	40.00 lb	5. Turn on steam and cook until a thin smooth sauce is formed, about 10 min.
CHEDDAR CHEESE, WHEEL	1.50 lb	3.00 lb	4.50 lb	6.00 lb	6. Add grated cheese and salt to cream sauce and stir until blended.
					7. Slice ham twice on slicer set on No. 30, then cut with knife into .5 inch cubes.
					8. Combine well-drained macaroni and cubed ham with cheese sauce and pour 1.5 gal into each pan.
					9. Top each pan with 6 oz grated cheese and bake in oven at 350°F. for 15 min. or until golden brown.
					Cooking time: total approx 1 hr
					Cooking temp: 350°F. in oven
					Equipment: steam kettle, conv oven

1570	BARBECUED PORK ON BUN				ENTREES—Pork
Recipe No.	**Recipe Name**				**Category**

Serving Standards:

20- by 12- by 6-in.	128	4.5 oz	3 oz Ladle	Hot
Pan	**Portions/Pan**	**Portion Size**	**Utensil**	**Temperature**

Ingredients	Portions				Procedure
	96	**192**	**480**	**960**	
Yield	3.00 gal	6.00 gal	15.00 gal	30.00 gal	1. Place pork on roasting pans and cook at 300°F. until the internal temp is 160°F., approx 2.5 hr.
BOSTON BUTT, US CHO, BNLS, No. 407, 5 lb	15.00 lb	30.00 lb	75.00 lb	150.00 lb	2. While pork is cooking, prepare barbecue sauce.
BARBECUE SAUCE, Recipe 0610	2.00 gal	4.00 gal	10.00 gal	20.00 gal	3. Remove pork from oven and slice on slicer, No. 5 manual, or No. 7 automatic.
ROLLS, HAMBURGER, pkg/12-4 in., rd	8.00 doz	16.00 doz	40.00 doz	80.00 doz	4. Add cooked sliced pork to barbecue sauce and heat to 160°F. in steam kettle. Use 1 gal barbecue sauce to 5 lb cooked pork.
					5. Place 4 gal barbecued pork in 20- by 12- by 6-in. counter pans.
					6. Serve barbecue from a 3 oz ladle on to warm hamburger buns.
					Cooking time: 2.5 hr
					Cooking temp: 300°F.
					Equipment: rotary oven, steam kettle

1580	BREADED PORK CHOPS	ENTREES—Pork
Recipe No.	Recipe Name	Category

Serving Standards:

20- by 12- by 2.5-in.	20	4 oz	Tongs	Hot
Pan	Portions/Pan	Portion Size	Utensil	Temperature

Ingredients	Portions				Procedure
	50	100	300	500	
FLOUR, 25 lb bag	6.00 oz	1.25 lb	3.75 lb	6.25 lb	1. Mix flour, salt, pepper and paprika.
SALT, 100 lb bag	1.25 oz	2.50 oz	7.50 oz	12.50 oz	2. Dredge chops in flour mixture.
PEPPER, BLACK, GROUND,	.50 tsp	1.00 tsp	1.00 tbs	1.00 tbs	3. Reconstitute milk in water and stir in eggs with
6 lb				2.00 tsp	wire whip.
PAPRIKA, GROUND, 6 lb	1.25 tsp	2.50 tsp	2.00 tbs	.25 cup	4. Dip floured chops into egg-milk mixture.
			1.50 tsp	.50 tsp	5. Dip chops in bread crumbs, coating both sides.
PORK CHOPS, END TO END,	12.50 lb	25.00 lb	75.00 lb	125.00 lb	6. Place chops on greased sheet pans.
4 oz					7. Bake in preheated conv oven at 275ºF. for 1 hr or
EGGS, 6/5 lb/cs	6.00 oz	.75 lb	2.25 lb	3.75 lb	to internal temp of 160ºF.
MILK, INST NONFAT DRY,	1.25 oz	2.50 oz	7.50 oz	12.50 oz	*Note:* Portion size is raw weight of chop.
6/5 lb					Cooking time: 1 hr
WATER, cold	1.50 cup	3.00 cup	2.00 qt	3.00 qt	Cooking temp: 275ºF.
			1.00 cup	3.00 cup	Equipment: conv oven
BREAD CRUMBS	1.50 lb	3.00 lb	9.00 lb	15.00 lb	
SHORTENING, LIQUID,	.33 cup	.66 cup	2.00 cup	3.30 cup	
for deep fat 5 gal					

1591					BAKED PORK CHOPS	ENTREES—Pork

Recipe No.   **Recipe Name**   **Category**

Serving Standards: <u>20- by 12- by 2.5-in.</u>   <u>6 oz</u>   <u>Tongs</u>   <u>Hot</u>
                                              Pan   Portions/Pan   Portion Size   Utensil   Temperature

Ingredients	Portions				Procedure
	50	200	500	1000	
PORK CHOPS, END TO END, 6 oz	18.75 lb	75.00 lb	187.50 lb	375.00 lb	1. Dip pork chops into water then drain and coat well with oven breader.
BREADING, PREPARED OVEN-FRY, 6/5 lb	1.00 lb	4.00 lb	10.00 lb	20.00 lb	2. Place in single layer on sheet pans and bake at 300°F. in conv oven for 50 min. to 1 hr, depending on thickness of chops.
					3. Place in counter pans and garnish appropriately.
					Cooking time: 50 min. to 1 hr
					Cooking temp: 300°F.
					Equipment: conv oven

1600	PORK CHOW MEIN					ENTREES—Pork
Recipe No.	Recipe Name					Category

Serving Standards: __20- by 12- by 6-in.__   __76__   __5.25 oz__   __3 oz Ladle__   __Hot__
                       Pan   Portions/Pan   Portion Size   Utensil   Temperature

Ingredients	Portions				E*	Procedure
	67	201	402	804		
Yield	2.62 gal	7.87 gal	15.75 gal	31.50 gal		1. Season pork with salt and pepper. Place in roasting pans and cook at 300°F. until the internal temp is 160°F., approx 2.5 hr. Save drippings.
BOSTON BUTT, BNLS, US CHO, No. 407, 5 lb	10.00 lb	30.00 lb	60.00 lb	120.00 lb		
SALT, 100 lb bag	1.50 tsp	1.00 tbs 1.50 tsp	3.00 tbs	.25 cup 2.00 tbs		2. Remove pork from oven and slice twice on slicer set on No. 30, then cut with knife into half-inch cubes.
PEPPER, BLACK, GROUND, 6 lb	.50 tsp	1.50 tsp	1.00 tbs	2.00 tbs		3. Skim off most of the fat from the drippings.
WATER, hot, 180°F.	3.00 cup	2.00 qt 1.00 cup	1.00 gal 2.00 cup	2.00 gal 1.00 qt		4. To the remaining drippings add enough hot water to equal the amt of water in recipe and place in steam kettle.
VEGETABLES, CHOW MEIN, 4/4 lb/cs	18.00 lb	54.00 lb	108.00 lb	216.00 lb		5. Add thawed vegetables and simmer until tender but firm, about 20 to 25 min.
SOY SAUCE, 4/1 gal/cs	.50 cup	1.50 cup	3.00 cup	1.00 qt 2.00 cup		6. Add soy sauce and stir.
NOODLES, CHINESE, 6/10/cs	2.50 can	7.50 can	15.00 can	30.00 can		7. Add cooked pork and heat to serving temp, 160°F. Stir carefully to avoid breaking up vegetables and pork.

8. Place 3 gal of pork mixture into 20- by 12- by 6-in. counter pans.

9. Serve 3 oz ladle of pork over .75 oz of Chinese noodles.

Variations: 1) In mix 1 (67 portions), substitute 6.25 lb cooked chicken and add 4 oz chicken soup base; 2) same as variation 1 except use T.V.P. diced chicken and increase soy sauce to one and one-half the amt in recipe; 3) serve over rice.

Note: 7 lb of cooked pork may be substituted for 10 lb of raw Boston butts. Yield is 25.5 servings per gal. Chinese noodles No. 10 can is 1.25 lb.

Cooking time: total about 3 hr

Cooking temp: 300°F.

Equipment: rotary oven, steam kettle

*Early Prep: Thaw vegetables 1 day ahead.

1620	ROAST PORK				ENTREES—Pork
Recipe No.	Recipe Name				Category

Serving Standards: __20- by 12- by 2.5-in.__   __35__   __2.5 oz__   _____Tongs_____   _____Hot_____
                  Pan   Portions/Pan   Portion Size   Utensil   Temperature

Ingredients	Portions				Procedure
	35	105	210	420	
HAM, FRESH, BNLS, TIED, CHO, 14 lb No. 1402R	10.00 lb 6.00 oz	31.00 lb 2.00 oz	62.25 lb	124.50 lb	1. Season pork with salt and pepper. 2. Place pork in roasting pans and cook at 300°F. in rotary oven until the internal temp is 160°F. (4 to 4.5 hr).
SALT, 100 lb bag	1.50 tsp	1.00 tbs 1.50 tsp	3.00 tbs	.25 cup 2.00 tbs	3. Remove pork from oven and allow to cool.
PEPPER, BLACK, GROUND, 6 lb	.50 tsp	1.50 tsp	1.00 tbs	2.00 tbs	4. Slice pork into 2.5 oz pieces with slicer on approx No. 14 or 15. 5. Make au jus out of pork drippings. Pour enough over pork slices to prevent drying out while in holding equipment and on hot line. *Note:* Yield is 3.37 serv per lb of raw. Cooking time: 4 to 4.5 hr Cooking temp: 300°F. Equipment: rotary oven

1624	ROAST PORK WITH DRESSING				ENTREES—Pork
Recipe No.	Recipe Name				Category

Serving Standards: 20- by 12- by 2.5-in.   15   2 oz   Solid Spatula   Hot

                              Pan   Portions/Pan   Portion Size   Utensil   Temperature

Ingredients	Portions				Procedure
	60	240	480	960	
HAM, FRESH, BNLS, CHO, 14 lb No. 1402R	14.25 lb	57.00 lb	114.00 lb	228.00 lb	1. Season pork with salt and pepper. 2. Place pork in roasting pans and cook at 300°F. in rotary oven until internal temp is 160°F. (4 to 4.5 hr).
SALT, 100 lb bag	2.25 tsp	3.00 tbs	.25 cup 2.00 tbs	.75 cup	
PEPPER, BLACK, GROUND, 6 lb	.75 tsp	1.00 tbs	2.00 tbs	.25 cup	3. Remove pork from oven and allow to cool. 4. Slice pork into 2 oz slices with slicer and serve over a No. 16 scoop of dressing.
DRESSING, BREAD, Recipe 3396	1.25 gal	5.00 gal	10.00 gal	20.00 gal	5. Pour about 2 oz of light brown gravy over each portion.
LIGHT BROWN GRAVY, Recipe 0520	1.00 gal	4.00 gal	8.00 gal	16.00 gal	Cooking time: 4 to 4.5 hr Cooking temp: 300°F. Equipment: rotary oven

1632	BAKED STUFFED PORK CHOP				ENTREES—Pork
Recipe No.	Recipe Name				Category

Serving Standards: <u>20- by 12- by 2.5-in.</u>   <u>20</u>   <u>4 oz</u>   <u>Solid Spatula</u>   <u>Hot</u>

                   Pan   Portions/Pan   Portion Size   Utensil   Temperature

Ingredients	Portions				Procedure
	100	300	600	1200	
PORK CHOPS, END TO END, 4 oz	25.00 lb	75.00 lb	150.00 lb	300.00 lb	1. Place 20 chops on each sheet pan.
SALT, 100 lb bag	3.00 oz	9.00 oz	1.00 lb 2.00 oz	2.25 lb	2. Sprinkle chops with salt. 3. Place No. 16 scoop raw stuffing on each chop. 4. Bake for 50 min. to 1 hr in conv oven at 300°F.
DRESSING, STUFFING, Recipe 3397	2.08 gal	6.24 gal	12.49 gal	24.99 gal	5. Place chops in 20- by 12- by 2.5-in. counter pans (20 chops/pan). Cooking time: 50 min. to 1 hr Cooking temp: 300°F. Equipment: conv oven

1649	SAUSAGE PATTIES		ENTREES—Pork
Recipe No.	Recipe Name		Category

Serving Standards: _____ _____ __2 oz__ __Tongs__ __Hot__
                     Pan   Portions/Pan   Portion Size   Utensil   Temperature

Ingredients	Portions				Procedure
	8	48	192	768	
SAUSAGE, PATTIE, 40 pcnt fat, 2 oz	1.00 lb	6.00 lb	24.00 lb	96.00 lb	1. Heat conv oven to 350°F. 2. Cook on sheet pan 8 to 10 min. 3. Or cook on 300°F. grill until brown on both sides.

1661	LINK SAUSAGE		ENTREES—Pork
Recipe No.	Recipe Name		Category

Serving Standards: _____ _____ __2 ea__ __Tongs__ __Hot__
                     Pan   Portions/Pan   Portion Size   Utensil   Temperature

Ingredients	Portions				Procedure
	8	192	480	1008	
SAUSAGE, LINKS, 6 lb box, 16 link/lb	1.00 lb	24.00 lb	60.00 lb	126.00 lb	1. Place on sheet pans and cook in conv oven at 350°F. for 8 to 10 min. 2. Or cook on 300°F. grill, turning until brown on all sides.

1671	BACON, CHEESE AND TOMATO GRILL				ENTREES—Pork
Recipe No.	Recipe Name				Category

Serving Standards: __20- by 12- by 2.5-in.__   __12__   __Half Bun__   __Solid Spatula__   __Hot__

     Pan   Portions/Pan   Portion Size   Utensil   Temperature

Ingredients	Portions				Procedure
	48	192	480	960	
BACON, precooked, 600 slc/8 lb/cs	.16 cs	.66 cs	1.66 cs	3.32 cs	1. Warm bacon in conv oven at 350°F. for 1 to 2 min. Drain.
ROLLS, HAMBURGER, pkg/12-4 in., rd	2.00 doz	8.00 doz	20.00 doz	40.00 doz	2. Place bun halves on sheet pans with cut surfaces up. Brush with melted margarine. Place in conv oven at 400°F. until toasted, about 5 min.
MARGARINE, SOLID, 1 lb	.50 lb	2.00 lb	5.00 lb	10.00 lb	
TOMATOES, FNCY, 38 lb	2.00 lb 10.00 oz	10.50 lb	26.25 lb	52.50 lb	3. Wash tomatoes and slice on slicer set on No. 13 automatic. Tomatoes are AP.
AMERICAN CHEESE, pre-cut 6/5 lb	2.50 lb	10.00 lb	25.00 lb	50.00 lb	4. Place 1 slice of tomato on each bun half. Follow with 2 slices of bacon and 1 slice of cheese.
OLIVES, STUFFED, 340 to 360 ct, 4/1 gal	2.25 cup	2.00 qt 1.00 cup	1.00 gal 1.00 qt 2.50 cup	2.00 gal 3.00 qt 1.00 cup	5. Return to oven at 350°F. until cheese begins to melt, 2 to 3 min.
					6. Slice the stuffed olives into 3 circles each.
					7. Garnish each sandwich with 3 slices of olive.
					8. Place 12 sandwiches in pan 20- by 12- by 2.5-in.
					Cooking time: about 10 min. total
					Cooking temp: 400°F. to toast bread and 350°F. for bacon and to melt cheese
					Equipment: conv oven

1673	BACON (PRECOOKED)				ENTREES—Pork
Recipe No.	Recipe Name				Category

Serving Standards: 20- by 12- by 2.5-in.   2 slc   Tongs   Hot
               Pan   Portions/Pan   Portion Size   Utensil   Temperature

Ingredients	Portions				Procedure
	15	300	600	1050	
BACON, PRECOOKED, 600 slc/8 lb/cs	.05 cs	1.00 cs	2.00 cs	3.50 cs	1. Heat on 350°F. grill 20 seconds or in oven at 350°F. for 2 min.

1674	GRILLED BACON AND CHEESE SANDWICH				ENTREES—Pork
Recipe No.	Recipe Name				Category

Serving Standards: 12- by 20- by 2.5-in.   16   1 ea   Spatula   Hot
               Pan   Portions/Pan   Portion Size   Utensil   Temperature

Ingredients	Portions				Procedure
	45	180	495	990	
BACON, PRECOOKED, 600 slc/8 lb/cs	.15 cs	.60 cs	1.65 cs	3.30 cs	1. Heat bacon on 350°F. grill 20 seconds or in oven at 350°F. for 2 min.
BREAD, SANDWICH, WHITE, 32 oz	3.00 lf	12.00 lf	33.00 lf	66.00 lf	2. Assemble 1 slice cheese and 2 slices of bacon between 2 slices of bread.
AMERICAN CHEESE, PRE-CUT 6/5 lb	2.00 lb 6.00 oz	9.50 lb	26.00 lb 2.00 oz	52.25 lb	3. Brush tops with melted margarine.
MARGARINE, SOLID, 1 lb	.75 lb	3.00 lb	8.25 lb	16.50 lb	4. Place on 300°F. grill for 7 min., margarine side down.

5. Brush top with melted margarine. Turn and brown other side.
6. Place in 12- by 20- by 2.5-in. counter pans (16 ea).
Cooking temp: 350°F.—oven, 300°F.—grill
Equipment: conv oven, grill

1760	CREOLE SHRIMP	ENTREES—Fish and Shellfish
Recipe No.	Recipe Name	Category

Serving Standards:	20- by 12- by 2.5-in.	36	6 oz	Solid Spoon	Hot
	Pan	Portions/Pan	Portion Size	Utensil	Temperature

Ingredients	Portions				Procedure
	144	288	432	576	
Yield	6.00 gal	12.00 gal	18.00 gal	24.00 gal	1. Cook shrimp in boiling water 2 min. and remain in liquid 10 min.
SHRIMP, FNCY, PDQ, 130 to 150 ct	20.00 lb	40.00 lb	60.00 lb	80.00 lb	1. Cook shrimp in boiling water 2 min. and let remain in liquid 10 min.
WATER, hot	4.00 gal	8.00 gal	12.00 gal	16.00 gal	2. Wash and clean if necessary.
PEPPERS, DEHYD, DICED, GRN, 1.25 lb XSTD 6/10	1.00 oz	2.00 oz	3.00 oz	.25 lb	3. Rehydrate green peppers and onions in specified amt of water for 20 min.
ONIONS, DEHYD, CHOP, 2.5 lb XSTD 6/10	3.00 oz	6.00 oz	9.00 oz	.75 lb	4. Saute green peppers and onions in margarine in steam kettle.
WATER, cold	2.00 cup	1.00 qt	1.00 qt 2.00 cup	2.00 qt	5. Add tomato paste, tomato puree, parsley, Worcestershire sauce, salt and pepper and simmer 10 min.
MARGARINE, SOLID, 1 lb	1.75 lb	3.50 lb	5.25 lb	7.00 lb	6. In steam kettle cook rice in ample amt of salted water until tender.
TOMATO PASTE, HVY, 33 pcnt sld 6/10	.66 can	1.32 can	2.00 can	2.64 can	7. Drain water from rice.
TOMATO PUREE, 1.06 FNCY, 6/10/cs	1.50 can	3.00 can	4.50 can	6.00 can	8. Add rice and shrimp to tomato mixture and combine well.
PARSLEY, DEHYD, FLK, XSTD 6/10	.25 cup	.50 cup	.75 cup	1.00 cup	9. Place 1.5 gal mixture into counter pans 20- by 12- by 2.5-in.
WORCESTERSHIRE SAUCE, 4/1 gal/cs	.33 cup	.66 cup	1.00 cup	1.32 cup	10. Cook in conv oven at 350°F. for 20 min.
SALT, 100 lb bag	.33 cup	.66 cup	1.00 cup	1.32 cup	11. Remove pans from oven and top each with 12 oz grated cheese.
PEPPER, BLACK, GROUND, 6 lb	1.00 tbs 1.00 tsp	2.00 tbs 2.00 tsp	.25 cup	.25 cup 1.00 tbs 1.00 tsp	12. Return pans to oven until cheese is melted.
RICE, CONVERTED, 6/10 lb	7.00 lb	14.00 lb	21.00 lb	28.00 lb	Cooking time: see above
CHEDDAR CHEESE, WHEEL	3.00 lb	6.00 lb	9.00 lb	12.00 lb	Cooking temp: 350°F. Equipment: steam kettle, conv oven

1770	**FRIED SHRIMP WITH TARTAR SAUCE**				**ENTREES**—Fish and Shellfish
Recipe No.	Recipe Name				Category

Serving Standards:

20- by 12- by 2.5-in.		5 ea	Tongs	Hot
Pan	Portions/Pan	Portion Size	Utensil	Temperature

Ingredients	Portions				Procedure
	23	184	460	920	
SHRIMP, BRD FANTAIL, 21 to 25 ct 5 lb bx	5.00 lb	40.00 lb	100.00 lb	200.00 lb	1. Fill deep fat fryer with oil and heat to 350°F.
TARTAR SAUCE, 4/gal/cs	.75 qt	1.00 gal 2.00 qt	3.00 gal 3.00 qt	7.00 gal 2.00 qt	2. Place 5 lb shrimp in a fryer basket and fry until golden brown, about 3 min. 3. Drain shrimp and place in counter pans. 4. Place tartar sauce on condiment stand. *Note:* Yield is 4.6 servings per pound AP of shrimp. Tartar sauce is 1 oz per serving. Portion size: 5 ea is 3 oz cooked weight Cooking time: 3 min. Cooking temp: 350°F. Equipment: deep fat fryer

1785	SHRIMP CHOW MEIN				ENTREES—Fish and Shellfish
Recipe No.	Recipe Name				Category

Serving Standards: 10- by 12- by 2.5-in. <u>Pan</u>   12 <u>Portions/Pan</u>   5.25 oz <u>Portion Size</u>   3 oz Ladle <u>Utensil</u>   Hot <u>Temperature</u>

Ingredients	Portions				E*	Procedure
	12	192	480	960		
SHRIMP CHOW MEIN, 4/4 lb/cs NOODLES, CHINESE, 6/10/cs	4.00 lb .20 can	64.00 lb 3.20 can	160.00 lb 8.00 can	320.00 lb 16.00 can		1. Heat thawed shrimp chow mein in conv oven at 400°F. in disposable aluminum pan with lid on for approx 35 min. or until hot. 2. Serve with 3 oz ladle. 3. Garnish with .25 oz of chow mein noodles. 4. May be served over rice or chow mein noodles. Cooking time: 35 min. Cooking temp: 400°F. Equipment: conv oven *Early Prep: Thaw shrimp chow mein in refrigerator one day ahead.

| 1789 | SHRIMP MARENGO | ENTREES—Fish and Shellfish |
| Recipe No. | Recipe Name | Category |

Serving Standards: <u>10- by 12- by 4-in.</u>   <u>4.5 oz</u>   <u>3 oz Ladle</u>   <u>Hot</u>
             Pan   Portions/Pan   Portion Size   Utensil   Temperature

| Ingredients | Portions | | | | Procedure |
	50	200	500	1000	
Yield	1.65 gal	6.60 gal	16.50 gal	33.00 gal	
WATER, cold	2.00 cup	2.00 qt	1.00 gal 1.00 qt	2.00 gal 2.00 qt	1. Rehydrate green pepper and onion in specified amt of water 20 min.
PEPPERS, DEHYD, DICED, GRN, XSTD 6/10	1.50 oz	6.00 oz	15.00 oz	1.00 lb 14.00 oz	2. Cook thawed shrimp in boiling water 2 min. Let remain in water 10 min.
ONIONS, DEHYD, CHOP, 2.5 lb XSTD 6/10	2.25 oz	9.00 oz	1.00 lb 6.50 oz	2.00 lb 13.00 oz	3. Wash and clean shrimp if necessary.
SHRIMP, PDQ, FNCY, 130 to 150 ct	6.25 lb	25.00 lb	62.50 lb	125.00 lb	4. Saute onions, green peppers and chopped garlic in margarine (use bacon drippings if available) in steam kettle.
MARGARINE, SOLID, 1 lb	6.00 oz	1.50 lb	3.75 lb	7.50 lb	5. Add tomato puree, undrained mushrooms, msg, basil, salt, chicken base, black pepper and sugar to sauteed vegetables.
GARLIC, BULBS, CELLO PK 1 lb	.25 oz	1.00 oz	2.50 oz	5.00 oz	
TOMATO PUREE, 1.06 FNCY, 6/10/cs	1.50 can	6.00 can	15.00 can	30.00 can	6. Simmer slowly for 25 min. 7. Mix cornstarch and water together to form a paste.
MUSHROOMS, STEMS/PCS, XSTD 24/16 oz	.75 can	3.00 can	7.50 can	15.00 can	8. Add slowly to sauce and stir until thickened. 9. Add cooked shrimp and simmer for 10 min.
MONOSODIUM GLUTAMATE, 2 lb can	.75 tsp	1.00 tbs	2.00 tbs 1.50 tsp	.25 cup 1.00 tbs	10. Serve over rice.
BASIL, 1 lb can	1.00 tbs 1.50 tsp	.25 cup 2.00 tbs	.75 cup 3.00 tbs	1.75 cup 2.00 tbs	Cooking time: see above Equipment: steam kettle
SALT, 100 lb bag	1.00 oz	.25 lb	10.00 oz	1.25 lb	
CHICKEN SOUP BASE, 12/1 lb/cs	.75 oz	3.00 oz	7.50 oz	15.00 oz	
PEPPER, BLACK, GROUND, 6 lb	.75 tsp	1.00 tbs	2.00 tbs 1.50 tsp	.25 cup 1.00 tbs	

(cont. on facing page)

1789 SHRIMP MARENGO (cont.)

Ingredients	Portions				Procedure
	50	200	500	1000	
SUGAR, GRAN, 100 lb	1.50 tsp	2.00 tbs	.25 cup 1.00 tbs	.50 cup 2.00 tbs	
CORNSTARCH, 24/1 lb/cs	2.25 oz	9.00 oz	1.00 lb 6.50 oz	2.00 lb 13.00 oz	
WATER, cold	1.50 cup	1.00 qt 2.00 cup	3.00 qt 3.00 cup	1.00 gal 3.00 qt 2.00 cup	
BUTTERED RICE, Recipe 3350	1.25 gal	5.00 gal	12.50 gal	25.00 gal	

1810 BROILED FLOUNDER

| Recipe No. | Recipe Name | | | ENTREES—Fish and Shellfish
Category |

Serving Standards: __20- by 12- by 2.5-in.__ / Pan __12__ / Portions/Pan __4 oz__ / Portion Size __Slotted Spatula__ / Utensil __Hot__ / Temperature

Ingredients	Portions				Procedure
	20	100	200	600	
MARGARINE, SOLID, 1 lb	6.00 oz	1.00 lb 14.00 oz	3.75 lb	11.25 lb	1. Melt margarine and cool to room temp. 2. Add lemon juice, Worcestershire sauce, salt and paprika. Stir to combine. 3. Place frozen fish in counter pans and brush each fillet with sauce being careful not to get sauce on sides of pan. If margarine solidifies, place pan of sauce in warm water to make it easy to spread. 4. Place fish in conv oven at 300°F. until tender, 25 to 30 min. 5. Slice lemons on No. 13 on slicer (8 slices ea) and garnish each piece of fish with a circle of lemon. Cooking time: 25 to 30 min. Cooking temp: 300°F. Equipment: conv oven *Variations:* sole, haddock
LEMON JUICE, RECONSTI- TUTED, 12/qt jars	2.00 tbs 2.00 tsp	.75 cup 1.00 tbs 1.00 tsp	1.50 cup 2.00 tbs 2.00 tsp	1.00 qt 1.00 cup	
WORCESTERSHIRE SAUCE, 4/1 gal/cs	1.00 tbs 1.00 tsp	.25 cup 2.00 tbs 2.00 tsp	.75 cup 1.00 tbs 1.00 tsp	2.50 cup	
PAPRIKA, GROUND, 6 lb	.25 oz	1.25 oz	2.50 oz	7.50 oz	
SALT, 100 lb bag	.50 tsp	2.50 tsp	1.00 tbs 2.00 tsp	.25 cup 1.00 tbs	
FLOUNDER, UNBRD, 4 oz, lb	5.00 lb	25.00 lb	50.00 lb	150.00 lb	
LEMONS, FNCY, FRESH, 200 ct	2.50 ea	1.00 doz .50 ea	2.00 doz 1.00 ea	6.00 doz 3.00 ea	

1813   BAKED STUFFED FLOUNDER

ENTREES—Fish and Shellfish

| Recipe No. | Recipe Name | | | | Category |

Serving Standards:

20- by 12- by 2.5-in.	12	4 oz	Solid Spatula	Hot
Pan	Portions/Pan	Portion Size	Utensil	Temperature

Ingredients	Portions				Procedure
	100	200	500	1000	
DRESSING, STUFFING, Recipe 3397	2.08 gal	4.16 gal	10.41 gal	20.83 gal	1. Prepare corn bread stuffing, but do not cook.
FLOUNDER, UNBRD, 4 oz, lb	25.00 lb	50.00 lb	125.00 lb	250.00 lb	2. Place frozen fish in counter pans 20- by 12- by 2.5-in.
MARGARINE, SOLID, 1 lb	1.00 lb	2.00 lb	5.00 lb	10.00 lb	3. Melt margarine and add salt.
SALT, 100 lb bag	1.25 tsp	2.50 tsp	2.00 tbs	.25 cup	4. Brush fish with margarine.
			.25 tsp	.50 tsp	5. Place a No. 16 scoop of dressing on each portion of fish and spread to cover fish. Sprinkle with paprika.
PAPRIKA, GROUND, 1 lb	.25 oz	.50 oz	1.25 oz	2.50 oz	6. Bake in conv oven at 300°F. for about 40 to 50 min. or until done.

6. (cont.)

Cooking time: 40 to 50 min.
Cooking temp: 300°F.

1820   FRIED FLOUNDER

ENTREES—Fish and Shellfish

| Recipe No. | Recipe Name | | | | Category |

Serving Standards:

20- by 12- by 2.5-in.	20	4 oz	Solid Spatula	Hot
Pan	Portions/Pan	Portion Size	Utensil	Temperature

Ingredients	Portions				Procedure
	20	100	400	800	
FLOUNDER, BRD, 4 oz, lb	5.00 lb	25.00 lb	100.00 lb	200.00 lb	1. Fill deep fryer with oil and heat to 350°F.
TARTAR SAUCE, 4/gal/cs	.75 qt	3.75 qt	3.00 gal	7.00 gal	2. Place 5 lb flounder in deep fat fryer and cook 4 to 5 min. or until golden brown.
			3.00 qt	2.00 qt	3. Drain flounder and place in counter pans.

4. Place tartar sauce on condiment stand.

Note: Tartar sauce is 1 oz per serving.

Variations: sole, perch, ocean trout, haddock, whiting and stuffed flounder.

Cooking time: 4 to 5 min.
Cooking temp: 350°F.
Equipment: deep fat fryer

1841	FRIED SCALLOPS WITH TARTAR SAUCE					ENTREES—Fish and Shellfish
Recipe No.	Recipe Name					Category

Serving Standards: 10- by 12- by 2.5-in. / Pan   6 ea / Portion Size   Tongs / Utensil   Hot / Temperature

Ingredients	Portions				Procedure
	50	200	500	1000	
SCALLOPS, BRD, 30/lb	10.00 lb	40.00 lb	100.00 lb	200.00 lb	1. Fill deep fryer with oil and heat to 350°F.
TARTAR SAUCE, 4/gal/cs	1.50 qt	1.00 gal	3.00 gal	7.00 gal	2. Place 5 lb breaded scallops in a fryer basket and fry until golden brown, about 3 to 4 min.
		2.00 qt	3.00 qt	2.00 qt	3. Drain and place in counter pans.
					4. Place tartar sauce on condiment stand.
					Cooking time: 3 to 4 min.
					Cooking temp: 350°F.
					Equipment: deep fat fryer

1860	FISH SANDWICH/BUN					ENTREES—Fish and Shellfish
Recipe No.	Recipe Name					Category

Serving Standards: 20- by 12- by 2.5-in. / Pan   3 oz / Portion Size   Solid Spatula / Utensil   Hot / Temperature

Ingredients	Portions				Procedure
	27	108	432	864	
WHITING, BRD, 3 oz, lb	5.00 lb	20.00 lb	80.00 lb	160.00 lb	1. Fill deep fryer with oil and heat to 350°F.
ROLLS, HAMBURGER,	2.25 doz	9.00 doz	36.00 doz	72.00 doz	2. Fry fish in deep fat fryer until golden brown, 4 to 5 min.
pkg/12-4 in., rd					3. Drain fish and serve on warm bun.
TARTAR SAUCE, 4/gal/cs	1.00 qt	1.00 gal	4.00 gal	8.00 gal	4. Place tartar sauce on condiment stand.
					Cooking time: 4 to 5 min.
					Cooking temp: 350°F.
					Equipment: deep fat fryer

1920	TUNA DOG				ENTREES—Fish and Shellfish
Recipe No.	Recipe Name				Category

Serving Standards: <u>20- by 12- by 2.5-in.</u>   <u>20</u>   <u>3.25 oz</u>   <u>No. 12 Scoop</u>   <u>Warm</u>
                      Pan   Portions/Pan   Portion Size   Utensil   Temperature

Ingredients	Portions				Procedure
	40	120	240	480	
EGGS, FRESH, 30 doz/case	1.00 doz	3.00 doz	6.00 doz	12.00 doz	1. Hard cook eggs in high speed steam cooker.
ONIONS, DEHYD CHOP,	1.50 tsp	1.00 tbs	3.00 tbs	.25 cup	2. Rehydrate onions in water for 20 min.
2.5 lb XSTD 6/10		1.50 tsp		2.00 tbs	3. Drain tuna and break into large pieces.
WATER, cold	2.00 tsp	2.00 tbs	.25 cup	.50 cup	4. Trim and wash celery. Weight is EP.
TUNA, LIGHT,	1.00 can	3.00 can	6.00 can	12.00 can	5. Chop celery and eggs into .25 in. pieces in chopper.
6/66.5 oz cans/cs					6. Combine all ingredients by tossing lightly.
CELERY, FRESH, GRN,	2.00 lb	6.00 lb	12.00 lb	24.00 lb	7. Using a No. 12 scoop put 3.25 oz tuna mix on ea
FNCY, pascal, bun					hot dog bun.
RELISH, RED AND GREEN,	1.00 cup	3.00 cup	1.00 qt	3.00 qt	8. Cut each slice of cheese in half.
4/1 gal/cs			2.00 cup		9. Place half slice of cheese on top of tuna.
LEMON JUICE, RECONSTI-	.25 cup	.75 cup	1.50 cup	3.00 cup	10. Place tuna dogs on sheet pan and heat in conv oven
TUTED, 12/qt jars					at 350°F. for 2 to 3 min. until cheese melts.
SALAD DRESSING,	1.75 cup	1.00 qt	2.00 qt	1.00 gal	11. Put tuna dogs in 20- by 12- by 2.5-in. counter pan.
4/1 gal/cs		1.25 cup	2.50 cup	1.00 qt	Cooking time: 2 to 3 min.
				1.00 cup	Cooking temp: 350°F.
PEPPER, WHITE, GROUND,	.04 tsp	.12 tsp	.25 tsp	.50 tsp	Equipment: conv oven
1 lb					
SALT, 100 lb bag	.50 oz	1.50 oz	3.00 oz	6.00 oz	
ROLLS, WIENER,	3.33 doz	10.00 doz	20.00 doz	40.00 doz	
pkg/12-6 in.					
AMERICAN CHEESE,	1.00 lb	3.00 lb	6.00 lb	12.75 lb	
PRE-CUT 6/5 lb	1.00 oz	3.00 oz	6.00 oz		

1930	TUNA NOODLE CASSEROLE	ENTREES—Fish and Shellfish
Recipe No.	Recipe Name	Category

Serving Standards:	20- by 12- by 2.5-in.	32	6 oz	4 oz Ladle	Hot
	Pan	Portions/Pan	Portion Size	Utensil	Temperature

Ingredients	Portions				Procedure
	100	300	500	1000	
Yield	4.50 gal	13.50 gal	22.50 gal	45.00 gal	1. Cook noodles about 15 min. in an ample amt of boiling salted water until tender but firm.
NOODLES, MEDIUM, 10 lb	2.50 lb	7.50 lb	12.50 lb	25.00 lb	2. Drain and rinse with cold water.
MARGARINE, SOLID, 1 lb	1.25 lb	3.75 lb	6.25 lb	12.50 lb	3. Melt fat and blend with flour to make a roux.
FLOUR, 25 lb bag	1.00 lb	3.00 lb	5.00 lb	10.00 lb	4. Turn off steam.
WATER, hot, 180°F.	1.00 gal	5.00 gal	9.00 gal	18.00 gal	5. Add hot water and stir until smooth.
	3.00 qt	2.00 qt	1.00 qt	3.00 qt	6. Add dry milk and stir until dissolved.
	2.00 cup	2.00 cup	2.00 cup		7. Turn on steam. Add white pepper and salt and cook until thickened.
MILK, INST NONFAT DRY, 6/5 lb	1.50 lb	4.50 lb	7.50 lb	15.00 lb	8. Rehydrate onions in water.
PEPPER, WHITE, GROUND, 1 lb	.25 tsp	.75 tsp	1.25 tsp	2.50 tsp	9. Add drained tuna fish, frozen peas, onion, chopped pimento and cooked noodles to sauce.
SALT, 100 lb bag	.25 oz	.75 oz	1.25 oz	2.50 oz	10. Mix gently but thoroughly to combine.
TUNA, LIGHT, 6/66.5 oz cans/cs	2.00 can	6.00 can	10.00 can	20.00 can	11. Place 1.5 gal of mixture into 20- by 12- by 2.5-in. counter pans and bake in conv oven at 350°F. for 30 min.
PEAS, SM, FNCY, 20 lb box	5.00 lb	15.00 lb	25.00 lb	50.00 lb	12. Divide grated cheese evenly over all pans and return to oven just long enough to melt cheese.
ONIONS, DEHYD CHOP, 2.5 lb XSTD 6/10	5.00 oz	15.00 oz	1.00 lb 9.00 oz	3.00 lb 2.00 oz	Cooking time: 15 min., 30 min.
WATER, cold	.25 cup	.75 cup	1.25 cup	2.50 cup	Cooking temp: 350°F.
PIMENTOS, BROKEN PIECES, STD 24/2.5	1.25 cup	3.75 cup	1.00 qt 2.25 cup	3.00 qt .50 cup	Equipment: steam kettle, conv oven
CHEDDAR CHEESE, WHEEL	1.00 lb	3.00 lb	5.00 lb	10.00 lb	

1935	DEVILED CRAB WITH TARTAR SAUCE				ENTREES—Fish and Shellfish
Recipe No.	Recipe Name				Category

Serving Standards: __20- by 12- by 2.5-in.__ _____ __3 oz__ _____ __Tongs__ _____ __Hot__ _____

Pan .... Portions/Pan .... Portion Size .... Utensil ...... Temperature

Ingredients	Portions				Procedure
	24	96	192	480	
CRAB, DEV FNCY 3 oz 24/cs	2.00 doz	8.00 doz	16.00 doz	40.00 doz	1. Unwrap frozen crabs and place on sheet pans about
MARGARINE, SOLID, 1 lb	.25 lb	1.00 lb	2.00 lb	5.00 lb	40 per pan.
LEMON JUICE, RECONSTI-	1.00 tbs	.25 cup	.75 cup	1.75 cup	2. Melt margarine and cool to room temp.
TUTED, 12/qt jars	1.50 tsp	2.00 tbs		2.00 tbs	3. Add lemon juice, Worcestershire sauce, salt and
WORCESTERSHIRE SAUCE,	2.25 tsp	3.00 tbs	.25 cup	.75 cup	paprika. Stir to combine.
4/1 gal/cs			2.00 tbs	3.00 tbs	4. Brush each portion with sauce. If margarine solidi-
PAPRIKA, GROUND, 6 lb	1.75 tsp	2.00 tbs	.25 cup	.50 cup	fies, place pan of sauce in warm water to make it
		1.00 tsp	2.00 tsp	3.00 tbs	easy to spread.
				2.00 tsp	5. Place crabs in conv oven at 350°F. until done and
TARTAR SAUCE, 4/gal/cs	1.50 cup	1.00 qt	3.00 qt	1.00 gal	slightly browned, about 25 min.
		2.00 cup		3.00 qt	6. Place on counter pans and add appropriate garnish
				2.00 cup	such as sliced lemons or fresh parsley.

7. Place tartar sauce on condiment stand.

Note: Tartar sauce is 1 tbs (one-half oz) per serving.

Cooking time: about 25 min.

Cooking temp: 350°F.

Equipment: conv oven

1937	CRAB ROLLS WITH TARTAR SAUCE				ENTREES—Fish and Shellfish
Recipe No.	Recipe Name				Category

Serving Standards: __20- by 12- by 2.5-in.__   _____   __2 ea__   __Tongs__   __Hot__
                           Pan   Portions/Pan   Portion Size   Utensil   Temperature

Ingredients	Portions				Procedure
	12	96	480	960	
CRAB ROLLS, 12 bx/cs, 24 ea, 2 oz/bx	2.00 doz	16.00 doz	80.00 doz	160.00 doz	1. Fill deep fryer with oil and heat to 350°F.
					2. Fry in deep fat until golden brown.
TARTAR SAUCE, 4/gal/cs	.75 cup	1.00 qt	1.00 gal	3.00 gal	3. Place tartar sauce on condiment stand.
		2.00 cup	3.00 qt	3.00 qt	Cooking temp: 350°F.
			2.00 cup		Equipment: deep fat fryer

1941	BROILED MACKEREL				ENTREES—Fish and Shellfish
Recipe No.	Recipe Name				Category

Serving Standards:

20- by 12- by 2.5-in.	7 to 8	5 oz	Slotted Spatula	Hot
Pan	Portions/Pan	Portion Size	Utensil	Temperature

Ingredients	Portions				Procedure
	60	120	240	480	
MARGARINE, SOLID, 1 lb	1.00 lb	2.00 lb	5.25 lb	10.50 lb	1. Melt margarine and cool to room temp.
	5.00 oz	10.00 oz			2. Add lemon juice, Worcestershire sauce, salt and
LEMON JUICE, RECONSTI-	.66 cup	1.33 cup	2.66 cup	1.00 qt	paprika and stir to combine.
TUTED, 12/qt jars				1.33 cup	3. Place frozen fish in counter pans and brush each
WORCESTERSHIRE SAUCE,	.33 cup	.66 cup	1.33 cup	2.66 cup	fillet with sauce, being careful not to get sauce on
4/1 gal/cs					sides of pan. If margarine solidifies, place pan of
PAPRIKA, GROUND, 6 lb	.33 cup	.66 cup	1.33 cup	2.66 cup	sauce in warm water to make it easy to spread.
SALT, 100 lb bag	.50 oz	1.00 oz	2.00 oz	.25 lb	4. Place in conv oven until tender, 25 to 30 min. at
MACKEREL, SPANISH,	20.00 lb	40.00 lb	80.00 lb	160.00 lb	300°F.
5 oz, lb					5. Slice lemons on No. 13 on slicer (8 slices per lem-
LEMONS, FNCY, FRESH,	8.00 ea	1.00 doz	2.00 doz	5.00 doz	on) and garnish each piece of fish with a circle of
200 ct		4.00 ea	8.00 ea	4.00 ea	lemon.
					Cooking time: 25 to 30 min.
					Cooking temp: 300°F.
					Equipment: conv oven

1979	SEAFOOD NEWBURG				ENTREES—Fish and Shellfish
Recipe No.	Recipe Name				Category

Serving Standards:

10- by 12- by 4-in.		4 oz	4 oz Ladle	Hot
Pan	Portions/Pan	Portion Size	Utensil	Temperature

Ingredients	Portions				Procedure
	56	112	224	448	
Yield	6.25 qt	12.50 qt	6.25 gal	12.50 gal	1. Rehydrate onions and green peppers.
ONIONS, DEHYD CHOP, 2.5 lb XSTD 6/10	2.00 oz	.25 lb	.50 lb	1.00 lb	2. Melt margarine in steam kettle. 3. Saute onions, green peppers and bay leaves in margarine for 3 min.
PEPPERS, DEHYD DICED, GRN, 1.25 lb XSTD 6/10	.50 oz	1.00 oz	2.00 oz	.25 lb	4. Remove bay leaves.
WATER, cold	1.25 cup	2.50 cup	1.00 qt 1.00 cup	2.00 qt 2.00 cup	5. Add flour, salt and pepper. Cook for 3 min. 6. Turn steam off and add second amt of water, then
MARGARINE, SOLID, 1 lb	1.00 lb 2.00 oz	2.25 lb	4.50 lb	9.00 lb	add dry milk. Turn steam on and cook until thickened.
BAY LEAVES, 1 lb can	3.00 ea	6.00 ea	1.00 doz	2.00 doz	7. Bake flounder and sole in conv oven at 350°F. un-
FLOUR, 25 lb bag	9.00 oz	1.00 lb 2.00 oz	2.25 lb	4.50 lb	til fish is flaky, about 20 min.
SALT, 100 lb bag	2.25 tsp	1.00 tbs 1.50 tsp	3.00 tbs	.25 cup 2.00 tbs	8. Steam shrimp in high speed steam cooker until tender, about 12 min., if frozen.
PEPPER, WHITE, GROUND, 1 lb	.75 tsp	1.50 tsp	1.00 tbs	2.00 tbs	9. Chop pimento. 10. Flake flounder and sole. Add with pimento and
MILK, INST NONFAT DRY, 6/5 lb	13.50 oz	1.00 lb 11.00 oz	3.00 lb 6.00 oz	6.75 lb	shrimp to sauce. Mix. 11. Add cooking sherry and mix. Place in counter pans
WATER, cold	1.00 gal 1.00 cup	2.00 gal 2.00 cup	4.00 gal 1.00 qt	8.00 gal 2.00 qt	10- by 12- by 4-in. 12. Serve according to instructions.
SOLE, UNBRD, 4 oz, lb	1.50 lb	3.00 lb	6.00 lb	12.00 lb	*Note:* Can be served with toast points, rice or English
FLOUNDER, UNBRD, 4 oz, lb	1.50 lb	3.00 lb	6.00 lb	12.00 lb	muffins.
SHRIMP, PDQ, FNCY 130 to 150 ct	1.50 lb	3.00 lb	6.00 lb	12.00 lb	Cooking time: 1.5 hr Cooking temp: simmer
PIMENTOS, BROKEN PIECES, STD 24/2.5	.75 cup	1.50 cup	3.00 cup	1.00 qt 2.00 cup	Equipment: conv oven, high speed steam cooker
COOKING SHERRY, gallons	.75 cup	1.50 cup	3.00 cup	1.00 qt 2.00 cup	

1980	SEAFOOD NEWBURG WITH TOAST POINTS	ENTREES—Fish and Shellfish
Recipe No.	Recipe Name	Category

Serving Standards: __10- by 12- by 4-in.__ _____ __4 oz__ __4 oz Ladle__ __Hot__
Pan   Portions/Pan   Portion Size   Utensil   Temperature

Ingredients	Portions				Procedure
	56	112	224	448	
BREAD, SANDWICH, WHITE, 32 oz	56.00 sli	112.00 sli	224.00 sli	448.00 sli	1. Cut each slice of bread diagonally and place on sheet pans.
SEAFOOD NEWBURG, Recipe 1979	1.00 gal 2.25 qt	3.00 gal .50 qt	6.00 gal 1.00 qt	12.00 gal 2.00 qt	2. Toast in conv oven at 400°F. for 5 min.
					3. Place toast points in counter pans.
					4. Serve a 4 oz ladle of Seafood Newburg over 2 toast points (1 slice of bread).
					Cooking time: 5 min.
					Cooking temp: 400°F.
					Equipment: conv oven

1990	SEAFOOD PATTIES WITH COCKTAIL SAUCE				ENTREES—Fish and Shellfish
Recipe No.	Recipe Name				Category

Serving Standards: 20- by 12- by 2.5-in. _____ **(2) 2 oz** _____ **Solid Spatula** _____ **Hot** _____

| | Pan | Portions/Pan | Portion Size | Utensil | Temperature |

Ingredients	Portions				Procedure
	50	100	200	500	
SEAFOOD PATTIES,	8.00 doz	16.00 doz	33.00 doz	83.00 doz	1. Place frozen patties on sheet pan.
6 ctn/24 pcs/2 oz	4.00 ea	8.00 ea	4.00 ea	4.00 ea	2. Bake in conv oven at 350°F. for 20 min. until
COCKTAIL SAUCE,	1.62 qt	3.25 qt	1.00 gal	4.00 gal	golden brown.
Recipe 0660			2.50 qt	.25 qt	3. Place in 20- by 12- by 2.5-in. counter pans.
					<div align="center">OR</div>
					1. Deep fry frozen patties at 350°F. for approx 4 min.
					2. Place in 20- by 12- by 2.5-in. counter pans.
					Note 1: Prepare cocktail sauce.
					Note 2: Serve two 2 oz patties; cocktail sauce may be placed on condiment stand.
					Cooking time: 20 min. or 4 min.
					Cooking temp: 350°F.
					Equipment: conv oven or deep fat fryer

2110	BARBECUED CHICKEN				ENTREES—Poultry
Recipe No.	Recipe Name				Category

Serving Standards: __20- by 12- by 2.5-in.__   __20__   __1 qtr__   __Tongs__   __Hot__
                              Pan   Portions/Pan   Portion Size   Utensil   Temperature

Ingredients	Portions				Procedure
	50	100	300	500	
FRYERS, QTR, 2.22 to 2.50 lb grade A 2.4 lb	12.50 hd	25.00 hd	75.00 hd	125.00 hd	1. Place chicken on sheet pans.
SALT, 100 lb bag	1.25 oz	2.50 oz	7.50 oz	12.50 oz	2. Combine salt, pepper, chili powder and paprika.
PEPPER, BLACK, GROUND, 6 lb	.25 tsp	.50 tsp	1.50 tsp	2.50 tsp	3. Brush chicken with oil and sprinkle lightly with seasoning mixture.
CHILI POWDER, 1 lb	.50 tsp	1.00 tsp	1.00 tbs	1.00 tbs 2.00 tsp	4. Bake for 1 hr in conv oven at 350°F. 5. Remove chicken from sheet pans and place in 20- by 12- by 2.5-in. counter pans.
PAPRIKA, GROUND, 6 lb	.75 tsp	1.50 tsp	1.00 tbs 1.50 tsp	2.00 tbs 1.50 tsp	6. Brush chicken with barbecue sauce. 7. Bake for 30 min. in conv oven at 300°F.
SHORTENING, LIQUID, for deep fat 5 gal	1.50 cup	3.00 cup	2.00 qt 1.00 cup	3.00 qt 3.00 cup	Cooking time: 1 hr—350°F.; 30 min.—300°F. Cooking temp: 350°F., 300°F.
BARBECUE SAUCE, Recipe 0610	1.00 gal	2.00 gal	6.00 gal	10.00 gal	Equipment: conv oven

| | | | 2120 | | BROILED CHICKEN HALVES | | ENTREES—Poultry |

2120   **BROILED CHICKEN HALVES**   **ENTREES—Poultry**

Recipe No.   Recipe Name   Category

Serving Standards: **20- by 12- by 2.5-in.**   **1 half**   **Tongs**   **Hot**

                     Pan   Portions/Pan   Portion Size   Utensil   Temperature

Ingredients	Portions 50	100	200	400	Procedure
FRYERS, HLV, 1.75 to 2 lb, grade A 1.9 lb	25.00 hd	50.00 hd	100.00 hd	200.00 hd	1. Melt margarine and cool to room temp.
					2. Add flour, salt and paprika. Mix well.
MARGARINE, SOLID, 1 lb	2.50 lb	5.00 lb	10.00 lb	20.00 lb	3. Add lemon juice gradually and mix well.
LEMON JUICE, RECONSTI-	1.25 cup	2.50 cup	1.00 qt	2.00 qt	4. Place clean chicken on sheet pans, skin side up.
TUTED, 12/qt jars			1.00 cup	2.00 cup	5. Brush each piece of chicken with the sauce, approx
PAPRIKA, GROUND, 6 lb	2.50 oz	5.00 oz	10.00 oz	1.25 lb	1 oz sauce on ea piece.
SALT, 100 lb bag	1.00 oz	2.00 oz	.25 lb	.50 lb	6. Place in conv oven at 300°F. until golden brown,
FLOUR, 25 lb bag	.25 lb	.50 lb	1.00 lb	2.00 lb	approx 1.25 hr.
					7. Place in 20- by 12- by 2.5-in. counter pans to serve.
					Cooking time: 1.25 hr
					Cooking temp: 300°F.
					Equipment: conv oven

2121	BROILED CHICKEN (QUARTERS)				ENTREES—Poultry
Recipe No.	Recipe Name				Category

Serving Standards:	20- by 12- by 6-in.	50	1 qtr	Tongs	Hot
	Pan	Portions/Pan	Portion Size	Utensil	Temperature

Ingredients	Portions				Procedure
	50	100	300	500	
MARGARINE, SOLID, 1 lb	1.25 lb	2.50 lb	7.50 lb	12.50 lb	1. Melt margarine and cool to room temp.
FLOUR, 25 lb bag	2.00 oz	.25 lb	.75 lb	1.25 lb	2. Add flour, salt and paprika. Mix well.
SALT, 100 lb bag	.50 oz	1.00 oz	3.00 oz	5.00 oz	3. Add lemon juice gradually and mix well.
PAPRIKA, GROUND, 6 lb	1.25 oz	2.50 oz	7.50 oz	12.50 oz	4. Place clean chicken on sheet pans, skin side up.
LEMON JUICE, RECONSTI-	.50 cup	1.25 cup	3.75 cup	1.00 qt	5. Brush ea piece of chicken with the sauce, approx
TUTED, 12/qt jars	2.00 tbs			2.25 cup	0.5 oz sauce on ea piece.
FRYERS, QTR 2.22 to 2.50 lb	12.50 hd	25.00 hd	75.00 hd	125.00 hd	6. Place in conv oven at 300°F. until golden brown,
grade A 2.4 lb					approx 1 hr.
					Cooking time: 1 hr
					Cooking temp: 300°F.
					Equipment: conv oven

2125			BROILED CHICKEN THIGHS				ENTREES—Poultry
Recipe No.			Recipe Name				Category

Serving Standards: 20- by 12- by 6-in.   50   2 ea   Tongs   Hot

                       Pan   Portions/Pan   Portion Size   Utensil   Temperature

Ingredients	Portions				E*	Procedure
	55	220	495	990		
MARGARINE, SOLID, 1 lb	1.25 lb	5.00 lb	11.25 lb	22.50 lb		1. Melt margarine and cool to room temp.
FLOUR, 25 lb bag	2.00 oz	.50 lb	1.00 lb	2.25 lb		2. Add flour, salt and paprika. Mix well.
			2.00 oz			3. Add lemon juice gradually and mix well.
SALT, 100 lb bag	.50 oz	2.00 oz	4.50 oz	9.00 oz		4. Place clean chicken on sheet pans, skin side up.
PAPRIKA, GROUND, 1 lb	1.25 oz	5.00 oz	11.25 oz	1.00 lb		5. Brush each piece of chicken with the sauce, approx
				6.50 oz		.25 oz sauce on each piece.
LEMON JUICE, RECONSTI-	.50 cup	2.50 cup	1.00 qt	2.00 qt		6. Place in conv oven at 300°F. until golden brown,
TUTED, 12/qt jars	2.00 tbs		1.50 cup	3.25 cup		approx 1 hr.
			2.00 tbs			Cooking time: 1 hr
CHICKEN THIGHS, 5 lb/box	25.00 lb	100.00 lb	225.00 lb	450.00 lb		Cooking temp: 300°F.
						Equipment: conv oven
						*Early Prep: Thaw chicken in refrigerator one day ahead.

2146	CHICKEN CHEESEBURGER					ENTREES—Poultry
Recipe No.	Recipe Name					Category

Serving Standards:	20- by 12- by 2.5-in.	12	1 ea	Solid Spatula	Hot
	Pan	Portions/Pan	Portion Size	Utensil	Temperature

Ingredients	Portions				E*	Procedure
	42	252	504	1008		
EGGS, FRESH, 30 doz/case	1.00 doz	6.00 doz	12.00 doz	24.00 doz		1. Hard cook eggs in steamer. Place in cold water, peel and chop into .5 inch pieces.
CHICKEN, BONED, SK, precooked, fro	2.50 lb	15.00 lb	30.00 lb	60.00 lb		2. Place thawed chicken in chopper and chop coarsely.
CELERY, FRESH, GRN, FNCY, pascal, bun	1.25 lb	7.50 lb	15.00 lb	30.00 lb		3. Chop celery in chopper not too fine. Weight of celery is EP.
LEMON JUICE, RECONSTI-TUTED, 12/qt jars	1.00 tbs	.25 cup 2.00 tbs	.75 cup	1.50 cup		4. Pour lemon juice over chicken.
ONIONS, DEHYD CHOP, 2.5 lb XSTD 6/10	1.00 tbs 1.00 tsp	.50 cup	1.00 cup	2.00 cup		5. Rehydrate onion with water; drain well.
WATER, cold	1.00 tbs 1.50 tsp	.50 cup 1.00 tbs	1.00 cup 2.00 tbs	2.25 cup		6. Drain pickle relish and combine with chicken. Add eggs, celery, onion, mayonnaise, salt and white pepper and mix lightly.
RELISH, RED AND GREEN, 4/1 gal/cs	1.00 cup	1.00 qt 2.00 cup	3.00 qt	1.00 gal 2.00 qt		7. Grate the American cheese.
MAYONNAISE, 4/1 gal/cs	1.25 cup	1.00 qt 3.50 cup	3.00 qt 3.00 cup	1.00 gal 3.00 qt 2.00 cup		8. Wash tomatoes and slice thinly. Wt AP.
						9. Arrange bun halves with cut surfaces up in counter pan 20- by 12- by 2.5-in.
SALT, 100 lb bag	2.25 tsp	.25 cup 1.50 tsp	.50 cup 1.00 tbs	1.00 cup 2.00 tbs		10. Top with a No. 20 scoop of chicken salad, about 2.25 oz.
PEPPER, WHITE, GROUND, 1 lb	.12 tsp	.75 tsp	1.50 tsp	1.00 tbs		11. Place slice of tomato on top of chicken salad and press down to spread the salad to the edges.
AMERICAN CHEESE, PRE-CUT 6/5 lb	10.50 oz	3.00 lb 15.00 oz	7.00 lb 14.00 oz	15.75 lb		12. Sprinkle .25 oz of grated American cheese over the tomato and garnish with dehyd parsley flakes.
TOMATOES, FNCY, 18 lb	2.25 lb	13.50 lb	27.00 lb	54.00 lb		13. Place in conv oven at 350°F. for about 5 min. until cheese melts.
ROLLS, KAISER, pkg/12-4 in.	1.75 doz	10.50 doz	21.00 doz	42.00 doz		14. Serve immediately.
PARSLEY, DEHYD FLK, XSTD 6/10	1.00 tbs	.25 cup 2.00 tbs	.75 cup	1.50 cup		Cooking time: 5 min.

Cooking temp: 350°F.

Equipment: conv oven

*Early Prep: Thaw chicken in refrigerator 1 day ahead.

2170	**CHICKEN AND DUMPLINGS**				**ENTREES—Poultry**
Recipe No.	Recipe Name				Category

Serving Standards:

12- by 20- by 8-in.		6.75 oz	4 oz Ladle	Hot
Pan	Portions/Pan	Portion Size	Utensil	Temperature

Ingredients	Portions				Procedure
	50	**200**	**500**	**1000**	
Yield	2.66 gal	10.64 gal	26.60 gal	53.20 gal	1. Combine flour, salt and baking powder and mix well.
FLOUR, 25 lb bag	2.25 lb	9.00 lb	22.50 lb	45.00 lb	2. Work lard into flour lightly by hand until small balls are formed.
BAKING POWDER, 4/10/bag	2.50 oz	10.00 oz	1.00 lb 9.00 oz	3.00 lb 2.00 oz	3. Reconstitute milk with water.
SALT, 100 lb bag	1.00 tbs 1.00 tsp	.25 cup 1.00 tbs 1.00 tsp	.75 cup 1.00 tbs 1.00 tsp	1.50 cup 2.00 tbs 2.00 tsp	4. Combine eggs and milk and add to flour mixture and mix. This should be a stiff dough.
LARD, 12/4 lb/cs	11.00 oz	2.75 lb	6.00 lb 14.00 oz	13.75 lb	5. Roll on floured surface to .25 in. thick and cut into strips 1 in. wide and 1.5 in. long. This can be dropped with a No. 30 scoop if desired.
MILK, INST NONFAT DRY, 6/5 lb	1.25 oz	5.00 oz	12.50 oz	1.00 lb 9.00 oz	
WATER, cold	1.50 cup	1.00 qt 2.00 cup	3.00 qt 3.00 cup	1.00 gal 3.00 qt 2.00 cup	6. Melt margarine in steam kettle and blend in second amt of flour to make a roux; cook for 2 min.
EGGS, 6/5 lb/cs	14.00 oz	3.50 lb	8.75 lb	17.50 lb	7. Add warm water and stir rapidly with wire whip until thin smooth gravy is formed.
MARGARINE, SOLID, 1 lb	.50 lb	2.00 lb	5.00 lb	10.00 lb	8. Add chicken base and blend well.
FLOUR, 25 lb bag	6.50 oz	1.00 lb 10.00 oz	4.00 lb 1.00 oz	8.00 lb 2.00 oz	9. Drop dumplings into hot gravy and cook for 15 min. or until tender.
WATER, warm	1.00 gal 2.00 qt 2.50 cup	6.00 gal 2.00 qt 2.00 cup	16.00 gal 2.00 qt 1.00 cup	33.00 gal 2.00 cup	10. Drain canned chicken and cut large pieces once across the fibers.
CHICKEN SOUP BASE, 12/1 lb/cs	5.00 oz	1.25 lb	3.00 lb 2.00 oz	6.25 lb	11. Add chicken to dumplings and fold together lightly. Turn off heat and serve.
CHICKEN, BONED, WHL, FNCY, 12/50 oz can	2.00 can	8.00 can	20.00 can	40.00 can	*Note:* Drained wt of 50 oz can of boned chicken is 2.5 lb.

Note: Drained wt of 50 oz can of boned chicken is 2.5 lb.
Cooking time: see above
Equipment: steam kettle
Pre-prep: Dumplings may be made 1 day ahead. Separate layers with waxed paper and sprinkle flour over each layer and refrigerate.

2190	CHICKEN TETRAZZINI					ENTREES—Poultry
Recipe No.	Recipe Name					Category

Serving Standards:

20- by 12- by 2.5-in.	34	6 oz	3 oz Ladle	Hot
Pan	Portions/Pan	Portion Size	Utensil	Temperature

Ingredients	Portions				E*	Procedure
	102	306	612	918		
Yield	4.50 gal	13.50 gal	27.00 gal	40.50 gal		
SPAGHETTI, LONG THIN, 20 lb	3.00 lb	9.00 lb	18.00 lb	27.00 lb		1. Break spaghetti into 3 pieces and cook in boiling salted water for 20 min. or until done. Drain.
ONIONS, DEHYD CHOP, 2.5 lb XSTD 6/10	2.00 oz	6.00 oz	.75 lb	1.00 lb 2.00 oz		2. Rehydrate onions and green peppers in water; dice the celery. Weight is EP.
PEPPERS, DEHYD DICED, GRN, XSTD 6/10	1.00 oz	3.00 oz	6.00 oz	9.00 oz		3. Dice the thawed chicken. Grate cheese.
WATER, cold	1.50 cup	1.00 qt .50 cup	2.00 qt 1.00 cup	3.00 qt 1.50 cup		4. Melt margarine and saute green peppers, onions, celery and drained mushrooms in it.
CELERY, FRESH, GRN, FNCY, PASCAL, bun	1.50 lb	4.50 lb	9.00 lb	13.50 lb		5. Add flour and blend well and turn steam off. 6. Add hot water and mix well.
MUSHROOMS, STEMS/PCS, XSTD 24/16 oz	1.50 can	4.50 can	9.00 can	13.50 can		7. Add nonfat dry milk and mix well. 8. Turn on steam and cook, stirring constantly until thickened.
CHICKEN, BONED, SK, precooked, fro	7.50 lb	22.50 lb	45.00 lb	67.50 lb		9. Add salt, white pepper, Worcestershire sauce and sherry and blend well.
CHEDDAR CHEESE, WHEEL	1.50 lb	4.50 lb	9.00 lb	13.50 lb		10. Add diced chicken and drained chopped pimento
MARGARINE, SOLID, 1 lb	1.00 lb	3.00 lb	6.00 lb	9.00 lb		and combine well.
FLOUR, 25 lb bag	1.00 lb	3.00 lb	6.00 lb	9.00 lb		11. Combine cooked spaghetti with sauce and place
WATER, hot, 180°F.	1.75 gal	5.25 gal	10.50 gal	15.75 gal		1.5 gal into 20- by 12- by 2.5-in. counter pans.
MILK, INST NONFAT DRY, 6/5 lb	1.75 lb	5.25 lb	10.50 lb	15.75 lb		12. Sprinkle each pan with parmesan cheese and paprika.
SALT, 100 lb bag	1.25 oz	3.75 oz	7.50 oz	11.00 oz		13. Bake in conv oven at 350°F. for 20 to 25 min.
PEPPER, WHITE, GROUND, 1 lb	.75 tsp	2.25 tsp	1.00 tbs 1.50 tsp	2.00 tbs .75 tsp		Cooking time: 20 to 25 min. Cooking temp: 350°F.
WORCESTERSHIRE SAUCE, 4/1 gal/cs	.25 cup 2.00 tbs	1.00 cup 2.00 tbs	2.25 cup	3.25 cup 2.00 tbs		Equipment: steam kettle; conv oven *Early Prep: Thaw chicken in refrigerator one day
COOKING SHERRY, gallons	.75 cup	2.25 cup	1.00 qt .50 cup	1.00 qt 2.75 cup		ahead.

(cont.)

2190   CHICKEN TETRAZZINI (cont.)

Ingredients	Portions				Procedure
	102	306	612	918	
PIMENTOS, BROKEN PIECES, STD 24/2.5	.50 can	1.50 can	3.00 can	4.50 can	
PARMESAN CHEESE, GRATED, 12/1 lb	.50 lb	1.50 lb	3.00 lb	4.50 lb	
PAPRIKA, GROUND, 6 lb	.50 tsp	1.50 tsp	1.00 tbs	1.00 tbs 1.50 tsp	

2210   FRIED CHICKEN—FOURTHS   ENTREES—Poultry

Recipe No.   Recipe Name   Category

Serving Standards: 20- by 12- by 6-in.   1 qtr   Tongs   Hot

        Pan   Portions/Pan   Portion Size   Utensil   Temperature

Ingredients	Portions				Procedure
	50	100	300	500	
FLOUR, 25 lb bag	1.00 lb	2.00 lb	6.00 lb	10.00 lb	1. Combine flour, salt, pepper and paprika.
SALT, 100 lb bag	1.37 oz	2.75 oz	8.25 oz	13.75 oz	2. Dredge each chicken part in flour mixture.
PEPPER, BLACK, GROUND, 6 lb	.50 tsp	1.00 tsp	1.00 tbs	1.00 tbs 2.00 tsp	3. Place chicken in deep fryer basket. 4. Fry in deep fryer preheated to 325°F. until golden brown, about 15 min.
PAPRIKA, GROUND, 6 lb	.33 oz	.66 oz	2.00 oz	3.30 oz	5. Place in 20- by 12- by 6-in. counter pans to serve.
FRYERS, QTR, 2.22 to 2.50 lb grade A 2.4 lb	12.50 hd	25.00 hd	75.00 hd	125.00 hd	Cooking time: 15 min. Cooking temp: 325°F. Equipment: deep fat fryer

2215	FRIED CHICKEN (PRECOOKED EIGHTHS)					ENTREES—Poultry
Recipe No.	Recipe Name					Category

Serving Standards: 20- by 12- by 6-in.   / Pan   Portions/Pan   2 pcs / Portion Size   Tongs / Utensil   Hot / Temperature

Ingredients	Portions				Procedure
	24	192	480	960	
CHICKEN, FROZEN, precooked, 48 1/8	1.00 cs	8.00 cs	20.00 cs	40.00 cs	1. Fry frozen chicken in deep fryer at 300°F. until golden brown, 5 to 6 min. Cooking time: 5 to 6 min. Cooking temp: 300°F. Equipment: deep fat fryer

2220	FRIED CHICKEN DRUMSTICKS					ENTREES—Poultry
Recipe No.	Recipe Name					Category

Serving Standards: 20- by 12- by 6-in.   / Pan   Portions/Pan   2 ea / Portion Size   Tongs / Utensil   Hot / Temperature

Ingredients	Portions				Procedure
	50	200	600	800	
FLOUR, 25 lb bag	1.00 lb	4.00 lb	12.00 lb	16.00 lb	1. Combine flour, salt, pepper and paprika.
SALT, 100 lb bag	1.37 oz	5.50 oz	1.00 lb .50 oz	1.00 lb 6.00 oz	2. Dredge each drumstick in flour mixture. 3. Place in deep fryer basket.
PEPPER, BLACK, GROUND, 6 lb	.50 tsp	2.00 tsp	2.00 tbs	2.00 tbs 2.00 tsp	4. Fry in deep fryer preheated to 300°F. until golden brown, approx 12 to 15 min.
PAPRIKA, GROUND, 6 lb	.33 oz	1.32 oz	4.00 oz	.25 lb 1.28 oz	5. Place in 20- by 12- by 6-in. counter pans to serve. Cooking time: 12 to 15 min.
CHICKEN DRUMSTICKS, 5 lb/box	20.00 lb	80.00 lb	240.00 lb	320.00 lb	Cooking temp: 300°F. Equipment: deep fat fryer

2230	OVEN FRIED CHICKEN	ENTREES—Poultry
Recipe No.	Recipe Name	Category

Serving Standards: **20- by 12- by 2.5-in.**   **1 qtr**   **Tongs**   **Hot**

| | Pan | Portions/Pan | Portion Size | Utensil | Temperature |

Ingredients	Portions				Procedure
	50	100	500	1000	
FLOUR, 25 lb bag	1.00 lb	2.00 lb	10.00 lb	20.00 lb	1. Combine flour, salt, pepper and paprika in large mixing bowl.
SALT, 100 lb bag	1.37 oz	2.75 oz	13.75 oz	1.00 lb	
				11.50 oz	2. Dredge each chicken part in flour mixture.
PEPPER, BLACK, GROUND,	.50 tsp	1.00 tsp	1.00 tbs	3.00 tbs	3. Place on sheet pans and brush oil over each piece
6 lb			2.00 tsp	1.00 tsp	of chicken.
PAPRIKA, GROUND, 6 lb	.33 oz	.66 oz	3.30 oz	6.60 oz	4. Place in conv oven at 300°F. for approx 1 hr and
FRYERS, QTR 2.22 to 2.50 lb	12.50 hd	25.00 hd	125.00 hd	250.00 hd	25 min. or until golden brown.
grade A 2.4 lb					5. Place in counter pans 20- by 12- by 2.5-in.
SHORTENING, LIQUID,	3.00 cup	1.00 qt	1.00 gal	3.00 gal	Cooking time: approx 1 hr and 25 min.
for deep fat 5 gal		2.00 cup	3.00 qt	3.00 qt	Cooking temp: 300°F.
			2.00 cup		Equipment: conv oven

2235	BAKED CHICKEN WITH DRESSING (QUARTERS)				ENTREES—Poultry
Recipe No.	Recipe Name				Category

Serving Standards:

20- by 12- by 2.5-in.	15	1 qtr	Solid Spatula	Hot
Pan	Portions/Pan	Portion Size	Utensil	Temperature

Ingredients	Portions				Procedure
	60	240	480	960	
DRESSING, BREAD, Recipe 3396	1.25 gal	5.00 gal	10.00 gal	20.00 gal	1. Prepare bread dressing.
MARGARINE, SOLID, 1 lb	1.50 lb	6.00 lb	12.00 lb	24.00 lb	2. Melt margarine and cool to room temp.
FLOUR, 25 lb bag	2.00 oz	.50 lb	1.00 lb	2.00 lb	3. Add flour and salt and mix well.
SALT, 100 lb bag	.50 oz	2.00 oz	.25 lb	.50 lb	4. Place clean chicken on sheet pans, skin side up.
FRYERS, QTR 2.22 to 2.50 lb grade A 2.4 lb	15.00 hd	60.00 hd	120.00 hd	240.00 hd	5. Brush each piece of chicken with margarine mixture.
CHICKEN GRAVY, Recipe 0530	1.00 gal	4.00 gal	8.00 gal	16.00 gal	6. Cook in conv oven at 300°F. until golden brown, approx 1 hr.
					7. Prepare chicken gravy.
					8. Using a No. 16 scoop place 15 mounds of cooked dressing in counter pan and place a quarter of chicken over each.
					9. Pour 1 qt of chicken gravy over each pan (about 2 oz gravy per portion).
					10. Garnish appropriately.
					Cooking time: 1 hr
					Cooking temp: 300°F.
					Equipment: conv oven

2250	SAUTEED CHICKEN LIVERS	ENTREES–Poultry
Recipe No.	Recipe Name	Category

Serving Standards: <u>20- by 12- by 2.5-in.</u>   <u>32</u>   <u>2.5 oz</u>   <u>Tongs</u>   <u>Hot</u>
                 Pan   Portions/Pan   Portion Size   Utensil   Temperature

Ingredients	Portions				Procedure
	65	130	260	520	
FRYER LIVERS, Grade A	10.00 lb	20.00 lb	40.00 lb	80.00 lb	1. Wash livers and drain thoroughly.
FLOUR, 25 lb bag	13.00 oz	1.00 lb	3.25 lb	6.50 lb	2. Remove any tough veins.
		10.00 oz			3. Combine flour, salt and pepper.
SALT, 100 lb bag	1.50 tsp	1.00 tbs	2.00 tbs	.25 cup	4. Dredge livers in flour mixture.
PEPPER, BLACK, GROUND,	.25 tsp	.50 tsp	1.00 tsp	2.00 tsp	5. Pour 1 cup oil in sheet pan.
6 lb					6. Place 5 lb floured livers in sheet pan.
SHORTENING, LIQUID,	3.00 cup	1.00 qt	3.00 qt	1.00 gal	7. Pour .5 cup oil over livers in each pan.
for deep fat 5 gal		2.00 cup		2.00 qt	8. Bake in conv oven at 400°F. for approx 20 min.
					9. Place in 20- by 12- by 2.5-in. counter pans to serve.
					Cooking time: 20 min.
					Cooking temp: 400°F.
					Equipment: conv oven

2260	SCALLOPED CHICKEN AND NOODLES	ENTREES—Poultry
Recipe No.	**Recipe Name**	**Category**

Serving Standards:

20- by 12- by 2.5-in.	34	6 oz	3 oz Ladle	Hot
Pan	**Portions/Pan**	**Portion Size**	**Utensil**	**Temperature**

Ingredients	Portions				Procedure
	50	**100**	**200**	**500**	
ONIONS, DEHYD CHOP, 2.5 lb XSTD 6/10	1.00 oz	2.00 oz	.25 lb	.50 lb 2.00 oz	1. Rehydrate onions in first amt of water.
WATER, cold	.50 cup	1.00 cup	2.00 cup	1.00 qt 1.00 cup	2. Cook noodles in boiling salted water about 20 min. Rinse and drain.
NOODLES, MEDIUM, 10 lb	1.50 lb	3.00 lb	6.00 lb	15.00 lb	3. Drain fat from chicken and weigh.
MARGARINE, SOLID, 1 lb	.25 lb	.50 lb	1.00 lb	2.50 lb	4. Melt margarine and add chicken fat. Add onions and saute.
CHICKEN FAT, DRAINED from canned chicken	.50 lb	1.00 lb	2.00 lb	5.00 lb	5. Add flour and stir. Turn off steam.
CHICKEN SOUP BASE, 12/1 lb/cs	1.75 oz	3.50 oz	7.00 oz	1.00 lb 1.50 oz	6. Add hot water, saving some to mix with eggs. Stir. 7. Add dry milk and stir to dissolve.
FLOUR, 25 lb bag	6.00 oz	.75 lb	1.50 lb	3.75 lb	8. Turn steam on and cook until smooth.
WATER, hot, 180°F.	3.00 qt 2.75 cup	1.00 gal 3.00 qt 1.50 cup	3.00 gal 2.00 qt 3.00 cup	9.00 gal 3.50 cup	9. Add eggs which have been mixed with small amt of hot water. 10. Cook 5 to 7 min. 11. Add salt.
MILK, INST NONFAT DRY, 6/5 lb	5.00 oz	10.00 oz	1.25 lb	3.00 lb 2.00 oz	12. In a large mixing bowl combine noodles, chicken and chopped pimentos.
EGGS, 6/5 lb/cs	3.00 oz	6.00 oz	.75 lb	1.00 lb 14.00 oz	13. Fold in sauce. 14. Place 1.5 gal in 20- by 12- by 2.5-in. counter pans.
SALT, 100 lb bag	.25 oz	.50 oz	1.00 oz	2.50 oz	15. Melt margarine and combine with bread crumbs. Place 6 oz bread crumb mixture on each pan of chicken.
CHICKEN, BONED, WHL, FNCY, 12/50 oz can	2.50 can	5.00 can	10.00 can	25.00 can	
PIMENTOS, BROKEN PIECES, STD 24/2.5	.66 can	1.32 can	2.64 can	6.60 can	16. Bake in conv oven at 350°F. until golden brown, 20 to 25 min.
BREAD CRUMBS	6.50 oz	13.00 oz	1.00 lb 10.00 oz	4.00 lb 1.00 oz	Cooking time: 30 min. steam kettle 20 to 25 min. conv oven
MARGARINE, SOLID, 1 lb	.25 lb	.50 lb	1.00 lb	2.50 lb	Cooking temp: 350°F. conv oven Equipment: steam kettle, conv oven

2370	**TURKEY CLUB SANDWICH**				**ENTREES—Poultry**
Recipe No.	Recipe Name				Category

Serving Standards: <u>18- by 26- by 1-in.</u>   <u>12</u>   <u>1 ea</u>   <u>Solid Spatula</u>   <u>Cold</u>

         Pan   Portions/Pan   Portion Size   Utensil   Temperature

Ingredients	Portions				E* Procedure
	48	192	384	960	
LETTUCE, HEAD, FNCY, ICEBERG	1.00 ea	4.00 ea	8.00 ea	1.00 doz 8.00 ea	1. Clean and shred lettuce on No. 13 automatic slicer.
TOMATOES, FNCY, 38 lb	2.50 lb	10.00 lb	20.00 lb	50.00 lb	2. Wash tomatoes and slice with slicer set on No. 13 automatic. Weight of tomatoes is AP.
BACON, precooked, 600 slc/8 lb/cs	.16 cs	.66 cs	1.32 cs	3.32 cs	3. Set slicer on No. 8 automatic and slice turkey into 1 oz slices.
TURKEY, ROLL, WHT, grade A 9 lb	3.00 lb	12.00 lb	24.00 lb	60.00 lb	4. Warm bacon in conv oven at 350°F. for 1 to 2 min. Drain.
ROLLS, HAMBURGER, SEEDED, pkg/12-4 in.	4.00 doz	16.00 doz	32.00 doz	80.00 doz	5. Place 12 opened buns on colored trays.

6. Arrange 1 oz slice of turkey and 2 slices of bacon on one half of seeded bun.
7. Arrange .5 oz lettuce and 1 slice tomato on other half of bun.
8. Serve open-faced.
Cooking time: 1 to 2 min.
Cooking temp: 350°F.
Equipment: conv oven, slicer
Variation: Kaiser rolls
*Early Prep: Thaw turkey 1 day in advance.

2372	HOT TURKEY SANDWICH (OPEN-FACED)					ENTREES—Poultry
Recipe No.	Recipe Name					Category

Serving Standards:	20- by 12- by 2.5-in.	12	2 oz	Solid Spatula	Hot
	Pan	Portions/Pan	Portion Size	Utensil	Temperature

Ingredients	Portions				E*	Procedure
	30	120	480	960		
TURKEY, ROLL, WHT, grade A 9 lb	1.00 lb 14.00 oz	7.50 lb	30.00 lb	60.00 lb		1. Set slicer on No. 8 automatic and slice turkey into 1 oz slices.
TURKEY, ROLL, DARK, grade A 9 lb	1.00 lb 14.00 oz	7.50 lb	30.00 lb	60.00 lb		2. Prepare chicken gravy.
CHICKEN GRAVY, Recipe 0530	.50 gal	2.00 gal	8.00 gal	16.00 gal		3. Place 1 oz of light and 1 oz of dark turkey on each slice of bread in counter pans. Add about 2 oz very hot gravy per portion.
BREAD, SANDWICH, WHITE, 32 oz	1.00 lf	4.00 lf	16.00 lf	32.00 lf		4. Place in holding unit to warm.
						*Early Prep: Thaw turkey 1 day in advance.

2380	**ROAST TURKEY WITH DRESSING**	ENTREES—Poultry
Recipe No.	Recipe Name	Category

Serving Standards: 20- by 12- by 2.5-in. / 15 / 2 oz / Solid Spatula / Hot

Pan / Portions/Pan / Portion Size / Utensil / Temperature

Ingredients	Portions				E*	Procedure
	60	240	480	960		
DRESSING, BREAD, Recipe 3396	1.25 gal	5.00 gal	10.00 gal	20.00 gal		1. Prepare bread dressing.
CHICKEN GRAVY, Recipe 0530	1.00 gal	4.00 gal	8.00 gal	16.00 gal		2. Prepare chicken gravy. 3. Slice turkey breasts into 1.5 oz slices and dark rolls into .5 oz slices.
TURKEY, BREAST, SKLS, BNLS, 3.5 lb avg	5.75 lb	23.00 lb	46.00 lb	92.00 lb		4. Using a No. 16 scoop place 15 mounds of dressing in counter pans.
TURKEY, ROLL, DARK, grade A 9 lb	2.00 lb	8.00 lb	16.00 lb	32.00 lb		5. Place .5 oz of dark meat and 1.5 oz of breast over each mound.

6. Place in warmer to heat and just prior to placing on counter, pour 2 oz of very hot gravy over each portion. Garnish appropriately.

Note: Dark rolls and fully cooked breasts (not rolls).

*Early Prep: Thaw turkey under refrigeration.

2520	ROAST VEAL AND DRESSING				ENTREES—Veal and Lamb
Recipe No.	Recipe Name				Category

Serving Standards: 20- by 12- by 2.5-in.   18   2 oz   Solid Spatula   Hot
_____Pan_____Portions/Pan____Portion Size____Utensil_____Temperature

Ingredients	Portions				Procedure
	60	120	480	960	
VEAL, LEG, BNLS, TIED, gd 12 lb No. 1335R	12.00 lb	24.00 lb	96.00 lb	192.00 lb	1. Place veal in roasting pans and rub salt and pepper on all sides.
SALT, 100 lb bag	1.00 tsp	2.00 tsp	2.00 tbs 2.00 tsp	.25 cup 1.00 tbs 1.00 tsp	2. Roast in rotary oven at 300°F. until the internal temp is 160°F., approx 2 to 2.5 hr.
PEPPER, BLACK, GROUND, 6 lb	.50 tsp	1.00 tsp	1.00 tbs 1.00 tsp	2.00 tbs 2.00 tsp	3. Slice into 2 oz portions on slicer (No. 13 to 15) and serve over a No. 16 scoop of dressing.
DRESSING, BREAD, Recipe 3396	1.25 gal	2.50 gal	10.00 gal	20.00 gal	4. Pour about 2 oz of light brown gravy over each portion.
LIGHT BROWN GRAVY, Recipe 0520	1.00 gal	2.00 gal	8.00 gal	16.00 gal	Cooking time: 2 to 2.5 hr Cooking temp: 300°F. Equipment: rotary oven

2530	VEAL CUTLET WITH CREOLE SAUCE					ENTREES—Veal and Lamb
Recipe No.	**Recipe Name**					**Category**

Serving Standards:
20- by 12- by 2.5-in.	20	1 ea	Solid Spatula	Hot
Pan	**Portions/Pan**	**Portion Size**	**Utensil**	**Temperature**

Ingredients	Portions				Procedure
	50	200	500	1000	
CREOLE SAUCE, Recipe 0670	2.50 qt	2.00 gal 2.00 qt	6.00 gal 1.00 qt	12.00 gal 2.00 qt	1. Prepare Creole sauce and turn off steam and hold. 2. Fill deep fat fryer with oil and heat to 350°F.
VEAL, CUTLET, BRD, US CHO, 4 oz	12.50 lb	50.00 lb	125.00 lb	250.00 lb	3. Place frozen veal cutlets in fryer basket and fry in deep fat 4 to 5 min. or until golden brown. 4. Place 20 cutlets in counter pans 20- by 12- by 2.5-in. and pour 1 qt of Creole sauce over each pan. Cooking time: 4 to 5 min. Cooking temp: 350°F. Equipment: deep fat fryer

2550	VEAL PARMESAN				ENTREES—Veal and Lamb
Recipe No.	Recipe Name				Category

Serving Standards: <u>20- by 12- by 2.5-in.</u>   <u>20</u>   <u>5 oz</u>   <u>Solid Spatula</u>   <u>Hot</u>
                    Pan   Portions/Pan   Portion Size   Utensil   Temperature

Ingredients	Portions				Procedure
	50	100	200	500	
VEAL, CUTLET, BRD, US CHO, 4 oz	12.50 lb	25.00 lb	50.00 lb	125.00 lb	1. Fry veal cutlets in deep fat fryer about 4 min. at 350°F.
MOZZARELLA CHEESE, 6/5 lb	1.87 lb	3.75 lb	7.50 lb	18.75 lb	2. Place 20 veal cutlets in 20- by 12- by 2.5-in. counter pans in 2 rows of 10 cutlets ea.
PARMESAN CHEESE, grated, 12/1 lb	.25 lb	.50 lb	1.00 lb	2.50 lb	3. Slice mozzarella cheese in 1 oz slices. Use No. 10 on slicer.
PIZZA SAUCE, PREPARED, 6/10	1.00 can	2.00 can	4.00 can	10.00 can	4. Place 6 slices of cheese over each row of cutlets, 12 slices of cheese per pan.

5. Pour approx one qt of pizza sauce over each pan of cutlets.
6. Sprinkle parmesan cheese over pizza sauce.
7. Cook in conv oven at 350°F. for 20 min.
Cooking time: 4 min. in deep fat fryer
               20 min. in conv oven
Cooking temp: 350°F. deep fat fryer
               350°F. conv oven
Equipment: deep fat fryer and conv oven

2560	VEAL SCALLOPINI	ENTREES—Veal and Lamb
Recipe No.	Recipe Name	Category

Serving Standards: 20- by 12- by 2.5-in. / 40 / 4 oz / Solid Spoon / Hot

Pan / Portions/Pan / Portion Size / Utensil / Temperature

Ingredients	Portions				Procedure
	40	120	400	1000	
ONIONS, DEHYD SLICED, 6/10	2.00 oz	6.00 oz	1.25 lb	3.00 lb 2.00 oz	1. Rehydrate onions in first amt of water.
WATER, cold	1.00 cup	3.00 cup	2.00 qt 2.00 cup	1.00 gal 2.00 qt 1.00 cup	2. Melt margarine in steam kettle and add onions and drained mushrooms and saute for 5 min.
MARGARINE, SOLID, 1 lb	5.00 oz	15.00 oz	3.00 lb 2.00 oz	7.00 lb 13.00 oz	3. Add flour and stir well. 4. Add beef base and water and stir.
MUSHROOMS, STEMS/PCS, XSTD 24/16 oz	.50 can	1.50 can	5.00 can	12.50 can	5. Cook until thickened and then add sherry, parmesan cheese, gravy flavoring and seasonings. Mix well. Turn off steam and hold.
FLOUR, 25 lb bag	5.00 oz	15.00 oz	3.00 lb 2.00 oz	7.00 lb 13.00 oz	6. Place 20 frozen steaks on sheet pans and cook 15 min. in conv oven at 325°F. Drain off fat.
BEEF SOUP BASE, 12/1 lb/cs	1.50 oz	4.50 oz	15.00 oz	2.00 lb 5.50 oz	7. Stack 40 steaks in long shallow counter pans, pouring gravy over each layer, using 3 qt per pan.
WATER, cold	2.50 qt	1.00 gal 3.50 qt	6.00 gal 1.00 qt	15.00 gal 2.50 qt	8. Return to conv oven at 325°F. for 12 to 15 min. Serve.
COOKING SHERRY, gallons	.50 cup	1.50 cup	1.00 qt 1.00 cup	3.00 qt .50 cup	Cooking time: 50 min. total Cooking temp: 325°F.
PARMESAN CHEESE, grated, 12/1 lb	2.00 oz	6.00 oz	1.25 lb	3.00 lb 2.00 oz	Equipment: steam kettle, conv oven
SALT, 100 lb bag	.75 tsp	2.25 tsp	2.00 tbs 1.50 tsp	.25 cup 2.00 tbs .75 tsp	
PEPPER, BLACK, GROUND 6 lb	.25 tsp	.75 tsp	2.50 tsp	2.00 tbs .25 tsp	
GRAVY MIX, 4/1 gal/cs	1.00 tbs	3.00 tbs	.50 cup 2.00 tbs	1.50 cup 1.00 tbs	
VEAL, CUTLET, REG US CHO, No. 1336, 4 oz	10.00 lb	30.00 lb	100.00 lb	250.00 lb	

2570	**ROAST LEG OF LAMB**				**ENTREES**—Veal and Lamb
Recipe No.	Recipe Name				Category

Serving Standards: 20- by 12- by 2.5-in.   2.5 oz   Solid Spatula   Hot
_____Pan_____Portions/Pan____Portion Size____Utensil____Temperature_

Ingredients	Portions				Procedure
	50	200	500	1000	
LAMB LEG, BNLS, TIED, CHO No. 1234 AR, 5 to 6 lb	12.50 lb	50.00 lb	125.00 lb	250.00 lb	1. Place lamb in roasting pans.
SALT, 100 lb bag	1.50 tsp	2.00 tbs	.25 cup 1.00 tbs	.50 cup 2.00 tbs	2. Mix together salt, pepper and garlic powder and rub on all sides of meat. 3. Roast in rotary oven at 300°F. until the internal
PEPPER, BLACK, GROUND, 6 lb	.50 tsp	2.00 tsp	1.00 tbs 2.00 tsp	3.00 tbs 1.00 tsp	temp is 160°F., approx 2 to 2.5 hr. 4. Remove from oven and allow to stand 30 min.
GARLIC POWDER, 1 lb	.25 tsp	1.00 tsp	2.50 tsp	1.00 tbs 2.00 tsp	then slice into 2.5 oz portions. 5. Place in counter pans and pour au jus over lamb.
					Cooking time: 2 to 2.5 hr
					Cooking temp: 300°F.
					Equipment: rotary oven

2640	HOT DOG/BUN/CHILI/RELISH					ENTREES—Misc
Recipe No.	Recipe Name					Category

Serving Standards:

			1 ea	2 oz Ladle	Hot
	Pan	Portions/Pan	Portion Size	Utensil	Temperature

Ingredients	Portions				Procedure
	45	180	450	900	
FRANKS, 9/lb, 7 in. long, 10 lb/box	5.00 lb	20.00 lb	50.00 lb	100.00 lb	1. Steam franks in high speed steam cooker for 2.5 min. If frozen, steam for 3 min.
CHILI W/BEANS, 12/52 oz	1.75 can	7.00 can	17.50 can	35.00 can	2. Heat chili with beans to serving temp. Serve with 2 oz ladle over hot dog.
ROLLS, WIENER, pkg/12-6 in.	3.75 doz	15.00 doz	37.50 doz	75.00 doz	3. Place buns in holding unit to warm.
RELISH, RED AND GREEN, 4/1 gal/cs	1.00 cup	1.00 qt	2.00 qt 2.00 cup	1.00 gal 1.00 qt	4. Place pickle relish on condiment stand for self service.
					5. Assemble hot dog at service counter.
					Cooking time: franks 2.5 to 3 min.
					Equipment: high speed steam cooker

2650	**FRANKFURTERS AND BAKED BEANS (WITH 10/LB FRANKS)**				**ENTREES**—Misc
Recipe No.	Recipe Name				Category

Serving Standards: 10- by 12- by 4-in.   2 ea   Solid Spoon   Hot

| Pan | Portions/Pan | Portion Size | Utensil | Temperature |

Ingredients	Portions				Procedure
	50	300	600	1200	
BEANS, BAKED, FNCY, 6/10	2.00 can	12.00 can	24.00 can	48.00 can	1. Place baked beans in counter pans and bake at 350°F. for 20 to 25 min.
FRANKS, 10/lb, 25 lb box	10.00 lb	60.00 lb	120.00 lb	240.00 lb	2. Steam franks in high speed steam cooker for 2.5 min. If frozen, steam for 3 min.
					3. Serve 2 frankfurters and 1 solid spoon of beans.
					Note: Beans can be heated to serving temp in steam kettle; approx 1 cup of water per can of beans should be added.
					Cooking time: beans 20 to 25 min.
					franks 2.5 to 3 min.
					Cooking temp: 350°F.
					Equipment: conv oven, high speed steam cooker

2651	FRANKFURTERS AND BAKED BEANS (DINNER FRANKS 8/LB)				ENTREES—Misc
Recipe No.	Recipe Name				Category

Serving Standards: 10- by 12- by 4-in. _____ Pan | 2 ea — Portion Size | Solid Spoon — Utensil | Hot — Temperature

Portions/Pan

Ingredients	Portions				Procedure
	40	200	500	1000	
BEANS, BAKED, FNCY, 6/10	1.50 can	7.50 can	18.75 can	37.50 can	1. Place baked beans in counter pan and bake at 350°F. for 20 to 25 min.
FRANKS, 8/LB, 10 lb box	10.00 lb	50.00 lb	125.00 lb	250.00 lb	2. Steam franks in high speed steam cooker for 2.5 min. If frozen, steam for 3 min.

3. Serve 2 frankfurters and 1 solid spoon of beans.
Note: Beans can be heated to serving temp in steam kettle; approx 1 cup of water per can of beans should be added.
Cooking time: beans 20 to 25 min.
                 franks 2.5 to 3 min.
Cooking temp: 350°F.
Equipment: conv oven, high speed steam cooker

2655	FRANKFURTERS AND SAUERKRAUT (WITH 10/LB FRANKS)				ENTREES—Misc
Recipe No.	Recipe Name				Category

Serving Standards: 20- by 12- by 2.5-in. <u>Pan</u>   34 <u>Portions/Pan</u>   2 ea <u>Portion Size</u>   Tongs <u>Utensil</u>   Hot <u>Temperature</u>

Ingredients	Portions				Procedure
	50	200	400	600	
FRANKS, 10/LB, 25 lb box	10.00 lb	40.00 lb	80.00 lb	120.00 lb	1. Place 7.5 lb franks in counter pans 20- by 12- by 2.5-in. and steam in high speed steam cooker for 2.5 min. If frozen, steam for 3 min.
KRAUT, SHREDDED, FNCY, 6/10	1.75 can	7.00 can	14.00 can	21.00 can	2. Place 1 can kraut in counter pan 10- by 12- by 4-in. and steam in high speed steam cooker for about 5 min. or until hot.
					3. Serve 2 franks and 3 oz kraut with tongs.
					Cooking time: see above
					Equipment: high speed steam cooker

2660	GRILLED CHEESE SANDWICH				ENTREES—Misc
Recipe No.	Recipe Name				Category

Serving Standards: 20- by 12- by 2.5-in. <u>Pan</u>   16 <u>Portions/Pan</u>   1 ea <u>Portion Size</u>   Spatula <u>Utensil</u>   Warm <u>Temperature</u>

Ingredients	Portions				Procedure
	45	180	495	990	
BREAD, SANDWICH, WHITE, 32 oz	3.00 lf	12.00 lf	33.00 lf	66.00 lf	1. Place 1 slice cheese between each 2 slices of bread.
AMERICAN CHEESE, PRE-CUT 6/5 lb	2.00 lb 6.00 oz	9.50 lb	26.00 lb 2.00 oz	52.25 lb	2. Brush tops with melted margarine. 3. Place on 300°F. grill for 7 min., margarine side down.
MARGARINE, SOLID, 1 lb	.75 lb	3.00 lb	8.25 lb	16.50 lb	4. Brush top with melted margarine. Turn and brown other side.
					5. Place in 20- by 12- by 2.5-in. counter pan (16 ea).
					Equipment: grill

2670	CHEESE PIZZAS OR TYPICAL PIZZA				ENTREES—Misc
Recipe No.	Recipe Name				Category

Serving Standards: _____ _____ __1 ea__ _____ __Hot__
Pan · Portions/Pan · Portion Size · Utensil · Temperature

Ingredients	Portions				Procedure
	36	108	540	1080	
PIZZA, CHEESE, 7-in., 36/6 oz/cs	1.00 cs	3.00 cs	15.00 cs	30.00 cs	1. Prepare according to instructions.

2675	KNOCKWURST				ENTREES—Misc
Recipe No.	Recipe Name				Category

Serving Standards: __10- by 12- by 4-in.__ _____ __1 ea__ __Tongs__ __Hot__
Pan · Portions/Pan · Portion Size · Utensil · Temperature

Ingredients	Portions				Procedure
	52	104	260	520	
Yield	10.00 lb	20.00 lb	50.00 lb	100.00 lb	
KNOCKWURST, 5.2/lb	10.00 lb	20.00 lb	50.00 lb	100.00 lb	1. Place in high speed steam cooker for 3 to 5 min. 2. Put in counter pan 10- by 12- by 4-in. and cover with hot water. 3. Serve 1 ea. *Note:* AP weight is 3 oz. Cooking time: 3 to 5 min. Cooking temp: steam Equipment: high speed steam cooker

2680	KNOCKWURST AND WHITE BEANS	ENTREES—Misc
Recipe No.	Recipe Name	Category

Serving Standards:
10- by 12- by 4-in.		3.5 oz	Solid Spoon	Hot
Pan	Portions/Pan	Portion Size	Utensil	Temperature

Ingredients	Portions				Procedure
	52	104	260	520	
KNOCKWURST, Recipe 2675	10.00 lb	20.00 lb	50.00 lb	100.00 lb	1. Prepare knockwurst.
BEANS, DRIED, GRT NORTH FNCY 6/10	2.00 can	4.00 can	10.00 can	20.00 can	2. Put beans and water in steam kettle.
WATER, cold	2.00 cup	1.00 qt	2.00 qt 2.00 cup	1.00 gal 1.00 qt	3. Add 2 oz of bacon drippings for each can of beans.

3. Add 2 oz of bacon drippings for each can of beans.
4. Simmer beans for 15 min.
Note: Omit bacon drippings if pre-seasoned beans are used and reduce water, if necessary.
5. Put knockwurst and white beans in separate counter pans, 10- by 12- by 4-in. for service.
6. Serve 1 solid spoon of beans with 1 knockwurst.
Cooking time: beans, 15 min.
Cooking temp: simmer
Equipment: steam kettle

2697	COTTAGE CHEESE CROQUETTE					ENTREES—Misc
Recipe No.	**Recipe Name**					**Category**

Serving Standards:
10- by 12- by 2.5-in.	12	1 ea	Tongs	Hot
Pan	Portions/Pan	Portion Size	Utensil	Temperature

Ingredients	Portions				E*	Procedure
	31	124	248	496		
PEPPERS, DEHYD DICED, GRN, XSTD 6/10	.62 oz	2.50 oz	5.00 oz	10.00 oz		1. Weigh green peppers and onions and rehydrate with cold water for at least 1 hr.
ONIONS, DEHYD CHOP, 2.5 lb XSTD 6/10	.33 oz	1.33 oz	2.66 oz	5.32 oz		2. Combine cottage cheese, first amt of bread crumbs, chopped pecans, drained green peppers, drained onions, paprika and salt and mix well.
WATER, cold	1.00 cup	1.00 qt	2.00 qt	1.00 gal		
COTTAGE CHEESE, 25 lb bag in box	6.00 lb	24.00 lb	48.00 lb	96.00 lb		3. Measure with a No. 10 scoop (wt 4.25 oz) and shape into a cone shaped croquette.
BREAD CRUMBS	1.50 lb	6.00 lb	12.00 lb	24.00 lb		4. Refrigerate overnight.
PECANS, MED FNCY, 30 lb/cs	.75 lb	3.00 lb	6.00 lb	12.00 lb		5. Dissolve dry milk in water and add thawed eggs and mix well.
PAPRIKA, GROUND, 6 lb	1.00 tsp	1.00 tbs 1.00 tsp	2.00 tbs 2.00 tsp	.25 cup 1.00 tbs 1.00 tsp		6. Roll croquettes in flour, dip in egg-milk mixture and roll in second amt of bread crumbs. 7. Prepare green pea sauce.
SALT, 100 lb bag	1.50 tsp	2.00 tbs	.25 cup	.50 cup		8. Fry in deep fat at 325ºF. until golden brown, about 3 min. Drain well.
MILK, INST NONFAT DRY, 6/5 lb	.50 oz	2.00 oz	.25 lb	.50 lb		9. Place in serving pans.
WATER, cold	.50 cup	2.00 cup	1.00 qt	2.00 qt		10. Serve 2 oz green pea sauce over each portion.
EGGS, 6/5 lb/cs	2.00 oz	.50 lb	1.00 lb	2.00 lb		Cooking time: 3 min.
FLOUR, 25 lb bag	3.00 oz	.75 lb	1.50 lb	3.00 lb		Cooking temp: 325ºF.
BREAD CRUMBS	6.00 oz	1.50 lb	3.00 lb	6.00 lb		Equipment: deep fat fryer
GREEN PEA SAUCE, Recipe 0690	.50 gal	2.00 gal	4.00 gal	8.00 gal		*Variation:* Parsley or pimento sauce *Early Prep: Croquette mix must be prepared 1 day in advance.

2700	RICE, MUSHROOMS AND ALMONDS	ENTREES—Misc
Recipe No.	Recipe Name	Category

Serving Standards:

20- by 12- by 2.5-in.	25	6 oz	Solid Spoon	Hot
Pan	Portions/Pan	Portion Size	Utensil	Temperature

Ingredients	Portions				Procedure
	100	200	400	500	
Yield	5.00 gal	10.00 gal	20.00 gal	25.00 gal	
RICE, CONVERTED, 6/10 lb	3.50 lb	7.00 lb	14.00 lb	17.50 lb	1. Stir rice into boiling salted water and simmer until tender, 20 to 25 min. Do not overcook.
ONIONS, DEHYD CHOP,	2.50 oz	.25 lb	.50 lb	.75 lb	
2.5 lb XSTD 6/10		1.00 oz	2.00 oz	.50 oz	2. Drain.
WATER, cold	1.25 cup	2.50 cup	1.00 qt	1.00 qt	3. Rehydrate onions in water.
			1.00 cup	2.25 cup	4. Brown almonds slightly in frying oil on sheet pan in oven at 475°F.; turn once and watch carefully to avoid burning.
ALMONDS, SLICED,	1.50 lb	3.00 lb	6.00 lb	7.50 lb	
BLANCHED, 6/10					
SHORTENING, LIQUID,	.25 cup	.75 cup	1.50 cup	1.75 cup	5. Melt margarine in steam kettle.
for deep fat 5 gal	2.00 tbs			2.00 tbs	6. Add rehydrated onions and saute for 5 min. Add chicken base.
MARGARINE, SOLID, 1 lb	4.00 lb	8.00 lb	16.00 lb	20.00 lb	
CHICKEN SOUP BASE,	.75 lb	1.50 lb	3.00 lb	3.75 lb	7. Add flour and blend well and simmer a few minutes.
12/1 lb/cs					
FLOUR, 25 lb bag	3.25 lb	6.50 lb	13.00 lb	16.25 lb	8. Add hot water and stir until thickened.
WATER, hot, 180°F.	3.00 gal	7.00 gal	14.00 gal	18.00 gal	9. Add salt and blend well.
	2.00 qt	1.00 qt	2.00 qt	2.00 cup	10. Add drained mushrooms and browned almonds to sauce.
	2.00 cup				
SALT, 100 lb bag	1.50 oz	3.00 oz	6.00 oz	7.50 oz	11. Place 1.25 gal sauce into 20- by 12- by 2.5-in. counter pans and using a No. 20 scoop, place 25 mounds of rice on each pan.
MUSHROOMS, STEMS/PCS,	4.00 can	8.00 can	16.00 can	20.00 can	
XSTD 24/16 oz					

Note: Portion size is 6 oz sauce and 1.75 oz of rice.
Equipment: steam kettle.

Vegetables

3002	AU GRATIN POTATOES				VEGETABLES—Potatoes and Corn
Recipe No.	Recipe Name				Category

Serving Standards: 20- by 12- by 2.5-in. ____   35 ____   4.5 oz ____   No. 12 Scoop ____   Hot ____
                     Pan   Portions/Pan   Portion Size   Utensil   Temperature

Ingredients	Portions				Procedure
	35	210	490	980	
POTATOES, AU GRATIN, DEHYD 6/2 lb 7 oz	1.00 bag	6.00 bag	14.00 bag	28.00 bag	1. Place 4.5 qt of boiling water into each long shallow counter pan 20- by 12- by 2.5-in.
WATER, hot, 180°F.	1.00 gal .50 qt	6.00 gal 3.00 qt	15.00 gal 3.00 qt	31.00 gal 2.00 qt	2. Stir in 2 packages cheese sauce mix (from 1 bag of potatoes).
					3. Add 1 bag potato slices and stir thoroughly.
					4. Bake in conv oven at 275°F. for 1 hr and 15 to 20 min.
					Cooking time: 1 hr and 15 to 20 min.
					Cooking temp: 275°F.
					Equipment: conv oven
					Suggested garnish: fresh parsley sprigs

3004	BAKED POTATO WITH SOUR CREAM				VEGETABLES—Potatoes and Corn
Recipe No.	Recipe Name				Category

Serving Standards:

		1 ea	Tongs	Hot
Pan	Portions/Pan	Portion Size	Utensil	Temperature

Ingredients	Portions				Procedure
	25	100	500	1000	
POTATOES, BAKING, No. 1, 100 ct	.25 box	1.00 box	5.00 box	10.00 box	1. Wash potatoes and place on sheet pan.
					2. Bake in conv oven at 350°F. for 1 hr.
NON-DAIRY SOUR CREAM, 1/2 gal 4/cs	3.00 cup	3.00 qt	3.00 gal 3.00 qt	7.00 gal 2.00 qt	3. Pierce each potato with a meat fork to allow steam to escape; place in counter pans.
					Note: Place non-dairy sour cream topping on condiment stand.
					Cooking time: 1 hr
					Cooking temp: 350°F.
					Equipment: conv oven

3008	CANDIED SWEET POTATOES				VEGETABLES—Potatoes and Corn
Recipe No.	Recipe Name				Category

Serving Standards:	20- by 12- by 2.5-in.	35	1 ea	Solid Spoon	Hot
	Pan	Portions/Pan	Portion Size	Utensil	Temperature

Ingredients	Portions				Procedure
	25	200	500	1000	
POTATOES, SWT, WHL, FNCY, 22 to 30 6/10	1.00 can	8.00 can	20.00 can	40.00 can	1. Drain sweet potatoes and save liquid.
CORNSTARCH, 24/1 lb/cs	1.00 oz	.50 lb	1.25 lb	2.50 lb	2. In a steam kettle, combine all liquid from sweet potatoes, cornstarch, nutmeg, pineapple juice and sugar and stir until dissolved.
NUTMEG, GROUND, 1 lb	.12 tsp	1.00 tsp	2.50 tsp	1.00 tbs 2.00 tsp	3. Turn on steam and simmer until thickened—about 5 min.
PINEAPPLE JUICE, 12/46 foz can	.50 cup	1.00 qt	2.00 qt 2.00 cup	1.00 gal 1.00 qt	4. Turn off steam and add margarine and vanilla and mix well.
SUGAR, GRAN, 100 lb	.25 lb	2.00 lb	5.00 lb	10.00 lb	5. Place about 1.5 cans of potatoes in counter pans 20- by 12- by 2.5-in. and pour sauce over them.
MARGARINE, SOLID, 1 lb	2.00 oz	1.00 lb	2.50 lb	5.00 lb	6. Bake in rotary oven at 350°F. for about 40 min., basting with syrup as necessary.
VANILLA, case 12 qt	.37 tsp	1.00 tbs	2.00 tbs 1.50 tsp	.25 cup 1.00 tbs	Cooking time: 40 min. Cooking temp: 350°F. Equipment: rotary oven

3012	PARSLEY CREAMED WHOLE POTATOES				VEGETABLES—Potatoes and Corn
Recipe No.	Recipe Name				Category

Serving Standards: 10- by 12- by 4-in.   25   4 ea   Solid Spoon   Hot
                    _____   _____ _____   _____   _____
                         Pan   Portions/Pan Portion Size   Utensil   Temperature

Ingredients	Portions				Procedure
	25	100	500	1000	
POTATOES, WHL, wtrpk ct 100 6/10	1.00 can	4.00 can	20.00 can	40.00 can	1. Drain off half the liquid and place potatoes and remaining liquid in steam kettle and heat to serving temp, or drain and heat in high speed steam cooker about 5 min.
WHITE SAUCE (medium), Recipe 0640	.25 gal	1.00 gal	5.00 gal	10.00 gal	2. Prepare white sauce.
PARSLEY, FNCY, bunch	1.00 tbs	.25 cup	1.25 cup	2.50 cup	3. Pour white sauce over drained potatoes (1 qt white sauce to 3 qt potatoes or 1 can).
					4. Garnish with fresh chopped parsley.
					5. Serve 4 potatoes with 1.25 oz sauce using a solid spoon.
					Equipment: steam kettle or high speed steam cooker

3014	DUCHESS POTATOES				VEGETABLES—Potatoes and Corn
Recipe No.	Recipe Name				Category

Serving Standards:	10- by 12- by 4-in.	35	3 oz	No. 12 Scoop	Hot
	Pan	Portions/Pan	Portion Size	Utensil	Temperature

Ingredients	Portions				Procedure
	70	140	420	840	
Yield	2.00 gal	4.00 gal	12.00 gal	24.00 gal	1. Rehydrate onions in specified amt of water.
ONIONS, DEHYD CHOP,	1.00 oz	2.00 oz	6.00 oz	.75 lb	2. Grate cheese.
2.5 lb XSTD 6/10					3. Place hot water, salt and pepper in mixing bowl.
WATER, cold	.50 cup	1.00 cup	3.00 cup	1.00 qt	4. Slowly add potatoes while blending at low speed
				2.00 cup	(No. 1) until water is absorbed, about 30 sec to 1
CHEDDAR CHEESE,	10.00 oz	1.25 lb	3.75 lb	7.50 lb	min.
WHEEL					5. Mix at No. 3 speed for 2 more min.
WATER, hot, 180°F.	1.00 gal	2.00 gal	8.00 gal	16.00 gal	6. Remove some of the potatoes from mixing bowl
	1.50 qt	3.00 qt	1.00 qt	2.00 qt	and add to eggs, mixing rapidly.
SALT, 100 lb bag	1.50 tsp	1.00 tbs	3.00 tbs	.25 cup	7. Add egg mixture, rehydrated onions and cheese to
				2.00 tbs	remaining potatoes, mixing 1 to 2 min. on speed
PEPPER, WHITE, GROUND,	.50 tsp	1.00 tsp	1.00 tbs	2.00 tbs	No. 3 until light and fluffy.
1 lb					8. Grease pans with margarine and place 1 gal of mix-
POTATOES, GRD DEHYD,	.50 can	1.00 can	3.00 can	6.00 can	ture in each counter pan 10- by 12- by 4-in.
Idho inst w/mk 6/10					9. Bake in conv oven at 300°F. until lightly browned,
EGGS, 6/5 lb/cs	10.00 oz	1.25 lb	3.75 lb	7.50 lb	about 1 hr.
MARGARINE, SOLID, 1 lb	.25 lb	.50 lb	1.50 lb	3.00 lb	Cooking time: 1 hr
					Cooking temp: 300°F.
					Equipment: mixer, conv oven

3016	ESCALLOPED POTATOES				VEGETABLES—Potatoes and Corn
Recipe No.	Recipe Name				Category

Serving Standards: **20- by 12- by 2.5-in.** / Pan   **40** / Portions/Pan   **4.5 oz** / Portion Size   **No. 12 Scoop** / Utensil   **Hot** / Temperature

Ingredients	Portions				Procedure
	60	240	480	960	
Yield	2.25 gal	9.00 gal	18.00 gal	36.00 gal	1. Rehydrate onions in specified amt of water for about 20 min.
ONIONS, DEHYD CHOP, 2.5 lb XSTD 6/10	.37 oz	1.50 oz	3.00 oz	.25 lb 2.00 oz	2. Melt margarine in steam kettle and add onions and saute.
WATER, cold	3.00 tbs	.75 cup	1.50 cup	3.00 cup	3. Blend flour into margarine and cook about 5 min.
MARGARINE, SOLID, 1 lb	1.00 lb 2.00 oz	4.50 lb	9.00 lb	18.00 lb	4. Turn off steam and add second amt of water, stirring constantly.
FLOUR, 25 lb bag	.50 lb	2.00 lb	4.00 lb	8.00 lb	5. Add dry milk while stirring.
WATER, hot, 180°F.	1.00 gal	4.00 gal	8.00 gal	16.00 gal	6. Cook until a thin smooth sauce is formed, about 10 min. Add salt and white pepper. Remove from heat.
MILK, INST NONFAT DRY, 6/5 lb	13.00 oz	3.25 lb	6.50 lb	13.00 lb	7. In steam kettle, bring an ample amt of water to boil and add salt as needed.
SALT, 100 lb bag	.75 oz	3.00 oz	6.00 oz	.75 lb	8. Add dehydrated potatoes and cook until tender, about 20 min.
PEPPER, WHITE, GROUND, 1 lb	.12 tsp	.50 tsp	1.00 tsp	2.00 tsp	9. Drain well and add to sauce and combine.
POTATOES, SLICED, DEHYD, 4/5 lb bag	2.50 lb	10.00 lb	20.00 lb	40.00 lb	10. Place 1.5 gal of potatoes into counter pan 20- by 12- by 2.5-in.
PAPRIKA, GROUND, 6 lb	.25 tsp	1.00 tsp	2.00 tsp	1.00 tbs 1.00 tsp	11. Sprinkle paprika lightly over each pan.

12. Bake in conv oven at 300°F. for 30 min.
Cooking time: see above
Cooking temp: 300°F.
Equipment: steam kettle, conv oven

3018	FRENCH FRIED POTATOES	VEGETABLES—Potatoes and Corn
Recipe No.	Recipe Name	Category

Serving Standards: 10- by 12- by 4-in. / Pan   Portions/Pan   2.75 oz / Portion Size   Tongs / Utensil   Hot / Temperature

Ingredients	Portions				Procedure
	22	220	440	880	
POTATOES, FRENCH FRIES, CR-CUT, 6/5 lb	5.00 lb	50.00 lb	100.00 lb	200.00 lb	1. Fill deep fryer with oil and preheat to 350°F. 2. Place 5 lb potatoes in large fryer basket and fry for 2 min. 3. Drain. 4. Place in counter pans to serve. *Note:* Yield is 4.4 servings per lb AP. Cooking time: 2 min. Cooking temp: 350°F. Equipment: deep fat fryer

3020	HOT GERMAN POTATO SALAD	VEGETABLES—Potatoes and Corn
Recipe No.	Recipe Name	Category

Serving Standards: 20- by 12- by 2.5-in. / Pan   Portions/Pan   3.25 oz / Portion Size   No. 12 Scoop / Utensil   Hot / Temperature

Ingredients	Portions				Procedure
	15	180	450	900	
GERMAN POTATO SALAD, 12/52 oz/cs	1.00 can	12.00 can	30.00 can	60.00 can	1. Place potato salad in counter pans 20- by 12- by 2.5-in. and heat in conv oven at 350°F. until hot, about 20 to 25 min. 2. Garnish appropriately. Cooking time: 20 to 25 min. Cooking temp: 350°F. Equipment: conv oven

3022	**HASH BROWN POTATOES**				**VEGETABLES**—Potatoes and Corn
Recipe No.	Recipe Name				Category

Serving Standards: __10- by 12- by 4-in.__   _____   __3 oz__   __No. 12 Scoop__   __Hot__
         Pan   Portions/Pan   Portion Size   Utensil   Temperature

Ingredients	Portions				Procedure
	50	**100**	**200**	**400**	
POTATOES, SLICED, DEHYD, 4/5 lb bag	2.50 lb	5.00 lb	10.00 lb	20.00 lb	1. Bring water to boil in steam kettle. Add salt as needed.
PAPRIKA, GROUND, 6 lb	1.00 tbs 1.50 tsp	3.00 tbs	.25 cup 2.00 tbs	.75 cup	2. Add dehyd potatoes and cook until tender, about 20 min. Run cold water over potatoes to stop cooking. Drain well.
MARGARINE, SOLID, 1 lb	1.00 lb	2.00 lb	4.00 lb	8.00 lb	3. Oil grill with 3 lb margarine.

3. Oil grill with 3 lb margarine.
4. Place 4 gal potatoes on grill. Brown about 8 min. on 1 side, turn and brown about 7 min. on the other side at 350°F.
5. Sprinkle .25 cup paprika over ea full grill of potatoes.
6. Repeat Steps 3, 4, 5, as necessary.
7. Serve in 10- by 12- by 4-in. counter pans.

Cooking time: 20 min.—steam kettle
                15 min.—grill
Cooking temp: 350°F.—grill
Equipment: steam kettle, grill

3023	COTTAGE FRIED POTATOES				VEGETABLES—Potatoes and Corn
Recipe No.	Recipe Name				Category

Serving Standards: 10- by 12- by 4-in. | | 15 sl | Tongs | Hot
Pan | Portions/Pan | Portion Size | Utensil | Temperature

Ingredients	Portions				Procedure
	30	**180**	**540**	**1080**	
POTATOES, COTTAGE FRIES, 6/5 lb	5.00 lb	30.00 lb	90.00 lb	180.00 lb	1. Place 5 lb frozen fries into fryer basket. 2. Fry in deep fat at 350°F. for 2.5 to 3 min. Drain. 3. Place in counter pans 10- by 12- by 4-in. *Note:* Cooked weight per portion is about 1.5 oz. Cooking time: 2.5 to 3 min. Cooking temp: 350°F. Equipment: deep fat fryer

3026
Recipe No.

LYONNAISE POTATOES
Recipe Name

VEGETABLES–Potatoes and Corn
Category

Serving Standards: 20- by 12- by 2.5-in.
_____
Pan

3 oz
_____
Portions/Pan Portion Size

No. 12 Scoop
_____
Utensil

Hot
_____
Temperature

Ingredients	Portions				Procedure
	50	100	400	1000	
POTATOES, SLICED DEHYD, 4/5 lb bag	2.50 lb	5.00 lb	20.00 lb	50.00 lb	1. Bring water to boil in steam kettle. Add salt as needed.
ONIONS, DEHYD CHOP, 2.5 lb XSTD 6/10	2.00 oz	.25 lb	1.00 lb	2.50 lb	2. Add dehyd potatoes and cook until tender, about 20 min. Run cold water over potatoes to stop cooking. Drain well.
WATER, cold	1.00 cup	2.00 cup	2.00 qt	1.00 gal 1.00 qt	3. Rehydrate onions in specified amt of water for 20 min.
MARGARINE, SOLID, 1 lb	1.00 lb 2.00 oz	2.25 lb	9.00 lb	22.50 lb	4. Melt margarine and combine with potatoes.
PAPRIKA, GROUND, 1 lb	2.25 tsp	1.00 tbs 1.50 tsp	.25 cup 2.00 tbs	.75 cup 3.00 tbs	5. Add onions to potatoes and mix well. 6. Place 1.5 gal mixture in counter pans 20- by 12- by 2.5-in. and sprinkle with paprika.
PARSLEY, DEHYD FLK, XSTD 6/10	2.00 tbs	.25 cup	1.00 cup	2.50 cup	7. Place in conv oven at 350°F. for about 20 min. 8. Remove from oven and garnish with dehyd parsley.

Cooking time: 20 min.–steam kettle
                      20 min.–conv oven
Cooking temp: 350°F.
Equipment: steam kettle, conv oven

3028	MASHED POTATOES WITH GRAVY				VEGETABLES—Potatoes and Corn
Recipe No.	Recipe Name				Category

Serving Standards: <u>10- by 12- by 4-in.</u> <u>42</u> <u>3.5 oz</u> <u>No. 12 Scoop
1 oz Ladle</u> <u>Hot</u>

| | Pan | | Portions/Pan | Portion Size | Utensil | Temperature |

Ingredients	Portions				Procedure
	60	**120**	**480**	**960**	
Yield	2.12 gal	4.25 gal	17.00 gal	34.00 gal	
WATER, hot, 180°F.	1.50 gal	3.00 gal	12.00 gal	24.00 gal	1. Place hot water in mixing bowl.
SALT, 100 lb bag	1.00 tbs	3.00 tbs	.75 cup	1.50 cup	2. Add salt.
	1.50 tsp				3. Slowly add instant potatoes while blending at slow speed, using wire whip attachment until water is absorbed, about 1 min.
POTATOES, GRD DEHYD,	.50 can	1.00 can	4.00 can	8.00 can	
IDHO INST w/mk 6/10					
MARGARINE, SOLID, 1 lb	1.50 oz	3.00 oz	.75 lb	1.50 lb	4. Scrape down mixer bowl and mix on speed No. 2 until light and fluffy, about 10 to 15 min. If mixing bowl is not too full, use speed No. 3 instead for a shorter time.
BROWN GRAVY,	.25 gal	.50 gal	2.00 gal	4.00 gal	
Recipe 0520					5. Place 1.5 gal of potatoes in counter pans and garnish each pan with 2 tbs of melted margarine.
					6. Prepare brown gravy and place in separate counter pan. Serve with 1 oz ladle. The amt of gravy is enough for about half of customers to choose gravy. Equipment: mixer

3032	NEW POTATOES IN JACKET	VEGETABLES—Potatoes and Corn
Recipe No.	Recipe Name	Category

Serving Standards: 10- by 12- by 8-in. _____ | 2 to 3 ea _____ | Tongs _____ | Hot _____

| | Pan | Portions/Pan | Portion Size | Utensil | Temperature |

Ingredients	Portions				Procedure
	200	400	800	1000	
POTATOES, NEW, B SIZE, 50 lb bag	50.00 lb	100.00 lb	200.00 lb	250.00 lb	1. Wash potatoes. 2. Cover with water in steam kettle.
MARGARINE, SOLID, 1 lb	2.50 lb	5.00 lb	10.00 lb	12.50 lb	3. Add margarine. 4. Simmer until done (approx 30 min.). 5. Serve in counter pan 10- by 12- by 8-in. 6. One portion of 2 to 3 each is about 4 oz. Cooking time: 30 min. Equipment: steam kettle.

3034	O'BRIEN POTATOES				VEGETABLES—Potatoes and Corn
Recipe No.	Recipe Name				Category

Serving Standards: <u>20- by 12- by 2.5-in.</u> <u> </u> <u>3 oz</u> <u>No. 12 Scoop</u> <u>Hot</u>
                  Pan   Portions/Pan   Portion Size   Utensil   Temperature

Ingredients	Portions				Procedure
	50	300	600	1200	
POTATOES, DICED DEHYD-FRO 6/5 lb/cs	5.00 lb	30.00 lb	60.00 lb	120.00 lb	1. Place ample amt of cold water and salt in steam kettle and stir.
ONIONS, DEHYD CHOP, 2.5 lb XSTD 6/10	3.00 oz	1.00 lb 2.00 oz	2.25 lb	4.50 lb	2. Add potatoes and heat to boiling; reduce heat and simmer until tender, 25 to 30 min. Drain.
WATER, cold	1.50 cup	2.00 qt 1.00 cup	1.00 gal 2.00 cup	2.00 gal 1.00 qt	3. While potatoes are cooking, rehydrate onions in specified amt of water for 20 min.
MARGARINE, SOLID, 1 lb	1.00 lb	6.00 lb	12.00 lb	24.00 lb	4. Melt margarine in steam kettle and saute onions for about 10 min.
PIMENTOS, BROKEN PIECES, STD 24/2.5	.33 can	2.00 can	4.00 can	8.00 can	5. Combine cooked potatoes, sauteed onions with margarine, chopped pimentos and white pepper.
PEPPER, WHITE, GROUND, 1 lb	.50 tsp	1.00 tbs	2.00 tbs	.25 cup	6. Place in counter pans and heat in conv oven at 350°F. for about 20 min. **Garnish with bacon** crumbs.
BACON, PRECOOKED, 600 slc/8 lb/cs	3.00 oz	1.00 lb 2.00 oz	2.25 lb	4.50 lb	Cooking time: see above Cooking temp: 350°F. Equipment: steam kettle, conv oven

3036	OVEN BROWNED POTATOES				VEGETABLES—Potatoes and Corn
Recipe No.	Recipe Name				Category

Serving Standards: 10- by 12- by 4-in.   5 ea   Solid Spoon   Hot
                          Pan   Portions/Pan   Portion Size   Utensil   Temperature

Ingredients	Portions				Procedure
	20	180	360	720	
POTATOES, WHL, wtrpk, ct 100 6/10	1.00 can	9.00 can	18.00 can	36.00 can	1. Drain potatoes.
SHORTENING, LIQUID, for deep fat 5 gal	.25 cup	2.25 cup	1.00 qt .50 cup	2.00 qt 1.00 cup	2. Place potatoes in mixing bowl and add cooking oil. 3. Turn potatoes so all sides are coated with fat. 4. Combine seasonings and add to potatoes and turn again.
SALT, 100 lb bag	1.00 tbs	.50 cup 1.00 tbs	1.00 cup 2.00 tbs	2.25 cup	5. Place in shallow roasting pans.
PAPRIKA, GROUND, 6 lb	1.50 tsp	.25 cup 1.50 tsp	.50 cup 1.00 tbs	1.00 cup 2.00 tbs	6. Bake at 400°F. for 35 min. 7. Turn occasionally for potatoes to be evenly browned.
PEPPER, WHITE, GROUND, 1 lb	.25 tsp	2.25 tsp	1.00 tbs 1.50 tsp	3.00 tbs	8. Place in counter pans for service.

1. Drain potatoes.
2. Place potatoes in mixing bowl and add cooking oil.
3. Turn potatoes so all sides are coated with fat.
4. Combine seasonings and add to potatoes and turn again.
5. Place in shallow roasting pans.
6. Bake at 400°F. for 35 min.
7. Turn occasionally for potatoes to be evenly browned.
8. Place in counter pans for service.
Note: Cooked weight of 1 serving is approx 3.5 oz or 5 potatoes.
Cooking time: 35 min.
Cooking temp: 400°F.
Equipment: conv oven

3038   **PARSLIED BUTTERED POTATOES**   **VEGETABLES—Potatoes and Corn**

Recipe No.   Recipe Name   Category

Serving Standards: 10- by 12- by 4-in.   5 ea   Slotted Spoon   Hot

                     Pan   Portions/Pan   Portion Size   Utensil   Temperature

Ingredients	Portions				Procedure
	20	**240**	**480**	**960**	
POTATOES, WHL, wtrpk, ct 100 6/10	1.00 can	12.00 can	24.00 can	48.00 can	1. Drain off half the liquid and place potatoes and remaining liquid in steam kettle.
SALT, 100 lb bag	1.00 tsp	.25 cup	.50 cup	1.00 cup	2. Add salt and margarine and heat to serving temp.
MARGARINE, SOLID, 1 lb	3.00 oz	2.25 lb	4.50 lb	9.00 lb	3. Place in serving pan with a small amt of the liquid.
PARSLEY, FNCY, bunch	1.00 tbs	.75 cup	1.50 cup	3.00 cup	4. Garnish with chopped fresh parsley.
					Equipment: steam kettle

3044   **FRIED POTATO GEMS**   **VEGETABLES—Potatoes and Corn**

Recipe No.   Recipe Name   Category

Serving Standards: 10- by 12- by 4-in.   8 ea   Slotted Spoon   Hot

                     Pan   Portions/Pan   Portion Size   Utensil   Temperature

Ingredients	Portions				Procedure
	30	**180**	**540**	**1080**	
POTATOES, TOT OR GEMS, 6/5 lb/cs	5.00 lb	30.00 lb	90.00 lb	180.00 lb	1. Preheat deep fat fryer to 350°F.
					2. Place 5 lb of potato gems in fryer basket and fry for 1.5 to 2 min.
					3. Drain and place in counter pans to serve.
					Note: 8 each equals 2.25 oz cooked weight and is 1 spoonful.
					Cooking time: 1.5 to 2 min.
					Cooking temp: 350°F.
					Equipment: deep fat fryer

3050	STEAK HOUSE FRIED POTATOES				VEGETABLES—Potatoes and Corn
Recipe No.	Recipe Name				Category

Serving Standards: <u>20- by 12- by 2.5-in.</u>   <u>20</u>   <u>2.75 oz</u>   <u>Tongs</u>   <u>Hot</u>
                             Pan   Portions/Pan   Portion Size   Utensil   Temperature

Ingredients	Portions				Procedure
	20	100	200	500	
POTATOES, STEAK HOUSE FRIED, 6/5 lb	5.00 lb	25.00 lb	50.00 lb	125.00 lb	1. Heat deep fat fryer to 350°F. 2. Pour a 5 lb bag of potatoes into fryer basket and fry potatoes 6 min. 3. One serving is 2.75 oz or about 5 whole pieces. Cooking time: 6 min. Cooking temp: 350°F. Equipment: deep fat fryer

3052	**SWEET POTATO PUDDING**				**VEGETABLES—Potatoes and Corn**
Recipe No.	Recipe Name				Category

Serving Standards:	20- by 12- by 2.5-in.	40	3.25 oz	No. 12 Scoop	Hot
	Pan	Portions/Pan	Portion Size	Utensil	Temperature

Ingredients	Portions				Procedure
	80	**160**	**320**	**480**	
POTATOES, SWT, WHL, FNCY, 22 to 30 ct 6/10	3.00 can	6.00 can	12.00 can	18.00 can	1. Drain potatoes, place in mixing bowl and mash well.
SUGAR, GRAN, 100 lb	1.25 lb	2.50 lb	5.00 lb	7.50 lb	2. Mix sugar, dry milk, water, eggs, margarine and nutmeg together in separate bowl and add to potatoes in mixing bowl while mixing at lowest speed. Mix thoroughly.
MILK, INST NONFAT DRY, 6/5 lb	2.00 oz	.25 lb	.50 lb	.75 lb	
WATER, cold	3.00 cup	1.00 qt 2.00 cup	3.00 qt	1.00 gal 2.00 cup	3. Grease lightly the bottoms of 20- by 12- by 2.5-in. counter pans.
EGGS, 6/5 lb/cs	.75 lb	1.50 lb	3.00 lb	4.50 lb	4. Pour 1.5 gal mixture into each pan.
MARGARINE, SOLID, 1 lb	6.00 oz	.75 lb	1.50 lb	2.25 lb	5. Bake in conv oven at 300°F. for 40 min. Remove pans from oven and top with marshmallows in 6 rows of 5 each. Increase heat to 375°F. and return pans to oven for a few min. for marshmallows to brown.
NUTMEG, GROUND, 1 lb	.25 tsp	.50 tsp	1.00 tsp	1.50 tsp	
VANILLA, case 12 qt	2.25 tsp	1.00 tbs 1.50 tsp	3.00 tbs	.25 cup 1.50 tsp	
MARSHMALLOWS, REGULAR, 12/1 lb	1.00 lb	2.00 lb	4.00 lb	6.00 lb	*Note:* If marshmallows blow around, leave blower off until they begin to melt.
					Cooking time: about 40 min.
					Cooking temp: 300° and 375°F.
					Equipment: mixer, conv oven

3058	FRIED POTATO WEDGES	VEGETABLES—Potatoes and Corn
Recipe No.	Recipe Name	Category

Serving Standards: 20- by 12- by 2.5-in.   20   2 ea   Tongs   Hot

Pan   Portions/Pan   Portion Size   Utensil   Temperature

Ingredients	Portions				Procedure
	20	100	200	400	
POTATO WEDGES, 2 oz ea, 6/5 lb/cs	5.00 lb	25.00 lb	50.00 lb	100.00 lb	1. Place 5 lb potato wedges in fryer basket and fry until golden brown, about 4 min. at 350°F. 2. Place in 20- by 12- by 2.5-in. counter pans. *Note:* Portion size 2 each is 3 oz cooked weight. Cooking time: 4 min. Cooking temp: 350°F. Equipment: deep fat fryer

3076	CORN CHIPS	VEGETABLES—Potatoes and Corn
Recipe No.	Recipe Name	Category

Serving Standards: 1.25 oz

Pan   Portions/Pan   Portion Size   Utensil   Temperature

Ingredients	Portions				Procedure
	10	120	480	960	
CORN CHIPS, 12/13 oz/cs	1.00 pkg	12.00 pkg	48.00 pkg	96.00 pkg	1. Place corn chips in counter pan to serve. 2. Server wearing plastic gloves, serve 1 handful.

3078	CORN ON COB		VEGETABLES—Potatoes and Corn
Recipe No.	Recipe Name		Category

Serving Standards: 10- by 12- by 4-in. / Pan   1 ea / Portion Size   Tongs / Utensil   Hot / Temperature

Ingredients	Portions				Procedure
	48	192	480	960	
CORN, YELL COB, FNCY, 96 3 in./cs	.50 cs	2.00 cs	5.00 cs	10.00 cs	1. Bring an ample amt of water to boil. Add salt as needed. Add margarine.
MARGARINE, SOLID, 1 lb	1.00 oz	.25 lb	.50 lb 2.00 oz	1.25 lb	2. Add corn and more hot water to cover if needed. 3. Cook for 8 to 10 min. until done. 4. Place in counter pans with some of the water to prevent drying. Cooking time: 8 to 10 min. Equipment: steam kettle

3079	FRESH CORN ON COB		VEGETABLES—Potatoes and Corn
Recipe No.	Recipe Name		Category

Serving Standards: 10- by 12- by 4-in. / Pan   1 ea / Portion Size   Tongs / Utensil   Hot / Temperature

Ingredients	Portions				Procedure
	60	240	480	960	
CORN, FNCY, YELLOW, SWEET, COB, doz	5.00 doz	20.00 doz	40.00 doz	80.00 doz	1. Husk corn. Remove silks. Wash. Do not allow to stand in water.
MARGARINE, SOLID, 1 lb	2.00 oz	.50 lb	1.00 lb	2.00 lb	2. Bring water to boil. Add salt as needed. Add margarine. 3. Add corn and more hot water to cover if needed. 4. Cook for 10 to 15 min. until done 5. Place in counter pans with some of the water to prevent drying. Cooking time: 10 to 15 min. Equipment: steam kettle

3080	FRESH CORN ON COB (WRAPPED IN ALUMINUM FOIL)				VEGETABLES–Potatoes and Corn
Recipe No.	Recipe Name				Category

Serving Standards: _____　_____　__1 ea__　__Tongs__　__Hot__
　　　　　　　　　　　　　　Pan　　　　　Portions/Pan　　Portion Size　　Utensil　　Temperature

| Ingredients | Portions | | | | E* | Procedure |
	60	120	480	960		
CORN, FNCY YELLOW, SWEET, COB, doz	5.00 doz	10.00 doz	40.00 doz	80.00 doz		1. Remove shucks and silks from corn.
MARGARINE, SOLID, 1 lb	2.00 lb	4.00 lb	16.00 lb	32.00 lb		2. Melt margarine and dip each ear of corn in it. Sprinkle corn with salt.
						3. Wrap each ear of corn with aluminum foil and place on sheet pans.
						4. Cook in conv oven at 300°F. for 15 min.
						5. Remove from oven and place in counter pans.
						6. Serve 1 whole ear of corn.
						Cooking time: 15 min.
						Cooking temp: 300°F.
						Equipment: conv oven
						*Early Prep: Steps 1, 2 and 3 can be completed 1 day in advance; then store corn under refrigeration.

3086	CORN PUDDING	VEGETABLES—Potatoes and Corn
Recipe No.	Recipe Name	Category

Serving Standards: <u>20- by 12- by 2.5-in.</u>   <u>32</u>   <u>3.75 oz</u>   <u>No. 12 Scoop</u>   <u>Hot</u>
               Pan   Portions/Pan   Portion Size   Utensil   Temperature

Ingredients	Portions				Procedure
	80	160	240	320	
Yield	3.75 gal	7.50 gal	11.25 gal	15.00 gal	
MILK, INST NONFAT DRY,	1.00 lb	2.00 lb	3.00 lb	4.75 lb	1. Place dry milk in large bowl. Add water and dissolve milk.
6/5 lb	3.00 oz	6.00 oz	9.00 oz		2. Beat eggs slightly and add to milk.
WATER, cold	1.50 gal	3.00 gal	4.50 gal	6.00 gal	3. Add corn, sugar and bread crumbs to large bowl and stir well.
EGGS, 6/5 lb/cs	2.50 lb	5.00 lb	7.50 lb	10.00 lb	4. Melt margarine. Use part of margarine to oil the pans. The recipe for 80 portions yields 2.5 long pans.
CORN, GLD, CRM STYLE,	2.00 can	4.00 can	6.00 can	8.00 can	
FNCY 6/10					5. Add the remaining margarine to the mixture.
SUGAR, GRAN, 100 lb	.25 cup	.75 cup	1.00 cup	1.50 cup	6. Pour 1.5 gal mixture into pans 20- by 12- by 2.5-in.
	2.00 tbs		2.00 tbs		7. Bake at 350°F. for 50 min. to 1 hr or until custard sets and is golden brown. Test with a knife.
SALT, 100 lb bag	3.00 tbs	.25 cup	.50 cup	.75 cup	
		2.00 tbs	1.00 tbs		*Note:* For pans 10- by 12- by 2.5-in., pour 3 qt of mixture.
BREAD CRUMBS	3.00 lb	6.00 lb	9.00 lb	12.00 lb	Cooking time: 50 min. to 1 hr
MARGARINE, SOLID, 1 lb	1.00 lb	2.00 lb	3.00 lb	4.00 lb	Cooking temp: 350°F.
					Equipment: conv oven

3090	W K YELLOW CORN				VEGETABLES—Potatoes and Corn
Recipe No.	Recipe Name				Category

Serving Standards: 10- by 12- by 4-in.   3 oz   Slotted Spoon   Hot
_____
                         Pan   Portions/Pan   Portion Size   Utensil   Temperature

Ingredients	Portions				Procedure
	25	150	300	450	
CORN, GLD, WHL KERN, QK, COK, a, 70 dw 6/10	1.00 can	6.00 can	12.00 can	18.00 can	1. Place corn and liquid in steam kettle.
SALT, 100 lb bag	.50 tsp	1.00 tbs	2.00 tbs	3.00 tbs	2. Add salt and margarine and bring to boil and heat only long enough to bring it to serving temp. Turn off steam.
MARGARINE, SOLID, 1 lb	2.66 oz	1.00 lb	2.00 lb	3.00 lb	3. Place in counter pans with only a small amt of the liquid.
					4. Add appropriate garnish.
					5. Or for batch cooking: drain corn and place in 10- by 12- by 4-in. pan and add .5 tsp salt and 2.66 oz margarine per can and heat in high speed steam cooker about 3 min. or until hot.
					Equipment: steam kettle or high speed steam cooker

3114	GREEN BEANS, SOUTHERN	VEGETABLES—Beans and Peas
Recipe No.	**Recipe Name**	**Category**

Serving Standards: <u>10- by 12- by 4-in.</u>   <u>3 oz</u>   <u>Slotted Spoon</u>   <u>Hot</u>
            Pan   **Portions/Pan**   **Portion Size**   **Utensil**   **Temperature**

Ingredients	Portions				Procedure
	20	**120**	**480**	**960**	
WATER, cold	1.50 cup	2.00 qt	2.00 gal	4.00 gal	1. Wash and cut fatback into several pieces.
		1.00 cup	1.00 qt	2.00 qt	2. Boil fatback in water 35 min. in steam kettle.
FATBACK, salt, lb	2.75 oz	1.00 lb	4.00 lb	8.25 lb	*Note:* Optional—2 whole peeled onions, approx 8 oz,
		.50 oz	2.00 oz		may be added to boiling water.
BEANS, GRN, ct sv 5,	1.00 can	6.00 can	24.00 can	48.00 can	3. Add green beans, salt and sugar. Do not drain
bl dw 60 oz XSTD 6/10					green beans.
SALT, 100 lb bag	1.50 tsp	3.00 tbs	.75 cup	1.50 cup	4. Cook for 45 min. in steam kettle.
SUGAR, GRAN, 100 lb	1.50 tsp	3.00 tbs	.75 cup	1.50 cup	5. Drain excess water.
					6. Put in counter pans for service.
					Cooking time: see above
					Equipment: steam kettle

3122	BABY LIMA BEANS				VEGETABLES—Beans and Peas
Recipe No.	**Recipe Name**				**Category**

Serving Standards: <u>10- by 12- by 4-in.</u>   <u>3 oz</u>   <u>Slotted Spoon</u>   <u>Hot</u>
                          Pan   **Portions/Pan**   **Portion Size**   **Utensil**   **Temperature**

Ingredients	Portions				Procedure
	25	**100**	**500**	**1000**	
WATER, cold	1.50 qt	1.00 gal 2.00 qt	7.00 gal 2.00 qt	15.00 gal	1. Bring water to a boil in steam kettle.
					2. Add salt.
SALT, 100 lb bag	2.25 tsp	3.00 tbs	.75 cup 3.00 tbs	1.75 cup 2.00 tbs	3. Add baby lima beans and more hot water as necessary to just cover beans and bring to a boil.
MARGARINE, SOLID, 1 lb	.25 lb	1.00 lb	5.00 lb	10.00 lb	4. Add margarine.
LIMA BEANS, BABY, FNCY 20 lb/cs	5.00 lb	20.00 lb	100.00 lb	200.00 lb	5. Start timing when water returns to a boil and simmer for 20 to 25 min., uncovered, and less time if lid is used. Be careful not to overcook.
					6. Place lima beans in counter pans with a small amt of margarine-liquid from steam kettle.
					Cooking time: 20 to 25 min.
					Cooking temp: simmer
					Equipment: steam kettle

3126	FORDHOOK LIMA BEANS	VEGETABLES—Beans and Peas
Recipe No.	Recipe Name	Category

Serving Standards: <u>10- by 12- by 4-in.</u> _____ <u>3 oz</u> <u>Slotted Spoon</u> <u>Hot</u>
Pan Portions/Pan Portion Size Utensil Temperature

Ingredients	Portions				Procedure
	25	100	500	1000	
WATER, cold	1.50 qt	1.00 gal 2.00 qt	7.00 gal 2.00 qt	15.00 gal	1. Bring water to a boil in steam kettle. 2. Add salt.
SALT, 100 lb bag	2.25 tsp	3.00 tbs	.75 cup 3.00 tbs	1.75 cup 2.00 tbs	3. Add Fordhook lima beans and more hot water as necessary to just cover the limas, and bring to a boil.
MARGARINE, SOLID, 1 lb	.25 lb	1.00 lb	5.00 lb	10.00 lb	4. Add margarine.
LIMA BEANS, FORDHOOK, 20 lb cs	5.00 lb	20.00 lb	100.00 lb	200.00 lb	5. Start timing when water returns to a boil and simmer for 20 to 25 min., uncovered, and less time if lid is used. Be careful not to overcook. 6. Place lima beans in counter pans with a small amt of margarine-liquid from steam kettle. Cooking time: 20 to 25 min. Cooking temp: simmer Equipment: steam kettle

3128	SUCCOTASH				VEGETABLES—Beans and Peas
Recipe No.	**Recipe Name**				**Category**

Serving Standards: 10- by 12- by 4-in. _____   3 oz _____   Slotted Spoon _____   Hot _____
                       Pan   **Portions/Pan**   **Portion Size**   **Utensil**   **Temperature**

Ingredients	Portions				Procedure
	25	**100**	**500**	**1000**	
WATER, cold	1.50 qt	1.00 gal 2.00 qt	7.00 gal 2.00 qt	15.00 gal	1. Bring water to boil in steam kettle.
SALT, 100 lb bag	2.25 tsp	3.00 tbs	.75 cup 3.00 tbs	1.75 cup 2.00 tbs	2. Add salt. 3. Add succotash and more hot water as necessary to just cover the succotash.
MARGARINE, SOLID, 1 lb	.25 lb	1.00 lb	5.00 lb	10.00 lb	4. Add margarine.
SUCCOTASH, FNCY, 12/2.5 lb/cs	5.00 lb	20.00 lb	100.00 lb	200.00 lb	5. Start timing when water returns to boil and simmer for 20 to 25 min., uncovered, and less time if lid is used. Be careful not to overcook. 6. Place succotash in counter pans with a small amt of margarine-liquid from steam kettle. Cooking time: 20 to 25 min. Cooking temp: simmer Equipment: steam kettle

3130	MIXED VEGETABLES				VEGETABLES—Beans and Peas
Recipe No.	Recipe Name				Category

Serving Standards: 10- by 12- by 4-in.   3 oz   Slotted Spoon   Hot

                   Pan   Portions/Pan   Portion Size   Utensil   Temperature

Ingredients	Portions				Procedure
	25	100	500	1000	
WATER, cold	1.50 qt	1.00 gal 2.00 qt	7.00 gal 2.00 qt	15.00 gal	1. Bring water to boil in steam kettle. 2. Add salt.
SALT, 100 lb bag	2.25 tsp	3.00 tbs	.75 cup 3.00 tbs	1.75 cup 2.00 tbs	3. Add vegetables and more hot water as necessary to just cover the vegetables and bring to boil.
MARGARINE, SOLID, 1 lb	.25 lb	1.00 lb	5.00 lb	10.00 lb	4. Add margarine.
VEGETABLES, MIXED, FNCY 20 lb	5.00 lb	20.00 lb	100.00 lb	200.00 lb	5. Start timing when water returns to boil and simmer for 20 to 25 min., uncovered, and less time if lid is used. Be careful not to overcook. 6. Place vegetables in counter pans with a small amt of margarine-liquid from steam kettle. Cooking time: 20 to 25 min. Cooking temp: simmer Equipment: steam kettle

3134	PINTO BEANS				VEGETABLES—Beans and Peas
Recipe No.	Recipe Name				Category

Serving Standards: 10- by 12- by 4-in. ___ Pan   ___ Portions/Pan   3.5 oz ___ Portion Size   Solid Spoon ___ Utensil   Hot ___ Temperature

Ingredients	Portions				Procedure
	25	150	300	1200	
BEANS, PINTO, FNCY 6/10	1.00 can	6.00 can	12.00 can	48.00 can	1. Place pinto beans, water, margarine and black pepper in steam kettle.
WATER, cold	1.00 cup	1.00 qt	3.00 qt	3.00 gal	2. Turn on steam and cook for 30 min.
		2.00 cup			3. Pour 1 gal mixture into 10- by 12- by 4-in. counter pan.
MARGARINE, SOLID, 1 lb	.25 lb	1.50 lb	3.00 lb	12.00 lb	Cooking time: 30 min.
PEPPER, BLACK, GROUND, 6 lb	.50 tsp	1.00 tbs	2.00 tbs	.50 cup	Equipment: steam kettle

3136	PORK AND BEANS				VEGETABLES—Beans and Peas
Recipe No.	Recipe Name				Category

Serving Standards: 10- by 12- by 4-in. ___ Pan   ___ Portions/Pan   3.5 oz ___ Portion Size   Solid Spoon ___ Utensil   Hot ___ Temperature

Ingredients	Portions				Procedure
	25	300	600	1200	
BEANS, W/PORK, W/TOM SAUCE, FNCY 6/10	1.00 can	12.00 can	24.00 can	48.00 can	1. Place pork and beans in steam kettle and heat to serving temp. 2. Or for batch cooking, place in counter pan and heat in high speed steam cooker about 5 min. or until hot. Equipment: steam kettle or high speed steam cooker

3142	NORTHERN WHITE BEANS	VEGETABLES—Beans and Peas
Recipe No.	Recipe Name	Category

Serving Standards: __10- by 12- by 4-in.__ _____ __3.5 oz__ __Solid Spoon__ __Hot__
Pan   Portions/Pan   Portion Size   Utensil   Temperature

Ingredients	Portions				Procedure
	26	52	260	520	
BEANS, DRIED, GRT NORTH, FNCY 6/10	1.00 can	2.00 can	10.00 can	20.00 can	1. Put beans and water in steam kettle.
					2. Add 2 oz of bacon drippings for each can of beans.
WATER, cold	1.00 cup	2.00 cup	2.00 qt	1.00 gal	3. Simmer for 15 min.
			2.00 cup	1.00 qt	4. Place in counter pans 10- by 12- by 4-in.
BACON DRIPPINGS	2.00 oz	4.00 oz	1.25 lb	2.50 lb	*Note:* Omit bacon drippings if pre-seasoned beans are used and reduce water, if necessary
					Cooking time: 15 min.
					Cooking temp: simmer
					Equipment: steam kettle

3152	BLACKEYED PEAS	VEGETABLES—Beans and Peas
Recipe No.	Recipe Name	Category

Serving Standards: __10- by 12- by 4-in.__ _____ __3.5 oz__ __Slotted Spoon__ __Hot__
Pan   Portions/Pan   Portion Size   Utensil   Temperature

Ingredients	Portions				Procedure
	25	150	300	600	
PEAS, BLACKEYED, STD 6/10/cs	1.00 can	6.00 can	12.00 can	24.00 can	1. Place blackeyed peas, margarine and black pepper in steam kettle. Do not drain peas.
MARGARINE, SOLID, 1 lb	1.50 oz	.50 lb	1.00 lb	2.25 lb	2. Turn on steam and simmer for 30 min.
		1.00 oz	2.00 oz		3. Place in counter pans.
PEPPER, BLACK, GROUND, 6 lb	.25 tsp	1.50 tsp	1.00 tbs	2.00 tbs	Cooking time: about 30 min.
					Cooking temp: simmer
					Equipment: steam kettle

3158	BUTTERED GREEN PEAS (FROZEN GREEN PEAS)				VEGETABLES—Beans and Peas
Recipe No.	Recipe Name				Category

Serving Standards: 10- by 12- by 4-in. | 25 | 3 oz | Slotted Spoon | Hot

Pan   Portions/Pan   Portion Size   Utensil   Temperature

Ingredients	Portions				Procedure
	25	100	300	500	
PEAS, SM FNCY, 20 lb box	5.00 lb	20.00 lb	60.00 lb	100.00 lb	1. Put 5 lb green peas in 10- by 12- by 4-in. counter pan.
SALT, 100 lb bag	1.00 tsp	1.00 tbs 1.00 tsp	.25 cup	.25 cup 2.00 tbs 2.00 tsp	2. Add salt and stir. 3. Place in high speed steam cooker for 2 min. 4. Pour 3 oz melted margarine over each pan of green peas and stir.
MARGARINE, SOLID, 1 lb	3.00 oz	.75 lb	2.25 lb	3.75 lb	5. Serve 3 oz with slotted spoon. Cooking time: 2 min. Equipment: high speed steam cooker

3159	BUTTERED SWEET PEAS (CANNED)				VEGETABLES—Beans and Peas
Recipe No.	Recipe Name				Category

Serving Standards: 10- by 12- by 4-in. | | 3 oz | Slotted Spoon | Hot

Pan   Portions/Pan   Portion Size   Utensil   Temperature

Ingredients	Portions				Procedure
	23	138	276	552	
PEAS, GRN, FNCY, No. 4sv, dr wt 70 oz 6/10	1.00 can	6.00 can	12.00 can	24.00 can	1. Place undrained peas in steam kettle. 2. Add salt and margarine and heat to serving temp.
SALT, 100 lb bag	.50 tsp	1.00 tbs	2.00 tbs	.25 cup	3. Place in 10- by 12- by 4-in. counter pans with a small amt of liquid.
MARGARINE, SOLID, 1 lb	2.66 oz	1.00 lb	2.00 lb	4.00 lb	4. Or for batch cooking: drain peas and place 1 can in 10- by 12- by 4-in. pan and add 2.66 oz margarine and .5 tsp salt and steam in high speed steam cooker for 2 min. or until hot. Equipment: steam kettle or high speed steam cooker

3161	PEAS AND CARROTS	VEGETABLES—Beans and Peas
Recipe No.	Recipe Name	Category

Serving Standards: __10- by 12- by 4-in.__ _____ __3 oz__ __Slotted Spoon__ __Hot__
Pan Portions/Pan Portion Size Utensil Temperature

Ingredients	Portions				Procedure
	25	100	300	500	
PEAS/CARROTS, FNCY, 12/2.5 lb/cs	5.00 lb	20.00 lb	60.00 lb	100.00 lb	1. Put 5 lb peas and carrots in 10- by 12- by 4-in. counter pan.
SALT, 100 lb bag	1.00 tsp	1.00 tbs 1.00 tsp	.25 cup	.25 cup 2.00 tbs 2.00 tsp	2. Add salt and stir. 3. Place in high speed steam cooker for 2 min.
MARGARINE, SOLID, 1 lb	3.00 oz	.75 lb	2.25 lb	3.75 lb	4. Pour 3 oz melted margarine over each pan of peas and carrots and stir. 5. Serve 3 oz with slotted spoon. Cooking time: 2 min. Equipment: high speed steam cooker

3178	ASPARAGUS WITH CHEESE SAUCE	VEGETABLES—Green, Yellow, Red
Recipe No.	Recipe Name	Category

Serving Standards: <u>20- by 12- by 2.5-in.</u>   <u>48</u>   <u>3 oz</u>   <u>Solid Spoon</u>   <u>Hot</u>
                Pan   Portions/Pan   Portion Size   Utensil   Temperature

Ingredients	Portions				Procedure
	65	195	520	1040	
CHEESE SAUCE, Recipe 0620	2.00 qt	1.00 gal 2.00 qt	4.00 gal	8.00 gal	1. Prepare cheese sauce and hold. 2. Place 7.5 lb frozen asparagus in counter pans 20- by 12- by 2.5-in. with racks in pans. 3. Cook in high speed steam cooker until done, about 5 min. Remove rack and drain well. 4. Pour 1.5 qt of hot cheese sauce over each 7.5 lb asparagus just before serving. *Note:* Proportion is 2 cups cheese sauce per 2.5 lb raw **asparagus.** Cooking time: 5 min. Equipment: high speed steam cooker
ASPARAGUS, CUTS-TIPS, FNCY 2.5 lb box	10.00 lb	30.00 lb	80.00 lb	160.00 lb	

3181	BUTTERED GREEN CABBAGE	VEGETABLES—Green, Yellow, Red
Recipe No.	Recipe Name	Category

Serving Standards: __10- by 12- by 4-in.__ | _____ | __3 oz__ | __Slotted Spoon__ | __Hot__
Pan | Portions/Pan | Portion Size | Utensil | Temperature

Ingredients	Portions				Procedure
	25	200	500	1000	
CABBAGE, GREEN, FNCY 50 lb	7.50 lb	60.00 lb	150.00 lb	300.00 lb	1. Wash cabbage.
SALT, 100 lb bag	1.00 tsp	2.00 tbs	.25 cup	.75 cup	2. Remove unusable leaves saving all usable outer leaves.
		2.00 tsp	2.00 tbs	1.00 tbs	3. Cut cabbage into quarters and remove core.
			2.00 tsp	1.00 tsp	4. Chop with French knife into long pieces about 1.5 in. wide.
MARGARINE, SOLID, 1 lb	.25 lb	2.00 lb	5.00 lb	10.00 lb	5. Cook in boiling salted water with margarine until tender, about 10 to 15 min. or sprinkle with salt and cook in high speed steam cooker until tender, about 2 min.
					6. Drain cabbage and if cooked in steamer add melted margarine.
					Cooking time: see above
					Equipment: steam kettle or high speed steam cooker

3184	SCALLOPED BROCCOLI				VEGETABLES—Green, Yellow, Red
Recipe No.	**Recipe Name**				**Category**

Serving Standards: 20- by 12- by 2.5-in. _____ 50 _____ 4 oz _____ Solid Spoon _____ Hot _____
                Pan   Portions/Pan   Portion Size   Utensil   Temperature

Ingredients	Portions				Procedure
	50	100	200	500	
MILK, INST NONFAT DRY, 6/5 lb	6.00 oz	.75 lb	1.50 lb	3.75 lb	1. Dissolve milk in hot water.
WATER, hot, 180°F.	1.00 qt	3.00 qt	1.00 gal	4.00 gal	2. In small steam kettle melt margarine, add flour, and stir until smooth. Add salt. Add hot milk all at once, stirring constantly.
	3.50 cup	3.00 cup	3.00 qt	2.00 qt	
			2.00 cup	3.00 cup	3. Cook and stir as necessary until smooth and thick (15 to 20 min).
FLOUR, 25 lb bag	.25 lb	.50 lb	1.00 lb	2.50 lb	
MARGARINE, SOLID, 1 lb	.50 lb	1.00 lb	2.00 lb	5.00 lb	4. Steam frozen broccoli in high speed steam cooker approx 2.5 min. until tender. Drain well.
SALT, 100 lb bag	2.25 tsp	1.00 tbs	3.00 tbs	.25 cup	
		1.50 tsp		3.00 tbs	5. Combine cooked broccoli with white sauce in large mixing bowl.
				1.50 tsp	
BROCCOLI, CUTS, FNCY 2.5 lb box	10.00 lb	20.00 lb	40.00 lb	100.00 lb	6. Pour 1.5 gal broccoli mixture into 20- by 12- by 2.5-in. counter pans.
BREAD CRUMBS	.25 lb	.50 lb	1.00 lb	2.50 lb	7. Top each pan with 2 cups margarine and bread crumb mixture.
MARGARINE, SOLID, 1 lb	2.50 oz	5.00 oz	10.00 oz	1.00 lb	
				9.00 oz	8. Brown in conv oven at 350°F. about 15 min. until bubbly.

Cooking time: 20 min. steam kettle
                 15 min. conv oven
                 2.5 min. high speed steam cooker
Cooking temp: 350°F. conv oven
Equipment: steam kettle, conv oven, high speed steam cooker

3186	BROCCOLI SPEARS	VEGETABLES—Green, Yellow, Red
Recipe No.	Recipe Name	Category

Serving Standards: <u>20- by 12- by 2.5-in.</u>   <u>40</u>   <u>2 ea</u>   <u>Tongs</u>   <u>Hot</u>
                      Pan   Portions/Pan   Portion Size   Utensil   Temperature

Ingredients	Portions				Procedure
	10	100	200	500	
BROCCOLI, SPEARS, FNCY 2 lb box	1.00 box	10.00 box	20.00 box	50.00 box	1. Place 4 boxes (8 lb) frozen broccoli spears in 20- by 12- by 2.5-in. counter pan.
SALT, 100 lb bag	.25 tsp	2.50 tsp	1.00 tbs 2.00 tsp	.25 cup .50 tsp	2. Sprinkle 1 tsp salt over each pan. 3. Cook in high speed steam cooker for 2 to 2.5 min. until broccoli is tender and color is still bright green.
MARGARINE, SOLID, 1 lb	1.00 oz	10.00 oz	1.25 lb	3.00 lb 2.00 oz	4. Drain and add 4 oz melted margarine per pan. 5. Serve 2 spears.

4. Drain and add 4 oz melted margarine per pan.
5. Serve 2 spears.
Note: If service is slow, cook smaller quantities as needed.
Portion size: 2 cooked spears weigh approx 2.75 oz
Cooking time: 2 to 2.5 min.
Equipment: high speed steam cooker

3192	BRUSSELS SPROUTS	VEGETABLES–Green, Yellow, Red
Recipe No.	Recipe Name	Category

Serving Standards: 10- by 12- by 4-in. _____   24 _____   6 ea _____   Slotted Spoon _____   Hot _____
                          Pan   Portions/Pan   Portion Size   Utensil   Temperature

Ingredients	Portions				Procedure
	12	72	144	576	
BRUSSELS SPROUTS, FNCY, 2.5 lb box	2.00 lb	12.00 lb	24.00 lb	96.00 lb	1. Place 4 lb Brussels sprouts into steam table pan. Add salt (.5 tsp/pan).
SALT, 100 lb bag	.25 tsp	1.50 tsp	1.00 tbs	.25 cup	2. Cook in high speed steam cooker for 6 min. or until tender.
MARGARINE, SOLID, 1 lb	1.00 oz	6.00 oz	.75 lb	3.00 lb	3. Drain off excess liquid.
					4. Pour 2 oz margarine over each pan
					Note: Cooked weight per portion of 6 ea is about 2.5 oz.
					Cooking time: about 6 min.
					Equipment: high speed steam cooker

3194	COLLARD GREENS				VEGETABLES—Green, Yellow, Red
Recipe No.	**Recipe Name**				**Category**

Serving Standards: **10- by 12- by 4-in.**   **3 oz**   **Tongs**   **Hot**
_____Pan_____Portions/Pan___Portion Size_____Utensil_____Temperature

Ingredients	Portions				Procedure
	63	**252**	**504**	**1008**	
GREENS, CHOP COLL, FNCY 12/3 lb	18.00 lb	72.00 lb	144.00 lb	288.00 lb	1. Place fatback and water in steam kettle. Boil for 20 min.
FATBACK, salt, lb	.75 lb	3.00 lb	6.00 lb	12.00 lb	2. Add greens to boiling water.
WATER, cold	.50 gal	2.00 gal	4.00 gal	8.00 gal	3. Add salt and more water as necessary during cooking.
SALT, 100 lb bag	2.00 tbs	.50 cup	1.00 cup	2.00 cup	4. Bring to boil and simmer for about 1 hr and 10 min. or until done, stirring occasionally at first until greens are completely thawed.

4. Bring to boil and simmer for about 1 hr and 10 min. or until done, stirring occasionally at first until greens are completely thawed.

Note: Cooking time may vary with quantity of greens.

5. Drain greens and put into 10- by 12- by 4-in. pans for service.

Cooking time: approx 1 hr 10 min.

Cooking temp: simmer

Equipment: steam kettle

Variation: Use turnip and mustard greens.

3208	OKRA AND TOMATOES	VEGETABLES—Green, Yellow, Red
Recipe No.	Recipe Name	Category

Serving Standards:

10- by 12- by 4-in.		3 oz	Solid Spoon	Hot
Pan	Portions/Pan	Portion Size	Utensil	Temperature

Ingredients	Portions				Procedure
	55	110	220	440	
OKRA, CUT, FNCY, 3 lb box	5.00 lb	10.00 lb	20.00 lb	40.00 lb	1. Steam okra in high speed steam cooker until tender, approx 4 to 6 min.
TOMATOES, BROKEN, dr wt 64 oz XSTD 6/10	1.00 can	2.00 can	4.00 can	8.00 can	2. Break up tomatoes slightly if whole and save 1 cup of juice for every 2 oz of cornstarch to make a thin paste.
SUGAR, GRAN, 100 lb	.25 lb	.50 lb	1.00 lb	2.00 lb	3. Heat tomatoes, sugar and margarine in steam kettle.
MARGARINE, SOLID, 1 lb	3.00 oz	6.00 oz	.75 lb	1.50 lb	4. Dissolve cornstarch in tomato juice and add to tomatoes, stirring constantly.
CORNSTARCH, 24/1 lb bag/cs	2.00 oz	.25 lb	.50 lb	1.00 lb	5. Cook until clear in color.
SALT, 100 lb bag	1.50 tsp	1.00 tbs	2.00 tbs	.25 cup	6. Add cooked okra and salt. Mix well.
					7. Pour 1 gal into 10- by 12- by 4-in. counter pans.

Cooking time: 4 to 6 min. high speed steam cooker
                       15 min. steam kettle
Cooking temp: simmer—steam kettle
Equipment: high speed steam cooker, steam kettle

3210	BUTTERED SPINACH				VEGETABLES—Green, Yellow, Red
Recipe No.	Recipe Name				Category

Serving Standards: <u>10- by 12- by 4-in.</u>   <u>   </u>   <u>3 oz</u>   <u>Slotted Spoon</u>   <u>Hot</u>

             Pan   Portions/Pan   Portion Size   Utensil   Temperature

Ingredients	Portions				Procedure
	21	**126**	**252**	**504**	
SPINACH, FNCY chopped, 3 lb box	6.00 lb	36.00 lb	72.00 lb	144.00 lb	1. Place 2 qt water plus the amt of water in recipe in steam kettle and bring to boil. Add salt.
WATER, cold	1.00 cup	1.00 qt 2.00 cup	3.00 qt	1.00 gal 2.00 qt	2. Add spinach and simmer until thawed, stirring occasionally.
SALT, 100 lb bag	1.00 tsp	2.00 tbs	.25 cup	.50 cup	3. After it is thawed, simmer approx 20 min. or until done. Add water as necessary during cooking.
MARGARINE, SOLID, 1 lb	2.66 oz	1.00 lb	2.00 lb	4.00 lb	4. Add margarine and stir. Drain and place in counter pans with only a small amt of liquid. Garnish.

Note: For small quantities, spinach may be cooked in high speed steam cooker approx 11 min. or until done.

Seasoning: use 1 tsp salt and 2.66 oz margarine for 6 lb spinach.

Equipment: steam kettle or high speed steam cooker

Variation: For each 6 lb of spinach, chop 4 hard-cooked eggs and sprinkle over cooked spinach.

3214	CREAMED SPINACH				VEGETABLES—Green, Yellow, Red
Recipe No.	Recipe Name				Category

Serving Standards: 12- by 10- by 4-in. Pan   24 Portions/Pan   3.5 oz Portion Size   No. 12 Scoop Utensil   Hot Temperature

Ingredients	Portions				Procedure
	48	96	192	576	
SPINACH, FNCY CHOPPED, 3 lb box	9.00 lb	18.00 lb	36.00 lb	108.00 lb	1. Place 2 qt water plus first amt in recipe in steam kettle and bring to boil.
WATER, cold	2.00 cup	1.00 qt	2.00 qt	1.00 gal 2.00 qt	2. Add spinach and simmer until thawed, stirring occasionally.
MARGARINE, SOLID, 1 lb	.50 lb	1.00 lb	2.00 lb	6.00 lb	3. After it is thawed, simmer approx 20 min. or until done. Add water as necessary during cooking.
FLOUR, 25 lb bag	.25 lb	.50 lb	1.00 lb	3.00 lb	Drain well.
WATER, hot, 180°F.	2.00 qt	1.00 gal	2.00 gal	6.00 gal	*Note:* For small quantities, spinach may be cooked
MILK, INST NONFAT DRY, 6/5 lb	6.00 oz	.75 lb	1.50 lb	4.50 lb	in high speed steam cooker approx 11 min. or until done.
SALT, 100 lb bag	2.00 tsp	1.00 tbs 1.00 tsp	2.00 tbs 2.00 tsp	.50 cup	4. Melt margarine in steam kettle. 5. Add flour and mix well.
PEPPER, WHITE, GROUND, 1 lb	.75 tsp	1.50 tsp	1.00 tbs	3.00 tbs	6. Turn off steam and add second amt of water. Mix well.
					7. Stir in dry milk until dissolved.
					8. Turn on steam and simmer until thickened, about 8 to 10 min.
					9. Add salt and pepper.
					10. Combine cooked drained spinach with cream sauce and place in counter pans.
					Cooking time: see above
					Cooking temp: simmer
					Equipment: steam kettle

3254   **HARVARD BEETS (SLICED BEETS)**   **VEGETABLES**—Green, Yellow, Red

Recipe No.   Recipe Name   Category

Serving Standards: 10- by 12- by 4-in.   28   3 oz   Solid Spoon   Hot

                       Pan   Portions/Pan   Portion Size   Utensil   Temperature

Ingredients	Portions				Procedure
	21	**84**	**126**	**252**	
BEETS, SLC, FNCY med, dr wt 68 oz 6/10	1.00 can	4.00 can	6.00 can	12.00 can	1. Drain beets and save juice.
MARGARINE, SOLID, 1 lb	5.33 oz	1.00 lb 5.32 oz	2.00 lb	4.00 lb	2. Melt margarine in steam kettle. Add sugar and dissolve.
SUGAR, GRAN, 100 lb	14.00 oz	3.50 lb	5.25 lb	10.50 lb	3. Substitute beet juice from Step 1 for the water in recipe and dissolve cornstarch in it.
WATER, cold	2.66 cup	2.00 qt 2.64 cup	1.00 gal	2.00 gal	4. Add cornstarch-beet juice mixture, vinegar and seasonings to steam kettle.
CORNSTARCH, 24/1 lb/cs	2.00 oz	.50 lb	.75 lb	1.50 lb	5. Simmer until it thickens and becomes glossy, about 10 min.
VINEGAR, COLORED, DIST, 4/1 gal/cs	.66 cup	2.64 cup	1.00 qt	2.00 qt	6. Add beets and heat about 5 min.
SALT, 100 lb bag	1.00 tbs	.25 cup	.25 cup 2.00 tbs	.75 cup	7. Place 1 gal in counter pan 10- by 12- by 4-in.
CLOVES, WHOLE, 1 lb	.12 tsp	.50 tsp	.75 tsp	1.50 tsp	*Note:* Portion size is 3 oz of beets only plus about 1 oz of sauce. This 3 oz is approx 7 slices. There are approx 150 slices/can.

Note: Portion size is 3 oz of beets only plus about 1 oz of sauce. This 3 oz is approx 7 slices. There are approx 150 slices/can.

Service: If served on the entree plate, use a slotted spoon.

Cooking time: 15 min.

Cooking temp: simmer

Equipment: steam kettle

Variation: Whole beets.

3266	BUTTERED CARROTS WITH PARSLEY				VEGETABLES—Green, Yellow, Red
Recipe No.	Recipe Name				Category

Serving Standards:	10- by 12- by 4-in.	23	3 oz	Slotted Spoon	Hot
	Pan	Portions/Pan	Portion Size	Utensil	Temperature

Ingredients	Portions				Procedure
	23	92	276	552	
CARROT, CHK, FNCY, 69 dw 6/10	1.00 can	4.00 can	12.00 can	24.00 can	1. Drain carrots and place in counter pans, 1 can per pan.
SUGAR, GRAN, 100 lb	1.00 tbs	.25 cup	.75 cup	1.50 cup	2. Sprinkle each pan with 1 tsp of salt and 1 tbs of sugar.
SALT, 100 lb bag	1.00 tsp	1.00 tbs	.25 cup	.50 cup	3. Heat in high speed steam cooker for 2 to 3 min. or until hot.
		1.00 tsp			4. Melt margarine and pour 3 oz over each pan.
MARGARINE, SOLID, 1 lb	3.00 oz	.75 lb	2.25 lb	4.50 lb	5. Chop the parsley and sprinkle 1 tbs over each pan.
PARSLEY, FNCY bunch	1.00 tbs	.25 cup	.75 cup	1.50 cup	6. For large quantities, drain half of the liquid from the carrots and place carrots with remaining liquid and seasonings in steam kettle and heat to serving temp. Place in counter pans with some of the liquid and garnish with chopped parsley.
					7. Serve one slotted spoonful of carrots, about 3 oz.
					Cooking time: 2 to 3 min.
					Equipment: high speed steam cooker

3270		FRENCH FRIED CARROTS			VEGETABLES–Green, Yellow, Red	
Recipe No.		Recipe Name			Category	

Serving Standards: **20- by 12- by 2.5-in.**   **35**   **2.75 oz**   **Solid Spoon**   **Hot**
                    Pan   Portions/Pan   Portion Size   Utensil   Temperature

Ingredients	Portions				Procedure
	70	140	420	700	
CARROTS, FNCY bulk, 50 lb, no tops	12.50 lb	25.00 lb	75.00 lb	125.00 lb	1. Trim carrots and wash.
					2. Cook in high speed steam cooker 5 to 8 min.
BREAD CRUMBS	2.50 lb	5.00 lb	15.00 lb	25.00 lb	3. Remove from steamer and peel.
FLOUR, 25 lb bag	1.00 lb	2.00 lb	6.00 lb	10.00 lb	4. Cut carrots in half and then in fourths (3 in. long and .5 in. thick).
SALT, 100 lb bag	2.00 tbs	.25 cup	.75 cup	1.25 cup	
MILK, INST NONFAT DRY, 6/5 lb	2.50 oz	5.00 oz	15.00 oz	1.00 lb 9.00 oz	5. Add salt to flour.
					6. Reconstitute dry milk in amt water specified. Add eggs and mix well.
WATER, cold	.75 qt	1.00 qt	1.00 gal .50 qt	1.00 gal 3.50 qt	7. Roll sliced carrots in flour, dip in egg batter and coat with bread crumbs.
EGGS, 6/5 lb/cs	.25 lb	.50 lb	1.50 lb	2.50 lb	8. Fry in deep fat fryer set at 300°F. until brown (approx 3 min.).
					9. Pour into 20- by 12- by 2.5-in. counter pans.

Cooking time: 5 to 8 min. in high speed steam cooker
              3 min. in deep fat fryer
Cooking temp: 300°F. deep fat fryer
Equipment: high speed steam cooker, deep fat fryer

3282	**BAKED ACORN SQUASH**			**VEGETABLES**—Green, Yellow, Red
Recipe No.	Recipe Name			Category

Serving Standards: __20- by 12- by 2.5-in.__   __16__   __4 oz__   __Solid Spoon__   __Hot__
                          Pan   Portions/Pan   Portion Size   Utensil   Temperature

Ingredients	Portions				Procedure
	25	**100**	**300**	**600**	
SQUASH, ACORN, FNCY	10.00 lb	40.00 lb	120.00 lb	240.00 lb	1. Wash squash.
SUGAR, LIGHT BROWN,	10.00 oz	2.50 lb	7.50 lb	15.00 lb	2. Cook in high speed steam cooker for 3 min.
24/1 lb/cs					3. Slice off ends and slice in fourths, lengthwise. Remove seeds.
MARGARINE, SOLID, 1 lb	.25 lb	1.00 lb	3.00 lb	6.00 lb	4. Place squash in counter pans in high speed steam cooker for 4 min. Drain, leaving some water in pan to prevent burning.
NUTMEG, GROUND, 1 lb	1.25 tsp	1.00 tbs	.25 cup	.50 cup	
		2.00 tsp	1.00 tbs	2.00 tbs	5. Put 1 tbs of brown sugar and 1 tsp melted margarine in each piece.
CHERRIES, RED MARAS-	.25 cup	1.00 cup	3.00 cup	1.00 qt	6. Sprinkle with nutmeg.
CHINO, HLVS FNCY 6/.5 gal				2.00 cup	7. Place in conv oven at 350°F. and bake 20 to 25 min.

8. Garnish each piece with a maraschino cherry half.
9. Serve one large fourth or two small fourths, depending on size.
Note: Portion size of 1 quarter is 4 oz cooked weight.
Cooking time: see above
Cooking temp: 350°F.
Equipment: high speed steam cooker and conv oven

3286	SCALLOPED SQUASH/CHICKEN SOUP				VEGETABLES—Green, Yellow, Red
Recipe No.	Recipe Name				Category

Serving Standards:

20- by 12- by 2.5-in.	45	3.5 oz	Solid Spoon	Hot
Pan	Portions/Pan	Portion Size	Utensil	Temperature

Ingredients	Portions				Procedure
	90	180	360	540	
SQUASH, YELLOW CROOK-NECK, 12/3 lb	18.00 lb	36.00 lb	72.00 lb	108.00 lb	1. Place frozen squash in steamer pans on rack.
SOUP, CRM OF CHICKEN, 12/50 oz/cs	1.50 can	3.00 can	6.00 can	9.00 can	2. Cook in high speed steam cooker until tender (approx 4 to 6 min.).
MARGARINE, SOLID, 1 lb	.50 lb	1.00 lb	2.00 lb	3.00 lb	3. Remove pans from steamer and drain squash well.
SALT, 100 lb bag	2.00 tbs	.25 cup	.50 cup	.75 cup	4. Place squash in large mixing bowl and add melted margarine, chicken soup and salt.
BREAD CRUMBS	.75 lb	1.50 lb	3.00 lb	4.50 lb	5. Pour 1 gal and 1.5 cup squash mixture into each 20- by 12- by 2.5-in. counter pan.
MARGARINE, SOLID, 1 lb	6.00 oz	.75 lb	1.50 lb	2.25 lb	6. Melt second amt margarine and combine with bread crumbs.

7. Sprinkle 2 cups crumb mixture over each pan of squash.

8. Bake in conv oven at 350°F. until golden brown (approx 10 to 15 min.).

Cooking time: 4 to 6 min. in steamer
                      10 to 15 min. in conv oven

Cooking temp: 350°F. conv oven

Equipment: high speed steam cooker, conv oven

Variation: Mushroom soup.

3292	YELLOW SQUASH WITH CHEESE CRUMBS	VEGETABLES—Green, Yellow, Red
Recipe No.	Recipe Name	Category

Serving Standards:	20- by 12- by 2.5-in.	10	2 hlv	Solid Spoon	Hot
	Pan	Portions/Pan	Portion Size	Utensil	Temperature

Ingredients	Portions				Procedure
	62	124	248	372	
SQUASH, YELLOW CROOK-NECK, FNCY	.50 bsh	1.00 bsh	2.00 bsh	3.00 bsh	1. Wash, trim and slice squash in half. Place squash cut sides up compactly in counter pans.
BREAD CRUMBS	1.00 lb 2.00 oz	2.25 lb	4.50 lb	6.75 lb	2. Cook in high speed steam cooker until tender, approx 3 min., depending on size of squash.
MARGARINE, SOLID, 1 lb	6.00 oz	.75 lb	1.50 lb	2.25 lb	3. Remove pans from steamer and drain squash.
CHEDDAR CHEESE, WHEEL	6.00 oz	.75 lb	1.50 lb	2.25 lb	4. Combine first amt melted margarine and grated cheese with bread crumbs.
MARGARINE, SOLID, 1 lb	1.00 lb	2.00 lb	4.00 lb	6.00 lb	5. Melt second amt margarine and cover squash.
SALT, 100 lb bag	3.00 tbs	.25 cup 2.00 tbs	.75 cup	1.00 cup 2.00 tbs	6. Sprinkle salt and pepper mixture over buttered squash.
PEPPER, WHITE, GROUND, 1 lb	1.00 tsp	2.00 tsp	1.00 tbs 1.00 tsp	2.00 tbs	7. Sprinkle approx 1.75 cups crumb mixture over each pan of squash and bake in conv oven at 350°F. for 20 min.

Note: The weight of 2 hlv cooked is approx 3.75 oz. If squash is unusually large, serve only one hlv per portion.

Cooking time: 3 min.—steamer

               20 min.—conv oven

Cooking temp: 350°F.

Equipment: conv oven, high speed steam cooker

3296	BROILED TOMATOES	VEGETABLES—Green, Yellow, Red
Recipe No.	Recipe Name	Category

Serving Standards:

20- by 12- by 2.5-in.	28	5.25 oz	Solid Spoon	Hot
Pan	Portions/Pan	Portion Size	Utensil	Temperature

Ingredients	Portions				Procedure
	57	114	171	228	
TOMATOES, FNCY, 38 lb	19.00 lb	38.00 lb	57.00 lb	76.00 lb	1. Wash tomatoes and remove core.
MARGARINE, SOLID, 1 lb	.50 lb	1.00 lb	1.50 lb	2.00 lb	2. Place tomatoes in counter pans 20- by 12- by 2.5-
SALT, 100 lb bag	1.00 tbs	3.00 tbs	.25 cup	.25 cup	in.
	1.50 tsp		1.50 tsp	2.00 tbs	3. Melt first amt margarine and cover tomatoes.
PEPPER, WHITE, GROUND,	.50 tsp	1.00 tsp	1.50 tsp	2.00 tsp	4. Combine salt and pepper and sprinkle over toma-
1 lb					toes.
CHEDDAR CHEESE,	.25 lb	.50 lb	.75 lb	1.00 lb	5. Chop cheese on chopper, grind bread crumbs and
WHEEL					melt second amt margarine. Combine these ingredi-
BREAD CRUMBS	10.00 oz	1.25 lb	1.00 lb	2.50 lb	ents.
			14.00 oz		6. Top each tomato with crumb mixture (2 cups/pan).
MARGARINE, SOLID, 1 lb	.75 lb	1.50 lb	2.25 lb	3.00 lb	7. Cook in conv oven at 350°F. approx 35 min.
					Cooking time: 35 min.
					Cooking temp: 350°F.
					Equipment: conv oven

3298	ESCALLOPED TOMATOES		VEGETABLES—Green, Yellow, Red
Recipe No.	Recipe Name		Category

Serving Standards: __10- by 12- by 4-in.__   __25__   __3 oz__   __Solid Spoon__   __Hot__

                Pan   Portions/Pan   Portion Size   Utensil   Temperature

Ingredients	Portions				Procedure
	25	100	200	500	
TOMATOES, BROKEN, dr wt 64 oz XSTD 6/10	1.00 can	4.00 can	8.00 can	20.00 can	1. Cube first amt of bread into 1/2-in. cubes.
BREAD, DRY LEFT-OVER	.50 lb	2.00 lb	4.00 lb	10.00 lb	2. Combine tomatoes, cubed bread, first amt of margarine melted, sugar, salt and dehyd onions.
MARGARINE, SOLID, 1 lb	.25 lb	1.00 lb	2.00 lb	5.00 lb	3. Place 3 qt of mixture in 10- by 12- by 4-in. counter pans.
SUGAR, GRAN, 100 lb	1.00 oz	.25 lb	.50 lb	1.25 lb	4. Grind second amt of bread and combine with second amt of margarine melted. Sprinkle 1 cup over each pan.
ONIONS, DEHYD CHOP, 2.5 lb XSTD 6/10	.25 oz	1.00 oz	2.00 oz	5.00 oz	5. Bake in conv oven at 350°F. about 15 min. or until crumbs are golden brown.
BREAD CRUMBS	2.00 oz	.50 lb	1.00 lb	2.50 lb	Cooking time: 15 min.
MARGARINE, SOLID, 1 lb	1.25 oz	5.00 oz	10.00 oz	1.00 lb 9.00 oz	Cooking temp: 350°F. Equipment: conv oven

3299	TOMATO DUMPLINGS				VEGETABLES—Green, Yellow, Red
Recipe No.	Recipe Name				Category

Serving Standards:	10- by 12- by 4-in.		4 oz	Solid Spoon	Hot
	Pan	Portions/Pan	Portion Size	Utensil	Temperature

Ingredients	Portions				E*	Procedure
	35	210	350	525		
FLOUR, 25 lb bag	15.00 oz	5.00 lb	9.00 lb	14.00 lb		1. Combine flour, salt and baking powder and mix well.
		10.00 oz	6.00 oz	1.00 oz		
BAKING POWDER, 4/10/bag	.75 oz	4.50 oz	7.50 oz	11.25 oz		2. Work lard into flour lightly by hand until small balls are formed.
SALT, 100 lb bag	1.50 tsp	3.00 tbs	.25 cup	.25 cup		
			1.00 tbs	3.00 tbs		3. Reconstitute milk with water.
				1.50 tsp		4. Combine eggs and milk and add to flour mixture and mix. This should be a stiff dough.
LARD, 12/4 lb/cs	.25 lb	1.50 lb	2.50 lb	3.75 lb		
MILK, INST NONFAT DRY, 6/5 lb	.50 oz	3.00 oz	5.00 oz	7.50 oz		5. Roll on floured surface to .25 in. thick and cut into strips 1 in. wide and 1.5 in. long. Use second amt of flour for rolling.
WATER, cold	.50 cup	3.00 cup	1.00 qt	1.00 qt		
			1.00 cup	3.50 cup		6. Place tomatoes in steam kettle and use a wire whip to break them up more.
EGGS, 6/5 lb/cs	5.00 oz	1.00 lb	3.00 lb	4.00 lb		
		14.00 oz	2.00 oz	11.00 oz		7. Add margarine, sugar, dehyd onions and water and bring to boiling and reduce to simmer.
FLOUR, 25 lb bag	2.00 oz	.75 lb	1.25 lb	1.00 lb		
				14.00 oz		8. Drop dumplings into hot tomatoes and cook for 15 min. or until done. Avoid overstirring which breaks the dumplings.
TOMATOES, BROKEN, dr wt 64 oz XSTD 6/10	1.00 can	6.00 can	10.00 can	15.00 can		
MARGARINE, SOLID, 1 lb	.25 lb	1.50 lb	2.50 lb	3.75 lb		9. Place in counter pans 10- by 12- by 4-in.
SUGAR, GRAN, 100 lb	2.00 oz	.75 lb	1.25 lb	1.00 lb		Cooking time: about 20 min. total
				14.00 oz		Equipment: steam kettle
ONIONS, DEHYD CHOP, 2.5 lb XSTD 6/10	.25 oz	1.50 oz	2.50 oz	3.75 oz		*Early Prep: Dumplings may be made 1 day ahead. Separate layers with waxed paper and sprinkle flour over each layer and refrigerate.
WATER, cold	2.00 cup	3.00 qt	1.00 gal	1.00 gal		
			1.00 qt	3.00 qt		
				2.00 cup		

3302	STEWED TOMATOES				VEGETABLES—Green, Yellow, Red
Recipe No.	Recipe Name				Category

Serving Standards: __10- by 12- by 4-in.__   __22__   __3 oz__   __Solid Spoon__   __Hot__
   Pan   Portions/Pan   Portion Size   Utensil   Temperature

Ingredients	Portions				Procedure
	22	110	330	550	
TOMATOES, WHOLE, CALIF, dr wt 67 oz 6/10	1.00 can	5.00 can	15.00 can	25.00 can	1. Pour 1 can of tomatoes into a 10- by 12- by 4-in. pan.
SALT, 100 lb bag	1.00 tsp	1.00 tbs 2.00 tsp	.25 cup 1.00 tbs	.50 cup 1.00 tsp	2. Add 1 tsp salt, 1 tbs sugar and 2 oz margarine and heat in high speed steam cooker to serving temp, about 4 min.
SUGAR, GRAN, 100 lb	1.00 tbs	.25 cup 1.00 tbs	.75 cup 3.00 tbs	1.50 cup 1.00 tbs	3. Garnish with fresh parsley sprigs.
MARGARINE, SOLID, 1 lb	2.00 oz	10.00 oz	1.00 lb 14.00 oz	3.00 lb 2.00 oz	4. Serve 1 whole tomato (3 oz) plus juice, with solid spoon.
PARSLEY, FNCY bunch	1.00 tbs	.25 cup 1.00 tbs	.75 cup 3.00 tbs	1.50 cup 1.00 tbs	Cooking time: 4 min. Equipment: high speed steam cooker

3332	PARSLIED BUTTERED CAULIFLOWER				VEGETABLES—White and Starches
Recipe No.	Recipe Name				Category

Serving Standards: 10- by 12- by 4-in. __Pan__ 20 __Portions/Pan__ 3 oz __Portion Size__ Slotted Spoon __Utensil__ Hot __Temperature__

Ingredients	Portions				Procedure
	10	100	200	500	
CAULIFLOWER, FNCY, 2 lb box	2.00 lb	20.00 lb	40.00 lb	100.00 lb	1. Place 4 lb cauliflower in 10- by 12- by 4-in. pan. Break apart frozen cauliflower.
SALT, 100 lb bag	.25 tsp	2.50 tsp	1.00 tbs 2.00 tsp	.25 cup .50 tsp	2. Add salt (.5 tsp per 4 lb). 3. Cook in high speed steam cooker for 2.5 to 3 min.
MARGARINE, SOLID, 1 lb	1.00 oz	10.00 oz	1.25 lb	3.00 lb 2.00 oz	4. Pour 2 oz of margarine over each pan. 5. Garnish with fresh chopped parsley.
PARSLEY, FNCY bunch	.25 tsp	2.50 tsp	1.00 tbs 2.00 tsp	.25 cup .50 tsp	Cooking time: 2.5 to 3 min. Equipment: high speed steam cooker

3334	CAULIFLOWER AU GRATIN					VEGETABLES–White and Starches
Recipe No.	Recipe Name					Category

Serving Standards: <u>10- by 12- by 4-in.</u>   <u>28</u>   <u>3 oz</u>   <u>Solid Spoon</u>   <u>Hot</u>
                   Pan   Portions/Pan   Portion Size   Utensil   Temperature

Ingredients	Portions				Procedure
	70	210	700	1050	
CHEESE SAUCE,	2.00 qt	1.00 gal	5.00 gal	7.00 gal	1. Prepare cheese sauce and hold.
Recipe 0620		2.00 qt		2.00 qt	2. Place 4 lb cauliflower in 10- by 12- by 4-in. pans.
CAULIFLOWER, FNCY,	10.00 lb	30.00 lb	100.00 lb	150.00 lb	Break frozen cauliflower apart.
2 lb box					3. Cook in high speed steam cooker 2.5 to 3 min. or
					until tender.
					4. Remove from steamer and drain.
					5. Pour approx 3 cups of cheese sauce over each pan
					of cauliflower just before serving. (1.5 cups of
					cheese sauce for each 2 lb of cauliflower)
					6. Serve with solid spoon.
					Cooking time: 2.5 to 3 min.
					Equipment: high speed steam cooker, steam kettle

3336	BUTTERED NOODLES	VEGETABLES—White and Starches
Recipe No.	Recipe Name	Category

Serving Standards: 10- by 12- by 8-in.   4.5 oz   Slotted Spoon   Hot

                      Pan   Portions/Pan   Portion Size   Utensil   Temperature

Ingredients	Portions				Procedure
	50	100	200	500	
Yield	2.00 gal	4.00 gal	8.00 gal	20.00 gal	
					1. Place water and salt in steam kettle. Bring to a boil.
NOODLES, MEDIUM, 10 lb	2.75 lb	5.50 lb	11.00 lb	27.50 lb	2. Stir in noodles. Bring to a boil again, stirring frequently. Cook until noodles are tender but firm, about 15 min. Drain and rinse with warm water if necessary to prevent sticking.
MARGARINE, SOLID, 1 lb	.25 lb	.50 lb	1.00 lb	2.50 lb	3. Add margarine and enough warm water to cover noodles.
					4. Pour 3 gal of noodles in 10- by 12- by 8-in. counter pan.
					Note: Oil may be added during cooking to prevent foaming.
					Cooking time: 15 min.
					Cooking temp: boiling
					Equipment: steam kettle

3340	MACARONI AND CHEESE				VEGETABLES—White and Starches
Recipe No.	Recipe Name				Category

Serving Standards: __20- by 12- by 2.5-in.__   __30__   __6 oz__   __4 oz Ladle__   __Hot__
                            Pan   Portions/Pan   Portion Size   Utensil   Temperature

Ingredients	Portions				Procedure
	60	240	480	960	
Yield	3.00 gal	12.00 gal	24.00 gal	48.00 gal	1. Add macaroni to boiling water (salted) and cook 20 min.
MACARONI, ELBOW, 20 lb box	2.50 lb	10.00 lb	20.00 lb	40.00 lb	2. Drain macaroni and rinse with cold water.
MARGARINE, SOLID, 1 lb	10.00 oz	2.50 lb	5.00 lb	10.00 lb	3. Melt margarine in steam kettle.
FLOUR, 25 lb bag	10.00 oz	2.50 lb	5.00 lb	10.00 lb	4. Add flour and blend together to make a roux.
WATER, hot, 180°F.	1.25 gal	5.00 gal	10.00 gal	20.00 gal	5. Turn off steam and add hot water and blend well.
MILK, INST NONFAT DRY, 6/5 lb	1.25 lb	5.00 lb	10.00 lb	20.00 lb	6. Add dry milk and stir with wire whip to dissolve. 7. Turn steam on and cook, stirring occasionally, until a smooth sauce is formed, about 10 min.
CHEDDAR CHEESE, WHEEL	2.25 lb	9.00 lb	18.00 lb	36.00 lb	8. Grate both amts of cheddar cheese and set second amt aside to sprinkle on top of each pan.
SALT, 100 lb bag	2.25 tsp	3.00 tbs	.25 cup 2.00 tbs	.75 cup	9. Add first amt of grated cheese and salt to sauce and blend until cheese is melted.
CHEDDAR CHEESE, WHEEL	.50 lb	2.00 lb	4.00 lb	8.00 lb	10. Add well-drained macaroni to sauce and mix well.
					11. Place 1.5 gal of mixture into each counter pan 20- by 12- by 2.5-in.
					12. Sprinkle 4 oz of grated cheese on top of each pan.
					13. Bake in conv oven at 350°F. for 15 min., until golden brown.
					Cooking time: see above
					Cooking temp: 350°F.
					Equipment: steam kettle, conv oven

3342	FRENCH FRIED ONION RINGS				VEGETABLES—White and Starches
Recipe No.	Recipe Name				Category

Serving Standards: _____ _____ 2.25 oz _____ Hot

| | Pan | Portions/Pan | Portion Size | Utensil Tongs | Temperature |

Ingredients	Portions				Procedure
	12	96	192	384	
ONION RINGS, BRD, FNCY, 8/2.5 lb/cs	2.00 lb	16.00 lb	32.00 lb	64.00 lb	1. Place frozen onion rings in deep fat fryer at 350°F. 2. Fry for 1.5 min. or until golden brown. 3. Serve 4 onion rings, some small and some large ones. *Note:* Portion size is cooked weight. Cooking time: 1.5 min. Cooking temp: 350°F. Equipment: deep fat fryer

3348	SAVORY ONIONS		VEGETABLES—White and Starches
Recipe No.	Recipe Name		Category

Serving Standards: 20- by 12- by 2.5-in.   25   3.5 oz   Slotted Spoon   Hot
                                    Pan   Portions/Pan   Portion Size   Utensil   Temperature

Ingredients	Portions				Procedure
	84	168	252	504	
ONIONS, YELLOW, JUMBO, FNCY, 50 lb	16.50 lb	33.00 lb	49.50 lb	99.00 lb	1. Peel onions and slice one-half in. thick.
MARGARINE, SOLID, 1 lb	5.00 oz	10.00 oz	15.00 oz	1.00 lb 14.00 oz	2. Arrange onions in 20- by 12- by 2.5-in. counter pans with draining rack.
SUGAR, LIGHT BROWN, 25 lb bag	7.00 oz	14.00 oz	1.00 lb 5.00 oz	2.00 lb 10.00 oz	3. Place in high speed steam cooker about 3 min. until tender. Drain and remove rack.
SALT, 100 lb bag	1.00 tbs 2.00 tsp	3.00 tbs 1.00 tsp	.25 cup 1.00 tbs	.50 cup 2.00 tbs	4. Melt margarine and combine with brown sugar, salt and chili sauce.
CHILI SAUCE, 6/10	1.00 can	2.00 can	3.00 can	6.00 can	5. 5 lb onions AP should yield 1 pan.

6. Top each pan of onions with 4 cups of sauce.

7. Bake in conv oven at 350°F. about 25 min., until onions are glazed.

Note: Weight of onions is AP.

Cooking time: 3 min. high speed steam cooker
                       25 min. conv oven

Cooking temp: 350°F. conv oven

Equipment: high speed steam cooker, conv oven

3350	BUTTERED RICE	VEGETABLES—White and Starches
Recipe No.	**Recipe Name**	**Category**

Serving Standards:	10- by 12- by 4-in.	50	2.75 oz	No. 12 Scoop	Hot
	Pan	**Portions/Pan**	**Portion Size**	**Utensil**	**Temperature**

Ingredients	Portions				Procedure
	50	**200**	**500**	**1000**	
Yield	1.25 gal	5.00 gal	12.50 gal	25.00 gal	1. Stir rice into boiling salted water and simmer until tender, 20 to 25 min. Do not overcook.
RICE, CONVERTED, 6/10 lb	2.50 lb	10.00 lb	25.00 lb	50.00 lb	2. Drain and rinse with warm water, if necessary to prevent sticking.
MARGARINE, SOLID, 1 lb	1.00 oz	.25 lb	10.00 oz	1.25 lb	3. Add melted margarine and toss lightly.

4. Place 1.25 gal of rice into counter pans 10- by 12- by 4-in.

5. Suggested garnishes: fresh parsley, pimento, fresh green pepper.

Note: No. 12 scoop rice is 2.75 oz weight approx.

No. 16 scoop rice is 2 oz weight approx.

No. 20 scoop rice is 1.75 oz weight approx.

1 lb uncooked rice yields approx 3.5 lb cooked rice and measures approx 2 qt.

1 gal cooked rice weighs approx 7 lb.

Cooking time: 20 to 25 min.

Cooking temp: simmer

Equipment: steam kettle

3396	DRESSING, BREAD (TO BE COOKED ALONE IN PANS)				VEGETABLES—White and Starches
Recipe No.	Recipe Name				Category

Serving Standards:	20- by 12- by 2.5-in.		2.25 oz	No. 16 Scoop	Hot
	Pan	Portions/Pan	Portion Size	Utensil	Temperature

Ingredients	Portions				Procedure
	60	240	480	600	
Yield	1.25 gal	5.00 gal	10.00 gal	12.50 gal	
ONIONS, DEHYD CHOP, 2.5 lb XSTD 6/10	3.00 oz	.75 lb	1.50 lb	1.00 lb 14.00 oz	1. Rehydrate onions and celery in specified amt of water.
CELERY, SLICED STALKS, DEHYD, XSTD 6/10	.37 oz	1.50 oz	3.00 oz	3.75 oz	2. Melt margarine and mix with vegetables.
WATER, cold	1.50 cup	1.00 qt 2.00 cup	3.00 qt	3.00 qt 3.00 cup	3. Add sage, black pepper, monosodium glutamate, garlic powder, salt and chicken base to margarine and vegetables and mix well.
MARGARINE, SOLID, 1 lb	6.00 oz	1.50 lb	3.00 lb	3.75 lb	4. Grind corn bread and bread coarsely and mix well. Add to above mixture and mix lightly.
SAGE, RUBBED, 1 lb	.25 oz	1.00 oz	2.00 oz	2.50 oz	
PEPPER, BLACK, GROUND, 6 lb	.12 oz	.50 oz	1.00 oz	1.25 oz	5. Add eggs and water to the above mixture. Mix thoroughly but lightly.
MONOSODIUM GLUTAMATE, 2 lb can	.12 oz	.50 oz	1.00 oz	1.25 oz	6. Grease 20- by 12- by 2.5-in. counter pans with oil.
GARLIC POWDER, 1 lb	.50 tsp	2.00 tsp	1.00 tbs 1.00 tsp	1.00 tbs 2.00 tsp	7. Place 1.75 gal mixture in 20- by 12- by 2.5-in. pans or 2.5 gal in shallow roasting pans.
SALT, 100 lb bag	.62 oz	2.50 oz	5.00 oz	6.25 oz	8. Bake for 2 hr in rotary oven at 350°F. or 1.5 hr in conv oven at 300°F.
CHICKEN SOUP BASE, 12/1 lb/cs	.87 oz	3.50 oz	7.00 oz	8.75 oz	Cooking time: 2 hr or 1.5 hr
CORN BREAD SHEET	2.00 lb 14.00 oz	11.50 lb	23.00 lb	28.75 lb	Cooking temp: 350°F. or 300°F.
BREAD CRUMBS	1.00 lb 6.00 oz	5.50 lb	11.00 lb	13.75 lb	Equipment: rotary oven or conv oven
EGGS, 6/5 lb/cs	.75 lb	3.00 lb	6.00 lb	7.50 lb	
WATER, cold	2.00 qt .50 cup	2.00 gal 2.00 cup	4.00 gal 1.00 qt	5.00 gal 1.00 qt 1.00 cup	

3397	DRESSING, STUFFING (TO BE COOKED WITH A MEAT ITEM)				VEGETABLES—White and Starches
Recipe No.	**Recipe Name**				**Category**

Serving Standards:

Pan	Portions/Pan	2.25 oz Portion Size	No. 16 Scoop Utensil	Temperature

Ingredients	Portions				Procedure
	100	**200**	**300**	**600**	
Yield	2.08 gal	4.16 gal	6.24 gal	12.48 gal	1. Rehydrate onions and celery in specified amt of water.
ONIONS, DEHYD CHOP, 2.5 lb XSTD 6/10	5.00 oz	10.00 oz	15.00 oz	1.00 lb 14.00 oz	2. Melt margarine and mix with vegetables.
CELERY, SLICED STALKS, DEHYD XSTD 6/10	.50 oz	1.00 oz	1.50 oz	3.00 oz	3. Add sage, black pepper, monosodium glutamate, garlic powder, salt and chicken base to margarine and vegetables and mix well.
WATER, cold	2.50 cup	1.00 qt 1.00 cup	1.00 qt 3.50 cup	3.00 qt 3.00 cup	4. Grind corn bread and bread coarsely and mix well. Add to above mixture and mix lightly.
MARGARINE, SOLID, 1 lb	9.50 oz	1.00 lb 3.00 oz	1.00 lb 12.50 oz	3.50 lb 1.00 oz	5. Add eggs and water to the above mixture and mix lightly but thoroughly.
SAGE, RUBBED, 1 lb	.33 oz	.66 oz	1.00 oz	2.00 oz	6. Portion as necessary for desired use.
PEPPER, BLACK, GROUND, 6 lb	.25 oz	.50 oz	.75 oz	1.50 oz	7. Cook as directed for desired use.
MONOSODIUM GLUTAMATE, 2 lb can	.25 oz	.50 oz	.75 oz	1.50 oz	
GARLIC POWDER, 1 lb	.75 tsp	1.50 tsp	2.25 tsp	1.00 tbs 1.50 tsp	
SALT, 100 lb bag	1.50 oz	3.00 oz	4.50 oz	9.00 oz	
CHICKEN SOUP BASE, 12/1 lb/cs	1.00 oz	2.00 oz	3.00 oz	6.00 oz	
CORN BREAD SHEET	4.50 lb	9.00 lb	13.50 lb	27.00 lb	
BREAD CRUMBS	2.25 lb	4.50 lb	6.75 lb	13.50 lb	
EGGS, 6/5 lb/cs	1.25 lb	2.50 lb	3.75 lb	7.50 lb	
WATER, cold	3.00 qt 1.50 cup	1.00 gal 2.00 qt 3.00 cup	2.00 gal 2.00 qt .50 cup	5.00 gal 1.00 cup	

3398	HUSH PUPPIES				VEGETABLES—White and Starches
Recipe No.	Recipe Name				Category

Serving Standards: <u>20- by 12- by 2.5-in.</u>   <u>48</u>   <u>2 oz</u>   <u>Tongs</u>   <u>Hot</u>
                    Pan   Portions/Pan   Portion Size   Utensil   Temperature

Ingredients	Portions				Procedure
	8	56	96	200	
HUSH PUPPIES, 12/1 lb bag/cs	1.00 bag	7.00 bag	12.00 bag	25.00 bag	1. Spread hush puppies on sheet pan. (6 bags) 2. Place in conv oven at 325°F. for 5 to 6 min. 3. Remove from oven and place in 20- by 12- by 2.5-in. counter pans. Give 4 to 5 ea/serving. (If they are large, 32 per lb, give 4/serving.) *Note:* Frying hush puppies makes them too greasy.

Hot Fruits

3412	BAKED APPLES				HOT FRUITS
Recipe No.	Recipe Name				Category

Serving Standards:	20- by 12- by 2.5-in.	30	1 ea	Solid Spoon	Hot
	Pan	Portions/Pan	Portion Size	Utensil	Temperature

Ingredients	Portions				Procedure
	20	**60**	**240**	**480**	
APPLES, BAKED, WHOLE, FNCY 20 ct, 6/10	1.00 can	3.00 can	12.00 can	24.00 can	1. Arrange apples in 20- by 12- by 2.5-in. pans with 2 cups juice from can. Approx 30 apples per pan.
MARGARINE, SOLID, 1 lb	1.33 oz	4.00 oz	1.00 lb	2.00 lb	2. Melt margarine and ladle 2 oz over each pan.
SUGAR, GRAN, 100 lb	2.00 tbs	.50 cup	2.00 cup	1.00 qt	3. Combine sugar and cinnamon and sprinkle .25 cup over each pan of buttered apples.
	2.00 tsp				4. Cook in conv oven at 375°F. for 15 min.
CINNAMON, GROUND, 1 lb	.12 tsp	.37 tsp	1.50 tsp	1.00 tbs	Cooking time: 15 min. Cooking temp: 375°F. Equipment: conv oven

3414	ESCALLOPED APPLES	HOT FRUITS
Recipe No.	Recipe Name	Category

Serving Standards:

10- by 12- by 4-in.	44	3 oz	No. 12 Scoop	Hot
Pan	Portions/Pan	Portion Size	Utensil	Temperature

Ingredients	Portions				Procedure
	40	100	200	400	
APPLES, SLI, FNCY, solid pk, 6/10 cs	1.00 can	2.50 can	5.00 can	10.00 can	1. Pour apples into large mixing bowl or small steam kettle.
SUGAR, GRAN, 100 lb	.50 lb	1.25 lb	2.50 lb	5.00 lb	2. Add granulated sugar and first amt of cinnamon to apples and mix well.
CINNAMON, GROUND, 1 lb	.25 tsp	.62 tsp	1.25 tsp	2.50 tsp	
BREAD CRUMBS	.50 lb	1.25 lb	2.50 lb	5.00 lb	3. Combine bread crumbs, brown sugar, second amt of cinnamon and melted margarine.
SUGAR, LIGHT BROWN, 24/1 lb/cs	.25 lb 1.00 oz	.75 lb .50 oz	1.50 lb 1.00 oz	3.00 lb 2.00 oz	4. Fill 10- by 12- by 4-in. counter pans with 1 gal of apples.
CINNAMON, GROUND, 1 lb	.50 tsp	1.25 tsp	2.50 tsp	1.00 tbs 2.00 tsp	5. Top each pan of apples with 2 to 2.5 cup bread crumb mixture.
MARGARINE, SOLID, 1 lb	.25 lb	10.00 oz	1.25 lb	2.50 lb	6. Cook in conv oven at 350°F. for 20 min.

6. Cook in conv oven at 350°F. for 20 min.
Cooking time: 20 min.
Cooking temp: 350°F.
Equipment: conv oven

3416	GLAZED APPLES					HOT FRUITS
Recipe No.	Recipe Name					Category

Serving Standards: 10- by 12- by 4-in. / Pan   Portions/Pan   3.5 oz / Portion Size   No. 12 Scoop / Utensil   Hot / Temperature

Ingredients	Portions				Procedure
	30	90	180	360	
APPLES, SLI, FNCY, solid pk, 6/10 cs	1.00 can	3.00 can	6.00 can	12.00 can	1. Pour apples into steam kettle.
SUGAR, GRAN, 100 lb	.75 lb	2.25 lb	4.50 lb	9.00 lb	2. Combine sugar and cinnamon and add to apples.
CINNAMON, GROUND, 1 lb	.50 tsp	1.50 tsp	1.00 tbs	2.00 tbs	3. Melt margarine, add to apples and combine well.
MARGARINE, SOLID, 1 lb	.25 lb	.75 lb	1.50 lb	3.00 lb	4. Cook in steam kettle approx 20 min. until liquid begins to thicken and apples have a glazed appearance.
					5. When done, pour 1 gal of apple mixture into 10- by 12- by 4-in. counter pans.
					6. To serve use a slightly heaped No. 12 scoop.
					Cooking time: 20 min.
					Equipment: steam kettle

3420	APPLESAUCE					HOT FRUITS
Recipe No.	Recipe Name					Category

Serving Standards: 10- by 12- by 4-in. / Pan   30 / Portions/Pan   3.5 oz / Portion Size   Solid Spoon / Utensil   Cold / Temperature

Ingredients	Portions				Procedure
	30	90	180	360	
APPLESAUCE, FNCY swt, 6/10 can/cs	1.00 can	3.00 can	6.00 can	12.00 can	1. Pour ea can of applesauce into a 10- by 12- by 4-in. counter pan. 2. Serve 3.5 oz with a solid spoon. This is served from the hot counter but is not heated.

3428 Recipe No.	**BROILED APRICOTS** Recipe Name				**HOT FRUITS** Category

Serving Standards: <u>10- by 12- by 4-in.</u> <u>20</u> <u>5 hlv</u> <u>Solid Spoon</u> <u>Hot</u>
Pan Portions/Pan Portion Size Utensil Temperature

Ingredients	Portions				Procedure
	40	120	200	360	
APRICOTS, HLV, FNCY, 6/10 can/cs, 95 ct	2.00 can	6.00 can	10.00 can	18.00 can	1. Drain apricots leaving about 1 cup juice in ea can. 2. Pour 1 can apricots into each 10- by 12- by 4-in. counter pan.
SUGAR, LIGHT BROWN, 24/1 lb/cs	.25 lb	.75 lb	1.25 lb	2.25 lb	3. Sprinkle 2 oz brown sugar (approx .25 cup) over each pan of apricots.
MARGARINE, SOLID, 1 lb	.25 lb	.75 lb	1.25 lb	2.25 lb	4. Melt margarine and pour 2 oz ladle over each pan. 5. Cook in conv oven at 350°F. for 25 min. *Note:* Portion size of 5 hlv is about 2.75 oz. Cooking time: 25 min. Cooking temp: 350°F. Equipment: conv oven

3430   **BROILED PEACHES**   **HOT FRUITS**
Recipe No.   Recipe Name   Category

Serving Standards: **20- by 12- by 2.5-in.**   **18**   **2 hlv**   **Solid Spoon**   **Hot**
                    Pan   Portions/Pan   Portion Size   Utensil   Temperature

Ingredients	Portions				Procedure
	18	**108**	**216**	**540**	
PEACHES, YC, HLVS, FNCY, 35 to 40 ct 6/10 cs	1.00 can	6.00 can	12.00 can	30.00 can	1. Drain peaches leaving about 1 cup of liquid in ea can.
SUGAR, LIGHT BROWN, 24/1 lb/cs	2.00 oz	.75 lb	1.50 lb	3.75 lb	2. Pour 1 can peaches into 20- by 12- by 2.5-in. counter pan. Place ea peach with the seed side up.
MARGARINE, SOLID, 1 lb	2.00 oz	.75 lb	1.50 lb	3.75 lb	3. Sprinkle 2 oz (approx .25 cup) of brown sugar over ea pan.
					4. Pour 2 oz melted margarine over ea pan.
					5. Place in conv oven at 300°F. for approx 25 min.
					6. Remove pans from oven and place in warming unit.
					Cooking time: 25 min.
					Cooking temp: 350°F.
					Equipment: conv oven

3432	CINNAMON PEARS				HOT FRUITS
Recipe No.	Recipe Name				Category

Serving Standards: 20- by 12- by 2.5-in.   18   3 oz   Solid Spoon   Hot

Pan   Portions/Pan   Portion Size   Utensil   Temperature

Ingredients	Portions				Procedure
	36	108	180	360	
PEARS, BARTLETT, HLVS, FNCY, 35 to 40 ct 6/10	2.00 can	6.00 can	10.00 can	20.00 can	1. Drain pears leaving 1 cup juice in ea can. 2. Arrange pear hlvs in 20- by 12- by 2.5-in. counter pan, 1 can per pan.
MARGARINE, SOLID, 1 lb	.25 lb	.75 lb	1.25 lb	2.50 lb	3. Melt margarine and pour 2 oz over pears in ea pan.
SUGAR. GRAN, 100 lb	.25 lb	.75 lb	1.25 lb	2.50 lb	4. Combine sugar and cinnamon and sprinkle 2 oz over buttered pears in ea pan.
CINNAMON, GROUND, 1 lb	1.00 tsp	1.00 tbs	1.00 tbs 2.00 tsp	3.00 tbs 1.00 tsp	5. Cook in conv oven at 350°F. approx 25 min.
CHERRIES, RED MARAS-CHINO, HLVS, FNCY, 6/.5 gal	.75 cup	2.25 cup	3.75 cup	1.00 qt 3.50 cup	6. Garnish ea pear with maraschino cherry half. Cooking time: 25 min. Cooking temp: 350°F. Equipment: conv oven

| | 3434 | **BROILED PINEAPPLE** | | | | **HOT FRUITS** |

3434   **BROILED PINEAPPLE**   **HOT FRUITS**
Recipe No.   Recipe Name   Category

Serving Standards: 10- by 12- by 4-in.   26   2.25 oz   Solid Spoon   Hot
       Pan   Portions/Pan   Portion Size   Utensil   Temperature

Ingredients	26	104	208	520	Procedure
PINEAPPLE, SLI, HAW, FNCY, 52 ct 6/10	1.00 can	4.00 can	8.00 can	20.00 can	1. Drain pineapple and place in 10- by 12- by 4-in. counter pans, 1 can per pan.
MARGARINE, SOLID, 1 lb	2.00 oz	.50 lb	1.00 lb	2.50 lb	2. Melt margarine and pour 2 oz over ea pan of pineapple.
SUGAR, LIGHT BROWN, 24/1 lb/cs	2.00 oz	.50 lb	1.00 lb	2.50 lb	3. Sprinkle 2 oz (.25 cup) brown sugar over ea pan of buttered pineapple.
CHERRIES, RED MARASCHINO, HLVS, FNCY, 6/.5 gal	2.50 cup	2.00 qt / 2.00 cup	1.00 gal / 1.00 qt	3.00 gal / 2.00 cup	4. Cook in conv oven at 350°F. for approx 25 min. 5. Garnish with maraschino cherry halves. 6. Serve 2 slices per serving. Cooking time: 25 min. Cooking temp: 350°F. Equipment: conv oven

Salads

4020	CHEF SALAD BOWL					SALADS—Leafy and Other
Recipe No.	Recipe Name					Category

Serving Standards: _____   _____   _____   _____   Cold_____

| | Pan | Portions/Pan | Portion Size | | Utensil | Temperature |

Ingredients	Portions				Procedure
	100	200	300	400	
HAM, PULLMAN, SIZE 4x4, 6/11 lb	6.25 lb	12.50 lb	18.75 lb	25.00 lb	1. Slice ham into 1 oz slices. Julienne ham and cheese in strips 4 in. long and 1/4 in. wide.
AMERICAN CHEESE, PRE-CUT 6/5 lb	6.25 lb	12.50 lb	18.75 lb	25.00 lb	2. Place eggs in steamer pan and cover with water. Steam in high speed steam cooker 15 min.
EGGS, FRESH, 30 doz/case	8.33 doz	16.66 doz	25.00 doz	33.32 doz	3. Peel eggs and cut into quarters.
					4. Wash tomatoes and cut into quarters.
TOMATOES, FNCY, 38 lb	33.00 lb	66.00 lb	99.00 lb	132.00 lb	5. Wash lettuce. Save all usable outside leaves. Cut heads into quarters and chop by hand, on slicer, or on automatic cutter into bite-size pieces.
LETTUCE, HEAD, FNCY Iceberg, 24 hd/crt	1.00 doz 8.00 ea	3.00 doz 4.00 ea	5.00 doz	6.00 doz 8.00 ea	6. Place 2.5 cups or 5 oz of chopped lettuce into salad bowl.
					7. Cover lettuce with 1 oz ham, 1 oz cheese, 1 egg quartered and 1 tomato quartered.

4025	COLE SLAW				SALADS—Leafy and Other
Recipe No.	Recipe Name				Category

Serving Standards: _____ _____ 2.25 oz | No. 16 Scoop | Cold

| Pan | Portions/Pan | Portion Size | Utensil | Temperature |

Ingredients	Portions				Procedure
	50	100	200	400	
Yield	3.50 qt	7.00 qt	3.50 gal	7.00 gal	
CABBAGE, GREEN, FNCY, 50 lb	10.00 lb	20.00 lb	40.00 lb	80.00 lb	1. Trim and wash cabbage. Weight is AP.
VINEGAR, COLORED, DIST, 4/1 gal/cs	3.00 tbs .75 tsp	.25 cup 2.00 tbs 1.50 tsp	.75 cup 1.00 tbs	1.50 cup 2.00 tbs	2. Chop cabbage on chopper. 3. Rehydrate green peppers in amt water specified. 4. Combine all ingredients and mix well.
SALAD DRESSING, 4/1 gal/cs	.75 cup	1.50 cup	3.00 cup	1.00 qt 2.00 cup	5. Serve into serving dishes with No. 16 scoop.
MAYONNAISE, 4/1 gal/cs	.75 cup	1.50 cup	3.00 cup	1.00 qt 2.00 cup	
SUGAR, GRAN, 100 lb	2.00 oz	.25 lb	.50 lb	1.00 lb	
SALT, 100 lb bag	1.00 tbs 1.50 tsp	3.00 tbs	.25 cup 2.00 tbs	.75 cup	
PEPPERS, DEHYD DICED, GRN, 1.25 lb XSTD 6/10	.50 oz	1.00 oz	2.00 oz	.25 lb	
WATER, cold	.25 cup	.50 cup	1.00 cup	2.00 cup	

4030	COMBINATION SALAD				SALADS—Leafy and Other
Recipe No.	Recipe Name				Category

Serving Standards:

Pan	Portions/Pan	2.25 oz	No. 12 Scoop	Cold
		Portion Size	Utensil	Temperature

Ingredients	Portions				Procedure
	54	108	216	864	
CABBAGE, GREEN, FNCY, 50 lb	8.75 lb	17.50 lb	35.00 lb	140.00 lb	1. Trim and wash cabbage and carrots. Weight is AP.
CARROTS, FNCY BULK, 50 lb, no tops	1.25 lb	2.50 lb	5.00 lb	20.00 lb	2. Shred cabbage and carrots. 3. Trim green peppers, wash and dice.
PEPPERS, GREEN, FNCY, 25 lb	1.25 lb	2.50 lb	5.00 lb	20.00 lb	4. Combine all ingredients and mix lightly. 5. Serve with a No. 12 scoop.
SALT, 100 lb bag	1.50 tsp	1.00 tbs	2.00 tbs	.50 cup	
SALAD DRESSING, 4/1 gal/cs	.50 cup	1.00 cup	2.00 cup	2.00 qt	
MAYONNAISE, 4/1 gal/cs	.50 cup	1.00 cup	2.00 cup	2.00 qt	

4035　　**FIESTA SALAD BOWL**　　　　　　　　　　　　**SALADS—Leafy and Other**

Recipe No.	Recipe Name				Category

Serving Standards: _____　　　　　　　**3 oz**　　　　　　　**Cold**

	Pan	Portions/Pan	Portion Size	Utensil	Temperature

Ingredients	Portions				Procedure
	62	124	248	496	
TOMATOES, FNCY, 38 lb	1.75 lb	3.50 lb	7.00 lb	14.00 lb	1. Wash tomatoes, trim and cut into .5 oz wedges. Weight is AP.
CUCUMBERS, FRESH, FNCY, 48 lb/bsh	1.50 lb	3.00 lb	6.00 lb	12.00 lb	2. Wash and slice cucumbers. Weight is AP.
LETTUCE, HEAD, FNCY, Iceberg, 24 hd/crt	.25 crt	.50 crt	1.00 crt	2.00 crt	3. Wash, peel and slice onions into rings. 4. Wash and slice lettuce on slicer—No. 45.
CELERY, FRESH, GRN, FNCY, pascal, bun	1.50 lb	3.00 lb	6.00 lb	12.00 lb	5. If usable, chop celery leaves. 6. Chop celery and slice radishes. Celery is EP weight.
ONIONS, RED, FNCY, med, 25 lb	.50 lb	1.00 lb	2.00 lb	4.00 lb	7. Toss vegetable mixture together with lettuce. Equipment: mixing bowl
RADISHES, FNCY CELLO, pk 6 oz	1.00 cel	2.00 cel	4.00 cel	8.00 cel	

4036	**GARDEN SALAD BOWL**				**SALADS–Leafy and Other**
Recipe No.	Recipe Name				Category

Serving Standards:

		3 oz		**Cold**
Pan	Portions/Pan	Portion Size	Utensil	Temperature

Ingredients	Portions				Procedure
	55	**110**	**220**	**440**	
CARROTS, FNCY BULK, 50 lb, no tops	.50 lb	1.00 lb	2.00 lb	4.00 lb	1. Trim and wash carrots, cucumbers and radishes. Weights are AP.
CUCUMBERS, FRESH, FNCY, 48 lb/bsh	1.50 lb	3.00 lb	6.00 lb	12.00 lb	2. Slice thinly the carrots, cucumbers and radishes.
RADISHES, FNCY CELLO, pk 6 oz	1.00 cel	2.00 cel	4.00 cel	8.00 cel	3. Peel the red onions (weight is AP) and slice into thin circles.
ONIONS, RED, FNCY, med, 25 lb	.50 lb	1.00 lb	2.00 lb	4.00 lb	4. Wash celery and save all usable leaves. Weight is EP. Thinly slice celery with leaves.
CELERY, FRESH, GRN, FNCY, pascal, bun	1.50 lb	3.00 lb	6.00 lb	12.00 lb	5. Remove unusable leaves and core from lettuce. 6. Wash lettuce and slice on No. 45 on slicer.
LETTUCE, HEAD, FNCY, Iceberg, 24 hd/crt	.25 crt	.50 crt	1.00 crt	2.00 crt	7. Serve as instructed.

4040	GREEN BEAN SALAD				SALADS—Leafy and Other
Recipe No.	Recipe Name				Category

Serving Standards:

	Pan	Portions/Pan	3 oz Portion Size	No. 12 Scoop Utensil	Cold Temperature

Ingredients	Portions				E*	Procedure
	80	**160**	**240**	**400**		
Yield	2.00 gal	4.00 gal	6.00 gal	10.00 gal		
BEANS, GRN, ct sv5, bl dw 60 oz XSTD 6/10	1.00 can	2.00 can	3.00 can	5.00 can		1. Drain all beans thoroughly. 2. Combine green peppers, onions, sugar, vinegar, salad oil, salt and pepper and pour over beans. Mix well but do not break up beans.
BEANS, CUT, WAX, FNCY, 6/10	1.00 can	2.00 can	3.00 can	5.00 can		
BEANS, KID DK RD, FNCY, dr wt 70 oz 6/10	1.00 can	2.00 can	3.00 can	5.00 can		3. Marinate overnight. 4. Serve with No. 12 scoop in small serving dishes. Do not drain but serve liquid also.
PEPPERS, DEHYD DICED, GRN, XSTD 6/10	1.00 oz	2.00 oz	3.00 oz	5.00 oz		*Early Prep: Prepare 1 day in advance and marinate in refrigerator.
ONIONS, DEHYD CHOP, 2.5 lb XSTD 6/10	.75 oz	1.50 oz	2.25 oz	3.75 oz		
SUGAR, GRAN, 100 lb	2.00 lb	4.00 lb	6.00 lb	10.00 lb		
VINEGAR, COLORED, DIST, 4/1 gal/cs	1.00 qt	2.00 qt	3.00 qt	1.00 gal 1.00 qt		
OIL, SALAD, 6 gal/cs	2.00 cup	1.00 qt	1.00 qt 2.00 cup	2.00 qt 2.00 cup		
SALT, 100 lb bag	2.00 tbs	.25 cup	.25 cup 2.00 tbs	.50 cup 2.00 tbs		
PEPPER, BLACK, GROUND, 6 lb	2.00 tbs	.25 cup	.25 cup 2.00 tbs	.50 cup 2.00 tbs		

4051	GARNISH, LEAF LETTUCE				SALADS—Leafy and Other
Recipe No.	Recipe Name				Category

Serving Standards: _____ _____ _____ _____ _____

Pan | Portions/Pan | Portion Size | Utensil | Temperature

Ingredients	Portions				Procedure
	20	80	200	400	
LETTUCE, LEAF, FNCY	.50 lb	2.00 lb	5.00 lb	10.00 lb	1. Separate lettuce leaves from core. 2. Wash leaves well. 3. Line serving dishes with lettuce.

4052	GARNISH, HEAD LETTUCE				SALADS—Leafy and Other
Recipe No.	Recipe Name				Category

Serving Standards: _____ _____ _____ _____ _____

Pan | Portions/Pan | Portion Size | Utensil | Temperature

Ingredients	Portions				Procedure
	35	105	210	560	
LETTUCE, HEAD, FNCY Iceberg, 24 hd/crt	.50 ea	1.50 ea	3.00 ea	8.00 ea	1. Trim and wash lettuce. 2. Tear leaves into pieces as liners for serving dishes.

4055	TOSSED SALAD				SALADS—Leafy and Other
Recipe No.	Recipe Name				Category

Serving Standards:

Pan	Portions/Pan	3 oz Portion Size	Utensil	Cold Temperature

Ingredients	Portions				Procedure
	70	**140**	**280**	**560**	
LETTUCE, HEAD, FNCY Iceberg, 24 hd/crt	.50 crt	1.00 crt	2.00 crt	4.00 crt	1. Remove outer leaves of lettuce and core. 2. Wash lettuce and drain well.
CARROTS, FNCY BULK, 50 lb, no tops	1.00 lb	2.00 lb	4.00 lb	8.00 lb	3. Slice on No. 45 slicer. 4. Trim and wash radishes and carrots. Weight is AP.
RADISHES, FNCY CELLO, pk 6 oz	1.00 cel	2.00 cel	4.00 cel	8.00 cel	5. Slice radishes and carrots thin with slicer attach- ment on chopper.
CABBAGE, RED OR PURPLE, FNCY, 25 lb	.50 lb	1.00 lb	2.00 lb	4.00 lb	6. Trim and wash red cabbage. Weight is AP. 7. Slice with slicer attachment on chopper. 8. If serving in large bowls, fill in layers of lettuce and vegetables. In each bowl use approx 17 lb let- tuce and 1.5 lb other vegetables.

4065	TOSSED LETTUCE WITH CARROTS				SALADS—Leafy and Other
Recipe No.	Recipe Name				Category

Serving Standards: _____   _____   __3 oz__   _____   __Cold__
            Pan   Portions/Pan   Portion Size   Utensil   Temperature

Ingredients	Portions				Procedure
	70	140	280	560	
LETTUCE, HEAD, FNCY Iceberg, 24 hd/crt	.50 crt	1.00 crt	2.00 crt	4.00 crt	1. Remove outer leaves of lettuce and core. 2. Wash lettuce and drain well. 3. Slice on No. 45 slicer.
CARROTS, FNCY BULK, 50 lb, no tops	2.00 lb	4.00 lb	8.00 lb	16.00 lb	4. Wash carrots and trim ends. Weight is AP. 5. Slice carrots thin with slicer attachment on chopper. 6. If serving in large bowls, fill with layers of lettuce and sliced carrots. *Note:* French knife could be used instead of slicer.

4070	TOSSED LETTUCE WITH CELERY				SALADS—Leafy and Other
Recipe No.	Recipe Name				Category

Serving Standards: _____   _____   __3 oz__   __Tongs__   __Cold__
            Pan   Portions/Pan   Portion Size   Utensil   Temperature

Ingredients	Portions				Procedure
	70	140	280	560	
LETTUCE, HEAD, FNCY Iceberg, 24 hd/crt	.50 crt	1.00 crt	2.00 crt	4.00 crt	1. Remove outer leaves of lettuce and core. 2. Wash lettuce and drain well. 3. Slice on No. 45 slicer.
CELERY, FRESH, GRN, FNCY, pascal, bun	2.00 lb	4.00 lb	8.00 lb	16.00 lb	4. Wash celery. Cut off unusable parts. Weight is AP. 5. Slice celery thin with slicer attachment on chopper. 6. If serving in large bowls, fill with layers of lettuce and celery.

4080						SALADS—Leafy and Other
Recipe No.	Recipe Name					Category

TOSSED LETTUCE WITH GREEN ONIONS

Serving Standards:

			3 oz		Cold
Pan	Portions/Pan		Portion Size	Utensil	Temperature

	Portions				Procedure
Ingredients	70	140	280	560	
LETTUCE, HEAD, FNCY Iceberg, 24 hd/crt	.50 crt	1.00 crt	2.00 crt	4.00 crt	1. Remove outer leaves of lettuce and core. 2. Wash lettuce and drain well. 3. Slice on No. 45 slicer.
ONIONS, SCALLIONS, FNCY, bu	1.00 lb	2.00 lb	4.00 lb	8.00 lb	4. Wash and trim onions, saving the green tops. Weight is AP. 5. Chop onions with French knife. 6. If serving in large bowls, fill with layers of lettuce and chopped onion.

4140						SALADS—Leafy and Other
Recipe No.	Recipe Name					Category

POTATO SALAD

Serving Standards:

			3.25 oz	No. 12 Scoop	Cold
Pan	Portions/Pan		Portion Size	Utensil	Temperature

	Portions				Procedure
Ingredients	16	48	192	384	
POTATO SALAD, MAYON- NAISE STYLE, 12/50 oz	1.00 can	3.00 can	12.00 can	24.00 can	1. Portion salad with a No. 12 scoop onto serving dish, lined with a lettuce leaf. Suggested garnishes: paprika, olives, pickles or pimento.

4145	**RELISH PLATTER**				**SALADS**—Leafy and Other
Recipe No.	Recipe Name				Category

Serving Standards: _____   _____   _____   _____   Cold

| | Pan | Portions/Pan | Portion Size | Utensil | Temperature |

Ingredients	Portions				Procedure
	50	300	600	1200	
CARROTS, FNCY BULK, 50 lb, no tops	1.00 lb	6.00 lb	12.00 lb	24.00 lb	1. Wash carrots and trim ends; cut into sticks 3 in. long.
OLIVES, STUFFED, 340 to 360 ct, 4/1 gal	2.66 cup	1.00 gal	2.00 gal	4.00 gal	2. Wash and trim radishes and make into rose radishes.
PICKLES, MIXED, 4/1 gal/cs	2.66 cup	1.00 gal	2.00 gal	4.00 gal	3. Place carrot sticks and rose radishes in ice water until crisp.
RADISHES, FNCY CELLO, pk 6 oz	1.50 cel	9.00 cel	18.00 cel	36.00 cel	4. Drain all items and arrange on platter for self-service.
					5. Or assemble a few of each item on lettuce-lined dish for individual service.

4165	SLICED TOMATOES WITH LETTUCE, GARNISH				SALADS—Leafy and Other
Recipe No.	Recipe Name				Category

Serving Standards: _____ _____ __1 sli__ _____ __Cold__
  Pan Portions/Pan Portion Size Utensil Temperature

Ingredients	Portions				Procedure
	48	192	384	960	
Yield	4.00 doz	16.00 doz	32.00 doz	80.00 doz	
LETTUCE, HEAD, FNCY Iceberg, 24 hd/crt	1.00 ea	4.00 ea	8.00 ea	1.00 doz 8.00 ea	1. Clean and shred lettuce on No. 13 automatic slicer.
TOMATOES, FNCY, 38 lb	2.50 lb	10.00 lb	20.00 lb	50.00 lb	2. Wash tomatoes and slice with slicer set on No. 13 automatic. Weight of tomatoes is AP.
					3. Place lettuce in large bowl and tomatoes on trays for service. Garnish tray of tomatoes with leaves of lettuce.

4205	STUFFED CELERY				SALADS—Protein
Recipe No.	Recipe Name				Category

Serving Standards:

Pan	Portions/Pan	3 ea Portion Size	Utensil	Cold Temperature

Ingredients	Portions				Procedure
	19	38	76	114	
CHEDDAR CHEESE, WHEEL	.75 lb	1.50 lb	3.00 lb	4.50 lb	1. Grate cheese.
PIMENTOS, BROKEN PIECES, STD 24/2.5	.25 cup 2.00 tbs	.75 cup	1.50 cup	2.25 cup	2. Chop pimentos and add to cheese along with salt, sugar and Worcestershire sauce. Mix until well blended. Do not mix in chopper.
SALT, 100 lb bag	.12 tsp	.25 tsp	.50 tsp	.75 tsp	3. Add salad dressing and mix.
WORCESTERSHIRE SAUCE, 4/1 gal/cs	.75 tsp	1.50 tsp	1.00 tbs	1.00 tbs 1.50 tsp	4. Place cheese mixture in pastry bag. 5. Trim and wash celery. Weight is EP.
SUGAR, GRAN, 100 lb	.75 tsp	1.50 tsp	1.00 tbs	1.00 tbs 1.50 tsp	6. Cut celery 2.5 in. long. 7. Fill celery sticks with pimento cheese.
SALAD DRESSING, 4/1 gal/cs	.50 cup	1.00 cup	2.00 cup	3.00 cup	8. Serve 3 stuffed sticks on crisp lettuce leaf.
CELERY, FRESH, GRN, FNCY, pascal, bun	1.00 lb	2.00 lb	4.00 lb	6.00 lb	*Note:* 3 stuffed celery sticks weigh 2.25 oz. Cheese mix is approx 1 oz and celery is approx 1.25 oz.

4210	COTTAGE CHEESE				SALADS—Protein
Recipe No.	Recipe Name				Category

Serving Standards:

Pan	Portions/Pan	3 oz Portion Size	No. 12 Scoop Utensil	Cold Temperature

Ingredients	Portions				Procedure
	26	130	260	520	
COTTAGE CHEESE, 25 lb bag in box	5.00 lb	25.00 lb	50.00 lb	100.00 lb	1. Place No. 12 scoop of cottage cheese on serving dish, lined with lettuce. 2. Garnish appropriately

4220	DEVILED EGG SALAD				SALADS—Protein
Recipe No.	Recipe Name				Category

Serving Standards: _____ Pan _____ Portions/Pan __2 hlv__ Portion Size _____ Utensil __Cold__ Temperature

Ingredients	Portions				Procedure
	30	60	240	360	
EGGS, FRESH, 30 doz/case	2.50 doz	5.00 doz	20.00 doz	30.00 doz	1. Hard cook eggs in steamer.
SALAD DRESSING,	.75 cup	1.50 cup	1.00 qt	2.00 qt	2. Remove shell and cut eggs in half lengthwise.
4/1 gal/cs			2.00 cup	1.00 cup	3. Place yolks in bowl with remaining ingredients.
VINEGAR, COLORED,	2.00 tbs	.25 cup	1.00 cup	1.50 cup	Blend until smooth.
DIST, 4/1 gal/cs					4. Use decorator's tube to fill egg white halves.
SALT, 100 lb bag	1.00 tsp	2.00 tsp	2.00 tbs	.25 cup	5. Serve 2 egg halves on a lettuce leaf.
			2.00 tsp		6. Garnish with paprika or freshly chopped parsley.
PAPRIKA, GROUND,	.50 tsp	1.00 tsp	1.00 tbs	2.00 tbs	*Note:* Weight of 2 halves stuffed is 2 oz.
6 lb			1.00 tsp		
PARSLEY, DEHYD FLK,	2.25 tsp	1.00 tbs	.25 cup	.50 cup	
XSTD 6/10		1.50 tsp	2.00 tbs	1.00 tbs	
MUSTARD, PURE,	2.00 tsp	1.00 tbs	.25 cup	.50 cup	
4/1 gal/cs		1.00 tsp	1.00 tbs		
			1.00 tsp		
WORCESTERSHIRE SAUCE,	1.00 tsp	2.00 tsp	2.00 tbs	.25 cup	
4/1 gal/cs			2.00 tsp		
HOT SAUCE, 4/gal/cs	.25 tsp	.50 tsp	2.00 tsp	1.00 tbs	
RELISH, RED AND	.50 cup	1.00 cup	1.00 qt	1.00 qt	
GREEN, 4/1 gal/cs				2.00 cup	

4225	HARD-COOKED EGGS				SALADS—Protein
Recipe No.	Recipe Name				Category

Serving Standards:

		1 ea		
Pan	Portions/Pan	Portion Size	Utensil	Temperature

Ingredients	Portions				Procedure
	12	120	360	1080	
EGGS, FRESH, 30 doz/case	1.00 doz	10.00 doz	30.00 doz	60.00 doz 8.00 ea	1. Place eggs in steam kettle and cover with warm water. 2. Bring water to boil and simmer until eggs are hard cooked, about 14 min. Be careful not to overcook the eggs. 3. For cold eggs, cool with ice water. 4. Serve or use as directed. Cooking time: about 14 min. Equipment: steam kettle

4235	MACARONI SALAD				SALADS—Protein

Recipe No.   Recipe Name   Category

Serving Standards: _____ _____ 3 oz No. 12 Scoop Cool

Pan   Portions/Pan   Portion Size   Utensil   Temperature

| Ingredients | Portions | | | | E* Procedure |
	50	100	200	500	
Yield	4.68 qt	9.36 qt	4.68 gal	11.70 gal	
ONIONS, DEHYD CHOP, 2.5 lb XSTD 6/10	.50 oz	1.00 oz	2.00 oz	5.00 oz	1. Rehydrate onions and green peppers in first amt of water for 20 min. Add ice for more crispness. Drain.
PEPPERS, DEHYD DICED, GRN, 1.25 lb XSTD 6/10	.50 oz	1.00 oz	2.00 oz	5.00 oz	2. Cook macaroni in boiling, salted water for about 20 to 25 min. Drain and rinse. Cool
WATER, cold	1.00 cup	2.00 cup	1.00 qt	2.00 qt 2.00 cup	3. Chop parsley and celery. Celery is EP.
ICE, crushed	.25 lb	.50 lb	1.00 lb	2.50 lb	4. Cube cheese to 0.25 in.
MACARONI, ELBOW, 20 lb box	1.75 lb	3.50 lb	7.00 lb	17.50 lb	5. Combine all ingredients except pimento. Mix lightly.
PARSLEY, FNCY, bunch	2.00 tbs	.25 cup	.50 cup	1.25 cup	6. Portion with a No. 12 scoop and place on lettuce.
CELERY, FRESH, GRN, FNCY, pascal, bun	1.25 lb	2.50 lb	5.00 lb	12.50 lb	7. Cut pimentos into 15 to 16 strips. Garnish ea portion with 1 strip of pimento.
CHEDDAR CHEESE, WHEEL	.50 lb	1.00 lb	2.00 lb	5.00 lb	8. Refrigerate.
SALAD DRESSING, 4/1 gal/cs	2.25 cup	1.00 qt .50 cup	2.00 qt 1.00 cup	1.00 gal 1.00 qt 2.50 cup	*Early Prep: Cook macaroni several hr ahead and cool in refrigerator. It may be cooked 1 day in advance.
SALT, 100 lb bag	.25 oz	.50 oz	1.00 oz	2.50 oz	
RELISH, RED AND GREEN, 4/1 gal/cs	.50 cup	1.00 cup	2.00 cup	1.00 qt 1.00 cup	
PIMENTOS, BROKEN PIECES, STD, 24/2.5	.25 can	.50 can	1.00 can	2.50 can	

4240	CHICKEN SALAD				SALADS—Protein
Recipe No.	Recipe Name				Category

Serving Standards:

Pan	Portions/Pan	3.25 oz Portion Size	No. 12 Scoop Utensil	Cold Temperature

Ingredients	Portions				Procedure
	30	120	240	480	
Yield	3.00 qt	3.00 gal	6.00 gal	12.00 gal	
EGGS, FRESH, 30 doz/case	1.00 doz	4.00 doz	8.00 doz	16.00 doz	1. Hard cook eggs in steamer. Cool, peel and dice.
CHICKEN, BONED, WHL, FNCY, 12/50 oz can	1.00 can	4.00 can	8.00 can	16.00 can	2. Drain chicken and chop in chopper.
CELERY, FRESH, GRN, FNCY, pascal, bun	1.25 lb	5.00 lb	10.00 lb	20.00 lb	3. Chop celery in chopper. Weight is EP. 4. Combine all ingredients, mixing lightly.
LEMON JUICE, RECONSTI-TUTED, 12/qt jars	2.00 tbs	.50 cup	1.00 cup	2.00 cup	5. If serving on a cold plate, use a No. 12 scoop.
RELISH, RED AND GREEN, 4/1 gal/cs	1.00 cup	1.00 qt	2.00 qt	1.00 gal	*Note:* Dr wt 1 can chicken is approx 2.5 lb.
MAYONNAISE, 4/1 gal/cs	1.50 cup	1.00 qt 2.00 cup	3.00 qt	1.00 gal 2.00 qt	
SALT, 100 lb bag	1.50 tsp	2.00 tbs	.25 cup	.50 cup	

4245	T.V.P. CHICKEN SALAD				SALADS–Protein
Recipe No.	Recipe Name				Category

Serving Standards: _____   _____   __3.25 oz__   __No. 12 Scoop__   __Cold__

Pan   Portions/Pan   Portion Size   Utensil   Temperature

Ingredients	Portions				Procedure
	30	120	240	480	
EGGS, FRESH, 30 doz/case	1.00 doz	4.00 doz	8.00 doz	16.00 doz	1. Hard cook eggs in steamer. Place in cold water. Peel and chop into .5 in. pieces.
CHICKEN, T.V.P. DICE,	2.50 lb	10.00 lb	20.00 lb	40.00 lb	
3/5 lb box/cs					2. Place frozen T.V.P. chicken in chopper and chop coarsely or chop with French knife.
CELERY, FRESH, GRN,	1.25 lb	5.00 lb	10.00 lb	20.00 lb	
FNCY, pascal, bun					3. Chop celery in chopper not too fine. Weight of celery is EP.
LEMON JUICE, RECONSTI-	2.00 tbs	.50 cup	1.00 cup	2.00 cup	
TUTED, 12/qt jars					4. Pour lemon juice over T.V.P. chicken.
ONIONS, DEHYD CHOP,	1.00 tbs	.25 cup	.50 cup	1.25 cup	5. Rehydrate onions with water; drain well.
2.5 lb XSTD 6/10	1.00 tsp	1.00 tbs	2.00 tbs	1.00 tbs	6. Drain pickle relish and combine all ingredients and mix lightly.
		1.00 tsp	2.00 tsp	1.00 tsp	
WATER, cold	1.00 tbs	.25 cup	.75 cup	1.50 cup	7. Serve on lettuce leaf.
	1.50 tsp	2.00 tbs			
RELISH, RED AND	1.00 cup	1.00 qt	2.00 qt	1.00 gal	
GREEN, 4/1 gal/cs					
MAYONNAISE, 4/1 gal/cs	1.25 cup	1.00 qt	2.00 qt	1.00 gal	
		1.00 cup	2.00 cup	1.00 qt	
SALT, 100 lb bag	1.25 tsp	3.00 tbs	.25 cup	.75 cup	
			2.00 tbs		
PEPPER, WHITE, GROUND,	.06 tsp	.25 tsp	.50 tsp	1.00 tsp	
1 lb					

4250	HAM SALAD					SALADS—Protein
Recipe No.	Recipe Name					Category

Serving Standards:

	3.25 oz	No. 12 Scoop	Cold·
Pan	Portions/Pan	Portion Size	Utensil	Temperature

Ingredients	Portions				Procedure
	30	**120**	**240**	**360**	
EGGS, FRESH, 30 doz/case	1.00 doz	4.00 doz	8.00 doz	12.00 doz	1. Hard cook eggs in steamer. Cool, peel and dice.
HAM, PULLMAN, SIZE 4x4, 6/11 lb	2.50 lb	10.00 lb	20.00 lb	30.00 lb	2. Chop ham in chopper, not too fine.
CELERY, FRESH, GRN, FNCY, pascal, bun	1.25 lb	5.00 lb	10.00 lb	15.00 lb	3. Trim and wash celery and chop in chopper, not too fine. Weight is EP.
PARSLEY, FNCY bunch	2.00 tbs	.50 cup	1.00 cup	1.50 cup	4. Chop parsley, then measure.
RELISH, RED AND GREEN, 4/1 gal/cs	1.00 cup	1.00 qt	2.00 qt	3.00 qt	5. Combine eggs, ham, celery, parsley, relish and salad dressing. Mix lightly.
SALAD DRESSING, 4/1 gal/cs	1.50 cup	1.00 qt 2.00 cup	3.00 qt	1.00 gal 2.00 cup	6. Serve a No. 12 scoop of mix on crisp lettuce leaf.

4255	MEAT SALAD				SALADS—Protein
Recipe No.	Recipe Name				Category

Serving Standards:

		3.25 oz	No. 12 Scoop	Cold
Pan	Portions/Pan	Portion Size	Utensil	Temperature

Ingredients	Portions				Procedure
	60	120	240	360	
EGGS, FRESH, 30 doz/case	2.00 doz	4.00 doz	8.00 doz	12.00 doz	1. Hard cook eggs in steamer. Peel and dice.
ONIONS, DEHYD CHOP,	2.50 tsp	1.00 tbs	3.00 tbs	.25 cup	2. Rehydrate onions in water.
2.5 lb XSTD 6/10		2.00 tsp	1.00 tsp	1.00 tbs	3. Chop meat in chopper.
WATER, cold	1.00 tbs	2.00 tbs	.25 cup	.25 cup	4. Trim and wash celery, dice in .33 in. pieces.
				2.00 tbs	5. Chop parsley fine.
COOKED ROAST BEEF,	5.00 lb	10.00 lb	20.00 lb	30.00 lb	6. Combine all ingredients and mix lightly.
Recipe 1145					7. If serving on a cold plate, use a No. 12 scoop.
CELERY, FRESH, GRN,	2.50 lb	5.00 lb	10.00 lb	15.00 lb	
FNCY, pascal, bun					
PARSLEY, FNCY bunch	.25 cup	.50 cup	1.00 cup	1.50 cup	
RELISH, RED AND GREEN,	2.00 cup	1.00 qt	2.00 qt	3.00 qt	
4/1 gal/cs					
SALAD DRESSING,	3.00 cup	1.00 qt	3.00 qt	1.00 gal	
4/1 gal/cs		2.00 cup		2.00 cup	
SALT, 100 lb bag	1.00 tbs	2.00 tbs	.25 cup	.25 cup	
				2.00 tbs	
PEPPER, WHITE, GROUND,	.12 tsp	.25 tsp	.50 tsp	.75 tsp	
1 lb					

4270	TUNA FISH SALAD				SALADS—Protein
Recipe No.	Recipe Name				Category

Serving Standards:

Pan	Portions/Pan	3.25 oz Portion Size	No. 12 Scoop Utensil	Cold Temperature

Ingredients	Portions				Procedure
	40	**120**	**240**	**520**	
Yield	1.00 gal	3.00 gal	6.00 gal	13.00 gal	
EGGS, FRESH, 30 doz/case	1.00 doz	3.00 doz	6.00 doz	13.00 doz	1. Hard cook eggs in high speed steam cooker, cool, peel and chop into 0.5 in. pieces.
ONIONS, DEHYD CHOP,	1.50 tsp	1.00 tbs	3.00 tbs	.25 cup	
2.5 lb XSTD 6/10		1.50 tsp		2.00 tbs	2. Rehydrate onions in water for 20 min.
				1.50 tsp	3. Drain tuna and break into large pieces.
WATER, cold	2.00 tsp	2.00 tbs	.25 cup	.50 cup	4. Add lemon juice to tuna.
				2.00 tsp	5. Chop celery in chopper but not too fine. Weight
TUNA, LIGHT,	1.00 can	3.00 can	6.00 can	13.00 can	is EP.
6/66.5 cans/cs					6. Combine all ingredients by tossing lightly.
CELERY, FRESH, GRN,	2.00 lb	6.00 lb	12.00 lb	26.00 lb	7. Using a No. 12 scoop, serve on lettuce.
FNCY, pascal, bun					
RELISH, RED AND GREEN,	1.00 cup	3.00 cup	1.00 qt	3.00 qt	
4/1 gal/cs			2.00 cup	1.00 cup	
LEMON JUICE, RECONSTI-	.25 cup	.75 cup	1.50 cup	3.25 cup	
TUTED, 12/qt jars					
SALAD DRESSING,	1.75 cup	1.00 qt	2.00 qt	1.00 gal	
4/1 gal/cs		1.25 cup	2.50 cup	1.00 qt	
				2.75 cup	
SALT, 100 lb bag	.50 oz	1.50 oz	3.00 oz	6.50 oz	
PEPPER, WHITE, GROUND,	.08 tsp	.25 tsp	.50 tsp	1.00 tsp	
1 lb					

| 4275 | TURKEY SALAD | | | | SALADS–Protein |
| Recipe No. | Recipe Name | | | | Category |

Serving Standards: _____   _____   __3.25 oz__   __No. 12 Scoop__   __Cold__

Pan   Portions/Pan   Portion Size   Utensil   Temperature

| Ingredients | Portions | | | | Procedure |
	30	120	240	480	
EGGS, FRESH, 30 doz/case	1.00 doz	4.00 doz	8.00 doz	16.00 doz	1. Hard cook eggs in steamer. Cool, peel and dice.
TURKEY, ROLL, WHITE, grade A, 9 lb	1.25 lb	5.00 lb	10.00 lb	20.00 lb	2. Chop turkey in chopper, not too fine.
TURKEY, ROLL, DARK, grade A, 9 lb	1.25 lb	5.00 lb	10.00 lb	20.00 lb	3. Trim and wash celery. Chop in chopper. Weight is EP.
CELERY, FRESH, GRN, FNCY, pascal, bun	1.25 lb	5.00 lb	10.00 lb	20.00 lb	4. Pour lemon juice over turkey. 5. Combine all ingredients by mixing lightly.
LEMON JUICE, RECONSTI-TUTED, 12/qt jars	2.00 tbs	.50 cup	1.00 cup	2.00 cup	6. If serving on a cold plate, use a No. 12 scoop.
RELISH, RED AND GREEN, 4/1 gal/cs	1.00 cup	1.00 qt	2.00 qt	1.00 gal	
MAYONNAISE, 4/1 gal/cs	1.50 cup	1.00 qt 2.00 cup	3.00 qt	1.00 gal 2.00 qt	
SALT, 100 lb bag	1.50 tsp	2.00 tbs	.25 cup	.50 cup	

4305		AMBROSIA				SALADS—Fruits
Recipe No.		**Recipe Name**				**Category**

Serving Standards: _____

	Pan	Portions/Pan	3 oz Portion Size	No. 12 Scoop Utensil	Cold Temperature

Ingredients	Portions				Procedure
	64	128	256	512	
ORANGE SEC, FNCY, 4/1 gal	1.00 gal	2.00 gal	4.00 gal	8.00 gal	1. Drain orange and grapefruit sections.
GRAPEFRUIT SEC, FNCY,	1.00 gal	2.00 gal	4.00 gal	8.00 gal	2. Combine orange and grapefruit sections and coco-
4/1 gal					nut. Mix well.
COCONUT, DRY, 10 lb box	.50 lb	1.00 lb	2.00 lb	4.00 lb	3. Place a No. 12 scoop of fruit mixture on lettuce.
CHERRIES, RED MARAS-	.50 cup	1.00 cup	2.00 cup	1.00 qt	4. Garnish with maraschino cherry.
CHINO, HLVS, FNCY,					
6/.5 gal					

4310		APPLE WEDGES WITH FRUIT COCKTAIL				SALADS—Fruits
Recipe No.		**Recipe Name**				**Category**

Serving Standards: _____

	Pan	Portions/Pan	3 oz Portion Size	No. 30 Scoop Utensil	Cold Temperature

Ingredients	Portions				Procedure
	50	100	500	1000	
APPLES, WINESAP	5.50 lb	11.00 lb	55.00 lb	110.00 lb	1. Wash apples.
FRUIT COCKTAIL, FNCY,	1.00 can	2.00 can	10.00 can	20.00 can	2. Cut in fourths and core.
6/10					3. Cut fourths of apples in half lengthwise.
CHERRIES, RED MARAS-	.50 cup	1.00 cup	1.00 qt	2.00 qt	4. Put apples in orange juice to keep from turning
CHINO, HLVS, FNCY,			1.00 cup	2.00 cup	dark.
6/.5 gal					5. Assemble 3 apple wedges and a No. 30 scoop of
					fruit cocktail on lettuce.
					6. Garnish with maraschino cherry half.

	Recipe No.	Recipe Name				Category
4311		**APPLE WEDGE WITH GRAPEFRUIT**				**SALADS—Fruits**

Serving Standards: _____ Pan _____ Portions/Pan __3 oz__ Portion Size _____ Utensil __Cold__ Temperature

Ingredients	Portions				Procedure
	56	112	224	448	
GRAPEFRUIT SEC, FNCY, 4/1 gal	1.00 gal	2.00 gal	4.00 gal	8.00 gal	1. Drain grapefruit sections and save juice.
APPLES, WINESAP	6.00 lb	12.00 lb	24.00 lb	48.00 lb	2. Wash apples, cut in fourths and remove core.
					3. Cut fourths of apples in half lengthwise.
					4. Dip apples in juice from Step 1 to avoid darkening.
					5. Arrange 3 apple wedges and 3 grapefruit sections on individual dish lined with lettuce.
					6. Or place in large bowls for self-service.

	Recipe No.	Recipe Name				Category
4315		**BANANA NUT ROLL**				**SALADS—Fruits**

Serving Standards: _____ Pan _____ Portions/Pan __4 oz__ Portion Size _____ Utensil __Cold__ Temperature

Ingredients	Portions				Procedure
	50	100	200	300	
BANANAS, 20 lb box, fresh	14.00 lb	28.00 lb	56.00 lb	84.00 lb	1. Peel bananas and cut into halves or thirds depending on size. Weight is AP.
SALAD DRESSING, 4/1 gal/cs	1.75 cup	3.75 cup	1.00 qt	2.00 qt	2. Mix salad dressing and milk.
	2.00 tbs		3.50 cup	3.25 cup	3. Dip bananas in dressing mixture.
MILK, FRESH, HOMO, 6 gal can	1.25 cup	2.50 cup	1.00 qt	1.00 qt	4. Place 2 chunks of banana in serving dish lined with lettuce.
			1.00 cup	3.50 cup	5. Chop nuts and sprinkle generously over bananas.
PEANUTS, SALTED, ROASTED, 6/5 lb cs	2.00 lb	4.00 lb	8.00 lb	12.00 lb	

4325	BANANA SPLIT SALAD				SALADS—Fruits
Recipe No.	Recipe Name				Category

Serving Standards:

Pan	Portions/Pan	3 oz	No. 30 Scoop	Cold
Pan	Portions/Pan	Portion Size	Utensil	Temperature

Ingredients	Portions				Procedure
	50	100	150	300	
BANANAS, 20 lb box, fresh	7.00 lb	14.00 lb	21.00 lb	42.00 lb	1. Drain fruit cocktail.
SALAD DRESSING, 4/1 gal/cs	1.25 cup	2.50 cup	3.75 cup	1.00 qt	2. Peel bananas and cut into thirds or halves depend-
				3.50 cup	ing on size. Then slice the cubes into sixths or
MILK, FRESH, HOMO,	.50 cup	1.00 cup	1.50 cup	3.00 cup	fourths. Weight is AP.
6 gal can					3. Mix salad dressing and milk.
FRUIT COCKTAIL, FNCY, 6/10	1.00 can	2.00 can	3.00 can	6.00 can	4. Coat banana slices in salad dressing mixture.
CHERRIES, RED MARAS-	.50 cup	1.00 cup	1.50 cup	3.00 cup	5. Place two banana slices in serving dish lined with
CHINO, HLVS, FNCY,					lettuce.
6/.5 gal					6. Top bananas with a No. 30 scoop of fruit cocktail.
					7. Garnish with maraschino cherry half.

4335	FIESTA PEACH SALAD				SALADS—Fruits
Recipe No.	Recipe Name				Category

Serving Standards: _____ _____ __1 ea__ __No. 40 Scoop__ __Cold__
                Pan   Portions/Pan   Portion Size   Utensil   Temperature

Ingredients	Portions				Procedure
	37	111	555	1110	
SUGAR, GRAN, 100 lb	2.00 tbs	.25 cup 2.00 tbs	1.75 cup 2.00 tbs	3.75 cup	1. Combine sugar, orange juice and cream cheese in chopper and mix until light and fluffy.
ORANGE JUICE, cold	2.00 tbs	.25 cup 2.00 tbs	1.75 cup 2.00 tbs	3.75 cup	2. Measure maraschino cherries but do not drain.
					3. Add to cream cheese in chopper and mix until cherries are chopped but not too fine.
CREAM CHEESE, 6/3 lb	1.50 lb	4.50 lb	22.50 lb	45.00 lb	4. Place a peach half on lettuce leaf and fill center with No. 40 scoop of cream cheese mixture (about .75 oz).
CHERRIES, RED MARAS-CHINO, HLVS, 6/.5 gal	2.00 tbs	.25 cup 2.00 tbs	1.75 cup 2.00 tbs	3.75 cup	
PEACHES, YC, HLVS, FNCY, 35 to 40 ct. 6/10 cs	1.00 can	3.00 can	15.00 can	30.00 can	Equipment: chopper

4340	FRUIT SALAD WITH WHIP TOPPING	SALADS—Fruits
Recipe No.	Recipe Name	Category

Serving Standards:

		3 oz	No. 12 Scoop	Cold
Pan	Portions/Pan	Portion Size	Utensil	Temperature

Ingredients	Portions				Procedure
	60	120	240	480	
PEACHES, YC, SLI, FNCY, 6/10/cs	1.00 can	2.00 can	4.00 can	8.00 can	1. Drain all fruit well and place into large bowl.
PINEAPPLE TIDBITS, HVY SYRUP, XSTD 6/10	1.00 can	2.00 can	4.00 can	8.00 can	2. Whip the whip topping and fold into fruit mixture.
GRAPES, WHT, SEEDLESS, HVY SYRUP, XSTD 10	.25 can	.50 can	1.00 can	2.00 can	3. Serve with a No. 12 scoop on individual dish lined with lettuce and garnish with maraschino cherry halves.
ORANGES, MAND SECT, HVY SRP, FNCY 6/10	.25 can	.50 can	1.00 can	2.00 can	4. Or place in large serving bowl for self-service and garnish with cherries.
WHIP TOPPING, 12/32 foz can	.50 can	1.00 can	2.00 can	4.00 can	
CHERRIES, RED MARAS-CHINO, HLVS, FNCY, 6/.5 gal	.50 cup 1.00 tbs	1.00 cup 2.00 tbs	2.25 cup	1.00 qt .50 cup	

4350	FRUITMALLOW SALAD				SALADS—Fruits
Recipe No.	Recipe Name				Category

Serving Standards: _____   _____   2 oz   No. 12 Scoop   Cold
  Pan   Portions/Pan   Portion size   Utensil   Temperature

Ingredients	Portions				Procedure
	92	368	552	920	
FRUIT COCKTAIL, FNCY 6/10	2.00 can	8.00 can	12.00 can	20.00 can	1. Whip the whip topping.
WHIP TOPPING, 12/32 foz can	1.00 can	4.00 can	6.00 can	10.00 can	2. Add drained fruit cocktail and marshmallows. Mix well.
MARSHMALLOWS,	2.00 lb	8.00 lb	12.00 lb	20.00 lb	3. Serve with No. 12 scoop.
MINIATURE, 12/1 lb					

4355	HAWAIIAN DELIGHT SALAD				SALADS—Fruits
Recipe No.	Recipe Name				Category

Serving Standards:

		1 sl	No. 30 Scoop	Cold
Pan	Portions/Pan	Portion Size	Utensil	Temperature

Ingredients	Portions				Procedure
	50	100	200	300	
RAISINS, SEEDLESS, FNCY, 30 lb box	2.00 oz	.25 lb	.50 lb	.75 lb	1. Soak raisins in hot water 10 min. until plump. Drain.
PINEAPPLE TIDBITS, HVY SRP, XSTD 6/10	3.00 cup	1.00 qt 2.00 cup	3.00 qt	1.00 gal 2.00 cup	2. Chop celery. Weight is EP. Combine raisins with next 4 ingredients. Chill.
CELERY, FRESH, GRN, FNCY, pascal, bun	.50 lb	1.00 lb	2.00 lb	3.00 lb	3. Roll pineapple slice edge in strawberry gelatin.
SALAD DRESSING, 4/1 gal/cs	1.00 cup	2.00 cup	1.00 qt	1.00 qt 2.00 cup	4. Place 1 slice pineapple on lettuce leaf.
CHERRIES, RED MARAS-CHINO, HLVS, FNCY, 6/.5 gal	.25 cup	.50 cup	1.00 cup	1.50 cup	5. Top with No. 30 scoop of fruit mixture. Serve.
PINEAPPLE, SLI HAW, FNCY, 52 ct, 6/10	1.00 can	2.00 can	4.00 can	6.00 can	
GELATIN, STRAWBERRY, 12/24 oz/cs	.25 box	.50 box	1.00 box	1.50 box	

4359	MANDARIN ORANGE/COCONUT TOSS				SALADS—Fruits
Recipe No.	Recipe Name				Category

Serving Standards: _____ / _____ / __3 oz__ / __No. 12 Scoop__ / __Cold__
Pan / Portions/Pan / Portion Size / Utensil / Temperature

Ingredients	Portions				Procedure
	21	126	252	504	
ORANGES, MAND SECT, HVY SRP, FNCY 6/10	1.00 can	6.00 can	12.00 can	24.00 can	1. Drain mandarin oranges. 2. Combine coconut and mandarin oranges and mix well. 3. Place a No. 12 scoop of mixture on lettuce. 4. Garnish with maraschino cherry half.
COCONUT, DRY, 10 lb box	3.00 oz	1.00 lb 2.00 oz	2.25 lb	4.50 lb	
CHERRIES, RED MARAS-CHINO, HLVS, FNCY, 6/.5 gal	3.00 tbs	1.00 cup 2.00 tbs	2.25 cup	1.00 qt .50 cup	

4360	ORANGE COCONUT TOSS				SALADS—Fruits
Recipe No.	Recipe Name				Category

Serving Standards: _____ / _____ / __3 oz__ / __No. 12 Scoop__ / __Cold__
Pan / Portions/Pan / Portion Size / Utensil / Temperature

Ingredients	Portions				Procedure
	32	128	256	512	
ORANGE SEC, FNCY, 4/1 gal COCONUT, DRY, 10 lb box CHERRIES, RED MARAS-CHINO, HLVS, FNCY, 6/.5 gal	1.00 gal .25 lb .25 cup	4.00 gal 1.00 lb 1.00 cup	8.00 gal 2.00 lb 2.00 cup	16.00 gal 4.00 lb 1.00 qt	1. Drain orange sections. 2. Combine orange sections with coconut and mix well. 3. Place a No. 12 scoop of fruit mixture on lettuce. 4. Garnish with maraschino cherry half.

4365	PEACH HALF WITH FRUIT COCKTAIL				SALADS—Fruits
Recipe No.	Recipe Name				Category

Serving Standards:

_____	_____	1 hlv	No. 30 Scoop	Cold
Pan	Portions/Pan	Portion Size	Utensil	Temperature

Ingredients	Portions				Procedure
	37	74	111	222	
PEACHES, YC, HLVS, FNCY, 35 to 40 ct, 6/10 cs	1.00 can	2.00 can	3.00 can	6.00 can	1. Place a peach half in serving dish lined with lettuce and fill with No. 30 scoop of fruit cocktail.
FRUIT COCKTAIL, FNCY, 6/10	.75 can	1.50 can	2.25 can	4.50 can	2. Garnish with maraschino cherry half.
CHERRIES, RED MARASCHINO, HLVS, FNCY, 6/.5 gal	.33 cup	.66 cup	1.00 cup	2.00 cup	

4370	PEACH WITH COTTAGE CHEESE				SALADS—Fruits
Recipe No.	Recipe Name				Category

Serving Standards:

_____	_____	1 hlv	No. 40 Scoop	Cold
Pan	Portions/Pan	Portion Size	Utensil	Temperature

Ingredients	Portions				Procedure
	55	110	330	550	
PEACHES, YC, HLVS, FNCY, 35 to 40 ct, 6/10 cs	1.50 can	3.00 can	9.00 can	15.00 can	1. Place peach half on lettuce.
GRAPES, RED SEEDLESS, HVY SRP, XSTD 6/10	1.00 cup	2.00 cup	1.00 qt 2.00 cup	2.00 qt 2.00 cup	2. Fill center of peach with No. 40 scoop of cottage cheese.
COTTAGE CHEESE, 25 lb bag in box	3.50 lb	7.00 lb	21.00 lb	35.00 lb	3. Garnish with 4 maraschino grapes.

4371	PEACH, COTTAGE CHEESE, RAISINS, NUTS				SALADS—Fruits
Recipe No.	Recipe Name				Category

Serving Standards:

			1 hlv	No. 40 Scoop	Cold
Pan		Portions/Pan	Portion Size	Utensil	Temperature

Ingredients	Portions				Procedure
	37	111	333	555	
COTTAGE CHEESE, 25 lb bag in box	2.00 lb	6.00 lb	18.00 lb	30.00 lb	1. Combine cottage cheese, raisins and pecans.
RAISINS, SEEDLESS, FNCY, 30 lb box	.25 lb	.75 lb	2.25 lb	3.75 lb	2. Place 1 peach half on individual serving dish lined with lettuce.
PECANS, FNCY, med, 30 lb/cs	.25 lb	.75 lb	2.25 lb	3.75 lb	3. Fill peach half with No. 40 scoop of cottage cheese mixture.
PEACHES, YC, HLVS, FNCY, 35 to 40 ct, 6/10 cs	1.00 can	3.00 can	9.00 can	15.00 can	4. Garnish with maraschino cherry half.
CHERRIES, RED MARAS- CHINO, HLVS, FNCY, 6/.5 gal	.33 cup	1.00 cup	3.00 cup	1.00 qt 1.00 cup	

4378	PEACH HALF/CREAM CHEESE/OLIVE/NUT	SALADS—Fruits
Recipe No.	Recipe Name	Category

Serving Standards:

		1 hlv	No. 40 Scoop	Cold
Pan	Portions/Pan	Portion Size	Utensil	Temperature

Ingredients	Portions				Procedure
	37	111	555	1110	
CREAM CHEESE, 6/3 lb	1.50 lb	4.50 lb	22.50 lb	45.00 lb	1. Combine cream cheese and warm water in chopper and mix until light and fluffy.
WATER, warm	2.00 tbs	.25 cup	1.75 cup	3.75 cup	
		2.00 tbs	2.00 tbs		2. Add drained olives and pecans and mix until they are chopped but not too fine.
OLIVES, STUFFED,	2.00 tbs	.25 cup	1.75 cup	3.75 cup	
340 to 360 ct, 4/1 gal		2.00 tbs	2.00 tbs		3. Place a peach half on lettuce leaf and fill center with a No. 40 scoop of cream cheese mixture (about .75 oz).
PECANS, FNCY, med,	1.00 oz	3.00 oz	15.00 oz	1.00 lb	
30 lb/cs				14.00 oz	
PEACHES, YC, HLVS,	1.00 can	3.00 can	15.00 can	30.00 can	Equipment: chopper
FNCY, 35 to 40 ct, 6/10 cs					*Variation:* Pears

4390	SLICED PEACHES/COTTAGE CHEESE				SALADS—Fruits
Recipe No.	Recipe Name				Category

Serving Standards:

		3 sl	No. 30 Scoop	Cold
Pan	Portions/Pan	Portion Size	Utensil	Temperature

Ingredients	Portions				Procedure
	33	99	198	495	
PEACHES, YC, SLI, FNCY, 6/10/cs	1.00 can	3.00 can	6.00 can	15.00 can	1. Drain sliced peaches.
COTTAGE CHEESE, 25 lb bag in box	2.00 lb 10.00 oz	7.00 lb 14.00 oz	15.75 lb	39.00 lb 6.00 oz	2. Place No. 30 scoop cottage cheese and 3 peach slices on serving dish lined with lettuce.
CHERRIES, RED MARAS-CHINO, HLVS, FNCY, 6/.5 gal	.33 cup	1.00 cup	2.00 cup	1.00 qt 1.00 cup	3. Garnish with maraschino cherry half.

4405	PEAR WITH COTTAGE CHEESE				SALADS—Fruits
Recipe No.	Recipe Name				Category

Serving Standards:

		1 hlv	No. 30 Scoop	Cold
Pan	Portions/Pan	Portion Size	Utensil	Temperature

Ingredients	Portions				Procedure
	37	111	222	333	
PEARS, BARTLETT, HLVS, FNCY, 35 to 40 ct, 6/10	1.00 can	3.00 can	6.00 can	9.00 can	1. Drain pear halves.
COTTAGE CHEESE, 25 lb bag in box	3.00 lb	9.00 lb	18.00 lb	27.00 lb	2. Place pear half in serving dish lined with lettuce. 3. Fill center of pear half with No. 30 scoop of cottage cheese.
CHERRIES, RED MARAS-CHINO, HLVS, FNCY, 6/.5 gal	.25 cup	.75 cup	1.50 cup	2.25 cup	4. Garnish with maraschino cherry half.

4410	PEAR WITH CREAM CHEESE AND NUTS			SALADS—Fruits
Recipe No.	Recipe Name			Category

Serving Standards:

Pan	Portions/Pan	1 hlv Portion Size	No. 40 Scoop Utensil	Cold Temperature

Ingredients	Portions				Procedure
	37	111	555	1110	
CREAM CHEESE, 6/3 lb	1.50 lb	4.50 lb	22.50 lb	45.00 lb	1. Combine cream cheese and warm water in chopper and mix until light and fluffy.
WATER, warm	2.00 tbs	.25 cup	1.75 cup	3.75 cup	
		2.00 tbs	2.00 tbs		2. Add pecans and mix until they are chopped but not too fine.
PECANS, FNCY, med, 30 lb/cs	1.00 oz	3.00 oz	15.00 oz	1.00 lb 14.00 oz	3. Place a pear half on lettuce leaf and fill center with a No. 40 scoop of cream cheese mixture (about .75 oz).
PEARS, BARTLETT, HLVS, FNCY, 35 to 40 ct, 6/10	1.00 can	3.00 can	15.00 can	30.00 can	Equipment: chopper

4420	PEAR WITH GRATED CHEESE			SALADS—Fruits
Recipe No.	Recipe Name			Category

Serving Standards:

Pan	Portions/Pan	1 hlv Portion Size	Utensil	Cold Temperature

Ingredients	Portions				Procedure
	37	111	222	333	
PEARS, BARTLETT, HLVS, FNCY, 35 to 40 ct, 6/10	1.00 can	3.00 can	6.00 can	9.00 can	1. Drain pear halves.
CHEDDAR CHEESE, WHEEL	10.00 oz	1.00 lb 14.00 oz	3.75 lb	5.00 lb 10.00 oz	2. Place pear half in serving dish lined with lettuce. 3. Grate cheese and top each pear half with .25 oz cheese.
CHERRIES, RED MARAS-CHINO, HLVS, FNCY, 6/.5 gal	.25 cup 2.00 tbs	1.00 cup 2.00 tbs	2.25 cup	3.25 cup 2.00 tbs	4. Garnish each serving with a maraschino cherry half.

4425   **PEAR WITH MANDARIN ORANGES**

Recipe No.   Recipe Name   Category

Serving Standards:

		2.25 oz		Cold
Pan	Portions/Pan	Portion Size	Utensil	Temperature

Ingredients	Portions				Procedure
	40	80	160	480	
PEARS, BARTLETT, HLVS, FNCY, 35 to 40 ct, 6/10	1.00 can	2.00 can	4.00 can	12.00 can	1. Drain pears and mandarin oranges.
ORANGES, MAND SECT, HVY SRP, FNCY, 6/10	.50 can	1.00 can	2.00 can	6.00 can	2. Line serving dishes with lettuce.
					3. Place pear half in each serving dish.
					4. On each pear half place .75 oz mandarin orange sections (approx 5).

4435   **PINEAPPLE AMBROSIA**

Recipe No.   Recipe Name   Category

Serving Standards:

		3 oz	No. 12 Scoop	Cold
Pan	Portions/Pan	Portion Size	Utensil	Temperature

Ingredients	Portions				Procedure
	35	70	210	420	
PINEAPPLE TIDBITS, HVY SRP, XSTD 6/10	1.00 can	2.00 can	6.00 can	12.00 can	1. Drain pineapple and orange sections.
ORANGE SEC, FNCY, 4/1 gal	.50 gal	1.00 gal	3.00 gal	6.00 gal	2. Combine pineapple, oranges and coconut. Mix well.
COCONUT, DRY, 10 lb box	.25 lb	.50 lb	1.50 lb	3.00 lb	3. Place a No. 12 scoop of fruit mixture on lettuce.
CHERRIES, RED MARASCHINO, HLVS, FNCY, 6/.5 gal	.25 cup	.50 cup	1.50 cup	3.00 cup	4. Garnish with maraschino cherry.

4440	PINEAPPLE WITH APRICOT					SALADS—Fruits
Recipe No.	Recipe Name					Category

Serving Standards:

		1 sl		Cold
Pan	Portions/Pan	Portion Size	Utensil	Temperature

Ingredients	Portions				Procedure
	50	100	200	500	
PINEAPPLE, SLI HAW FNCY, 52 ct, 6/10	1.00 can	2.00 can	4.00 can	10.00 can	1. Drain pineapple and apricot halves.
APRICOTS, HLV, FNCY, 95 ct, 6/10can/cs	.50 can	1.00 can	2.00 can	5.00 can	2. Place pineapple slice on lettuce leaf. 3. Place apricot half in center of slice.
CHERRIES, RED MARASCHINO, HLVS, FNCY, 6/.5 gal	50 cup	1.00 cup	2.00 cup	1.00 qt 1.00 cup	4. Garnish each serving with a maraschino cherry half.

4445	PINEAPPLE WITH GRATED CHEESE					SALADS—Fruits
Recipe No.	Recipe Name					Category

Serving Standards:

		1 sl		Cold
Pan	Portions/Pan	Portion Size	Utensil	Temperature

Ingredients	Portions				Procedure
	50	100	200	500	
PINEAPPLE, SLI HAW FNCY, 52 ct, 6/10	1.00 can	2.00 can	4.00 can	10.00 can	1. Drain pineapple.
CHEDDAR CHEESE, WHEEL	14.00 oz	1.75 lb	3.50 lb	8.75 lb	2. On lettuce leaf place one pineapple slice. 3. Grate cheese and top each pineapple slice with .25 oz cheese.
CHERRIES, RED MARASCHINO, HLVS, FNCY, 6/.5 gal	.50 cup	1.00 cup	2.00 cup	1.00 qt 1.00 cup	4. Garnish each serving with a maraschino cherry half.

4450	PINEAPPLE WITH COTTAGE CHEESE				SALADS—Fruits
Recipe No.	Recipe Name				Category

Serving Standards:

		1 sl		Cold
Pan	Portions/Pan	Portion Size	Utensil	Temperature

Ingredients	Portions				Procedure
	50	**100**	**300**	**500**	
PINEAPPLE, SLI HAW FNCY, 52 ct, 6/10	1.00 can	2.00 can	6.00 can	10.00 can	1. Drain pineapple.
					2. Arrange pineapple on serving dish lined with lettuce.
COTTAGE CHEESE, 25 lb bag in box	3.50 lb	7.00 lb	21.00 lb	35.00 lb	3. Fill center of pineapple with No. 40 scoop of cottage cheese.
CHERRIES, RED MARASCHINO, HLVS, FNCY, 6/.5 gal	.50 cup	1.00 cup	3.00 cup	1.00 qt 1.00 cup	4. Garnish with maraschino cherry half.

4460	WALDORF SALAD				SALADS—Fruit
Recipe No.	Recipe Name				Category

Serving Standards:

Pan	Portions/Pan	2.5 oz	No. 12 Scoop	Cold
		Portion Size	Utensil	Temperature

Ingredients	Portions				Procedure
	60	120	240	300	
APPLES, WINESAP	6.00 lb	12.00 lb	24.00 lb	30.00 lb	1. Wash apples, slice into fourths and core.
LEMON JUICE, RECONSTI- TUTED, 12/qt jars	.75 cup	1.50 cup	3.00 cup	3.75 cup	2. Cut apples into 1/2 in. by 1/4 in. pieces.
WATER, cold	.75 cup	1.50 cup	3.00 cup	3.75 cup	3. Put apples into lemon-juice water mixture immedi- ately after cutting to prevent browning.
CELERY, FRESH, GRN, FNCY, pascal, bun	2.00 lb	4.00 lb	8.00 lb	10.00 lb	4. Trim and wash celery. Weight of celery is EP. Chop in chopper but not too fine.
RAISINS, SEEDLESS, FNCY, 30 lb box	.75 lb	1.50 lb	3.00 lb	3.75 lb	5. Add celery, raisins, pecans and salad dressing to apples. Mix well.
PECANS, FNCY, med, 30 lb/cs	.50 lb	1.00 lb	2.00 lb	2.50 lb	6. Serve a level No. 12 scoop into serving dish lined with lettuce.
SALAD DRESSING, 4/1 gal/cs	2.00 cup	1.00 qt	2.00 qt	2.00 qt 2.00 cup	*Note:* Weight of apples is AP.

4505	CONGEALED APPLESAUCE					SALADS—Gelatins
Recipe No.	**Recipe Name**					**Category**

Serving Standards:

Pan	Portions/Pan	4 oz Portion Size	Utensil	Cold Temperature

Ingredients	Portions				E* Procedure
	60	**120**	**360**	**480**	
GELATIN, LIME, 12/24 oz/cs	1.00 box	2.00 box	6.00 box	8.00 box	1. Dissolve gelatin in hot water.
WATER, hot, 180°F.	2.00 qt	1.00 gal	3.00 gal	4.00 gal	2. Add ice and stir until dissolved.
ICE, crushed	2.00 lb	4.00 lb	12.00 lb	16.00 lb	3. Chop celery. Weight is EP.
APPLESAUCE, FNCY,	1.00 can	2.00 can	6.00 can	8.00 can	4. Add applesauce, lemon juice and celery; mix well.
swt, 6/10 can/cs					5. Pour .5 cup gelatin mixture into molds.
CELERY, FRESH, GRN,	.50 lb	1.00 lb	3.00 lb	4.00 lb	6. Refrigerate.
FNCY, pascal, bun					7. Unmold on lettuce leaf.
LEMON JUICE, RECONSTI-	2.00 tbs	.25 cup	.75 cup	1.00 cup	*Early Prep: Prepare gelatin 1 day ahead of serving
TUTED, 12/qt jars					day.

4515	BLACKBERRY ISLE	SALADS—Gelatins
Recipe No.	Recipe Name	Category

Serving Standards:

Pan	Portions/Pan	4 oz Portion Size	Utensil	Cold Temperature

Ingredients	Portions				E*	Procedure
	50	100	400	1000		
GELATIN, BLACKBERRY, 12/24 oz/cs	.50 box	1.00 box	4.00 box	10.00 box		1. Drain pineapple and save juice.
GELATIN, LEMON, 12/24 oz/cs	.50 box	1.00 box	4.00 box	10.00 box		2. Dissolve gelatin in hot water. 3. Use juice plus enough water to equal amt cold water in recipe.
WATER, hot, 180°F.	.50 gal	1.00 gal	4.00 gal	10.00 gal		4. Stir in cold water-juice mixture.
WATER, cold	1.00 qt	2.00 qt	2.00 gal	5.00 gal		5. Add ice and stir until dissolved.
ICE, crushed	2.00 lb	4.00 lb	16.00 lb	40.00 lb		6. Chop celery in chopper. Weight is EP.
CELERY, FRESH, GRN, FNCY, pascal, bun	.50 lb	1.00 lb	4.00 lb	10.00 lb		7. When gelatin begins to thicken, add remaining ingredients.
PINEAPPLE, HAW, CRU, HVY SRP. XSTD, 6/10	.50 can	1.00 can	4.00 can	10.00 can		8. Pour .5 cup gelatin mixture into individual molds. 9. Refrigerate.
PECANS, FNCY, med, 30 lb/cs	.50 lb	1.00 lb	4.00 lb	10.00 lb		10. Unmold on lettuce. *Early Prep: Prepare gelatin 1 day ahead of serving day.

| 4521 | LIME FRUITED GELATIN | | | | SALADS—Gelatins |
| Recipe No. | Recipe Name | | | | Category |

Serving Standards: _____   _____   __4 oz__   _____   __Cold__
                        Pan   Portions/Pan   Portion Size   Utensil   Temperature

| Ingredients | Portions | | | | E* Procedure |
	50	100	300	500	
GELATIN, LIME, 12/24 oz/cs	1.00 box	2.00 box	6.00 box	10.00 box	1. Dissolve gelatin in hot water.
WATER, hot, 180°F.	.50 gal	1.00 gal	3.00 gal	5.00 gal	2. Add cold water and stir.
WATER, cold	1.00 qt	2.00 qt	1.00 gal	2.00 gal	3. Add ice and stir until dissolved.
			2.00 qt	2.00 qt	4. Chill and allow to thicken slightly.
ICE, crushed	2.00 lb	4.00 lb	12.00 lb	20.00 lb	5. Drain fruit cocktail.
FRUIT COCKTAIL,	1.00 can	2.00 can	6.00 can	10.00 can	6. When gelatin has congealed slightly, add fruit cocktail. Mix well.
FNCY, 6/10					7. Pour .5 cup gelatin mixture into molds.
					8. Refrigerate.
					9. Unmold on lettuce.
					*Early Prep: Prepare gelatin 1 day ahead of serving day.

4525	CHERRY GELATIN	SALADS—Gelatins
Recipe No.	Recipe Name	Category

Serving Standards:

Pan	Portions/Pan	3 oz Portion Size	Utensil	Cold Temperature

Ingredients	Portions				E* Procedure
	45	90	360	540	
GELATIN, CHERRY, 12/24 oz/cs	1.00 box	2.00 box	8.00 box	12.00 box	1. Dissolve gelatin in hot water.
WATER, hot, 180°F.	2.00 qt	1.00 gal	4.00 gal	6.00 gal	2. Stir in cold water. 3. Add ice and stir until dissolved.
WATER, cold	1.00 qt	2.00 qt	2.00 gal	3.00 gal	4. Pour into pans.
ICE, crushed	2.00 lb	4.00 lb	16.00 lb	24.00 lb	5. Refrigerate until firm.
WHIP TOPPING, 12/32 foz can	.25 can	.50 can	2.00 can	3.00 can	6. Cut into cubes. 7. Serve approx one-third cup heaped. 8. Whip the topping and using pastry tube, garnish each serving with 4 tsp.

Variation: Pour into ind molds to serve on fruit plate.

*Early Prep: Prepare gelatin 1 day in advance.

4530	BING CHERRY AND ALMOND GELATIN				SALADS—Gelatins
Recipe No.	Recipe Name				Category

Serving Standards: _____ _____ 4 oz _____ Cold
　　　　　　　　　　 Pan　　　　　　 Portions/Pan　　 Portion Size　　 Utensil　　　 Temperature

Ingredients	Portions				E*	Procedure
	40	80	240	400		
CHERRIES, BING, PITTED, HVY SRP, 6/10	.50 can	1.00 can	3.00 can	5.00 can		1. Drain cherries.
						2. Dissolve gelatin in boiling water.
GELATIN, CHERRY, 12/24 oz/cs	1.00 box	2.00 box	6.00 box	10.00 box		3. When gelatin is thoroughly dissolved, add cold water and stir.
WATER, hot, 180°F.	1.50 qt	3.00 qt	2.00 gal	3.00 gal		4. Add ice and let melt, stirring occasionally.
			1.00 qt	3.00 qt		5. Place gelatin in refrigerator until it begins to thicken.
WATER, cold	1.00 qt	2.00 qt	1.00 gal	2.00 gal		
			2.00 qt	2.00 qt		6. Add almonds and cherries.
ICE, crushed	2.00 lb	4.00 lb	12.00 lb	20.00 lb		7. Pour .5 cup gelatin mixture into molds.
ALMONDS, SLICED, BLANCHED, 6/10	.50 lb	1.00 lb	3.00 lb	5.00 lb		8. Refrigerate until firm.
						9. Unmold on lettuce leaf.
						*Early Prep: Prepare gelatin 1 day ahead of serving day.

| 4535 | CONGEALED FRUIT | SALADS—Gelatins |
| Recipe No. | Recipe Name | Category |

Serving Standards:

| | | 4 oz | | Cold |
| Pan | Portions/Pan | Portion Size | Utensil | Temperature |

| Ingredients | Portions | | | | E* Procedure |
	50	100	300	500	
GELATIN, CHERRY, 12/24 oz/cs	1.00 box	2.00 box	6.00 box	10.00 box	1. Dissolve gelatin in hot water.
WATER, hot, 180°F.	.50 gal	1.00 gal	3.00 gal	5.00 gal	2. Add cold water and stir.
WATER, cold	1.00 qt	2.00 qt	1.00 gal	2.00 gal	3. Add ice and stir until dissolved.
			2.00 qt	2.00 qt	4. Chill and allow to thicken slightly.
ICE, crushed	2.00 lb	4.00 lb	12.00 lb	20.00 lb	5. Drain fruit cocktail.
FRUIT COCKTAIL, FNCY, 6/10	1.00 can	2.00 can	6.00 can	10.00 can	6. When gelatin has congealed slightly, add fruit cocktail. Mix well.
					7. Pour .5 cup gelatin mixture into molds.
					8. Refrigerate.
					9. Unmold on lettuce.
					*Early Prep: Prepare gelatin 1 day ahead of serving day.

	4540		**CONGEALED WALDORF**			**SALADS**—Gelatins

Recipe No.　　　**Recipe Name**　　　　　　　　　　　　　　　　　　　**Category**

Serving Standards: _____　_____　__4 oz__　_____　__Cold__

　　　　　　　　　　Pan　　　　　**Portions/Pan**　　**Portion Size**　　　**Utensil**　　**Temperature**

Ingredients	Portions				E* Procedure
	42	**126**	**252**	**420**	
GELATIN, LEMON, 12/24 oz/cs	1.00 box	3.00 box	6.00 box	10.00 box	1. Dissolve gelatin in hot water.
WATER, hot, 180°F.	1.50 qt	1.00 gal .50 qt	2.00 gal 1.00 qt	3.00 gal 3.00 qt	2. Add cold water. 3. Add ice and stir until dissolved. 4. Cool and allow to thicken slightly.
WATER, cold	1.00 qt	3.00 qt	1.00 gal 2.00 qt	2.00 gal 2.00 qt	5. Trim and wash celery. Chop in food chopper but not too fine. Weight of celery is EP.
ICE, crushed	2.00 lb	6.00 lb	12.00 lb	20.00 lb	6. Weight of apples is AP. Core apples, but do not
CELERY, FRESH, GRN, FNCY, pascal, bun	.50 lb	1.50 lb	3.00 lb	5.00 lb	peel. Cut into .5 inch by .25 inch pieces. Pour lemon juice over apples.
APPLES, WINESAP	1.50 lb	4.50 lb	9.00 lb	15.00 lb	7. When gelatin has begun to thicken, add celery, ap-
LEMON JUICE, RECONSTI-TUTED, 12/qt jars	1.00 tbs	3.00 tbs	.25 cup 2.00 tbs	.50 cup 2.00 tbs	ples, pecans and raisins. 8. Pour .5 cup of mixture into molds.
PECANS, FNCY, med, 30 lb/cs	.25 lb	.75 lb	1.50 lb	2.50 lb	9. Refrigerate to congeal. 10. Unmold on lettuce leaf.
RAISINS, SEEDLESS, FNCY, 30 lb box	.25 lb	.75 lb	1.50 lb	2.50 lb	*Early Prep: Prepare gelatin 1 day ahead of serving day.

4545	CONGEALED CRANBERRY SALAD				SALADS—Gelatins
Recipe No.	Recipe Name				Category

Serving Standards: _____ _____ __4 oz__ _____ __Cold__

| Pan | Portions/Pan | Portion Size | Utensil | Temperature |

Ingredients	Portions				E*	Procedure
	80	160	240	320		
GELATIN, LEMON, 12/24 oz/cs	1.00 box	2.00 box	3.00 box	4.00 box		1. Dissolve gelatin in hot water.
GELATIN, CHERRY, 12/24 oz/cs	1.00 box	2.00 box	3.00 box	4.00 box		2. Add whole cranberry sauce and dissolve. 3. Add cold water and stir well.
WATER, hot, 180°F.	3.00 qt	1.00 gal 2.00 qt	2.00 gal 1.00 qt	3.00 gal		4. Chill and allow to thicken slightly. 5. Chop celery in chopper. Weight is EP.
WATER, cold	2.00 qt	1.00 gal	1.00 gal 2.00 qt	2.00 gal		6. Rinse orange sections with cold water and drain; cut by hand into half-inch pieces.
CRANBERRY SAUCE, WHOLE, 6/10/cs	1.00 can	2.00 can	3.00 can	4.00 can		7. When gelatin is slightly thickened, add celery, oranges and pecans and mix well.
CELERY, FRESH, GRN, FNCY, pascal, bun	.50 lb	1.00 lb	1.50 lb	2.00 lb		8. Pour .5 cup gelatin mixture into individual molds. 9. Refrigerate to congeal.
ORANGE SEC, FNCY, 4/1 gal	2.50 lb	5.00 lb	7.50 lb	10.00 lb		10. Serve on lettuce leaf.
PECANS, FNCY, med, 30 lb/cs	.50 lb	1.00 lb	1.50 lb	2.00 lb		*Early Prep: Prepare gelatin 1 day ahead of serving day.

4555	FLUFFY APRICOT SALAD				SALADS—Gelatins
Recipe No.	Recipe Name				Category

Serving Standards: _____ _____ __4 oz__ _____ __Cold__
 Pan Portions/Pan Portion Size Utensil Temperature

Ingredients	Portions				E*	Procedure
	49	98	196	294		
GELATIN, ORANGE, 12/24 oz/cs	1.00 box	2.00 box	4.00 box	6.00 box		1. Drain apricots and save juice.
						2. Dissolve gelatin in hot water.
WATER, hot, 180°F.	.50 gal	1.00 gal	2.00 gal	3.00 gal		3. Add ice and stir until melted.
ICE, crushed	2.00 lb	4.00 lb	8.00 lb	12.00 lb		4. Stir in apricot nectar. Substitute apricot juice
APRICOT NECTAR, 12/46 foz can	.50 can	1.00 can	2.00 can	3.00 can		from above for water. Add.
						5. Allow to cool and thicken slightly.
WATER, cold	1.00 cup	2.00 cup	1.00 qt	1.00 qt 2.00 cup		6. When slightly thickened, add mayonnaise and beat until fluffy with a wire whip.
MAYONNAISE, 4/1 gal/cs	1.00 cup	2.00 cup	1.00 qt	1.00 qt 2.00 cup		7. Dice apricots and add with pecans to gelatin mixture.
APRICOTS, HLV, FNCY, 95 ct, 6/10 can/cs	.50 can	1.00 can	2.00 can	3.00 can		8. Place 4 to 5 miniature marshmallows in bottom of each mold. Pour .5 cup in each mold.
PECANS, FNCY, med, 30 lb/cs	.50 lb	1.00 lb	2.00 lb	3.00 lb		9. Refrigerate.
						10. Serve on lettuce leaf.
MARSHMALLOWS, MINIATURE, 12/1 lb	.25 lb	.50 lb	1.00 lb	1.50 lb		*Early Prep: Prepare gelatin 1 day ahead of serving day.

4560	FROSTED FRUIT GELATIN	SALADS—Gelatins
Recipe No.	Recipe Name	Category

Serving Standards:

20- by 12- by 2.5-in.	40	4 oz		Cold
Pan	Portions/Pan	Portion Size	Utensil	Temperature

Ingredients	Portions				E* Procedure
	60	120	480	960	
GELATIN, CHERRY, 12/24 oz/cs	1.00 box	2.00 box	8.00 box	16.00 box	1. Dissolve gelatin in hot water.
WATER, hot, 180°F.	.50 gal	1.00 gal	4.00 gal	8.00 gal	2. Stir in cold water.
WATER, cold	1.00 qt	2.00 qt	2.00 gal	4.00 gal	3. Add ice and stir until dissolved.
ICE, crushed	2.00 lb	4.00 lb	16.00 lb	32.00 lb	4. Chill and allow to thicken slightly.
PEARS, BARTLETT, HLVS, FNCY, 6/10	.50 can	1.00 can	4.00 can	8.00 can	5. Drain pears and dice.
GRAPES, WHT, SEEDLESS, HVY SRP, XSTD 6/10	.50 can	1.00 can	4.00 can	8.00 can	6. Drain grapes.
MARSHMALLOWS, MINIATURE, 12/1 lb	1.00 lb	2.00 lb	8.00 lb	16.00 lb	7. When gelatin is slightly congealed, add pears, grapes and marshmallows.
WHIP TOPPING, 12/32 foz can	.50 can	1.00 can	4.00 can	8.00 can	8. Into 20- by 12- by 2.5-in. counter pans pour 1 gal and 1 cup gelatin mixture.

9. Refrigerate to congeal.

10. Just before serving, whip the whip topping and divide evenly among pans. Spread with a spatula. Cut into 40 portions and serve each on lettuce leaf.

*Early Prep: Prepare gelatin 1 day ahead of serving day.

4565	FROSTED PINEAPPLE SALAD					SALADS—Gelatins
Recipe No.	Recipe Name					Category

Serving Standards: __20- by 12- by 2.5-in.__   __40__   __4 oz__   _____   __Cold__

                 Pan   Portions/Pan   Portion Size   Utensil   Temperature

Ingredients	Portions				E*	Procedure
	40	**160**	**320**	**960**		
GELATIN, LEMON,	.50 box	2.00 box	4.00 box	12.00 box		1. Dissolve gelatin in hot water.
12/24 oz/cs						2. Stir in cold water.
WATER, hot, 180°F.	.25 gal	1.00 gal	2.00 gal	6.00 gal		3. Add ice and stir until dissolved.
WATER, cold	2.00 cup	2.00 qt	1.00 gal	3.00 gal		4. Allow to cool and thicken slightly.
ICE, crushed	1.00 lb	4.00 lb	8.00 lb	24.00 lb		5. Drain pineapple and save juice.
PINEAPPLE, HAW, CRU,	.50 can	2.00 can	4.00 can	12.00 can		6. Peel and slice bananas. Weight of bananas is AP.
HVY SRP, XSTD 6/10						7. Add bananas, pineapple and marshmallows to slight-
BANANAS, 20 lb box, fresh	1.50 lb	6.00 lb	12.00 lb	36.00 lb		ly congealed gelatin.
MARSHMALLOWS,	.50 lb	2.00 lb	4.00 lb	12.00 lb		8. Pour 1 gal + 1.5 cup gelatin mixture into 20- by 12-
MINIATURE, 12/1 lb						by 2.5-in. counter pans.
FLOUR, 25 lb bag	1.00 oz	.25 lb	.50 lb	1.50 lb		9. Refrigerate until firm.
SUGAR, GRAN, 100 lb	.25 cup	1.00 cup	2.00 cup	1.00 qt		10. Combine flour and sugar in small steam kettle.
				2.00 cup		11. Substitute pineapple juice from Step 5 for water.
						Add to flour and sugar mixture.
WATER, cold	2.00 cup	2.00 qt	1.00 gal	3.00 gal		12. Add beaten eggs and salt.
SALT, 100 lb bag	.12 tsp	.50 tsp	1.00 tsp	1.00 tbs		13. Turn on steam and cook until thickened—approx
EGGS, 6/5 lb/cs	3.50 oz	14.00 oz	1.75 lb	5.25 lb		5 min.
WHIP TOPPING, 12/32 foz can	.25 can	1.00 can	2.00 can	6.00 can		14. Cool.
CHEDDAR CHEESE,	3.00 oz	.75 lb	1.50 lb	4.50 lb		15. Whip the topping and fold into cooked mixture.
WHEEL						16. Top 20- by 12- by 2.5-in. counter pans with ap-
						prox 1.75 lb (1.25 qt) of topping.
						17. Refrigerate until firm.
						18. Cut 4 by 10. Garnish with grated cheese.
						19. Serve on lettuce leaf.
						*Early Prep: Prepare gelatin 1 day ahead of serving day.

| 4570 | | | | | | | SALADS—Gelatins |

4570   **FROZEN FRUIT SALAD**

Recipe No.   Recipe Name

SALADS—Gelatins
Category

Serving Standards:

| Pan | Portions/Pan | 4.5 oz
Portion Size | Utensil | Frozen
Temperature |

Ingredients	Portions				E*	Procedure
	50	100	200	400		
GELATIN, PLAIN, 12/1 lb/cs	2.00 oz	.25 lb	.50 lb	1.00 lb		1. Sprinkle gelatin over cold water and soak 10 min.
WATER, cold	1.00 cup	2.00 cup	1.00 qt	2.00 qt		2. Drain crushed pineapple, mandarin oranges and sliced peaches and substitute juices for boiling water in recipe.
PINEAPPLE, HAW, CRU, HVY SRP, XSTD 6/10	.50 can	1.00 can	2.00 can	4.00 can		
ORANGES, MAND SECT, HVY SRP, FNCY, 6/10	.50 can	1.00 can	2.00 can	4.00 can		3. Heat fruit juice and pour over gelatin and dissolve. 4. Cool mixture and let thicken slightly.
PEACHES, YC, SLI, FNCY, 6/10/cs	.50 can	1.00 can	2.00 can	4.00 can		5. Whip the whip topping and fold into the gelatin mixture.
WATER, hot, 180°F.	3.50 cup	1.00 qt 3.00 cup	3.00 qt 2.00 cup	1.00 gal 3.00 qt		6. Fold in the salad dressing. 7. Dice bananas. Weight of bananas is AP. (3 lb of bananas AP equals 2 lb EP)
WHIP TOPPING, 12/32 foz can	.50 can	1.00 can	2.00 can	4.00 can		8. Fold in remaining ingredients and pour into individual 4-oz molds. Freeze.
SALAD DRESSING, 4/1 gal/cs	1.00 cup	2.00 cup	1.00 qt	2.00 qt		
BANANAS, 20 lb box, fresh	3.00 lb	6.00 lb	12.00 lb	24.00 lb		9. Unmold on lettuce leaf.
PECANS, FNCY, med, 30 lb/cs	.75 lb	1.50 lb	3.00 lb	6.00 lb		*Early Prep: Prepare salad 1 day ahead of serving day.

CHERRIES, RED MARAS-
  CHINO, HLVS, FNCY,
  6/.5 gal
	1.00 cup	2.00 cup	1.00 qt	2.00 qt		

MARSHMALLOWS, MINIATURE, 12/1 lb	.50 lb	1.00 lb	2.00 lb	4.00 lb		

4575	**HEAVENLY HASH**				SALADS—Gelatins
Recipe No.	Recipe Name				Category

Serving Standards:

20- by 12- by 2.5-in.	40	2.5 oz		Cold
Pan	Portions/Pan	Portion Size	Utensil	Temperature

Ingredients	Portions				E*	Procedure
	80	160	320	480		
GELATIN, LEMON, 12/24 oz/cs	.50 box	1.00 box	2.00 box	3.00 box		1. Dissolve gelatin in hot water.
WATER, hot, 180°F.	1.00 qt	2.00 qt	1.00 gal	1.00 gal 2.00 qt		2. Add cold water. 3. Add ice and stir until dissolved. 4. Chill and allow gelatin to thicken slightly.
WATER, cold	2.00 cup	1.00 qt	2.00 qt	3.00 qt		5. Drain oranges, pineapple and fruit cocktail.
ICE, crushed	1.00 lb	2.00 lb	4.00 lb	6.00 lb		6. Whip the whip topping.
ORANGES, MAND SECT, HVY SRP, FNCY, 6/10	.50 can	1.00 can	2.00 can	3.00 can		7. Fold drained fruit and whipped topping into slightly congealed gelatin.
PINEAPPLE TIDBITS, HVY SRP, XSTD, 6/10	.50 can	1.00 can	2.00 can	3.00 can		8. Pour approx 1 gal and 1.5 cups mixture into 20- by 12- by 2.5-in. pans.
FRUIT COCKTAIL, FNCY, 6/10	.50 can	1.00 can	2.00 can	3.00 can		9. Refrigerate and allow to thicken.
MARSHMALLOWS, MINIATURE, 12/1 lb	1.00 lb	2.00 lb	4.00 lb	6.00 lb		10. Cut slices so each pan will yield 40 servings. 11. Place in serving dish lined with lettuce.
WHIP TOPPING, 12/32 foz can	1.00 can	2.00 can	4.00 can	6.00 can		*Early Prep: Prepare gelatin 1 day ahead of serving day.

4600	MANDARIN ORANGE/ORANGE GELATIN	SALADS—Gelatins
Recipe No.	Recipe Name	Category

Serving Standards:

		4 oz		Cold
Pan	Portions/Pan	Portion Size	Utensil	Temperature

Ingredients	Portions				E* Procedure
	48	96	288	480	
GELATIN, ORANGE, 12/24 oz/cs	1.00 box	2.00 box	6.00 box	10.00 box	1. Dissolve gelatin in hot water.
WATER, hot, 180°F.	.50 gal	1.00 gal	3.00 gal	5.00 gal	2. Add cold water and stir.
WATER, cold	1.00 qt	2.00 qt	1.00 gal	2.00 gal	3. Add ice and stir until dissolved.
			2.00 qt	2.00 qt	4. Chill and allow to thicken slightly.
ICE, crushed	2.00 lb	4.00 lb	12.00 lb	20.00 lb	5. Drain mandarin oranges.
ORANGES, MAND SECT, HVY SRP, FNCY, 6/10	1.00 can	2.00 can	6.00 can	10.00 can	6. When gelatin has congealed slightly, add mandarin oranges. Mix well.
					7. Pour .5 cup gelatin mixture into molds.
					8. Refrigerate until congealed.
					9. Unmold on lettuce.
					*Early Prep: Prepare gelatin 1 day ahead of serving day.

4605	ORANGE SHERBET SALAD				SALADS–Gelatins
Recipe No.	Recipe Name				Category

Serving Standards: _____ _____ __4 oz__ _____ __Cold__
        Pan   Portions/Pan   Portion Size   Utensil   Temperature

Ingredients	Portions				E*	Procedure
	56	112	168	280		
GELATIN, ORANGE, 12/24 oz/cs	1.00 box	2.00 box	3.00 box	5.00 box		1. Dissolve gelatin in boiling water.
						2. Add sherbet and stir until dissolved.
WATER, hot, 180°F.	3.00 qt	1.00 gal	2.00 gal	3.00 gal		3. Chill until sirupy.
		2.00 qt	1.00 qt	3.00 qt		4. Drain mandarin oranges and add to mixture.
SHERBET, ORANGE, 3 gal	2.00 qt	1.00 gal	1.00 gal	2.00 gal		5. Pour .5 cup gelatin mixture into individual molds.
			2.00 qt	2.00 qt		6. Place in refrigerator to congeal.
ORANGES, MAND SECT, HVY SRP, FNCY, 6/10	1.00 can	2.00 can	3.00 can	5.00 can		*Note:* 1 gal sherbet equals 6.5 lb.
						*Early Prep: Prepare 1 day in advance.

4608	PEACHES IN STRAWBERRY GELATIN	SALADS—Gelatins
Recipe No.	Recipe Name	Category

Serving Standards:

Pan	Portions/Pan	4 oz Portion Size	Utensil	Cold Temperature

Ingredients	Portions				E* Procedure
	50	100	300	500	
GELATIN, STRAWBERRY, 12/24 oz/cs	1.00 box	2.00 box	6.00 box	10.00 box	1. Dissolve gelatin in hot water.
WATER, hot, 180°F.	.50 gal	1.00 gal	3.00 gal	5.00 gal	2. Add cold water and stir.
WATER, cold	1.00 qt	2.00 qt	1.00 gal	2.00 gal	3. Add ice and stir until dissolved.
			2.00 qt	2.00 qt	4. Chill and allow to thicken slightly.
ICE, crushed	2.00 lb	4.00 lb	12.00 lb	20.00 lb	5. Drain peaches.
PEACHES, YC, FNCY, SLI 6/10 cs	1.00 can	2.00 can	6.00 can	10.00 can	6. When gelatin has congealed slightly, add peaches. Mix well.

7. Pour .5 cup gelatin mixture into molds.
8. Refrigerate until firm.
9. Unmold on lettuce.
*Early Prep: Prepare gelatin 1 day ahead of serving day.

4610	**PEAR IN LIME GELATIN**					**SALADS—Gelatins**
Recipe No.	Recipe Name					Category

Serving Standards: _____ _____ __4 oz__ _____ __Cold__

Pan Portions/Pan Portion Size Utensil Temperature

Ingredients	Portions				E* Procedure
	55	110	330	550	
GELATIN, LIME, 12/24 oz/cs	1.00 box	2.00 box	6.00 box	10.00 box	1. Dissolve gelatin in hot water.
WATER, hot, 180°F.	.50 gal	1.00 gal	3.00 gal	5.00 gal	2. Stir in cold water.
WATER, cold	1.00 qt	2.00 qt	1.00 gal	2.00 gal	3. Add ice and stir until dissolved.
			2.00 qt	2.00 qt	4. Chill and allow to thicken slightly.
ICE, crushed	2.00 lb	4.00 lb	12.00 lb	20.00 lb	5. Drain pears and dice.
PEARS, BARTLETT, HLVS, FNCY, 35 to 40 ct, 6/10	1.00 can	2.00 can	6.00 can	10.00 can	6. Fill molds with .5 cup gelatin mixture.

7. Refrigerate.
8. Unmold on lettuce.
*Early Prep: Prepare gelatin 1 day ahead of serving day.

4615	RASPBERRY ARGENTINE	SALADS–Gelatins
Recipe No.	Recipe Name	Category

Serving Standards:

		4 oz		Cold
Pan	Portions/Pan	Portion Size	Utensil	Temperature

Ingredients	Portions				E*	Procedure
	45	90	135	180		
GELATIN, RASPBERRY, 12/24 oz/cs	1.00 box	2.00 box	3.00 box	4.00 box		1. Dissolve gelatin, sugar and salt in boiling water in mixing bowl.
SUGAR, GRAN, 100 lb	.50 cup	1.00 cup	1.50 cup	2.00 cup		2. Measure crushed pineapple, then drain it and add enough cold water to pineapple juice to equal amt of cold water needed.
SALT, 100 lb bag	1.00 tsp	2.00 tsp	1.00 tbs	1.00 tbs 1.00 tsp		
WATER, hot, 180°F.	2.00 qt	1.00 gal	1.00 gal 2.00 qt	2.00 gal		3. Add cold water-juice mixture to ingredients in mixing bowl. Mix well.
WATER, cold	1.00 qt	2.00 qt	3.00 qt	1.00 gal		4. Add crushed ice and stir slowly to dissolve.
ICE, crushed	2.00 lb	4.00 lb	6.00 lb	8.00 lb		5. Chop prunes with a French knife, not on the chopper.
PINEAPPLE, HAW, CRU, HVY SRP, XSTD, 6/10	1.00 qt .33 cup	2.00 qt .66 cup	3.00 qt 1.00 cup	1.00 gal 1.33 cup		6. When gelatin begins to thicken slightly, add remaining ingredients.
PRUNES, prepared, STD, 6/10	1.25 lb	2.50 lb	3.75 lb	5.00 lb		7. Pour .5 cup gelatin mixture into molds and refrigerate.
PECANS, FNCY, med, 30 lb/cs	.25 lb	.50 lb	.75 lb	1.00 lb		8. Unmold on lettuce leaf.

*Early Prep: Prepare gelatin 1 day ahead of serving day.

4621	**RIBBON GELATIN**				**SALADS—Gelatins**
Recipe No.	Recipe Name				Category

Serving Standards: 20- by 12- by 2.5-in. Pan / 40 Portions/Pan / 4.5 oz Portion Size / Utensil / Cold Temperature

Ingredients	Portions				E*	Procedure
	120	240	360	600		
GELATIN, LIME, 12/24 oz/cs	1.00 box	2.00 box	3.00 box	5.00 box		1. Drain pineapple and save juice.
WATER, hot, 180°F.	.50 gal	1.00 gal	1.50 gal	2.50 gal		2. Dissolve lime gelatin in hot water.
WATER, cold	1.00 qt	2.00 qt	3.00 qt	1.00 gal		3. Add cold water. Add ice and stir until melted.
				1.00 qt		4. Allow to cool and thicken slightly.
ICE, crushed	2.00 lb	4.00 lb	6.00 lb	10.00 lb		5. Divide pineapple equally among 20- by 12- by 2.5-in. pans.
PINEAPPLE TIDBITS, HVY SRP, XSTD, 6/10	1.00 can	2.00 can	3.00 can	5.00 can		6. Divide lime gelatin mixture evenly over pineapple in pans.
GELATIN, LEMON, 12/24 oz/cs	1.00 box	2.00 box	3.00 box	5.00 box		7. Refrigerate until firm.
WATER, hot, 180°F.	.50 gal	1.00 gal	1.50 gal	2.50 gal		8. Dissolve lemon gelatin in hot water.
WATER, cold	1.00 qt	2.00 qt	3.00 qt	1.00 gal		9. Add cold water. Add ice and stir until melted.
				1.00 qt		10. Mix salad dressing and cream cheese together until soft and smooth.
ICE, crushed	2.00 lb	4.00 lb	6.00 lb	10.00 lb		11. Combine with lemon gelatin mixture using a wire whip.
SALAD DRESSING, 4/1 gal/cs	2.66 cup	1.00 qt 1.32 cup	2.00 qt	3.00 qt 1.30 cup		
CREAM CHEESE, 6/3 lb	2.00 lb	4.00 lb	6.00 lb	10.00 lb		12. Divide lemon gelatin mixture over each congealed layer of lime gelatin.
GELATIN, RASPBERRY, 12/24 oz/cs	1.00 box	2.00 box	3.00 box	5.00 box		13. Refrigerate until firm.
						14. Weigh bananas. Weight is AP.
WATER, hot, 180°F.	.50 gal	1.00 gal	1.50 gal	2.50 gal		15. Peel and slice bananas and place in pineapple juice from Step 1.
WATER, cold	1.00 qt	2.00 qt	3.00 qt	1.00 gal		
				1.00 qt		16. Dissolve raspberry gelatin in hot water.
ICE, crushed	2.00 lb	4.00 lb	6.00 lb	10.00 lb		17. Pour in cold water. Add ice and stir until melted.
BANANAS, 40 lb box, fresh	5.00 lb	10.00 lb	15.00 lb	25.00 lb		18. Allow to cool and thicken slightly.
						19. Add drained, sliced bananas to slightly congealed raspberry gelatin.
						(cont. on next page)

4621	RIBBON GELATIN (cont.)		SALADS—Gelatins
Recipe No.	Recipe Name		Category

Procedure

20. Divide raspberry gelatin mixture evenly over second congealed layer in each pan.
21. Refrigerate until firm.
22. For service, cut each pan of gelatin into 40 portions and serve on lettuce leaf on individual serving dish.

*Early Prep: Prepare gelatin 1 day ahead of serving day.

4625	ROSY FRUIT MOLD		SALADS—Gelatins
Recipe No.	Recipe Name		Category

Serving Standards:

Pan	Portions/Pan	4 oz — Portion Size	Utensil	Cold — Temperature

Ingredients	Portions				E*	Procedure
	50	100	200	300		
GELATIN, RASPBERRY, 12/24 oz/cs	1.00 box	2.00 box	4.00 box	6.00 box		1. Drain fruit cocktail.
WATER, hot, 180°F.	1.50 qt	3.00 qt	1.00 gal 2.00 qt	2.00 gal 1.00 qt		2. Dissolve gelatin in hot water. 3. Add cold water and stir.
WATER, cold	2.00 cup	1.00 qt	2.00 qt	3.00 qt		4. Stir in ice until melted.
ICE, crushed	2.00 lb	4.00 lb	8.00 lb	12.00 lb		5. Add lemon juice.
LEMON JUICE, RECONSTITUTED, 12/qt jars	1.00 cup	2.00 cup	1.00 qt	1.00 qt 2.00 cup		6. Chill and allow to thicken slightly. 7. Soften cream cheese using warm water specified.
PINEAPPLE, HAW, SLI, FNCY, 52 ct, 6/10	1.00 can	2.00 can	4.00 can	6.00 can		8. Put softened cream cheese into pastry bag and squeeze a ball into bottom of molds. 9. Sprinkle cream cheese with chopped pecans.
FRUIT COCKTAIL, FNCY, 6/10	1.00 can	2.00 can	4.00 can	6.00 can		10. When gelatin is slightly congealed, fold in drained fruit cocktail.
CREAM CHEESE, 6/3 lb	.50 lb	1.00 lb	2.00 lb	3.00 lb		11. Pour .5 cup gelatin mixture into molds and refrigerate.
WATER, warm	2.00 tsp	1.00 tbs 1.00 tsp	2.00 tbs 2.00 tsp	.25 cup		12. Unmold over pineapple slices on lettuce.
PECANS, FNCY, med, 30 lb/cs	2.00 oz	.25 lb	.50 lb	.75 lb		*Early Prep: Prepare gelatin 1 day before serving day.

4640 SPRINGTIME SALAD						SALADS—Gelatins
Recipe No. Recipe Name						Category

Serving Standards: _____ Pan _____ Portions/Pan   **4 oz** Portion Size _____ Utensil   **Cold** Temperature

Ingredients	Portions				E*	Procedure
	76	**152**	**304**	**532**		
GELATIN, LIME, 12/24 oz/cs	1.00 box	2.00 box	4.00 box	7.00 box		1. Dissolve gelatin in hot water.
WATER, hot, 180°F.	1.50 qt	3.00 qt	1.00 gal 2.00 qt	2.00 gal 2.50 qt		2. Cool to room temp, but do not allow to begin congealing. 3. Stir in the evaporated milk.
MILK, EVAPORATED, 48/14.5 oz	5.00 can	10.00 can	20.00 can	35.00 can		4. Chop celery fine. Wt is EP. 5. Measure crushed pineapple—do not drain.
CELERY, FRESH, GRN, FNCY, pascal, bun	1.00 lb	2.00 lb	4.00 lb	7.00 lb		6. Add remaining ingredients and mix well. 7. Fill molds with .5 cup gelatin mixture.
PINEAPPLE, HAW, CRU, HVY SRP, XSTD, 6/10	2.25 qt	1.00 gal .50 qt	2.00 gal 1.00 qt	3.00 gal 3.75 qt		8. Refrigerate to congeal. 9. Unmold on lettuce leaf.
LEMON JUICE, RECONSTI-TUTED, 12/qt jars	.50 cup	1.00 cup	2.00 cup	3.50 cup		Caution: Evaporated milk and other ingredients must be added at just the right time. If milk is added while mixture is hot, it will curdle. But if milk and the crushed pineapple are added after mixture begins to congeal, the liquids will not congeal with the water. and the product will be too soft.
COTTAGE CHEESE, 25 lb bag in box	4.00 lb	8.00 lb	16.00 lb	28.00 lb		
PECANS, FNCY, med, 30 lb/cs	1.00 lb	2.00 lb	4.00 lb	7.00 lb		*Early Prep: Prepare 1 day ahead of serving day.
MAYONNAISE, 4/1 gal/cs	2.00 cup	1.00 qt	2.00 qt	3.00 qt 2.00 cup		

4645	STRAWBERRY GLAZE				SALADS—Gelatins
Recipe No.	Recipe Name				Category

Serving Standards:

Pan	Portions/Pan	4 oz Portion Size	Utensil	Cold Temperature

Ingredients	Portions				E*	Procedure
	60	120	180	360		
GELATIN, STRAWBERRY, 12/24 oz/cs	1.00 box	2.00 box	3.00 box	6.00 box		1. Dissolve gelatin in hot water.
GELATIN, LEMON, 12/24 oz/cs	.50 box	1.00 box	1.50 box	3.00 box		2. Add ice and stir until dissolved. 3. Cool gelatin in refrigerator until bottom of bowl is no longer warm.
WATER, hot, 180°F.	3.00 qt	1.00 gal 2.00 qt	2.00 gal 1.00 qt	4.00 gal 2.00 qt		4. When cool, add thawed strawberries.
ICE, crushed	2.00 lb	4.00 lb	6.00 lb	12.00 lb		5. Soften cream cheese with water in chopper.
STRAWBERRIES, FNCY, SLI, 6/6.5 lb/cs	1.00 can	2.00 can	3.00 can	6.00 can		6. Fill pastry tube with cream cheese and place a small amt in bottom of individual molds.
PECANS, FNCY, med, 30 lb/cs	.25 lb	.50 lb	.75 lb	1.50 lb		7. Sprinkle a few pecans over cream cheese in each mold.
CREAM CHEESE, 6/3 lb	.75 lb	1.50 lb	2.25 lb	4.50 lb		8. Pour .5 cup gelatin into molds.
WATER, cold	1.00 tbs	2.00 tbs	3.00 tbs	.25 cup 2.00 tbs		9. Refrigerate to congeal. 10. Unmold on lettuce leaf. *Early Prep: Prepare gelatin 1 day ahead of serving day. Thaw strawberries 2 days ahead of serving day.

4650	SUNSHINE SALAD						SALADS—Gelatins
Recipe No.	Recipe Name						Category

Serving Standards:

	Pan	Portions/Pan	4 oz Portion Size	Utensil	Cold Temperature

Ingredients	Portions				E*	Procedure
	50	**100**	**200**	**400**		
GELATIN, LEMON, 12/24 oz/cs	1.00 box	2.00 box	4.00 box	8.00 box		1. Drain pineapple. Save juice. 2. Dissolve gelatin in hot water.
WATER, hot, 180°F.	.50 gal	1.00 gal	2.00 gal	4.00 gal		3. Add pineapple juice and enough cold water to make the specified amt of cold water.
WATER, cold	1.00 qt	2.00 qt	1.00 gal	2.00 gal		4. Add ice and stir until dissolved.
ICE, crushed	2.00 lb	4.00 lb	8.00 lb	16.00 lb		5. Chill and allow to thicken slightly.
PINEAPPLE, HAW, CRU, HVY SRP, XSTD, 6/10	.50 can	1.00 can	2.00 can	4.00 can		6. Grate carrots. 7. When gelatin has congealed slightly, add crushed pineapple and grated carrots.
CARROTS, FNCY, bulk, 50 lb, no tops	1.00 lb 6.00 oz	2.75 lb	5.50 lb	11.00 lb		8. Pour .5 cup mixture into molds. 9. Refrigerate and allow to congeal. 10. Unmold in serving dishes lined with lettuce. *Early Prep: Prepare gelatin 1 day ahead of serving day.

Breakfast Items

6014	POACHED EGG				BREAKFAST ITEMS
Recipe No.	**Recipe Name**				**Category**

Serving Standards: _____ _____ <u>2 oz</u> _____ <u>Hot</u>
               Pan   **Portions/Pan**   **Portion Size**   **Utensil**   **Temperature**

Ingredients	Portions				Procedure
	12	**60**	**120**	**240**	
EGGS, FRESH, 30 doz/case	1.00 doz	5.00 doz	10.00 doz	20.00 doz	1. Break eggs in side dish. Place in high speed steam cooker for 1 min. for light and 2 min. for regular. Cooking time: 1 to 2 min. Equipment: high speed steam cooker

6016	SCRAMBLED EGGS				BREAKFAST ITEMS
Recipe No.	Recipe Name				Category

Serving Standards: <u>20- by 12- by 2.5-in.</u>   <u>   </u>   <u>2 oz</u>   <u>No. 24 Scoop</u>   <u>Hot</u>
                          Pan   Portions/Pan   Portion Size   Utensil   Temperature

Ingredients	Portions				Procedure
	40	80	240	480	

EGGS, 6/5 lb/cs
SHORTENING, oil for
  grill frying
	5.00 lb
	.25 cup
		10.00 lb
		.50 cup
			30.00 lb
			1.50 cup
				60.00 lb
				3.00 cup
					1. Beat eggs with wire whip for 3 min. on No. 3
					   speed.
					2. Heat grill to 350°F.
					3. Coat grill with oil.
					4. Pour beaten eggs onto grill.
					5. Scramble eggs for 3 min.
					6. Put eggs into 20- by 12- by 2.5-in. counter pans
					   and place in heat-holding cabinet.
					Cooking time: 3 min.
					Cooking temp: 350°F.
					Equipment: grill

6036	CHEESE OMELET	BREAKFAST ITEMS
Recipe No.	Recipe Name	Category

Serving Standards: __20- by 12- by 2.5-in.__   __3 oz__   __Solid Spatula__   __Hot__
　　　　　　　　　　　Pan　　　　Portions/Pan　　Portion Size　　Utensil　　Temperature

Ingredients	Portions				Procedure
	5	50	100	150	
EGGS, 6/5 lb/cs	1.00 lb	10.00 lb	20.00 lb	30.00 lb	1. Beat the eggs with wire whip for 3 min. on No. 3 speed. Grate cheese.
CHEDDAR CHEESE,	2.50 oz	1.50 lb	3.00 lb	4.50 lb	2. Heat grill to 350°F.
WHEEL		1.00 oz	2.00 oz	3.00 oz	3. Coat grill with oil
SHORTENING, oil for	1.50 tsp	.25 cup	.50 cup	.75 cup	4. Using a 3 oz ladle, deposit eggs on grill.
grill frying		1.00 tbs	2.00 tbs	3.00 tbs	5. Sprinkle .5 oz (about 2 tbs) of grated cheese on omelet.
					6. When firm enough, fold and continue to cook until done. Omelet should be tender and moist and browning should be evident only as a light tannish covering.
					7. Serve immediately.
					Note: These eggs can be beaten with the ones for scrambled eggs.
					Cooking temp: 350°F.
					Equipment: grill, mixer

6052	PANCAKES				BREAKFAST ITEMS
Recipe No.	Recipe Name				Category

Serving Standards: 20- by 12- by 2.5-in. _Pan_   _Portions/Pan_   2 ea _Portion Size_   Solid Spatula _Utensil_   Hot _Temperature_

Ingredients	Portions				Procedure
	12	24	96	144	
PANCAKE MIX,	.50 box	1.00 box	4.00 box	6.00 box	1. Pour two-thirds of total water into mixing bowl.
6/5 lb box					2. Add dry mix and using a wire whip, whip mix until
WATER, cold	1.00 qt	2.00 qt	2.00 gal	4.00 gal	well blended.
	1.50 cup	3.25 cup	3.00 qt	3.50 cup	3. Add remaining one-third water and blend well.
	2.00 tbs		1.00 cup		4. Using a 3-oz ladle, deposit batter on preheated
SHORTENING, oil for	.25 cup	.75 cup	3.00 cup	1.00 qt	oiled grill at 375°F.
grill frying	2.00 tbs			.50 cup	5. When brown on one side, turn and brown on other
SYRUP, IND PANCAKE,	.12 cs	.25 cs	1.00 cs	1.50 cs	side.
100/1.5 oz/cs					6. Pancakes are approx 5.5 in. diameter.
					Note 1: Place syrup on condiment stand.
					Note 2: Cooked weight of 2 pancakes is approx 5 oz.
					Cooking temp: 375°F.
					Equipment: grill

6054					BREAKFAST ITEMS

6054 Recipe No. **BLUEBERRY PANCAKES** Recipe Name

BREAKFAST ITEMS Category

Serving Standards: **20- by 12- by 2.5-in.** Pan **Portions/Pan** **2 ea** Portion Size **Solid Spatula** Utensil **Hot** Temperature

Ingredients	Portions				Procedure
	12	**24**	**96**	**144**	
PANCAKE MIX, 6/5 lb box	.50 box	1.00 box	4.00 box	6.00 box	1. Drain blueberries.
WATER, cold	1.00 qt .75 cup	2.00 qt 1.50 cup	2.00 gal 1.00 qt 2.00 cup	3.00 gal 2.00 qt 1.00 cup	2. Pour two-thirds of total water into mixing bowl. 3. Add the dry mix and, using a wire whip, mix until well blended. 4. Add remaining one-third water and blend well.
BLUEBERRIES, FNCY, 6/10, water pack	.25 can	.50 can	2.00 can	3.00 can	5. Add blueberries, mix lightly.
SHORTENING, oil for grill frying	.25 cup 2.00 tbs	.75 cup	3.00 cup	1.00 qt .50 cup	6. Using a 3-oz ladle, deposit batter on preheated oiled grill at 375°F. 7. When brown on one side, turn and brown on other side.
SYRUP, IND PANCAKE, 100/1.5 oz/cs	.12 cs	.25 cs	1.00 cs	1.50 cs	8. Pancake is approx 5.5 in. diameter. *Note 1:* Place syrup on condiment stand. *Note 2:* 1 can blueberries drained is approx 2 qt. Cooking temp: 375°F. Equipment: grill

6062	WAFFLES				BREAKFAST ITEMS
Recipe No.	Recipe Name				Category

Serving Standards: _____   _____   __1 ea__   __Tongs__   __Hot__

Pan   Portions/Pan   Portion Size   Utensil   Temperature

Ingredients	Portions				Procedure
	50	100	200	300	
WAFFLE MIX, 6/5 lb box	1.00 box	2.00 box	4.00 box	6.00 box	1. Pour two-thirds of total water in mixing bowl.
WATER, cold	2.00 qt	1.00 gal	2.00 gal	4.00 gal	2. Add the dry mix and use a wire whip to mix until well blended.
	3.25 cup	1.00 qt	3.00 qt	3.50 cup	3. Add remaining one-third water and blend well.
		2.50 cup	1.00 cup		4. Each time before pouring batter, coat waffle iron with frying oil.
SHORTENING, oil for	2.00 cup	1.00 qt	2.00 qt	3.00 qt	5. Deposit 3-oz ladle of batter into center of hot waffle iron.
grill frying					6. Bake at 380°F. until golden brown (approx 3 to 4 min.).
MARGARINE, SOLID, 1 lb	3.25 lb	6.50 lb	13.00 lb	19.50 lb	7. Melt margarine and serve a 1-oz ladle of margarine over each waffle.
SYRUP, IND, PANCAKE,	.50 cs	1.00 cs	2.00 cs	3.00 cs	*Note:* Cooked wt of waffle is 2 oz.
100/1.5 oz/cs					Cooking time: 3 to 4 min. ea
					Cooking temp: 380°F.
					Equipment: waffle iron

<u>6080</u>	**FRENCH TOAST**				**BREAKFAST ITEMS**
Recipe No.	Recipe Name				Category

Serving Standards: <u>20- by 12- by 2.5-in.</u>   <u>20</u>   <u>1 sl</u>   <u>Tongs</u>   <u>Hot</u>
                              Pan   Portions/Pan   Portion Size   Utensil   Temperature

Ingredients	Portions				Procedure
	25	50	100	200	
MILK, INST NONFAT DRY, 6/5 lb	1.50 oz	3.00 oz	6.00 oz	.75 lb	1. Dissolve dry milk in water.
WATER, cold	.50 cup	1.00 cup	2.00 cup	1.00 qt	2. Beat eggs and add to milk.
EGGS, 6/5 lb/cs	.50 lb	1.00 lb	2.00 lb	4.00 lb	3. Mix sugar, cinnamon and nutmeg together and blend into milk-egg mixture.
CINNAMON, GROUND, 1 lb	.75 tsp	1.50 tsp	1.00 tbs	2.00 tbs	4. Slice Italian bread into 16 to 17 1-oz slices on No. 15 slicer.
NUTMEG, GROUND, 1 lb	.50 tsp	1.00 tsp	2.00 tsp	1.00 tbs 1.00 tsp	5. Dip bread slices into egg-milk mixture and fry on grill at 375°F. covered with margarine. Cook until golden brown on both sides. Serve in 20- by 12- by 2.5-in. counter pans with 20 slices per pan.
SUGAR, GRAN, 100 lb	.25 lb	.50 lb	1.00 lb	2.00 lb	
ITALIAN BREAD, LOAF	1.50 lf	3.00 lf	6.00 lf	12.00 lf	
MARGARINE, SOLID, 1 lb	10.00 oz	1.25 lb	2.50 lb	5.00 lb	Cooking temp: 375°F.
SYRUP, IND, PANCAKE, 100/1.5 oz/cs	.25 cs	.50 cs	1.00 cs	2.00 cs	Equipment: grill

Fruits and Melons

7505	FRESH APPLES (RED DELICIOUS)				FRUITS and MELONS
Recipe No.	Recipe Name				Category

Serving Standards: _____ / Pan _____ / Portions/Pan | 1 ea / Portion Size | Utensil | Cool / Temperature

Ingredients	Portions				Procedure
	50	100	200	500	
APPLES, RED DEL, 100 ct	.50 box	1.00 box	2.00 box	5.00 box	1. Wash, drain and place in fruit bowl.

7526	APRICOT HALVES				FRUITS and MELONS
Recipe No.	Recipe Name				Category

Serving Standards: _____ / Pan _____ / Portions/Pan | 3 ea / Portion Size | Solid Spoon / Utensil | Cool / Temperature

Ingredients	Portions				Procedure
	31	93	217	496	
APRICOTS, HLV, FNCY, 95 ct, 6/10 can/cs	1.00 can	3.00 can	7.00 can	16.00 can	1. Dip and serve with juice in fruit dish.

7536	BANANAS				FRUITS and MELONS
Recipe No.	Recipe Name				Category

Serving Standards:

		1 ea		Room
Pan	Portions/Pan	Portion Size	Utensil	Temperature

Ingredients	Portions				Procedure
	120	240	480	960	
BANANAS, 40 lb box, fresh	1.00 box	2.00 box	4.00 box	8.00 box	1. Place bananas on serving tray.

7538	FRESH BLUEBERRIES				FRUITS and MELONS
Recipe No.	Recipe Name				Category

Serving Standards:

		.5 cup		Cool
Pan	Portions/Pan	Portion Size	Utensil	Temperature

Ingredients	Portions				Procedure
	4	48	96	192	
BLUEBERRIES, FRESH, US No. 1, pt	1.00 box	12.00 box	24.00 box	48.00 box	1. Wash blueberries. 2. Fill each serving dish with .5 cup of blueberries.

7545	FRESH BING CHERRIES				FRUITS and MELONS
Recipe No.	Recipe Name				Category

Serving Standards: _____ _____ __2 oz__ _____ _____
Pan · Portions/Pan · Portion Size · Utensil · Temperature

Ingredients	Portions				Procedure
	25	50	100	200	
CHERRIES, BING, FRESH, No. 1, sweet, lb	3.00 lb	6.00 lb	12.00 lb	24.00 lb	1. Wash cherries and drain—leave stems on. 2. Place 10 cherries in ea serving dish.

7547	WHOLE CRANBERRY SAUCE				FRUITS and MELONS
Recipe No.	Recipe Name				Category

Serving Standards: _____ _____ __2 oz__ __2 oz Ladle__ _____
Pan · Portions/Pan · Portion Size · Utensil · Temperature

Ingredients	Portions				Procedure
	50	200	300	600	
CRANBERRY SAUCE, WHOLE BERRY, 6/10/cs	1.00 can	4.00 can	6.00 can	12.00 can	1. Pour into counter pan and serve with 2-oz ladle.

7548	FRESH CRANBERRY SAUCE				FRUITS and MELONS
Recipe No.	Recipe Name				Category

Serving Standards: __10- by 12- by 4-in.__ / Pan _____ Portions/Pan __.8 oz__ / Portion Size __No. 40 Scoop__ / Utensil __Cold__ / Temperature

Ingredients	Portions				Procedure
	40	240	480	960	
Yield	1.00 qt	1.50 gal	3.00 gal	6.00 gal	1. Wash berries and remove stems.
CRANBERRIES, FRESH, US No. 1, lb	1.00 lb	6.00 lb	12.00 lb	24.00 lb	2. Place berries, sugar and water in steam kettle. 3. Bring to boil and boil until all berries pop open, 5 to 10 min.
SUGAR, GRAN, 100 lb	14.00 oz	5.25 lb	10.50 lb	21.00 lb	4. Remove from heat and cool under refrigeration.
WATER, cold	1.50 cup	2.00 qt	1.00 gal	2.00 gal	5. Serve with No. 40 scoop; for buffet, may serve with spoon.
		1.00 cup	2.00 cup	1.00 qt	Cooking time: 5 to 10 min. Equipment: steam kettle

7555	FRUIT COCKTAIL				FRUITS and MELONS
Recipe No.	Recipe Name				Category

Serving Standards: _____ / Pan _____ Portions/Pan __3 oz__ / Portion Size __No. 12 Scoop__ / Utensil __Cool__ / Temperature

Ingredients	Portions				Procedure
	25	100	200	500	
FRUIT COCKTAIL, FNCY, 6/10	1.00 can	4.00 can	8.00 can	20.00 can	1. Dip with No. 12 scoop and serve with juice in fruit dish.

7560	GRAPEFRUIT SECTIONS					FRUITS and MELONS
Recipe No.	Recipe Name					Category

Serving Standards: _____ _____ 3 oz ____ No. 12 Scoop ____ Cold ____
                   Pan   Portions/Pan   Portion Size   Utensil   Temperature

Ingredients	Portions				Procedure
	32	64	256	384	
GRAPEFRUIT SEC, FNCY, 4/1 gal	1.00 gal	2.00 gal	8.00 gal	12.00 gal	1. Fill serving dish with No. 12 scoop of grapefruit (4 sections). 2. Add a small amt of juice.

7561	HALF GRAPEFRUIT					FRUITS and MELONS
Recipe No.	Recipe Name					Category

Serving Standards: _____ _____ 1/2 ea ____ _____ Cold ____
                   Pan   Portions/Pan   Portion Size   Utensil   Temperature

Ingredients	Portions				Procedure
	17	68	204	544	
GRAPEFRUIT, WHITE, 32 to 36 ct	.25 box	1.00 box	3.00 box	8.00 box	1. Wash, cut in half and section.

7566	EMPEROR GRAPES				FRUITS and MELONS
Recipe No.	Recipe Name				Category

Serving Standards:

	Pan		Portions/Pan	3 oz Portion Size		Utensil	Cold Temperature

Ingredients	Portions				Procedure
	75	150	300	600	
GRAPES, FRESH, RED EMP, FNCY, 28 lb	14.00 lb	28.00 lb	56.00 lb	112.00 lb	1. Wash grapes and cut into 3 oz bunches. Remove excess stems. 2. Place in serving dish.

7575	WATERMELON				FRUITS and MELONS
Recipe No.	Recipe Name				Category

Serving Standards:

	Pan		Portions/Pan	1/16 ea Portion Size		Utensil	Cold Temperature

Ingredients	Portions				Procedure
	16	96	208	496	
MELONS, WATERMELON, No. 1, 22 to 27 lb	1.00 ea	6.00 ea	1.00 doz 1.00 ea	2.00 doz 7.00 ea	1. Wash and slice melon into 16 slices per melon.

7577	**FRESH MELON TRAY**					**FRUITS and MELONS**
Recipe No.	Recipe Name					Category

Serving Standards: _____ / _____ / 1 sli / _____ / Cold
Pan / Portions/Pan / Portion Size / Utensil / Temperature

Ingredients	Portions				Procedure
	32	96	192	384	
MELONS, WATERMELON, No. 1, 22 to 27 lb	1.00 ea	3.00 ea	6.00 ea	1.00 doz	1. Wash and slice watermelon into 16 slices per melon.
MELONS, CANTALOUPE, No. 1, 36 ct	1.00 ea	3.00 ea	6.00 ea	1.00 doz	2. Wash and remove seeds from cantaloupe and honey-dew melons. Slice into 8 pieces lengthwise.
MELONS, HONEYDEW, No. 1, 12 ct	1.00 ea	3.00 ea	6.00 ea	1.00 doz	3. Arrange on colored trays for self-service.

7580	**HONEYDEW MELON**					**FRUITS and MELONS**
Recipe No.	Recipe Name					Category

Serving Standards: _____ / _____ / 1/8 ea / _____ / Cold
Pan / Portions/Pan / Portion Size / Utensil / Temperature

Ingredients	Portions				Procedure
	48	96	192	480	
MELONS, HONEYDEW, No. 1, 12 ct	.50 crt	1.00 crt	2.00 crt	5.00 crt	1. Wash and seed melons. Cut each into 8 pieces, lengthwise.

7590	CANTALOUPE			FRUITS and MELONS

Recipe No. **Recipe Name** **Category**

Serving Standards: _____ _____ 1/8 ea _____ Cold

Pan   Portions/Pan   Portion Size   Utensil   Temperature

Ingredients	Portions				Procedure
	144	288	576	864	
MELONS, CANTALOUPE, No. 1, 36 ct	.50 crt	1.00 crt	2.00 crt	3.00 crt	1. Wash and seed melons. Cut each into 8 pieces, lengthwise.

7600	ORANGES			FRUITS and MELONS

Recipe No. **Recipe Name** **Category**

Serving Standards: _____ _____ 1 ea _____ Cool

Pan   Portions/Pan   Portion Size   Utensil   Temperature

Ingredients	Portions				Procedure
	50	100	200	500	
ORANGES, FNCY, Fla, 100 ct	.50 crt	1.00 crt	2.00 crt	5.00 crt	1. Wash, drain and place in fruit bowl.

7615	ORANGE SECTIONS				FRUITS and MELONS
Recipe No.	Recipe Name				Category

Serving Standards: _____ _____ __3 oz__ __No. 12 Scoop__ __Cold__
                            Pan   Portions/Pan   Portion Size   Utensil   Temperature

Ingredients	Portions				Procedure
	32	64	192	448	
ORANGE SEC, FNCY, 4/1 gal	1.00 gal	2.00 gal	6.00 gal	14.00 gal	1. Fill serving dish with No. 12 scoop of orange sections (8 sections). 2. Add a small amt of juice.

7618	ORANGE AND GRAPEFRUIT SECTIONS				FRUITS and MELONS
Recipe No.	Recipe Name				Category

Serving Standards: _____ _____ __3 oz__ __Solid Spoon__ __Cold__
                            Pan   Portions/Pan   Portion Size   Utensil   Temperature

Ingredients	Portions				Procedure
	64	192	384	768	
ORANGE SEC, FNCY, 4/1 gal	1.00 gal	3.00 gal	6.00 gal	12.00 gal	1. Dip and serve with juice in fruit dish.
GRAPEFRUIT SEC, FNCY, 4/1 gal	1.00 gal	3.00 gal	6.00 gal	12.00 gal	

7619   **FRESH PEACHES**   **FRUITS and MELONS**

Recipe No.   Recipe Name   Category

Serving Standards:

| | Pan | | Portions/Pan | 1 ea
Portion Size | Utensil | Cold
Temperature |

Ingredients	Portions				Procedure
	150	300	450	600	
PEACHES, FRESH, FREESTONE, No. 1	50.00 lb	100.00 lb	150.00 lb	200.00 lb	1. Wash, drain and place in fruit bowl.

7625   **PEACH HALVES**   **FRUITS and MELONS**

Recipe No.   Recipe Name   Category

Serving Standards:

| | Pan | | Portions/Pan | 1 hlv
Portion Size | Solid Spoon
Utensil | Cool
Temperature |

Ingredients	Portions				Procedure
	37	111	222	518	
PEACHES, YC, HLVS, FNCY, 35 to 40 ct, 6/10 cs	1.00 can	3.00 can	6.00 can	14.00 can	1. Dip and serve with juice in fruit dish.

7630	SLICED PEACHES				FRUITS and MELONS
Recipe No.	Recipe Name				Category

Serving Standards: _____   _____   __3 oz__   _____   __Cold__
                          Pan   Portions/Pan   Portion Size   Utensil   Temperature

Ingredients	Portions				Procedure
	25	100	200	500	
PEACHES, YC, FNCY, SLI, 6/10/cs	1.00 can	4.00 can	8.00 can	20.00 can	1. Place 4 slices with small amt of fruit juice in individual serving dish.

7635	PEAR HALVES				FRUITS and MELONS
Recipe No.	Recipe Name				Category

Serving Standards: _____   _____   __1 hlv__   __Solid Spoon__   __Cool__
                          Pan   Portions/Pan   Portion Size   Utensil   Temperature

Ingredients	Portions				Procedure
	37	111	222	999	
PEARS, BARTLETT, HLVS, FNCY, 35 to 40 ct, 6/10	1.00 can	3.00 can	6.00 can	27.00 can	1. Dip and serve with juice in fruit dish.

7640	FRESH BARTLETT PEARS				FRUITS and MELONS
Recipe No.	Recipe Name				Category

Serving Standards:

		1 ea		Cool
Pan	Portions/Pan	Portion Size	Utensil	Temperature

Ingredients	Portions				Procedure
	60	120	480	960	
PEARS, BARTLETT, FRESH, FNCY No. 1	.50 bsh	1.00 bsh	4.00 bsh	8.00 bsh	1. Wash, drain and place in fruit bowl.

7645	PINEAPPLE CHUNKS				FRUITS and MELONS
Recipe No.	Recipe Name				Category

Serving Standards:

		3 oz	No. 12 Scoop	Cool
Pan	Portions/Pan	Portion Size	Utensil	Temperature

Ingredients	Portions				Procedure
	30	210	510	1020	
PINEAPPLE, HAW, CHK, FNCY, 6/10	1.00 can	7.00 can	17.00 can	34.00 can	1. Dip 7 chunks, serve with juice in fruit dish with No. 12 scoop.

7650	PINEAPPLE TIDBITS					FRUITS and MELONS
Recipe No.	Recipe Name					Category

Serving Standards: _____   _____   3 oz   No. 12 Scoop   Cool
                         Pan   Portions/Pan   Portion Size   Utensil   Temperature

Ingredients	Portions				Procedure
	25	100	200	500	
PINEAPPLE TIDBITS, HVY SRP, XSTD, 6/10	1.00 can	4.00 can	8.00 can	20.00 can	1. Dip with No. 12 scoop and serve with juice in fruit dish.

7655	FRESH PINEAPPLE					FRUITS and MELONS
Recipe No.	Recipe Name					Category

Serving Standards: _____   _____   1/8   _____   Cold
                         Pan   Portions/Pan   Portion Size   Utensil   Temperature

Ingredients	Portions				Procedure
	64	128	256	384	
PINEAPPLE, HAW, No. 1, 8's	1.00 box	2.00 box	4.00 box	6.00 box	1. Cut fresh pineapple into quarters, remove core. Leaving top on is optional. 2. Slice quarters in half lengthwise. 3. Cut and loosen pineapple from shell, but keep in shell. 4. Partially slice each piece of pineapple into .5 in. slices. 5. Place pineapple portions in shell on individual serving plate.

| 7670 | PURPLE PLUMS | | | | FRUITS and MELONS |
| Recipe No. | Recipe Name | | | | Category |

Serving Standards:

| | | 3 ea | Solid Spoon | Cool |
| Pan | Portions/Pan | Portion Size | Utensil | Temperature |

| Ingredients | Portions | | | | Procedure |
	20	100	200	500	
PLUMS, PURPLE, STD, WHOLE, 6/10	1.00 can	5.00 can	10.00 can	25.00 can	1. Dip and serve with juice in fruit dish.

| 7680 | TANGERINES | | | | FRUITS and MELONS |
| Recipe No. | Recipe Name | | | | Category |

Serving Standards:

| | | 1 ea | | Cold |
| Pan | Portions/Pan | Portion Size | Utensil | Temperature |

| Ingredients | Portions | | | | Procedure |
	60	120	600	1200	
TANGERINES, FRESH, FNCY, 120 ct	.50 box	1.00 box	5.00 box	10.00 box	1. Wash, drain and place in fruit bowl.

7685	TANGELOS					FRUITS and MELONS
Recipe No.	Recipe Name					Category

Serving Standards: _____ _____ 1 ea _____ Cold

| | Pan | | Portions/Pan | Portion Size | Utensil | Temperature |

Ingredients	Portions				Procedure
	50	100	200	500	
TANGELOS, FRESH, FNCY, 100 ct	.50 box	1.00 box	2.00 box	5.00 box	1. Wash, drain and place in fruit bowl.

Miscellaneous

8020	BEEF NOODLE SOUP (TYPICAL SOUP)					MISCELLANEOUS
Recipe No.	Recipe Name					Category

Serving Standards: 12- by 10- by 8-in. _____ 6 foz 6 oz Ladle 180°F.

| | Pan | | Portions/Pan | Portion Size | Utensil | Temperature |

Ingredients	Portions				Procedure
	15	90	180	360	
SOUP, BEEF NOODLE, 12/51 oz/cs	1.00 can	6.00 can	12.00 can	24.00 can	1. Mix soup with hot water, bring to boil, stirring until well mixed.
WATER, hot, 180°F.	1.50 qt	2.00 gal 1.00 qt	4.00 gal 2.00 qt	9.00 gal	2. Pour into serving pans and maintain 180°F. temp. Cooking time: approx 5 min. for 90 servings Cooking temp: boiling Serving temp: 180°F. Equipment: steam kettle

| 8025 | OYSTER STEW | | | | MISCELLANEOUS |
| Recipe No. | Recipe Name | | | | Category |

Serving Standards: <u>12- by 10- by 8-in.</u>   <u>6 foz</u>   <u>6 oz Ladle</u>   <u>180°F.</u>
                  Pan   Portions/Pan   Portion Size   Utensil   Temperature

| Ingredients | Portions | | | | Procedure |
	10	80	160	240	
WATER, hot, 180°F.	3.75 cup	1.00 gal 3.00 qt 2.00 cup	3.00 gal 3.00 qt	5.00 gal 2.00 qt 2.00 cup	1. Place hot water in steam kettle and stir in dry milk. 2. Add soup and stir until mixed. 3. Bring to boil.
MILK, INST NONFAT DRY, 6/5 lb	3.75 oz	1.00 lb 14.00 oz	3.75 lb	5.00 lb 10.00 oz	4. Pour into serving pans. Cooking temp: boiling
SOUP, OYSTER STEW, 24/10 oz/cs	3.00 can	24.00 can	48.00 can	72.00 can	Equipment: steam kettle

8030	BEVERAGES (DINNER)				MISCELLANEOUS
Recipe No.	Recipe Name				Category

Serving Standards: _____ _____ _____ _____ _____

Pan   Portions/Pan   Portion Size   Utensil   Temperature

Ingredients	Portions				Procedure
	50	200	500	1000	
Yield	155.00 cup	620.00 cup	1550.00 cup	3100.00 cup	1. Connect or place in dispenser units according to directions on containers.
COFFEE, CONC, FRO, 12/42.7 oz can/cs	.02 can	.08 can	.20 can	.40 can	*Note:* The number of portions in this recipe denotes the number of people these quantities will serve when there are unlimited seconds.
TEA, INST, 12/6.75 oz jar/cs	.22 oz	.88 oz	2.22 oz	.25 lb .44 oz	
TEA, BAGS, 100 indv pk/box, 10 box/cs	2.74 ea	10.96 ea	2.00 doz 3.40 ea	4.00 doz 6.80 ea	
HOT CHOC MIX, 12/2 lb/cs	1.61 oz	.25 lb 2.46 oz	1.00 lb .16 oz	2.00 lb .32 oz	
COLA DRINK, 5 gal can	.07 can	.31 can	.79 can	1.58 can	
DIET COLA, 5 gal can	.02 can	.10 can	.25 can	.50 can	
SPRITE or 7-UP, 5 gal can	.02 can	.10 can	.25 can	.50 can	
ORANGE DRINK, 5 gal can	can	.03 can	.08 can	.16 can	
CO_2, drums, 20 lb	.01 dru	.06 dru	.17 dru	.34 dru	
MILK, FRESH HOMO, 6 gal can	3.14 gal	12.59 gal	31.49 gal	62.98 gal	
MILK, FRESH, CHOC, 6 gal can	.44 gal	1.76 gal	4.41 gal	8.82 gal	
MILK, FRESH, SKIM, 5 gal can	.40 gal	1.61 gal	4.04 gal	8.08 gal	

| 8035 | COFFEE | | | | MISCELLANEOUS |
| Recipe No. | Recipe Name | | | | Category |

Serving Standards:

| Pan | Portions/Pan | 6 foz Portion Size | Utensil | Hot Temperature |

| Ingredients | Portions | | | | Procedure |
	34	136	272	544	
COFFEE, CONC, FRO, 12/42.7 oz can/cs	.25 can	1.00 can	2.00 can	4.00 can	1. Follow directions on can.

| 8040 | GRAPEFRUIT JUICE (TYPICAL CANNED) | | | | MISCELLANEOUS |
| Recipe No. | Recipe Name | | | | Category |

Serving Standards:

| Pan | Portions/Pan | 4 foz Portion Size | Utensil | Cold Temperature |

| Ingredients | Portions | | | | E* Procedure |
	11	99	198	396	
GRAPEFRUIT JUICE, SW, 12/46 foz can	1.00 can	9.00 can	18.00 can	36.00 can	1. Open chilled juice and pour into dispenser for self-service. 2. Or pour into individual cups. *Early Prep: Place juice in refrig 1 day in advance.

8045	ORANGE JUICE (TYPICAL FROZEN)				MISCELLANEOUS
Recipe No.	Recipe Name				Category

Serving Standards: _____   _____   4 foz   _____   Cold
                          Pan   Portions/Pan   Portion Size   Utensil   Temperature

Ingredients	Portions				E*	Procedure
	32	96	192	384		
ORANGE JUICE, FRO, UNSWT, FNCY, 12/32 oz can	1.00 can	3.00 can	6.00 can	12.00 can		1. Mix orange juice according to directions on containers and pour into dispensers for self-service. *Early Prep: Place in refrig to thaw 1 day in advance.

8050	CHOCOLATE PUDDING (TYPICAL PUDDING)					MISCELLANEOUS
Recipe No.	Recipe Name					Category

Serving Standards:

			4 oz	No. 10 Scoop	Cold
Pan		Portions/Pan	Portion Size	Utensil	Temperature

Ingredients	Portions				Procedure
	40	80	240	480	
MILK, FRESH HOMO, 6 gal can	1.00 gal	2.00 gal	6.00 gal	12.00 gal	1. Pour chilled milk into mixer bowl.
PUDDING, CHOCOLATE INSTANT, 12/2 lb	1.00 box	2.00 box	6.00 box	12.00 box	2. Add pudding mix and whip at low speed until all powder is dampened, about 15 sec. Scrape bowl.
WHIP TOPPING, 12/32 foz can	.25 can	.50 can	1.50 can	3.00 can	3. Whip at medium speed until pudding is smooth and creamy, 1 to 2 min.
					4. Let stand 15 min. then portion with a No. 10 scoop.
					5. Whip the whip topping and, using a pastry tube, top each portion with about 1.5 tbs.
					6. Chill before serving.

8/ APPENDIX

INDEX
TO
THE CHARTS

Name of Chart	Chart Number	Page
TABLESPOONS PER OUNCE	1	322
PAN CAPACITY	2	322
FOOD MEASURES	3	323
LADLE AND SCOOP SIZE	4	323
COMMON CAN SIZES	5	323
MEASURE EQUIVALENTS	6	324
DECIMAL EQUIVALENTS	7	324
HEATING/PREPARATION	8	325
STANDARD ABBREVIATIONS	9	326
COST PER PORTION	10	328
CHANGING TO METRICS	11	332
METRIC CONVERSION TABLES	12	333

CHART 1
TABLESPOONS PER OUNCE

ITEM	TBS. PER OZ.	ITEM	TBS. PER OZ.	ITEM	TBS. PER OZ.
Allspice, Ground	5	Cream of Tartar	3	Onion Salt	3
Allspice, Whole	10	Cumin	4	Oregano, Ground	6
Baking Powder	3	Curry Powder	8	Paprika	6
Basil	8	Flour, All Purpose	4	Pepper, Ground Black	5
Cassia Buds	6	Garlic Salt	3	Pepper, Red	7
Celery Salt	4	Garlic Powder	4	Pepper, White	6
Celery Seed	6	Ginger, Ground	8	Pickling Spice	8
Chili Powder	4	Honey	1	Poppy Seeds	6
Cinnamon, Ground	6	Mace	6	Poultry Seasoning	10
Cloves, Ground	5	Margarine	2	Rosemary	10
Cloves, Whole	6	Marjoram	10	Sage, Ground	8
Cocoa	4	Milk, Dry	4	Salt	2
Coconut, Grated	6	Mustard, Dry	5	Shortening	2
Coffee	5	Mustard, Prepared	4	Soda, Baking	3
Coriander	10	Nutmeg, Ground	6	Thyme	12
Corn Meal	3	Onion Juice	2	Vanilla Extract	2
Cornstarch	3				

CHART 2
PAN CAPACITY

PAN SIZE	DEPTH OF PAN	NUMBER OF QUARTS	NUMBER OF ½-CUP PORTIONS (APPROX)
12 in. by 20 in.	2½ in.	9	70
	4 in.	15	120
	6 in.	22	175
1/2 Size	2½ in.	4	30
	4 in.	7	55
	6 in.	10	80
1/4 Size	2½ in.	2	16
	4 in.	3	24
	6 in.	4½	35
1/3 Size	2½ in.	3	20
	4 in.	4½	35
	6 in.	6½	50
18 in. by 26 in.	2½ in.	15	120
	3½ in.	23	185

CHART 3
FOOD MEASURES

3 teaspoons	=	1 tablespoon
2 tablespoons	=	1/8 cup or 1 fluid ounce
4 tablespoons	=	1/4 cup
8 tablespoons	=	1/2 cup
12 tablespoons	=	3/4 cup
16 tablespoons	=	1 cup
2 cups	=	1 pint
2 pints	=	1 quart
4 quarts	=	1 gallon
8 quarts	=	1 peck
4 pecks	=	1 bushel

CHART 4

LADLE SIZE

1/4 cup (2 ounces)
1/2 cup (4 ounces)
3/4 cup (6 ounces)
1 cup (8 ounces)

SCOOP SIZE

Scoop Measure	Level Measure
6	2/3 cup
8	1/2 cup
10	2/5 cup
12	1/3 cup
16	1/4 cup
20	3-1/5 tablespoons
24	2-2/3 tablespoons
30	2-1/5 tablespoons
40	1-3/5 tablespoons

CHART 5
COMMON CAN SIZES*

CAN SIZE	PRODUCT	APPROX. NO. CUPS
6-oz.	Used principally for frozen concentrated juices, as well as regular single-strength fruit and vegetable juices.	3/4
8-oz.	Used for most fruits and vegetables, as well as for ripe olives.	1
No. 1 (picnic)	Used principally for condensed soups, and some fruits, vegetables, meat, and fish products.	1-1/4
No. 2	Used for all vegetable items, plus a wide range of fruits and fruit and tomato juices.	2-1/2
No. 2-1/2	Used principally for fruits, such as peaches, pears, plums, and fruit cocktail, plus vegetables such as tomatoes, sauerkraut, and pumpkin.	3-1/2
46-oz. (No. 3 cylinder)	Used almost exclusively for vegetable and fruit juices. Whole chicken is also packed in this can.	5-3/4
No. 10	So-called "institutional" or "restaurant" size container. Most fruits and vegetables are packed in it. It is not ordinarily available in retail stores.	12-13

*American Can Company

CHART 6
GENERAL EQUIVALENTS

16 tablespoons	=	1 cup
1 cup (standard measure)	=	½ pint (8 fluid ounces)
2 cups	=	1 pint
16 ounces	=	1 pound
3 quarts (dry)	=	1 peck
4 pecks	:=	1 bushel
32 ounces	=	1 fluid quart
128 ounces	= 8 pounds =	1 fluid gallon
1 No. 10 can	=	13 cups
1 pound margarine	=	2 cups
1 pound flour	=	4 cups

The number of the scoop determines the number of servings in each quart of a mixture, i.e., with a No. 16 scoop, one quart of mixture will yield 16 servings.

CHART 7
DECIMAL EQUIVALENTS OF FRACTIONS

DECIMAL		FRACTION
.25	=	1/4
.33	=	1/3
.5	=	1/2
.66	=	2/3
.75	=	3/4

The abbreviation beside the fraction tells what unit of measure to use.

Examples

0.25 cup	=	1/4 cup
0.25 lb.	=	1/4 lb. or 4 oz.
0.33 cup	=	1/3 cup
0.5 lb.	=	1/2 lb. or 8 oz.
0.5 gal.	=	1/2 gal. or 2 qt.
0.66 cup	=	2/3 cup
1.66 cup	=	1-2/3 cup
0.75 cup	=	3/4 cup
2.75 lb.	=	2 lb. 12 oz.

CHART 8
TYPICAL PREPARATION TIME—HIGH SPEED STEAMER

HEATING/PREPARATION[1]

STEAM COOKER TIMING CHART*

Vegetables—Frozen

Item	Weight Per Pan	Size of Perforated Pan	No. of Pans	Time in Min.
Asparagus, Spears	3-2½ lb	12x20x2½ in.	1	3½-4
Beans green regular	3-2½ lb	12x20x2½ in.	1	3¼-3¾
Beans, lima	3-2½ lb	12x20x2½ in.	1	3-3½
Broccoli	3-2 lb	12x20x2½ in.	1	2-2½
Brussel Sprouts	3-2½ lb	12x20x2½ in.	1	2½-3½
Carrots, diced	3-2½ lb	12x20x2½ in.	1	2½-3
Cauliflower	3-2½ lb	12x20x2½ in.	1	3-3½
Corn	3-2½ lb	12x20x2½ in.	1	2¼-2½
Peas loose pack	3-2½ lb	12x20x2½ in.	1	1½-2

Frozen Prepared Entrees

Item	Weight Per Pan	Size of Perforated Pan	No. of Pans	Time in. Min.
Bulk pack ¾ in. depth	1 pkg. 3 lb	12x20x2½ in.	1	4½-5½
Individual Pouches	6-8 oz. per pouch	12x20x2½ in.	1	4½-5½
Shrimp C D P	3 lb	12x20x2½ in.	1	6-8
Shrimp, green	3 lb	12x20x2½ in.	1	8-10
Lobster Tails	6 lb	12x20x2½ in.	1	7-8

*Use of special insert.
*Starting temperature 0°F.

[1]*Frozen Food Opportunity Time, National Frozen Food Association, Institutions/VF Magazine, 1972-73, p. 30.*

CHART 9—

AD	Added		DEG	Degree
ANLTCL	Analytical		DEHYD	Dehydrated
AP	As Purchased		DK	Dark
APPROX	Approximately		DOZ	Dozen
ASSTD	Assorted		DRU	Drum
BET	Beet		DR WT	Drained Weight
BF	Beef		EA	Each
BG	Bag		EP	Edible Portion
BLK	Block		EVA	Evaporated
BNLS	Boneless		EX STD	Extra Standard
BNS	Beans		F	Fahrenheit
BSH	Bushel		FCY	Fancy
BSK	Basket		FOZ	Fluid Ounce
BTL	Bottle		FZ	Frozen
BUN	Bunch		GAL	Gallon
BX	Box		GD	Good
CEL	Cello		GR	Green
CHO	Choice		GRD	Ground
CKNG	Cooking		HC	Half Cup
CN	Can		HD	Head
CND	Canned		HLV	Half
CONC	Concentrate		HLVS	Halves
CR	Cream		HOMOG	Homogenized
CRT	Crate		HR	Hour
CS	Case		HVY	Heavy
CT	Count		IND	Individual
CTN	Carton		JAR	Jar
CUB	Cubed		LB	Pound
CUP	Cup		LF	Loaf

STANDARD ABBREVIATIONS

LG	Large	SHK	Shank
LK	Lake	SHT	Sheet
LO	Long	SLD	Solid
MED	Medium	SLI & SL	Slice
MIN	Minimum/Minute	SM	Small
NO	Number	SPRTS	Sprouts
OZ	Ounce	STD	Standard
PAN	Pan	SV	Sieve
PAT	Pattie	SWT	Sweet
PCNT	Per Cent	SWTND	Sweetened
PCS	Pieces	TBS	Tablespoon
PK	Pork	TEMP	Temperature
PKG	Package	TSP	Teaspoon
POWD	Powdered	TOM	Tomato
PROP	Proportion	TVP	Textured Veg. Protein
PT	Pint	UNCKD	Uncooked
PURP	Purpose	UNPTD	Unpitted
QC	Quarter (fourth) cup	UNSWTND	Unsweetened
QK	Quick	W/	With
QT	Quart	W/O	Without
QTR	Quarter	WHL	Whole
REG	Regular	WTR	Water
ROL	Roll	YC	Yellow Cling
RSP	Red Sour Pitted		

CHART 10–

PURCHASE COST PER POUND	1 oz.	2 oz.	2-1/4 oz.	3 oz.	4 oz.	5 oz.
.10	.00625	.0125	.0141	.0188	.0250	.0313
.11	.0069	.0138	.0155	.0206	.0275	.0343
.12	.0075	.0150	.0169	.0225	.0300	.0375
.13	.0081	.0163	.0183	.0244	.0325	.0406
.14	.0088	.0175	.0197	.0263	.0350	.0438
.15	.0094	.0188	.0211	.0281	.0375	.0469
.16	.0100	.0200	.0225	.0300	.0400	.0500
.17	.0106	.0213	.0239	.0319	.0425	.0531
.18	.0113	.0225	.0253	.0338	.0450	.0563
.19	.0119	.0236	.0267	.0356	.0475	.0594
.20	.0125	.0250	.0281	.0375	.0500	.0625
.21	.0131	.0263	.0295	.0394	.0525	.0656
.22	.0138	.0275	.0309	.0413	.0550	.0688
.23	.0148	.0288	.0323	.0432	.0575	.0719
.24	.0150	.0300	.0338	.0450	.0600	.0750
.25	.0156	.0313	.0352	.0469	.0625	.0781
.26	.0163	.0325	.0366	.0488	.0650	.0813
.27	.0169	.0338	.0380	.0507	.0675	.0844
.28	.0175	.0350	.0394	.0525	.0700	.0875
.29	.0181	.0362	.0408	.0544	.0725	.0906
.30	.0188	.0375	.0422	.0563	.0750	.0938
.31	.0194	.0388	.0436	.0582	.0775	.0969
.32	.0200	.0400	.0450	.0600	.0800	.1000
.33	.0206	.0413	.0464	.0619	.0825	.1031
.34	.0213	.0425	.0478	.0638	.0850	.1063
.35	.0219	.0438	.0492	.0656	.0875	.1093
.36	.0225	.0450	.0506	.0675	.0900	.1125

COST PER PORTION CHART

PURCHASE COST PER POUND	1 oz.	2 oz.	2-1/4 oz.	3 oz.	4 oz.	5 oz.
.37	.0231	.0463	.0520	.0694	.0925	.1156
.38	.0238	.0475	.0534	.0713	.0950	.1188
.39	.0244	.0488	.0549	.0731	.0975	.1219
.40	.0250	.0500	.0562	.0750	.1000	.1250
.41	.0256	.0513	.0577	.0769	.1025	.1281
.42	.0263	.0525	.0590	.0788	.1050	.1313
.43	.0269	.0538	.0605	.0806	.1075	.1344
.44	.0275	.0550	.0619	.0825	.1100	.1375
.45	.0281	.0563	.0633	.0844	.1125	.1406
.46	.0288	.0575	.0647	.0863	.1150	.1438
.47	.0294	.0588	.0661	.0881	.1175	.1469
.48	.0300	.0600	.0675	.0900	.1200	.1500
.49	.0306	.0613	.0691	.0919	.1225	.1531
.50	.0313	.0625	.0703	.0938	.1250	.1563
.51	.0319	.0638	.0717	.0956	.1275	.1594
.52	.0325	.0650	.0731	.0975	.1300	.1625
.53	.0331	.0663	.0746	.0994	.1325	.1656
.54	.0338	.0675	.0759	.1013	.1350	.1688
.55	.0344	.0688	.0773	.1031	.1375	.1719
.56	.0350	.0700	.0787	.1050	.1400	.1750
.57	.0356	.0713	.0802	.1069	.1425	.1781
.58	.0363	.0725	.0816	.1088	.1450	.1813
.59	.0369	.0738	.0820	.1106	.1475	.1844
.60	.0375	.0750	.0844	.1125	.1500	.1875
.61	.0381	.0763	.0858	.1144	.1525	.1906
.62	.0388	.0775	.0872	.1163	.1550	.1938
.63	.0394	.0788	.0886	.1182	.1575	.1969

CHART 10–

PURCHASE COST PER POUND	1 oz.	2 oz.	2-1/4 oz.	3 oz.	4 oz.	5 oz.
.64	.0400	.0800	.0900	.1201	.1600	.2000
.65	.0406	.0813	.0914	.1220	.1625	.2031
.66	.0413	.0825	.0928	.1237	.1650	.2063
.67	.0419	.0838	.0942	.1257	.1675	.2094
.68	.0425	.0830	.0956	.1278	.1700	.2125
.69	.0431	.0863	.0970	.1295	.1725	.2156
.70	.0438	.0875	.0985	.1313	.1750	.2188
.71	.0444	.0888	.1000	.1332	.1775	.2218
.72	.0450	.0900	.1013	.1351	.1800	.2250
.73	.0456	.0913	.1027	.1370	.1825	.2281
.74	.0463	.0925	.1041	.1388	.1850	.2313
.75	.0469	.0938	.1055	.1407	.1875	.2344
.76	.0475	.0950	.1068	.1425	.1900	.2375
.77	.0481	.0963	.1082	.1443	.1924	.2405
.78	.0487	.0975	.1096	.1461	.1948	.2435
.79	.0493	.0988	.1110	.1479	.1972	.2465
.80	.0500	.1000	.1125	.1500	.2000	.2500
.81	.0506	.1013	.1141	.1518	.2024	.2530
.82	.0512	.1025	.1156	.1536	.2048	.2560
.83	.0519	.1038	.1168	.1557	.2076	.2595
.84	.0525	.1050	.1182	.1575	.2100	.2625
.85	.0531	.1063	.1196	.1593	.2124	.2655
.86	.0537	.1075	.1210	.1611	.2148	.2685
.87	.0543	.1088	.1225	.1629	.2172	.2715
.88	.0550	.1100	.1241	.1650	.2200	.2750
.89	.0556	.1112	.1256	.1668	.2224	.2780
.90	.0563	.1125	.1268	.1689	.2252	.2815
.91	.0569	.1138	.1282	.1707	.2276	.2845

COST PER PORTION CHART (Cont.)

PURCHASE COST PER POUND	1 oz.	2 oz.	2-1/4 oz.	3 oz.	4 oz.	5 oz.
.92	.0575	.1150	.1296	.1725	.2300	.2875
.93	.0581	.1163	.1310	.1743	.2324	.2905
.94	.0588	.1175	.1325	.1764	.2352	.2940
.95	.0593	.1188	.1341	.1779	.2372	.2965
.96	.0600	.1200	.1350	.1800	.2400	.3000
.97	.0606	.1213	.1368	.1818	.2424	.3030
.98	.0612	.1225	.1382	.1836	.2448	.3060
.99	.0619	.1250	.1396	.1857	.2476	.3095
1.00	.0625	.1250	.1410	.1875	.2500	.3125
2.00	.1250	.2500	.2820	.3750	.5000	.6250
3.00	.1875	.3750	.4230	.5625	.7500	.9375
4.00	.2500	.5000	.5640	.7500	1.00	1.25
5.00	.3125	.6250	.7050	.9075	1.25	2.50

CHART 11
AIDS FOR CHANGING TO THE METRIC SYSTEM

The change to metric in the food industry depends upon the industries which produce, process, pack, and transport foods. Because of the range of products involved, the changeover will be a gradual process.

Timetables adopted will be influenced by the date of conversion or replacement of weighing equipment in retail shops, and by the dates of change to metric packs in foods which are supplied to the food service industry.

Changes That Can Be Anticipated

1.   Weighing equipment will need to be converted to weigh in kilograms (kg) or grams (g) instead of in pounds or ounces to show the price of each quantity weighed on the basis of the unit price per kilogram. Older machines not economically convertible will require replacement.

2.   Liquid measuring equipment where used will need to be replaced.

3.   Costing and pricing of goods in metric quantities will need to be recalculated.

4.   Commodities for which the price is now quoted on a per pound basis will be priced on a per kilogram basis.

5.   Employees must be trained to "Think Metric."

6.   Applicable Metric Units:

Food sold by the pound (lb) will be sold by the kilogram (kg)

With the Following Equivalents
1 kg	=	2.2 lbs
1 lb	=	0.454 kg

Food sold by the ounce (oz) will be sold by the gram (g)

With the Following Equivalents
1 g	-	0.0353 oz
1 oz	=	28.3 g

Beverages and some foods sold by the quart, pint, or fluid ounce will be sold by the liter (l) or milliliter (ml)

With the Following Equivalents
1 l.	=	1.76 pints
1 pint	=	568 ml
1 fl oz	=	28.4 ml

7.   The following condensed conversion tables are presented only in quantities applicable in these recipes

CHART 12
METRIC CONVERSION TABLES

LIQUIDS

Liters to Liquid Quarts
1 liter = 1.056 liquid quarts

Liters	Liquid Quarts
1	1.0567
2	2.1134
3	3.1701
4	4.2268

Liquid Quarts to Liters
1 liquid quart   =   0.946

Liquid Quarts	Liters
1	0.94635
2	1.89271
3	2.83906
4	3.78541

Gallons to Liters
1 gal.   =   3.785 liters

Gallons	Liters
1	3.7854
2	7.5708
3	11.3562
4	15.1416
5	18.9271
6	22.7125
7	26.4979
8	30.2833
9	34.0687

WEIGHTS

Grams to Ounces
1 gram   = 0.035

Grams	Ounces
1	0.035274
2	0.070548
3	0.105822
4	0.141096
5	0.176370
6	0.211644
7	0.246918
8	0.282192
9	0.317466
10	0.352740

Ounces to Grams
1 ounce   = 28.349 grams

Ounces	Grams
1	28.350
2	56.699
2	85.049
4	113.398
5	141.748
6	170.097
7	198.447
8	226.796
9	255.146
10	283.495
11	311.865
12	340.194
13	368.544
14	396.893
15	425.243
16.	453.592

Pounds to Kilograms
1 pound = 0.453 kilogram

Pounds	Kilogram
1	0.45359
2	0.90718
3	1.36078
4	1.81437
5	2.26796
6	2.72155
7	3.17515
8	3.62874
9	4.08233
10	4.53592

Kilograms to Pounds
1 kilogram = 2.204 pounds

Kilograms	Pounds
1	2.2046
2	4.4092
3	6.6139
4	8.8185
5	11.0231
6	13.2277
7	15.4324
8	17.6370
9	19.8416
10	22.0462

APPENDIX B

INDEX
TO
PURCHASING BID DOCUMENTS

Name of Document	Page
COVER LETTER	335
PRODUCT SPECIFICATION	336
GENERAL BID CONDITIONS	337
SPECIAL BID CONDITIONS	340
PRICE COMPARISON SHEET	341

COVER LETTER

(ADDRESS)

_____

Purchasing Manager

The _____ Food Service will receive quotations on our Annual Canned Goods Requirements until (DATE) **2:30 PM EST** at the Food Service Department Purchasing Office, (ADDRESS).

The following are attached to and made a part of this request for quotations:
1) Bid form one (1) page dated September 17, 1973. (two copies)
2) General Bid Conditions one (1) page.
3) Special Bid Conditions two (2) pages dated.

ACKNOWLEDGEMENT

All bidders must sign below and return with bid form prior to opening date and time shown above. Failure to sign and return the form may be considered as grounds for disqualification of bids submitted.

I certify that this bid is submitted in accordance with the terms and conditions contained herein.

_____   _____

Bidder's Firm Name   Street Address

BY _____   _____

    Signature of person authorized   City   State   Zip Code
    to sign bid

DELIVERY CAN BE MADE WITHIN CALENDAR DAYS ARO _____

TERMS: _____

FOB: _____

PRODUCT SPECIFICATION

ITEM NO.	QUANTITY	UNIT	DESCRIPTION	UNIT PRICE	AMOUNT
1	600	CS	Peaches, Yellow Cling, Halves, U. S. Grade A (Fancy), 35-40 count, 6/10/cs. BRAND_____		
2	600	CS	Peaches, Yellow Cling, Sliced U. S. Grade A (Fancy) in heavy syrup, Min. Dr. Wt. 66 oz., 6/10/cs. BRAND_____		
3	600	CS	Potatoes, Tiny Whole, Canned, U. S. Grade A (Fancy), 100-120 count, pack 6/10/cs. BRAND_____		
4	500	CS	Potatoes, Whole Sweet, Canned,U. S. Grade A (Fancy), in heavy syrup, 25 count avg. 6/10/cs. BRAND_____		
5	800	CS	Corn, Whole Kernel, Yellow, U. S. Grade A (Fancy), 6/10/cs. BRAND_____		

GENERAL BID CONDITIONS

A.

GBC-1   ACCEPTANCE AND REJECTION
The Institution reserves the right to reject any and all bids, to waive any informality in bids and, unless otherwise specified by the bidder, to accept any item in the bid. In the event that the Institution elects to award on an "all or none basis" this will be so stated in the Special Bid Conditions.

GBC-2   TIME OF ACCEPTANCE
If a bidder fails to state a time within which a bid must be accepted, it is understood and agreed that the Institution shall have thirty (30) days to accept.

GBC-3   ERRORS IN BIDS
In case of errors in the extension of prices in the bid, the unit price will govern.

GBC-4   DISCOUNTS
Discounts other than "Time Discounts" must be shown on the face of the bid opposite the item to which it applies.

GBC-5   SIGNATURE ON BIDS
Each bid must give the full name and business address of the bidder. The person signing the bid must show his title, and if requested by the Director of Purchasing, must furnish satisfactory proof of his authority to bind his company in contract. Bids must be written with typewriter, ink, or indelible pencil; otherwise, they may not be considered. A purchase order will be issued to the firm name appearing on the bid.

GBC-6   DELIVERY
The number of calendar days in which delivery will be made after receipt of order shall be stated in the bid in the space provided.

GBC-7   SPECIFICATIONS
It is understood that reference to available specifications shall be sufficient to make the terms of such specifications binding on the vendor. The use of the name of a manufacturer, or any special brand or make in describing an item does not restrict the bidder to that manufacturer or specific article, unless specifically stated, this means being used to simply indicate the character or quality of the article desired; but the articles on which the proposals are submitted must be equal to, or better than, that specified.

GBC-8   SUBSTITUTIONS
When offering substitutions, please so indicate, giving complete specifications, and submit catalog information to completely identify the item you propose to furnish.

GBC-9   SAMPLES
Samples of items (when requested) are to be furnished prior to the bid opening and will be returned upon the bidder's request; however, the Institution reserves the right to keep the sample of the low bidder. DO NOT submit samples unless you are specifically requested to do so.

GBC-10 BRANDS AND TRADE NAMES
The bidder must show the brand or trade name of the articles on which he is bidding, when applicable.

GBC-11 FOB POINT
All prices quoted are to be FOB delivered to the Institution (unless another FOB point is stated by the Institution on the bid form). The successful bidder must assume all responsibility for damage in transit.

GBC-12 TAXES
Do not include Federal Excise or State Sales Taxes in your bids (if applicable).

GBC-13 COMPARISON OF BIDS
In comparing the bids and making awards, the Institution may consider such factors as relative quality and adaptability of supplies or services, the bidders' financial responsibility, skill, experience, record of integrity in dealing, ability to furnish repairs and maintenance service, the time of delivery or performance offered, and any other element or factor in addition to that of the bid price which would affect the final cost to the Institution and whether the bidder has complied with the specifications.

GENERAL BID CONDITIONS (cont.)

GBC-14 AWARD INFORMATION AVAILABLE TO BIDDER

Any bidder may, seven (7) days after award has been made and for forty-five (45) thereafter, obtain additional information relative to awards by making application at the Purchasing Department (Address).

B.   WHEN AWARDED THE ORDER WILL BE SUBJECT TO THE TERMS AND CONDITIONS STATED BELOW

1.   THE ORDER

Furnish the material specified in full accordance with conditions printed on the face and back hereof, and any other attachment made a part of this order.

2.   IDENTIFICATION OF ORDER

THE PURCHASE ORDER AND REQUISITION NUMBERS MUST APPEAR ON ALL INVOICES, CORRESPONDENCE, CONTAINERS, SHIPPING PAPERS, and PACKING LISTS.

3.   CORRESPONDENCE

All Correspondence pertaining to this order must be addressed as follows: The Director of Purchasing.

4.   BILLING INSTRUCTIONS

a) Invoice in duplicate (unless otherwise shown on the order) within 5 days after shipment of material. Invoice must show trade and cash discounts.
b) Delivery tickets and invoices must show the Purchase Order and Requisition numbers, and must show car number when carload shipment is made.
c) Each shipment must be covered by a separate invoice in two copies (unless otherwise requested).
d) Render SEPARATE invoices for EACH AND EVERY shipment, and render invoices for returnable containers, stating terms and conditions for return thereof.

5.   TAXES

Do not include Federal Excise or State Sales Tax on your invoice, (if applicable).

6.   DISCOUNTS

Time, in connection with discounts offered, will be computed from date of the delivery of the supplies to carrier when final inspection and acceptance are at point of origin; or from date of delivery at destination and when final inspection and acceptance are at that point; or from date correct invoice is received if the latter date is later than the date of delivery.

7.   WARRANT OF SUPPLIES

The Vendor warrants that the supplies delivered hereunder shall be free from all defects in material and workmanship and shall comply with all the requirements of this order for a period of ninety (90) days from the date such supplies are delivered.

8.   PACKING LIST

A detailed packing list showing both the purchase order and requisition numbers must accompany all shipments.

9.   ASSIGNMENT

The Vendor shall not assign any monies due or to become due hereunder without the previous written consent.

10.   INSPECTION

All supplies purchased hereunder are subject to inspection and rejection upon receipt. Rejected supplies may be returned at the Vendor's expense. In addition to its right to return rejected supplies in the event of delivery of supplies not in accordance with the requirements of this order, the Institution may notify the Vendor of such damages or deficiencies, and if not repaired or corrected by the Vendor within ten (10) days after receipt of such notice, or such additional time as may be mutually agreed to by the Institution and the Vendor, the Institution shall have the right to correct any damages, defects, insufficiencies or improprieties therein, and do any other work necessary to put the supplies in condition for the use intended and the cost of such correction shall be deducted from monies due the Vendor under this order.

11. CHANGES

The buyer may at any time by written instructions make changes, within the general scope of this order, in any one or more of the following: (1) quantity or specifications; (2) method of shipment or packing; and (3) piace of delivery. If any such change causes an increase or decrease in the cost of, or the time required for performance of this order, an equitable adjustment shall be made in the order price or delivery schedule, or both, and the order shall be modified in writing accordingly. Any claim by the Vendor for adjustment under this paragraph must be asserted within thirty (30) days from the date of receipt by the Vendor of the notification of change.

12. PAYMENTS

The Vendor shall be paid, upon the submission of invoices or vouchers, the prices stipulated herein for supplies delivered and accepted or services rendered, less deducations, if any, as herein provided. Unless otherwise specified, partial payments shall not be made.

13. VARIATION IN QUANTITIES

Unless otherwise specified, any variation in the quantities herein called for, not exceeding 10 percent, will be accepted as compliance with the order when caused by conditions of loading, shipping, packing, or allowances in manufacturing processes, and payments shall be adjusted accordingly.

14. CANCELLATION OF ORDER

The right to cancel this order or any part thereof without penalty, if the Vendor fails to comply with the terms and conditions of this transaction, or fails to prosecute the work with promptness and diligence or fails to make shipment within the time agreed upon, except for causes beyond the Vendor's control.

15. ERRORS

In case of error in calculation or typing, the quoted unit price will be used as the basis for correction of this order.

16. EQUAL EMPLOYMENT

The contracting party will not discriminate against any employee or applicant for employment because of race, creed, color, sex, or natural origin. When awarded, this quotation is subject to the provisions of Title 7 of the Civil Rights Act of 1964 and parts of II, III, and IV of the Executive Order 11246, dated September 4, 1965 (30 F. R. 12319).

SPECIAL BID CONDITIONS
FOR
CANNED GOODS

SBC-1 SCOPE:

The Central Purchasing Office proposes to purchase the quantity stated with delivery to (ADDRESS). If you cannot quote on this list, indicate on form and return to us.

SBC-2 CONFLICTS IN BID CONDITIONS:

If there should be any conflicts between the general bid conditions and these special bid conditions, these special bid conditions shall take precedence.

SBC-3 SEALED BID:

The envelope in which bids are submitted must be identified by noting "annual canned goods" on the bottom left corner when submitting your bid. It is imperative that your name and address appear in the upper left corner of the envelope. Bids must be returned prior to the time stated on the bid form.

SBC-4 GRADES

Grades of items are based on those established by the U.S. Department of Agriculture. If an alternate grade is bid, the bidder must state the grade he is bidding.

SBC-5 SAMPLES:

The purchasing office will require two (2) number ten (10) samples of the product at no charge, on which you are quoting. Samples shall be submitted on or prior to closing of bids. Samples will not be returned to the bidders (samples shall be of the same grade and quality merchandise on which you are bidding). Submit samples to:

(ADDRESS)

The purchasing office after sampling and inspection will be the sole judge as to the quality, appearance, and acceptability of the products quoted.

SBC-6 DELIVERY:

State your best delivery in the space provided on the bid form since this may be a factor in awarding of the order(s).

SBC-7 SHIPMENT

Shipment shall be made to (ADDRESS). Central food stores has both truck and rail docks. All deliveries by truck shall be made between 7:30 am and 4:00 pm. A twenty-four hour prior notice of delivery will be required. Phone_____.

SBC-8 YEAR'S PACK:

All products shall be this year's crop.

SBC-9 FEDERAL GRADING CERTIFICATE

The successful bidder must furnish a federal grading certificate on each item at time of receipt of goods. The code numbers on the merchandise must be the same as those on the federal grading certificate.

SBC-10 BRAND

Each bidder must insert in the space provided on the bid form the brand of product, crop year, etc., he proposes to supply.

SBC-11 AWARD:

The right to award each item individually is reserved, to award all items on an all or none basis, or to award any combination of items that would be most advantageous to the purchaser.

Quality, price, and delivery will be considered in making the award.

SBC-12 CONTAINERS:

All containers and corrugated fiber cartons must be intact and in accordance with the federal container specifications at the time of receipt or be subject to rejection.

SBC-13 GRADE SPECIFICATIONS:

The right to refuse any or all merchandise not meeting U.S. Department of Agriculture grade specification is reserved. The removal of these products shall be at the expense of the purveyor.

SBC-14 FOB POINT

All prices are to be FOB, (LOCAL ADDRESS OF INSTITUTION).

CANNED PRODUCTS - PRICE COMPARISON CHART

PRODUCT	QUANTITY	SELECTED BRAND PRICE CASE	BRAND HIGHEST PRICE	BRAND LOWEST PRICE	PRICE CASE AT PRESENT	EXTENDED TOTALS			
						SELECTED BRAND	HIGHEST BRAND	LOWEST BRAND	PRESENT COST
Baked Beans	500 cs	No. 12 6.10/cs	No. 1 7.85/cs	No. 13 4.50/cs	6.19 cs	$3050.00	$3925.00	$2250.00	$3095.00
Green Beans	1300 cs	No. 14 4.35/cs	No. 2 6.29/cs	No. 15 4.04/cs	4.75 cs	$5655.00	$8177.00	$5252.00	$6175.00
W. K. Corn	600 cs	No. 16 5.40/cs	No. 3 5.62/cs	No. 17 5.25/cs	5.04 cs	$3240.00	$3372.00	$3150.00	$3024.00
Frt. Cocktail	600 cs	No. 18 7.25/cs	No. 4 8.77/cs	No. 18 7.25/cs	6.95 cs	$4350.00	$5262.00	$4350.00	$4170.00
Kidney Beans	500 cs	No. 19 3.94/cs	No. 5 5.55/cs	No. 19 3.94/cs	4.60 cs	$1970.00	$2775.00	$1970.00	$2300.00
Bartlett Pears	500 cs	No. 20 8.25/cs	No. 6 8.44/cs	No. 21 7.89/cs	7.63 cs	$4125.00	$4220.00	$3945.00	$3815.00
Inst. Potatoes	800 cs	No. 22 10.37/cs	No. 7 10.85/cs	No. 23 9.75/cs	10.94 cs	$8296.00	$8680.00	$7800.00	$8752.00
Tomato Catsup	900 cs	No. 24 5.40/cs	No. 8 6.75/cs	No. 24 5.40/cs	5.50 cs	$4860.00	$6075.00	$4860.00	$4950.00
Tomato Paste	300 cs	No. 25 6.00/cs	No. 9 9.75 cs	No. 25 6.00/cs	7.35 cs	$1800.00	$2925.00	$1800.00	$2205.00
Tomato Puree	300 cs	No. 26 4.28/cs	No. 10 6.18/cs	No. 26 4.28/cs	4.70 cs	$1284.00	$1854.00	$1284.00	$1410.00
Whole Tomatoes	500 cs	No. 27 4.68/cs	No. 11 6.22/cs	No. 27 4.68/cs	4.64 cs	$2340.00	$3110.00	$2340.00	$2320.00
					SUM	$40,970.00	$50,375.00	$39,001.00	$42,216.00

9/ GLOSSARY

Analyze Cost: To study, by separating into elements, the prices paid for each ingredient or step in the action of procurement, processing, and delivery of the end product.

As Purchased—"A.P.": The form in which the food item is received from the purveyor.

Automated Accounting System: The use of computers to process routine entry and posting of accounting data, to generate journals and trial balances, and also to develop detailed computations; e.g., payrolls, inventories, statistical forecasts.

Batch Cookery: The preparation of food in small quantities in amounts that equal the amounts that can be quickly consumed by the anticipated number of patrons. Foods are often those that can be prepared during a meal period.

Break-Out Space: An open area needed for the inspection and distribution of goods to storage or production.

Commercial Sector: Normally considered to be the hotel, motel, restaurant, cafeteria, and fast food segments of the food service industry or the food manufacturers that sell to those segments as well as to noncommercial operations.

Computerize: The development of programs to process data electronically.

Convection Oven: An oven that cooks with convected heat through the use of fan-forced air within the oven chamber. This type of equipment makes it possible to provide faster baking and roasting at lower temperatures.

Convenience Foods: Those foods that need a minimum of labor in their final preparation.

Cooking from Scratch: The preparation of food from its basic or raw form. Prior to the introduction of convenience foods, this was the primary method of combining ingredients in a recipe.

Cost Control: The process of controlling cost through the establishment of standards and the use of cost accounting methods.

Cost Per Meal Served: The actual dollar cost of the food ingredients used in menu items served to a single customer for a given meal.

Cycle Menu: A set of menus that is repeated within a prescribed period of time.

Deck Oven: Baking or roasting compartment designed to operate alone or in combination with other oven units. Compartments can be stacked one on top of the other.

E.D.P.—Electronic Data Processing: The computation of information using electronic equipment.

Extended Health Care Facilities: Term normally associated with convalescent homes or homes for the elderly.

Financial Statement: A written presentation of financial data prepared from accounting records, i.e., profit and loss statement (P & L).

Flow Chart: A chart showing the relationships among elements involved in an on-going process, e.g., the movement of food through a production kitchen.

Food Cost: Expenses associated with the purchase of raw ingredients and all activities required for delivery of the finished food item to the place where it is to be served.

Labor-Free Foods: Foods requiring a minimum of labor prior to their being served.

Line Number: A number associated with a particular item in a list or a line within a printed program.

Major Ingredients: Those food items representing the most significant cost of a recipe.

Meal Cost: The total cost of all food and labor required to produce each meal served.

On-Going Training Program: A continuous scheduled program of instruction.

Open Market Buying: The selection and purchase of food and supplies based on informal price quotes which are often obtained by telephone bids.

Post Cost: The actual cost of all food served for a given meal computed after the meal is served.

Pre-Cost: The estimated cost of all food to be served for a given meal.

Pre-Cost Method: A procedure in which all food ingredients needed to serve a given meal are listed and priced prior to the purchase of the food.

Pre-Preparation: All activity associated with readying of ingredients in advance of the actual preparation of a food item for service, e.g. mixing and forming a meat loaf or cleaning and chopping salad ingredients.

Pre-Prepared Entree: A meat or main dish food item that is delivered to the kitchen completely cooked and seasoned needing only to be heated prior to use.

Production Person: A food service worker who may combine, mix, cook, or portion food.

Raw Food Cost: The cost of all ingredients needed to produce the food served. Does not include cost of supplies, labor, and other overhead expenses.

Ready Foods: Items of food needing little or no labor prior to their being served or combined with other ingredients. Often referred to as "convenience foods."

Recipe Constraints: The limits within which a recipe can be expanded. In this book, one constraint was that recipes be written to use the maximum amount of an ingredient in the unit of issue, e.g., drained weight of a No. 10 can.

Rotary Oven: A multi-shelf oven constructed so that the shelves revolve; access is through a single door.

Schematic Drawing: A diagram outlining systematically the steps necessary to accomplish a plan or program.

Standard Recipes: A list of ingredients, their amounts, and the method required to combine them in order to produce a known quantity and quality of food.

Standardized Recipe File: A file of recipes that have been tested for a known quantity and quality of food. Individual recipes are referred to as standard recipes.

Stock File: A list of ingredients, their description, size of unit of purchase, issue, and use in recipe, with associated cost and source.

Stock Number: The number assigned each product used as an ingredient in a recipe. The number is needed to facilitate data processing.

Tilting Kettle: Or "Tilting Skillet," a deep-sided cooking device that can be used for frying or cooking, so mounted that its surface can be adjusted to change its level for braising or transfer of product.

Value Analysis: The organized and systematic study of every element of cost in a product or service being examined to make certain that it is being produced or accomplished at the lowest cost.

Vertical Cutter: Cutter/Mixer, which can be operated at variable speeds; designed to cut, mix, blend, whip, cream, grate, chop, or homogenize food products.

INDEX

BREAKFAST ITEMS ... 294-300
  Eggs: ... 294-96
    Omelet, Cheese (6036) ... 296
    Poached (6014) ... 294
    Scrambled (6016) ... 295
  Pancakes and Other: ... 297-300
    French Toast (6080) ... 300
    Pancakes (6052) ... 297
    Pancakes, Blueberry (6054) ... 298
    Waffles (6062) ... 299
ENTREES ... 71-164
  Beef: ... 71-104
    Braised (1350) ... 100
    Burger on Bun (1210) ... 87
    Burger on Bun, German (1213) ... 89
    Cheese Meat Loaf with Tomato Sauce (1251) ... 95
    Cheeseburger (1212) ... 88
    Chili Con Carne (1200) ... 85
    Chili Con Carne (1201) ... 86
    Chiliburgers (1190) ... 84
    Corned Beef and Cabbage (1380) ... 103
    Lasagne (1230) ... 93
    Liver with Onions, Grilled (1361) ... 101
    Liver with Onions, Smothered (1362) ... 102
    Meat Loaf with Tomato Sauce (1250) ... 94
    Reuben Sandwich, Hot (1390) ... 104
    Roast Beef Au Jus (1140) ... 81
    Roast Beef, Cooked (1145) ... 82
    Roast Beef Sandwich, Hot (1122) ... 79
    Sauerbraten (1132) ... 80
    Spaghetti, Italian (1220) ... 90
    Spaghetti with Italian Meat Balls (1221) ... 91
    Spaghetti with Meat Sauce (1225) ... 92
    Stew (1330) ... 98
    Stroganoff with Noodles (1340) ... 99
    Stuffed Pepper with Tomato Sauce (1280) ... 96
    Turnovers with Gravy (1180) ... 83
    Steak, Cantonese (1095) ... 76
    Steak, Charcoal Broiled Strip (1030) ... 71
    Steak, Country Fried (1050) ... 72
    Steak, Flank (1060) ... 74
    Steak on Bun, Smothered (1090) ... 75
    Steak Parmegiana, Italian (1103) ... 78
    Steak with Dill Pickle, Grilled (1079) ... 75
    Steak with Gravy, Salisbury (1291) ... 97
    Steak, Swiss (1101) ... 77
    Steak, Western (1052) ... 73
  Fish and Shellfish: ... 121-35
    Crab Rolls with Tartar Sauce (1937) ... 131
    Crab with Tartar Sauce, Deviled (1935) ... 130
    Fish Sandwich/Bun (1860) ... 127
    Flounder, Baked Stuffed (1813) ... 126
    Flounder, Broiled (1810) ... 125
    Flounder, Fried (1820) ... 126
    Mackerel, Broiled (1941) ... 132
    Scallops with Tartar Sauce, Fried (1841) ... 127
    Seafood Newburg (1979) ... 133
    Seafood Newburg with Toast Points (1980) ... 134
    Seafood Patties with Cocktail Sauce (1990) ... 135
    Shrimp Chow Mein (1785) ... 123
    Shrimp, Creole (1760) ... 121
    Shrimp Marengo (1789) ... 124
    Shrimp with Tartar Sauce, Fried (1770) ... 122
    Tuna Dog (1920) ... 128
    Tuna Noodle Casserole (1930) ... 129
  Miscellaneous: ... 157-64
    Cheese Pizza or Typical Pizza (2670) ... 161
    Cheese Sandwich, Grilled (2660) ... 160
    Cottage Cheese Croquette (2697) ... 163
    Frankfurters and Sauerkraut (with 10/lb Franks) (2655) ... 160
    Frankfurters with Baked Beans (Dinner Franks 8/lb) (2651) ... 159
    Frankfurters with Baked Beans (10/lb Franks) (2650) ... 158
    Hot Dog/Bun/Chili/Relish (2640) ... 157
    Knockwurst (2675) ... 161
    Knockwurst and White Beans (2680) ... 162
    Rice, Mushrooms and Almonds (2700) ... 164
  Pork: ... 105-20
    Bacon (1673) ... 120
    Bacon and Cheese Sandwich, Grilled (1674) ... 120
    Bacon, Cheese and Tomato Grille (1671) ... 119
    Barbecued Pork on Bun (1570) ... 111
    Chop, Baked Stuffed (1632) ... 117
    Chops, Baked (1591) ... 113
    Chops, Breaded (1580) ... 112
    Chow Mein (1600) ... 114
    Ham and Cheese on Bun (1550) ... 108
    Ham and Cheese Sandwich, Grilled (1552) ... 109
    Ham and Potatoes, Escalloped (1520) ... 106
    Ham, Macaroni and Cheese (1560) ... 110
    Ham Steak, Grilled (1530) ... 107
    Ham with Fruit Sauce, Baked (1510) ... 105
    Roast (1620) ... 115
    Roast, with Dressing (1624) ... 116
    Sausage, Link (1661) ... 118
    Sausage Patties (1649) ... 118
  Poultry: ... 136-51
    Chicken and Dumplings (2170) ... 141
    Chicken and Noodles, Scalloped (2260) ... 148
    Chicken, Barbecued (2110) ... 136
    Chicken Cheeseburger (2146) ... 140
    Chicken Drumsticks, Fried (2220) ... 144
    Chicken (Fourths), Fried (2210) ... 143
    Chicken Halves, Broiled (2120) ... 137
    Chicken Livers, Sauteed (2250) ... 147
    Chicken, Oven Fried (2230) ... 145
    Chicken (Pre-cooked Eighths), Fried (2215) ... 144
    Chicken (Quarters), Broiled (2121) ... 138
    Chicken Tetrazzini (2190) ... 142
    Chicken Thighs, Broiled (2125) ... 139
    Chicken with Dressing (Quarters), Baked (2235) ... 146
    Turkey Club Sandwich (2370) ... 149
    Turkey Sandwich (Open-Faced) Hot (2372) ... 150
    Turkey with Dressing, Roast (2380) ... 151
  Veal and Lamb: ... 152-64
    Lamb, Leg of, Roast (2570) ... 156
    Veal and Dressing, Roast (2520) ... 152
    Veal Cutlet with Creole Sauce (2530) ... 153
    Veal Parmesan (2550) ... 154
    Veal Scallopini (2560) ... 155
FRUITS AND MELONS ... 301-15
  Apples, Fresh (Red Delicious) (7505) ... 301
  Apricot Halves (7526) ... 301
  Bananas (7536) ... 302
  Blueberries, Fresh (7538) ... 302
  Cantaloupe (7590) ... 308
  Cherries, Fresh Bing (7545) ... 303
  Cranberry Sauce, Fresh (7548) ... 304
  Cranberry Sauce, Whole (7547) ... 303
  Fruit Cocktail (7555) ... 304
  Grapefruit, Half (7561) ... 305
  Grapefruit Sections (7560) ... 305
  Grapes, Emperor (7566) ... 306
  Melon, Honeydew (7580) ... 307
  Melon Tray, Fresh (7577) ... 307
  Orange and Grapefruit Sections (7618) ... 309
  Orange Sections (7615) ... 309
  Oranges (7600) ... 308
  Peach Halves (7625) ... 310
  Peaches, Fresh (7619) ... 310
  Peaches, Sliced (7630) ... 311
  Pear Halves (7635) ... 311
  Pears, Fresh Bartlett (7640) ... 312
  Pineapple Chunks (7645) ... 312
  Pineapple, Fresh (7655) ... 313
  Pineapple Tidbits (7650) ... 313
  Plums, Purple (7670) ... 314

Tangelos (7685) 315
Tangerines (7680) 314
Watermelon (7575) 306
HOT FRUITS 225-31
Apples, Baked (3412) 225
Apples, Escalloped (3414) 226
Apples, Glazed (3416) 227
Applesauce (3420) 227
Apricots, Broiled (3428) 228
Peaches, Broiled (3430) 229
Pears, Cinnamon (3432) 230
Pineapple, Broiled (3434) 231
MISCELLANEOUS 315-20
Beef Noodle Soup or Typical Soup (8020) 315
Beverages (Dinner) (8030) 317
Chocolate Pudding (Typical Pudding) (8050) 320
Coffee (8035) 318
Grapefruit Juice (Typical Canned) (8040) 318
Orange Juice (Typical Frozen) (8045) 319
Oyster Stew (8025) 316
SALADS 232-93
Fruits: 254-70
Ambrosia (4305) 254
Apple Wedge with Grapefruit (4311) 255
Apple Wedges with Fruit Cocktail (4310) 254
Banana Nut Roll (4315) 255
Banana Split Salad (4325) 256
Fruit Salad with Whip Topping (4340) 258
Fruitmallow Salad (4350) 259
Hawaiian Delight Salad (4355) 260
Mandarin Orange/Coconut Toss (4359) 261
Orange Coconut Toss (4360) 261
Peach, Cottage Cheese, Raisins, Nuts
(4371) 263
Peach Half/Cream Cheese/Olive/Nut
(4378) 264
Peach Half with Fruit Cocktail (4365) 262
Peach Salad, Fiesta (4335) 257
Peach with Cottage Cheese (4370) 262
Peaches/Cottage Cheese, Sliced (4390) 265
Pear with Cottage Cheese (4405) 265
Pear with Cream Cheese and Nuts (4410) 266
Pear with Grated Cheese (4420) 266
Pear with Mandarin Oranges (4425) 267
Pineapple Ambrosia (4435) 267
Pineapple with Apricot (4440) 268
Pineapple with Cottage Cheese (4450) 269
Pineapple with Grated Cheese (4445) 268
Waldorf Salad (4460) 270
Gelatins: 271-93
Applesauce, Congealed (4505) 271
Apricot Salad, Fluffy (4555) 279
Bing Cherry and Almond Gelatin (4530) 275
Blackberry Isle (4515) 272

Cherry Gelatin (4525) 274
Cranberry Salad, Congealed (4545) 278
Fruit, Congealed (4535) 276
Fruit Gelatin, Frosted (4560) 280
Fruit Mold, Rosy (4625) 290
Fruit Salad, Frozen (4570) 282
Heavenly Hash (4575) 283
Lime Fruited Gelatin (4521) 273
Mandarin Orange/Orange Gelatin (4600) 284
Orange Sherbet Salad (4605) 285
Peaches in Strawberry Gelatin (4608) 286
Pear in Lime Gelatin (4610) 287
Pineapple Salad, Frosted (4565) 281
Raspberry Argentine (4615) 288
Ribbon Gelatin (4621) 289
Springtime Salad (4640) 291
Strawberry Glaze (4645) 292
Sunshine Salad (4650) 293
Waldorf, Congealed (4540) 277
Lettuce and Cabbage and Other: 232-43
Chef Salad Bowl (4020) 232
Cole Slaw (4025) 233
Combination Salad (4030) 234
Fiesta Salad Bowl (4035) 235
Garden Salad Bowl (4036) 236
Garnish, Head Lettuce (4052) 238
Garnish, Leaf Lettuce (4051) 238
Green Bean Salad (4040) 237
Lettuce with Carrots, Tossed (4065) 240
Lettuce with Celery, Tossed (4070) 240
Lettuce with Green Onion, Tossed (4080) 241
Potato Salad (4140) 241
Relish Platter (4145) 242
Tomatoes, Sliced with Lettuce, Garnish
(4165) 243
Tossed Salad (4055) 239
Protein—Meat, Cheese, Eggs and TVP: 244-53
Celery, Stuffed (4205) 244
Chicken Salad (4240) 248
Chicken Salad, TVP (4245) 249
Cottage Cheese (4210) 244
Egg Salad, Deviled (4220) 245
Eggs, Hard Cooked (4225) 246
Ham Salad (4250) 250
Macaroni Salad (4235) 247
Meat Salad (4255) 251
Tuna Fish Salad (4270) 252
Turkey Salad (4275) 253
SAUCES AND GRAVIES 55-70
Barbecue Sauce (0610) 57
Brown Gravy (0520) 55
Caramel Sauce (for Bananas; for Ice Cream)
(0805) 67
Cheese Sauce (0620) 58

Chicken or Turkey Gravy (0530) 56
Cocktail Sauce (0660) 61
Creole Sauce (0670) 62
Custard Sauce (0622) 59
Fruit Sauce (0810) 68
Green Pea Sauce (0690) 63
Lemon Sauce (0820) 69
Sauerbraten Sauce (0708) 64
Tomato Sauce (0730) 65
Tomato Sauce, Italian (0731) 66
Vanilla Sauce (0830) 70
White Sauce (Medium) (0640) 60
VEGETABLES 165-224
Beans and Peas: 187-95
Beans, Baby Lima (3122) 188
Beans, Fordhook Lima (3126) 189
Beans, Green, Southern (3114) 187
Beans, Northern White (3142) 193
Beans, Pinto (3134) 192
Mixed Vegetables (3130) 191
Peas and Carrots (3161) 195
Peas, Blackeyed (3152) 193
Peas, Buttered Green (Frozen Green Peas)
(3158) 194
Peas, Buttered Sweet (Canned) (3159) 194
Pork and Beans (3136) 192
Succotash (3128) 190
Green, Yellow and Red Vegetables: 196-214
Acorn Squash, Baked (3282) 208
Asparagus with Cheese Sauce (3178) 196
Beets, Harvard (Sliced Beets) (3254) 205
Broccoli, Scalloped (3184) 198
Broccoli Spears (3186) 199
Brussels Sprouts (3192) 200
Cabbage, Green, Buttered (3181) 197
Carrots, French Fried (3270) 207
Carrots with Parsley, Buttered (3266) 206
Collard Greens (3194) 201
Okra and Tomatoes (3208) 202
Spinach, Buttered (3210) 203
Spinach, Creamed (3214) 204
Squash/Chicken Soup, Scalloped (3286) 209
Squash, Yellow, with Cheese Crumbs
(3292) 210
Tomato Dumplings (3299) 213
Tomatoes, Broiled (3296) 211
Tomatoes, Escalloped (3298) 212
Tomatoes, Stewed (3302) 214
Potatoes and Corn: 165-86
Corn Chips (3076) 182
Corn on Cob (3078) 183
Corn on Cob, Fresh (3079) 183
Corn on Cob, Fresh (Wrapped in Aluminum
Foil) (3080) 184

Corn Pudding (3086) 185
Corn, W. K. Yellow (3090) 186
Potato Gems, Fried (3044) 179
Potato Salad, Hot German (3020) 171
Potato Wedges, Fried (3058) 182
Potato with Sour Cream, Baked (3004) 166
Potatoes, Au Gratin (3002) 165
Potatoes, Cottage Fried (3023) 173
Potatoes, Duchess (3014) 169
Potatoes, Escalloped (3016) 170
Potatoes, French Fried (3018) 171
Potatoes, Hash Brown (3022) 172

Potatoes in Jacket, New (3032) 176
Potatoes, Lyonnaise (3026) 174
Potatoes, O'Brien (3034) 177
Potatoes, Oven Browned (3036) 178
Potatoes, Parslied Buttered (3038) 179
Potatoes, Steak House Fried (3050) 180
Potatoes, Whole, Parsley Creamed (3012) 168
Potatoes with Gravy, Mashed (3028) 175
Sweet Potato Pudding (3052) 181
Sweet Potatoes, Candied (3008) 167
White Vegetables and Starches: 215-24
    Cauliflower Au Gratin (3334) 216

Cauliflower, Parslied Buttered (3332) 215
Dressing, Bread (to Be Cooked Alone in Pans) (3396) 222
Dressing, Stuffing (to Be Cooked with Meat Item) (3397) 223
Hush Puppies (3398) 224
Macaroni and Cheese (3340) 218
Noodles, Buttered (3336) 217
Onion Rings, French Fried (3342) 219
Onions, Savory (3348) 220
Rice, Buttered (3350) 221

ABOUT THE AUTHORS

John C. Birchfield is Vice President of Business Affairs at Westminster Choir College, Princeton, N.J. Formerly he was Director of Residence Halls and Dining Services at the University of Tennessee. He is a graduate of the Cornell School of Hotel and Restaurant Administration and received the M.S. degree in institutional management from Rutgers University. Mr. Birchfield has held management positions in hotels and country clubs, and is currently involved in extensive consulting work in the layout and design of food service facilities.

Marilyn McCammon Davenport is Staff Dietitian in the Food Services Department at the University of Tennessee at Knoxville, where she received the B.S. degree in Dietetics and the M.S. degree in Food Service. A registered Dietitian, she took her internship at the Veterans Administration Center in Los Angeles.

Norman D. Hill has served eight years as Director of Food Services at the University of Tennessee at Knoxville, and was formerly on the Food Service staff at Princeton. Mr. Hill is President of Region 3, National Association of College and University Food Services. He holds a B.S. degree in Hotel and Restaurant Management from Cornell.

Richard M. Wingard is Director of Food Services at Auburn University, Auburn, Alabama, and was formerly Assistant Director of Food Services at the University of Tennessee at Knoxville. In 1974 he also served as Chairman of the Food Service Task Force for the State of Tennessee. Mr. Wingard holds a B.S. degree from Virginia Polytechnic Institute.